TRADERS IN MEN

TRADERS IN MEN

Merchants and the Transformation of the Transatlantic Slave Trade

NICHOLAS RADBURN

Yale

UNIVERSITY PRESS

New Haven and London

Published with assistance from the Annie Burr Lewis Fund and from the foundation established in memory of Amasa Stone Mather of the Class of 1907, Yale College.

Maps throughout this book were created using ArcGIS® software by Esri. ArcGIS® and ArcMap™ are the intellectual property of Esri and are used herein under license. Copyright © Esri. All rights reserved. For more information about Esri® software, visit www.esri.com.

Yale University Press books may be purchased in quantity for educational, business, or promotional use. For information, please email sales.press@yale.edu (U.S. office) or sales@yaleup.co.uk (U.K. office).

Set in Janson type by Newgen North America.
Printed in the United States of America.

Library of Congress Control Number: 2023930077
ISBN 978-0-300-25761-8 (hardcover : alk. paper)

A catalogue record for this book is available from the British Library.

This paper meets the requirements of ANSI/NISO Z39.48-1992 (Permanence of Paper).

10 9 8 7 6 5 4 3 2 1

To Kat

Contents

Acknowledgments

I DEVELOPED THIS PROJECT over a fifteen-year period in three different countries, and so I owe thanks to a lot of people across the globe. The seed of this book was planted at Victoria University of Wellington, New Zealand, where I had enrolled as an undergraduate in history after abandoning a career as an accountant in the United Kingdom. I thought I had put accounting behind me when I emigrated, but I discovered that the skills that I had developed when analyzing businesses in the English Midlands proved equally useful for studying the accounts of an eighteenth-century Liverpool slave trader. I owe my entry into slave trade studies to Steve Behrendt, who drew me into the subject through his passionate undergrad teaching at Vic and then his expert supervision of my M.A. James Campbell, Malcolm Craig, Michael Devine, and Kate Jordan were also great friends and colleagues in Vic's M.A. program, and I was also fortunate to receive guidance from Vic's faculty, especially Dolores Janiewski and Glyn Parry. My time in New Zealand was a particularly happy period thanks to the friendship of Josh and Alanah Clark, Geoff Hayward, Scott and Hannah Radburn, and Nick Ruane.

My work on slave-trading merchants might have ended when I finished my M.A. had David Eltis not encouraged me to apply to grad schools in the United States. I owe a great deal to David for the support he has given me since, including reading this manuscript in its entirety and serving on my doctoral dissertation committee. It was daunting to leave my friends and family to move to Johns Hopkins University for grad school, but I soon discovered that I had landed in my dream program. Phil Morgan was an ideal Ph.D. supervisor: generous with his time, knowledgeable, and always pushing me to think big. Like David, and Steve, Phil has become a close friend who has continued to help me think about how to convert my dissertation into this book. Numerous faculty members at Hopkins also helped me develop this project, especially Toby Ditz, Michael P. Johnson, Michael Kwass, the late Pier Larson, and Gabriel Paquette. My fellow grad students at Hopkins were equally important in helping to shape this work, particularly the members of the Early American Seminar: Katherine Arner, Joseph Clark, Sara Damiano, Meredith Gaffield, Stephanie Gamble, Claire Gherini, John Harris, Cole Jones, Alexey Krichtal, Lauren MacDonald, Emily Mokros, Dexnell Peters, Dave Schley, and Rachel Calvin Whitehead. And I owe a huge debt to my roommates at "History House" in Baltimore: Alvaro Caso Bello, Jonathan Gienapp, Craig Hollander, and Sarah Templier.

I received support from an equally expansive group of friends and colleagues after I left JHU. Peter Mancall selected me for an EMSI-Huntington Library postdoctoral fellowship when things were looking particularly bleak for me on the job market, which provided a crucial year to think about how I would structure this book. I also got to spend a year with a fantastic group of scholars, especially Scott Heerman, Lindsey O'Neill, Nathan Perl-Rosenthal, Keith Pluymers, Carole Shammas, Asheesh Siddique, Molly Warsh, and Jennifer Wells. Returning to the United Kingdom was never my plan, but I was fortunate to join Lancaster University's history department, where I've had the pleasure of working alongside some great colleagues, particularly Sophie Ambler, Sarah Barber, Tim Hickman, Mark Hurst, Paty Murietta-Flores, Will Pettigrew, Deb Sutton, Alex Wragg-Morley, and Marco Wyss. Seeing my old friends and family in the U.K.—Oli and Imogen Radburn, Jonathan Thompson, and Chris Wright—has also made finishing this book a lot more pleasurable.

Throughout my time at Lancaster, I have been a member of the *Slave Voyages* editorial team and so have had the fortune to meet weekly with leading scholars of the slave trade: Alex Borucki, Daniel Domingues da Silva, Jane Hooper, Nafees Khan, Kate McMahon, John Mulligan, Greg O'Malley, Jelmer Vos, and Jennie Williams.

Building two digital slave ship models with Arya Basu, Ian Burr, Bertrand Guillet, Paul Lachance, Alan Tullos, and Jane Webster also helped me develop the themes of chapter 3. And working with the Legacies of the British Slave Trade team—Nick Draper, Edmond Smith, James Dawkins, Lila Chambers, and Michael Bennet—aided my chapters on British merchants. Trevor Burnard, Marc Eagle, Melinda Elder, Sheryllynne Haggerty, Kathleen S. Murphy, Alan Rice, Justin Roberts, Anne Ruderman, David Wheat, and Nuala Zahedieh have all been generous with their time and provided sources that fed into this work. At Yale University Press, the three anonymous readers of my draft manuscript provided feedback that proved helpful in articulating my book's claims. I also owe thanks to my editor, Adina Berk, for seeing the potential in this project and steering it through publication. The feedback of audience members at conferences and workshops also shaped the book: the *Slave Voyages* launch conference at Emory; the American Historical Association in Chicago; BGEAH in Birmingham and Portsmouth; REDEHJA in Paris; the University of Ghana's seminar in Accra; the Trans-American Crossings conference at Brown; and the IHR's Economic and Social History seminar.

I am also indebted for the support of numerous funders and archivists. Victoria University of Wellington awarded me a scholarship that convinced me to undertake the M.A. rather than returning to accountancy. I would not have been able to undertake a Ph.D. without the support of JHU, who funded my graduate studies and provided additional support via the Kagan Fellowship. A sixth year of graduate funding, from the Doris G. Quinn Foundation and the Harry Frank Guggenheim Foundation, allowed me to concentrate on finishing my dissertation rather than teaching. An Economic History Society small grant also enabled me to explore the gunpowder industry's entanglements with the slave trade, a theme that fed into chapter 1 of the book. Numerous librarians shared their knowledge and collections with me, especially at the Bristol Archives; the British Library; the Historic Society of Pennsylvania; the Huntington Library; JHU's Milton S. Eisenhower Library; the John Carter Brown Library; the Liverpool Record Office; the Massachusetts Historical Society; the Merseyside Maritime Museum; the National Maritime Museum; the University of Liverpool Library; the Wilberforce

Institute; and the William L. Clements Library. Particular thanks are due to the staff at the National Archives at Kew, where much of the research for the book was undertaken, especially the Prize Papers Team—Amanda Bevan, Oliver Finnegan, and Randolph Cock.

My final thanks are reserved for my family. My parents, Steve and Naomi, provided their unwavering support for my pursuit of an academic career, even though it meant leaving them in New Zealand. While I have missed them, they have always been there for me as I have developed this book via frequent Skype calls and visits made much less frequent by the Covid pandemic. My in-laws, Steve, Mary, Zach, and Elizabeth, welcomed me into their family, making a home away from home while I was in the States. My daughter Willa was born twenty-four hours after I first submitted this manuscript, and my other daughter, Hazel, was born a week after I returned the copyedited version to the press. Their exuberance and love for life has made every day since their births a joy, albeit with a lot less sleep! My deepest thanks are for my wife, Katherine. We met at JHU and she has been there for me every step of the way since. She has been a sounding board for my ideas, the best editor and critical reader a writer could hope for, and a constant companion through the ups and downs of writing. The sacrifices she made so that I could pursue this book dwarf my own, as she moved across the Atlantic so that I could take a job in the U.K. and so left her own family behind. Without Katherine, this book would not exist, and so it is to her that I dedicate it.

TRADERS IN MEN

Introduction

IN 1775, BRITISH RADICAL Thomas Paine penned a devastating critique of what he called "Traders in Men"—the merchants who collectively organized the transatlantic slave trade. Focusing first on African slave traders, he termed them "desperate wretches" who were "willing to steal and enslave men by violence and murder for gain." Turning to British merchants, he described them as people who "sacrifice Conscience, and the character of integrity" at the "golden Idol" of profit. Finally, he poured scorn on "monstrous" British Americans for holding "so many hundred thousands in slavery." Through his condemnation of African, British, and American enslavers, Paine saw the extensiveness of the commercial networks that composed the slave trade by the late eighteenth century. As Paine wrote, merchants in myriad British cities organized slaving voyages by purchasing ships, loading them with trading cargoes sourced through complex commercial infrastructure, and dispatching them to the African coast. African brokers simultaneously marched captives to ports stretched across three thousand miles of coastline, where they sold enslaved people to arriving ships. American factors (brokers) received those ships as they dropped anchor after the Middle Passage and forced enslaved people into the plantation complex. The trade that these three groups of what Paine called "Men-Stealers" built together was, by 1775, immense. In that year alone, forty-five thousand men, women, and children were forcibly embarked on 175 British vessels in Africa. Despite the critiques of abolitionists such as Paine, the trade would grow further in the final quarter of the eighteenth century, peaking only in 1799. Across the entire eighteenth century, British slave traders shipped off 2.85 million Africans, almost half a million of whom perished on the Middle Passage. As Paine rightly noted, traders in men were responsible for the spilling of "so much innocent blood."[1]

That Britain's slave trade reached such enormous proportions by the time that Paine wrote is remarkable given the smallness of the business prior to the eighteenth century. In the two hundred years before 1700, English slave traders carried 430,000 people from Africa. Britons enslaved almost as many people in the ten-year period leading up to Paine's attack alone and shipped twice as many captives in the twenty-five years preceding the abolition of Britain's slave trade in 1807. The pre-eighteenth-century slave trade was also geographically confined. In Britain, the business was principally organized by government-backed companies and private merchants based in London, excluding traders in "outports" (ports outside the capital). The slave trade was likewise limited in Africa, because chartered companies principally purchased people from coastal forts. Almost half of the people enslaved by Britons before 1700 were consequently taken from the dungeons of slaving forts that lined a three-hundred-mile stretch of the several-thousand-mile-long African coastline. British American markets were equally constricted: of the 329,000 people who survived the Atlantic crossing, eight out of ten were sold in Barbados or Jamaica. As a result of its geographic concentration, small groups of merchants organized the pre-eighteenth-century slave trade. Although chartered companies had thousands of shareholders, they left the bloody business of slaving to small cadres of professional employees, ship captains, fort-based agents, and American factors. The narrowness of slaving in Africa meant that a minority of coastal people located in a few key sites were likewise engaged in selling people to Britons.[2]

This book explains how Paine's traders in men—thousands of enslavers in Africa, Britain, and the British Americas—collectively transformed Britain's slave trade into an Atlantic-wide system during the eighteenth century. It argues that slaving merchants devised a set of highly efficient—but incredibly brutal—methods for enslaving people, forcibly transporting them across the Atlantic and selling them in the Americas. The standardization and then expansion of these methods was what enabled slave traders to forcibly transport almost fifty thousand people a year by Paine's era. The spectacular growth of the slave trade sparked by these changes transformed the British Atlantic world. In Britain, ports such as Liverpool and Bristol grew into metropolises, aided by riches flowing from the slave trade. New ports were created in Africa to service visiting British ships, in the hinterland of which were powerful slaving societies that cast a metaphorical net over millions of people. And the frontier of slavery raced through the British Americas, propelled by the forced labor of Africans brought through the expansive slave trade. The slave trade was thus the engine that drove the expansion and integration of the British Atlantic world during the eighteenth century. The rapid growth of this cancerous system was premised on slave traders' presumption that enslaved people were a living commodity. The results for the millions of people who were pulled into the slave trade's vortex were unimaginably terrible, as they were mercilessly separated from family and friends, packed together in the holds of fetid slave ships, and shipped into slavery on the other side of the ocean.

Five years before Paine wrote his screed, Ottobah Cugoano (c. 1757– c. 1791), a thirteen-year-old boy in what is modern-day Ghana, became one of the millions of people ensnared by the traders in men. Cugoano was playing with a large group of children near his home, "a few days journey from the coast," when several pistol- and cutlass-wielding men claimed that the children had "committed a fault against their lord." After being separated from his playmates, Cugoano was driven to a nearby town and, six days later, marched to the sea. When he arrived at the water, a British slave trader purchased him for "a gun, a piece of cloth, and some lead." Three days later, Cugoano was rowed out to the dreaded slave ships. "There was nothing to be heard but rattling of chains, smacking of whips, and the groans and cries of our fellow men," he remembered. After a terrifying canoe trip over violent surf, Cugoano arrived at the ship where he and the other Africans were crowded together for months "in sight of our native land." He could not describe the "horrible scenes" and "base treatment" he faced aboard the slave ship, except

to say that one "succeeding woe, and dread, swelled up another."
After the Middle Passage, Cugoano and his shipmates were landed
at the British Caribbean island of Grenada, where he was sold and
then force-marched to a sugar plantation. There, he traumatically
witnessed enslaved people being beaten and tortured. Unlike most
of the Africans who undertook the Middle Passage, he was "delivered from . . . that horrid brutal slavery" when an English visitor
purchased him to work as a servant; he took Cugoano to Britain and
later freed him. Looking back on his enslavement, Cugoano could
barely describe his enslavement at the hands of numerous "barbarous robbers," except to say that the "thoughts which I then felt, still
pant in my heart." Although he escaped from slavery, it was "still
grievous" to him to imagine the tens of thousands of Africans who
suffered "in similar and greater distress" within Britain's slave trade
when he wrote his autobiography in 1787.[3]

Until recently, studies of the slave trade largely overlooked the
individual experiences of captives like Cugoano as historians sought
to instead quantify the size and complexity of the transatlantic slave
trade. In the past twenty years, though, a raft of books have focused
on the trade from the perspective of its victims, sparking a quiet revolution in slave trade studies. These "human histories" have demonstrated that the oceanic portion of an African's enslavement—*Slavery
at Sea*, or *Saltwater Slavery*, as it has been labeled—was just as traumatizing and formative as American plantation slavery. As Cugoano
described, enslaved people spent months aboard pestilential slave
ships where they endured crowding, poor food, and violence that
killed large numbers of people and wounded others. A cosmological
view that saw cannibalistic whites as demons who carried Africans on
endless voyages into an oceanic hell compounded enslaved people's
miseries. By unflinchingly detailing the horrors endured by captives
like Cugoano, human histories have also found that the slave trade
powerfully commoditized Africans before their arrival in the Americas. People first faced traumatic sales to alien whites on the coast,
marking the moment when "African Captives" were converted into
"Atlantic Commodities." Once at sea, Africans were made to endure
a daily regime that included forced exercise, to prevent muscular
atrophy, and starchy meals that were purposely designed to provide
maximum energy at minimum cost. Arrival in the Americas marked

the commencement of another traumatic stage, as enslaved people were shaved, glossed with oil, and then sold to colonists. By the conclusion of this three-stage process, Africans had been stripped of their identities and remade as "American slaves"—a generic commodity much like the sugar or tobacco that many captives would spend their lives growing. In addition to being a commerce, the slave trade was hence an "industry," as Sowande' Mustakeem has insightfully observed.[4]

Although recent scholarship has begun to sketch the three stages of the "human manufacturing process," particular regard has been paid to the Middle Passage. Slave ships have drawn attention because they were important sites of commodification, but also because they are well documented. Shipping generated reams of records in a way that slave trades on land typically did not, as owners, captains, and officials logged the movement of vessels around the Atlantic and corresponded across the oceans. Abolitionists also strategically fixed their campaign on shipping, and so they collected reams of testimony that vividly described the horrors of the ships—a treasure trove for historians examining the trade's human history. This focus on the Middle Passage has, however, left the terrestrial phases in Africa and the Americas neglected—despite those phases being perhaps just as formative to the Africans who endured them. Cugoano, for example, dwelt much more fulsomely on his enslavement in Africa and the Americas than he did on the Atlantic crossing—a common feature of slave narratives. The trauma of the Middle Passage no doubt forced many enslaved people to avoid reliving their experiences. But the relative shortness of the Atlantic crossing also helps to explain why enslaved people described their voyage so sparsely: at nine weeks, on average, the oceanic crossing was dwarfed by the months, and sometimes years, that captives sometimes spent within the slave trade in Africa and the Americas.[5]

In drawing so heavily on sources from the late eighteenth century to reconstruct a singular slave experience, recent scholarship has also inadvertently given the impression that Britain's slave trade changed little over the course of the eighteenth century. In reality, it was transformed during that period as expansive new pathways of forced migration were opened. Cugoano, for example, was enslaved on the Gold Coast and carried to Grenada—two places where the slave trade took off only in the eighteenth century. Had he been born a hundred years earlier, he would likely have lived his life as a free man on the Gold Coast. While quantitative studies have measured these important changes in the slave trade's size and contours, we lack adequate explanations of how the trade's processes were modified to facilitate the enslavement of millions of people. Understanding why Cugoano was enslaved necessitates an exploration of the important changes that occurred in Africa to fuel the export slave trade's expansion. The techniques that Britons utilized to trade people in Africa and the Americas likewise require scrutiny if we are to understand how the business of enslavement was modified to enable growth, as well as the impacts of those new techniques on the captives who endured them. Homing in on the experiences of enslaved people such as Cugoano in the late eighteenth century, while important, thus fails to capture when, why, and by whom the "human manufacturing process" was created, and how it changed over time.[6]

The lack of attention devoted to the changing character of Britain's slave trade is particularly remarkable given the scholarly attention that has been devoted to analyzing how American slavery was transformed as it expanded over time. African slavery in the British Caribbean, historians have found, was created through a careful process of experimentation on Barbados in the mid-seventeenth century. Barbadian planters dispensed with decentralized models of sugar production and instead contained all the steps of cultivation and processing on a single estate. Importantly, they also forced enslaved Africans, rather than indentured whites, to undertake every aspect of sugar work within large "gangs" organized by age, strength, and ability, with each gang made to work at a frenetic pace under a tropical sun by a whip-bearing driver. As this harsh new system of labor expanded across the island, Barbadian colonists devised new racial codes that permitted whites to beat, torture, and murder enslaved people. They simultaneously modified English gender norms, enabling women to be enslaved in the fields alongside men and be sexually abused at whim. The "Barbadian system" increased productivity and profits so radically that other Caribbean colonists soon adopted it; by 1750, the standardized Barbadian planting methods—along with the virulent racial and gender codes that accompanied them—were the bedrock of slavery across the British Caribbean. North American slavery likewise underwent seismic changes in the seventeenth and eighteenth centuries. In the first half of the seventeenth century, captive Africans toiled in conditions that were more akin to indentured servitude. As tobacco and rice planters began purchasing thousands of enslaved Africans in the late seventeenth century, though, they implemented regimented labor regimes similar to those of their Caribbean counterparts, as well as equally abusive racial and gender codes. The "charter generation" of Africans enslaved in the seventeenth century thus had experiences radically different to those of their successors in the "plantation generation" of the eighteenth century.[7]

Space was equally important for shaping the character of American slavery. Sugar plantations were, historians have found, very different to tobacco plantations: sugar estates held hundreds of enslaved people who occupied a plethora of skilled and unskilled positions, owing to the need to both grow and process sugar on site; tobacco plantations, by contrast, typically imprisoned fewer than thirty people, who each undertook a variety of tasks. The backbreaking labor needed to raise sugar under the Barbadian model ground enslaved people down, and so enslaved Africans were constantly purchased by sugar planters to replace the dead. The comparatively light labor regime needed to grow tobacco resulted in far fewer deaths and many more births. Two slave societies consequently emerged in the British Americas: a distinctly African society in the Caribbean; and a creole society in the Chesapeake. Further distinctions in the experiences of enslaved people prevailed among North American colonies and among individual Caribbean islands, with enslaved people on Carolina rice plantations enduring, for example, much heavier labor than their tobacco-growing counterparts in Virginia. As slavery expanded in the British Americas, numerous slave societies emerged, each with its own distinct labor regimes, cultures, and social structures.[8]

Analyzing how Britain's slave trade underwent a parallel, and connected, process of expansion necessitates a similarly nuanced attention to space and time. Cugoano, like other captives, experienced the slave trade as a three-stage process, and so equal regard must be devoted to the African and American wings of the slave trade and to the oft-studied Middle Passage. The slave trade was, however, so vast that it carried people from distant and distinct African regions and disembarked them in equally diverse American colonies. Examining how the slave trade grew and operated on either side of the Atlantic therefore requires attention to important regional differences, as well as commonalities in practices that simultaneously united those spaces. Whether we focus on Africa, the Middle Passage, or the Americas, we also need to appreciate how the slave trade's character changed over time. Quantifying the slave trade's ebbs and flows is important in gaining an understanding of when and where the trade expanded. But equal consideration needs to be devoted to how the practices within the slave trade were created and adapted to facilitate the trade's explosive growth. In this way, we can better grasp why Africans such as Cugoano were enslaved, and how they experienced their enslavement.

Studying the "barbarous robbers" who enslaved Cugoano and millions of other Africans can reveal how and by whom the slave trade was transformed, the way that its numerous stages operated, and the experiences of its victims across the vastness of the Atlantic world. As Paine realized, there was not one but three groups of slave traders in the British Atlantic world, each of whom was responsible for forcing captives along a different stage of the metaphorical conveyer belt into slavery: Africans enslaved people and sold them to ships owned by British merchants; these Britons' vessels forcibly transported enslaved people to the Americas; and "Guinea factors," as port-based slave traders were known in the Americas, sold arriving Africans to the colonists. By examining all three groups of slaving merchants, we can therefore grasp how Britain's slave trade operated at each stage of Africans' journeys into slavery—expanding the focus beyond the Middle Passage. Studying the business strategies of Atlantic slaving merchants can also reveal how the methods of enslavement that are now so recognizable to historians first emerged and operated. Moreover, the motivations of the trade's myriad investors need to be examined if we are to comprehend how the slave trade grew so large during the eighteenth century. By studying slaving merchants, this book thus sheds new light on how Britain's slave trade operated during the eighteenth century, while maintaining a focus on the "human history" of the people involved, both enslavers and the enslaved.[9]

Traders in Men focuses on slave traders within the British Atlantic world because they propelled the slave trade's growth during the eighteenth century. Viewed over the course of the trade's entire 350-year history, Portuguese merchants enslaved 5.85 million people, far more than the 3.25 million people taken by Britons. Like Britons, Portuguese merchants achieved their dominance by massively expanding the numbers of Africans whom they enslaved over time. Yet, the Portuguese were less important than Britons for spreading the slave trade in Africa because they concentrated south of the equator. Portuguese slave traders also sought few markets in the Americas because they disembarked most enslaved people in Brazil. Britons, by contrast, sought to circumvent Portugal's early control of the trade by enslaving people in new African and American markets north of the equator. Using these strategies, Britons inflated the slave trade and expanded its geography, enabling them to vault ahead of Portuguese merchants by the mid-eighteenth century. Britons also succeeded at slaving during the eighteenth century because they typically traded directly with Africans from the decks of ships, rather than operating in coastal forts or colonies. While French, Dutch, Danish, German, and American merchants pursued similar strategies, these groups were dwarfed by Britons, who enslaved more Africans than these numerous nations combined before 1808. Studying British merchants is thus crucial if we want to understand why the slave trade became so large in the eighteenth century, and especially why it expanded across the Atlantic world.[10]

Despite their importance to the slave trade's history, slaving merchants are under-studied. Human histories typically focus on the captains and crewmen of slave ships—the jailors whom captives faced and fought on the Middle Passage. When merchants feature in these works, they have been typically depicted as faceless capitalists who directed the commodification of enslaved people from afar, or African and American tyrants who tore enslaved people from each other. Business and economic historians have studied British slave traders to reveal their social background and aspirations, risk-reducing business strategies, and wildly fluctuating profits. Biographical studies of slaving merchants also provide snapshots of individual merchants' origins and varied career trajectories, demonstrating the trade's considerable risks and rewards. Slave traders elsewhere in the Atlantic world have received much less attention. Owing to a lack of records such as business accounts or diaries, few individual African slaving merchants have been examined.[11] Africanists have instead written a range of excellent works on individual slaving societies that have highlighted the important role of African merchants in the trade, particularly their agency when interacting with Europeans.[12] British American Guinea factors have received similarly scant attention, largely because they fall between extensive literatures on the slave trade and American slavery.[13] Especially lacking are works that examine the interlinked histories of British, African, and British American slave traders: no monograph has studied Atlantic slave traders collectively, and other works only touch on the connections between small groups of merchants in particular ports. Such a lacuna is especially remarkable given the extensive literature on the domestic slave trade in the Antebellum United States, which has effectively demonstrated the importance of merchants for shaping both the wider contours of the business and the formulation of its violent practices.[14]

Through an Atlantic-wide view of slaving merchants, *Traders in Men* makes five new and interrelated claims. First, it argues that British, African, and American merchants collectively expanded and transformed Britain's slave trade through their individual economic self-interest. At the opening of the eighteenth century, thousands of Atlantic merchants plunged into the recently liberalized slave trade in search of profits from the lucrative, but risky, business. Although each of these individuals acted selfishly, their collective actions rapidly spread the slave trade's frontiers across the Atlantic world and increased its volume. This process of expansion was enabled by the simultaneous formulation of a set of methods for enslaving people that were designed to enable myriad individuals to participate in a potentially perilous business. Slaving merchants knew that their victims were, as Paine labeled them, an "unnatural commodity," because people fought back, sickened, and died. Long-distance trade was also inherently fraught, especially cross-cultural exchange between Africans and Britons, who had very different goals and economic conceptions. To mitigate these risks, slave traders devised new business methods. In Africa, they developed the commercial infrastructure through which millions of people could be captured, moved swiftly to the coast, and exchanged for imports. British merchants simultaneously refined shipping methods that successfully curtailed resistance and reduced the numbers of captives who would typically perish at sea. American slave traders developed equally efficient techniques through which shiploads of captives could be sold to myriad colonial buyers, sometimes within an hour. The standardization and then widespread adoption of these methods was what enabled the slave trade's spectacular growth during the eighteenth century because it made the business a more secure and accessible investment. *Traders in Men* therefore contends that Britain's slave trade underwent a profound process of change that was crucial to the growth of Atlantic slavery.[15]

Second, this book demonstrates that this process of transformation was driven by individuals who shared similar backgrounds, motivations, and strategies. The slave trade's hazards deterred established merchants and attracted ambitious fortune hunters—usually non-elites who possessed limited stocks of capital that they were willing to chance in a high-risk, high-reward business. Those who succeeded vaulted the social ladder remarkably quickly, making the trade a powerful motor of social mobility in the British Atlantic world; those who crashed out were quickly replaced by newcomers. Regardless of whether they succeeded or failed, slave traders' shared social ambitions made them incredibly ruthless. Wherever they operated, traders in men adopted the same attitude: of viewing captives not as people but as goods that could be traded in the most efficient and profitable ways—regardless of the consequences for their victims. This mind-set was a fundamental prerequisite of slave trading; those who had compassion quit or were outcompeted by more merciless competitors. Slave traders' shared views were also crucial for the formulation and refinement of their business practices. Traders in men wrenched families and friends apart at slave sales on either side of the Atlantic to obtain healthy captives or people of a certain age; carefully computed how to pack people into cramped spaces aboard ships to maximize the carrying capacity of the ships; and utilized instrumental terror to effectively cow resistance. The book consequently demonstrates that violence was fundamental to slave traders' business methods throughout the Atlantic world, and that violence was underpinned by merchants' lowly social backgrounds and extreme ambition.

Third, *Traders in Men* argues that merchants structured the slave trade through the creation of Atlantic-wide commercial networks. Operating largely free of regulation, slave traders had to self-organize by forming business relations with one another. As the slave trade expanded, these small-scale partnerships collectively formed a vast transatlantic social network that resembled a complex crystalline structure. Although portions of this structure shattered as individuals fell out of the risky business of slaving, the network was self-repairing as new participants joined the trade. Decentralization made the slave trade incredibly resilient, enabling it to thrive throughout the turbulent and war-torn eighteenth century; one abolitionist astutely observed that Britain's slave trade was difficult to destroy precisely because it was a "hydra" made up of "many bodies of men." In addition to sustaining the trade's growth, merchant networks also conditioned the forced migration of enslaved people. Slave ships departed Britain and then moved to correspondents within their outfitters' networks, carrying enslaved people from particular African locales to specific American colonies. Enslavers' networks were also important for shaping the movements of enslaved people on both sides of the Atlantic. Ships moved through American waters, seeking markets in which to disembark enslaved people following paths established by ties between British merchants and American factors. African and American merchants formed their own subnetworks of slave sellers and buyers to quickly move people aboard and away from the ships. Merchants within these subnetworks transported enslaved people far beyond slaving ports, stretching the trade's tentacles deep inland on either side of the Atlantic. An enslaved person's fate was thus intimately tied to the enslavers' business decisions.[16]

Fourth, *Traders in Men* reveals that an enslaved person's age, sex, and especially health were crucial for determining the person's path through these networks because of the particular ways that slaving merchants organized their businesses. Slave buyers in both Africa and the Americas sought captives who met particular physical criteria because they wanted people who either could perform specific, often laborious, tasks or were in good enough health to survive arduous forced marches and oceanic voyages. Enslavers purchased captives who met their standards and marched them on one path, leaving those whom they rejected to take another route that might ultimately lead to a separate destination. Africans might, therefore, enter slavery with their family, villagers, or co-linguists but subsequently find themselves taking very different routes through the slave trade as merchants constantly sorted and separated them according to their physical characteristics. As enslaved people passed through the hands of numerous slave traders on both sides of the ocean, they endured a multistage "Long Middle Passage" that took several months—and sometimes years—to complete, dwarfing the ten-week ocean voyage that has been the focus of scholarly attention. Slave sales were the crucial junctions and crossroads in the slave trade because it was at these moments that enslaved people were collected or dispersed. A person's path into American slavery was not the straight leg of a transatlantic triangle but rather a potentially drawn-out journey through the complicated system of slaving routes that composed the Long Middle Passage.

Fifth, this book contends that Africans' experience of their enslavement varied considerably depending on their physical characteristics. A healthy person who arrived on the African coast would likely board a slave ship immediately, while an unhealthy companion would be forced aboard an entirely different vessel much later. Aboard the ships themselves, men, women, and children had varying experiences because slave traders divided people according to their age and sex. The experience of the slave trade in the Americas was equally diverse: men and women who arrived in good health were quickly marched from the port to a plantation, while their sickly shipmates were forced into complex secondary markets; children were often purchased to work as servants or apprentices. The amount of time that a person took to complete the Long Middle Passage also varied considerably. Healthy adults—especially men—might complete the journey from African to American slavery in the space of a few months; sickly captives spent longer periods, sometimes years, wending their way through tortuous slave routes on either side of the Atlantic. Through its focus on the importance of enslaved people's physical characteristics, this book departs from recent literature that has argued that enslaved people's "ethnicity" was the key determinant of people's forced movement through the slave trade. The book does not dispute that enslaved people possessed distinct African cultures that were crucial to individual captives and the wider cultural history of the Atlantic world. But it does contend that an enslaved person's age, gender, and health were what largely shaped their tortuous path through the Long Middle Passage—a complex network of slaving routes created by slaving merchants that stitched the Atlantic world together.[17]

Traders in Men sustains these five claims primarily through the analysis of records generated by slaving merchants. Despite the participation of at least four thousand private merchants in Britain's slave trade, only a handful of major collections of papers are extant.[18] Even so, these records are sufficiently detailed to analyze British merchants' strategies and the ways that their captains bought people in Africa, transported them across the Atlantic, and then sold them in the Americas. The voluminous papers of the Royal African Company and its successor firm also include key information on the formulation of methods of enslavement in the late seventeenth century.[19] Guinea factors' archives were, until recently, sparse. The discovery of two major collections now provides sufficient information to reconstruct the complex ways by which enslaved people were sold in the Americas, especially in late eighteenth-century Jamaica. Cross-referencing Guinea factors' records with colonial newspapers and the papers of slave buyers illuminates the subsequent fates of enslaved people after their sale. Complementing Atlantic slave traders' records are the voluminous reports generated by abolitionist debates in Parliament, which include the testimony of slaving merchants, fort-based officers, Guinea factors, planters, captains, and crewmen.[20]

In addition to drawing on a wealth of archival records that collectively detail how the slave trade developed and operated, *Traders in Men* also draws heavily upon *Slave Voyages*—a database of more than thirty-six thousand Atlantic slaving voyages.[21] By thus marrying quantitative and qualitative approaches, this book seeks to bridge a methodological divide that has emerged within slave trade studies.[22] An increasingly vocal group of scholars object to efforts to quantify the trade via large datasets. In 2008, for example, Marcus Rediker complained of a "violence of abstraction" that has "plagued the study of the slave trade from its beginning." Rediker's charge has been carried by numerous other scholars, some of whom have deliberately eschewed the use of numbers and statistics in their works. Other critics have noted that the *Slave Voyages* datasets include little information on the previous origins or subsequent destinations of enslaved people in Africa or the Americas. To respond to these critiques, I downloaded the 11,232 British voyages into a custom database and then added new fields that detail how enslaved people were sold to and from the ships, their experiences aboard the vessels, and their movement through the Americas. At the same time, I employ myriad qualitative sources—especially letters, slave narratives, and personal testimony—that maintain a close focus on the trade's human history. This book thus aims to demonstrate that quantification can shed new light on enslaved people's experiences within the slave trade, while simultaneously recognizing the importance of looking beyond numbers.[23]

These sources and methods collectively underpin five chapters, each of which examines a different stage in the process of enslavement. *Traders in Men* begins by offering a new explanation for the simultaneous and interlinked growth of the slave trade in Britain and Africa during the eighteenth century. After the collapse of the Royal African Company's monopoly in 1698, marginal but socially ambitious English outport merchants sought to enter the slave trade by dispatching vessels to areas of the African coast where they could purchase people direct from African brokers. The result was an explosion in the number of African ports engaged in the slave trade and a concomitant transformation of British ports such as Liverpool into major hubs of the business. Realizing that Britons could purchase enslaved people from myriad African ports, three groups of merchants on the Gold Coast and in the Bight of Biafra transformed their homes into efficient slaving ports that would draw British vessels. As a result of the business decisions of equally ambitious Britons and Africans, most captives arriving in the British Americas during the eighteenth century left a small number of busy African slaving ports aboard ships fitted out from an even smaller number of British cities.

Chapter 2 explains how slaving merchants simultaneously devised commercial practices through which millions of people could be traded across cultural lines. British and African merchants entered the slave market with very different goals: responding to the demands of American planters, British slave ship captains sought "prime slaves" who met specific standards of age and health; African brokers wanted exacting assortments of imported goods in exchange for captives. Traders in men developed complex new ways of selling people according to their age, sex, and health that enabled both groups to get what they wanted—at the expense of their enslaved victims. Captive Africans consequently suffered through numerous inspections, sales, and separations before they boarded a slave ship; many were rejected by whites and returned inland. The process by which captives were sold on the African coast thus had crucial implications for the direction that enslaved people took into slavery, and the amount of time that they spent trapped aboard the ships.

Chapter 3 follows slave ships to sea to show how British merchants' calculating business decisions shaped the experiences of enslaved people on the Middle Passage. It reveals that, by the opening of the eighteenth century, Britons had fixed upon a new method of shipping people that increased profitability by reducing both mortality rates and captive Africans' chances of successfully rebelling. Seeking to maximize the numbers of enslaved people who could be carried to the Americas, merchants packed as many enslaved people into their vessels as they could hold. On the typical British ship sailing before 1789, captives were consequently squeezed on their sides into tightly packed rooms unable to move from their painful position for sixteen hours a day; for the other eight hours, they were pressed together above deck into dense crowds. The implementation of these harsh techniques enabled merchants to transport millions of enslaved people to the Americas alive during the eighteenth century but led directly to the deaths of one in six embarked Africans, and the crippling of a fifth of the survivors.

Chapter 4 traces the movement of slave ships within American waters to reveal how slave traders determined the destinations of enslaved people. Thousands of ambitious American Guinea factors knitted the vast archipelago of British American slaving markets into a cohesive web of slaving markets by connecting with British slaving merchants. Slave ship captains were therefore able to use market intelligence provided by American slave traders to elect where to land their human cargoes, be it one of the diverse British Caribbean sugar islands or the North American rice and tobacco fields—powerfully shaping the fates of captive Africans. This chapter also demonstrates that slaving voyages within the Americas were formative stages in the Long Middle Passage. Journeys to often-distant American markets strained the mental and physical health of already exhausted people, killing captives that might have survived had they been disembarked in the first colony reached by a vessel. Because ships often sailed near land or anchored in ports, these voyages also enabled captive Africans to begin the difficult process of acclimatization before they made landfall.

Chapter 5 explores how Guinea factors sold enslaved Africans once ships reached their destination. In the late seventeenth century, slave traders across the British Americas embraced a standardized sales method with few variations: affluent planters entered the sale early and selected the healthiest "prime" adult slaves, leaving less affluent colonists to obtain children and sickly people; merchants and speculators purchased the remaining "refuse slaves" and sought to resell them locally or reexport them to neighboring colonies. Although the structure of slave sales was similar throughout the British Americas, this chapter demonstrates that sales nonetheless varied enormously in length: some were concluded within less than an hour, whereas some stretched on for months; the average length was almost four weeks. By following sickly Africans beyond their sale, this chapter also shows that the slave trade within the Americas was much more sophisticated and deadly than has been assumed. For many captives, slave sales were thus the crossroads that marked the end of a voyage through the transatlantic slave trade and the beginning of a potentially tortuous additional journey into American slavery.

By examining these five different stages of enslavement across the vastness of the Atlantic world, *Traders in Men* thus illuminates how merchants created an interlinked set of standardized techniques that proved insidiously effective at enslaving people. The epilogue explores how slave traders continued to benefit from these violent methods as their business was attacked and came to an end during the Age of Revolutions. The threat of abolition, coupled with the almost simultaneous outbreak of the Haitian Revolution in 1791, increased the American demand for enslaved people, as colonists sought to buy captives before the slave trade closed. The onset of the French Revolutionary Wars in 1793 opened new slaving markets to British merchants, further spreading the frontiers of slavery in the trade's closing years. Slaving merchants in Britain, Africa, and the Americas who could successfully navigate the risks of operating in an era of war and economic uncertainty could profit enormously from these transformations. When Britain's slave trade ended in 1808, many merchants were hence able to depart the business with fortunes purged of the taint of slavery, while their enslaved victims remained in bondage.

CHAPTER ONE

Connecting the Frontiers

British Merchants, African Middlemen,
and the Making of Atlantic Slaving Ports

I N JUNE 1780, THREE LEADING Efik slaving merchants at Old Calabar, a port in the Bight of Biafra, wrote a remarkable letter to their Liverpool trading partners. Owing to the American Revolutionary War (1775–1783), no slave ships had visited Calabar in the preceding two years. With alarm, the Efik brokers wrote to ask why the Liverpool merchants did not "Send Ship Sam[e] as Befor[e]" the war, when thirteen vessels had annually anchored in their river. The "Country" was "full" of captives that the Efik wanted to sell, and they "beg[ged]" their British partners to send ships and purchase them. If the ships did not come, they pleaded, Old Calabar would "Spoill" because the Efik had "nothing to Live [by] but Ship[s]." The Efik reliance on the slave trade was recent. In the mid-seventeenth century, Old Calabar was principally a collection of fishing villages nestled on the marshy banks of the Cross River. In the early eighteenth century, though, Efik merchants began selling thousands of people to visiting Britons, transforming their home into a booming Atlantic port. Writing nine years later, slaving merchant Robert Norris (d. 1791) likewise emphasized the traffic's key role in Liverpool's growth from fishing town to Atlantic port city. "At the Beginning of this Century," he observed, Liverpool "contained only about a thousand Houses, and five thousand Inhabitants." When Norris wrote in 1789, there were "above 10,000 Houses & 70,000 Inhabitants" and a series of docks that "excel every thing of the Kind in Europe." Of all the "branches" of trade, he wrote, Liverpool's "emerg[ence] from Obscurity" was "owing principally" to the slave trade. Norris deliberately overestimated the slave trade's prime responsibility for Liverpool's rise, but he correctly identified the town's astonishing expansion in slaving. In 1700, Liverpool merchants, like other merchants in outports, had little involvement in the trade. By the time of Norris's letter, a slave ship left Liverpool's docks every five days, making the town the largest slaving port in the Atlantic world.[1]

Although written by people separated by more than three thousand miles, these two letters capture how slaving ports were created in both Atlantic Africa and Britain during the eighteenth century—a phenomenon that was crucial to the slave trade's expansion. To satiate British American colonists' increasing demands for captive laborers, millions of people would be enslaved in Africa during the eighteenth century. African merchants sought to meet this demand by opening their homes to the slave trade, tripling the number of ports engaged in the slave trade with Britons, from twenty-nine locations before 1700 to eighty-seven during the eighteenth century. The growth of Britain's slave trade was likewise driven by the entry of new ports; slave ships left thirty towns in the eighteenth century, versus just nine before 1700. Even as the traffic's scope and scale widened, it remained concentrated in a handful of locations. Britons carried three-quarters of the 2.85 million people whom they enslaved during the eighteenth century from just ten African ports (Table 1.1). More than half of the captives carried from those ten ports were shipped to just three locations: Old Calabar in the eastern Bight of Biafra, Bonny in the western Bight, and Anomabu on the Gold Coast. All were insignificant slaving ports before the eighteenth century: just 37,548 people had been carried from them before 1700. The trade was even more concentrated in Britain; ships sailing from London, Bristol, and Liverpool carried almost nine of every ten enslaved Africans. Unlike London—the locus of England's seventeenth-century slave trade—Bristol and Liverpool handled little slave traffic until the eighteenth century. British and African slaving ports were thus made simultaneously.[2]

Table 1.1. The ten largest African ports by captives embarked on British vessels, 1514–1699 and 1700–1808

#	1514–1699 Port	1514–1699 Region	Captives Embarked	Captives Embarked	1700–1808 Region	1700–1808 Port	#
1	Whydah[F]	Bight of Benin	40,480	361,541	Bight of Biafra	Bonny	1
2	Old Calabar	Bight of Biafra	25,286	171,152	Bight of Biafra	Old Calabar	2
3	Ardra[F]	Bight of Benin	19,907	131,977	Gold Coast	Anomabu[a]	3
4	Gambia[F]	Senegambia	13,512	93,997	Senegambia	Gambia[F]	4
5	New Calabar	Bight of Biafra	13,116	92,119	Gold Coast	Cape Coast Castle[F]	5
6	Madagascar	Southeast Africa	7,958	82,376	Bight of Benin	Whydah[F]	6
7	Cape Coast Castle[F]	Gold Coast	7,221	80,235	Sierra Leone	Sierra Leone[F]	7
8	Kormantse[F]	Gold Coast	2,975	65,776	Bight of Biafra	New Calabar	8
9	Cabinda	West-Central Africa	2,648	34,167	West-Central Africa	Congo River	9
10	Sierra Leone[F]	Sierra Leone	1,927	33,555	Windward Coast	Cape Mount	10
	Subtotal at top ten ports		135,030	1,148,895	Subtotal at top ten ports		
	Subtotal at remaining 19 ports		9,956	362,593	Subtotal at remaining 82 ports		
	% share of top ten ports		93.1	76.0	% share of top ten ports		
	Unknown[b]		132,709	1,288,386			
	Estimated[c]		127,412	56,121			
	Total		405,107	2,853,995			

Source: Pre-1700 ports: https://www.slavevoyages.org/voyages/EG3raRVd. Post-1700 ports: https://www.slavevoyages.org/voyages/plxLkID). Estimates are from SV-*Estimates,* Flag; Great Britain, 1501–1699; 1700–1808. For the concentration of the trade at large African ports, see also Eltis and Richardson, *Atlas,* 90.
[F] Designates ports with forts/trading posts.
[a] The English and Dutch constructed forts at Anomabu, but these were both destroyed in the late seventeenth century. Although the British built a costly new fort there in 1757, it was ancillary to the port's slave trade, which was principally conducted directly between Africans and ship captains.
[b] "Unknown" refers to documented slaving voyages in which the region of trade is typically known but not the specific African port of embarkation. It is highly unlikely that these vessels traded at an unidentified major African slaving port.
[c] "Estimated" refers to voyages for which there is no documentation but which the authors of *SV* assume occurred. These vessels would have also traded at ports identified in the *SV,* including those listed above.

Historians have sought to explain the slave trade's geographic concentration in Africa and Europe by focusing on the market forces that gave ports particular economic advantages in either fitting out slave ships or forcibly exporting captives, such as location, experience in long-distance trade, proximity to trading hinterlands, and the development of complex credit mechanisms. Focusing on merchants reveals that these apparently abstract economic processes were driven by the actions of thousands of individual Britons and Africans who bore remarkable similarities. British merchants in outports such as Liverpool were socially marginal men who migrated to port towns to invest in risky Atlantic trades. They sought to grow their meager capital stock by scouring the African coast for underdeveloped markets where enslaved people could be purchased direct from coastal brokers for low prices. At the same time, Britons established the market infrastructure needed to source the complex assortments of trade goods demanded by African consumers in exchange for slaves, helping to drive the physical transformation of their adopted homes. Examining the African merchants who inhabited Bonny, Old Calabar, and Anomabu shows that they were equally fringe people who also saw opportunities to elevate themselves through slaving. Small groups of traders in these ports realized that their success hinged on making their homes efficient markets for the sale of people, attracting British vessels that might otherwise sail elsewhere. To achieve these ends, Africans cultivated ties with emergent slaving societies in the interior; developed the physical infrastructure through which thousands of captives could be moved to the coast; conquered neighboring ports; and forged close relations with visiting Britons. Commercial relationships between African and British merchants therefore connected the frontiers, linking previously peripheral people together in a mutually beneficial arrangement that enabled both groups to thrive in the slave trade—a business from which they had previously been excluded by more established merchants.[3]

When the Efik wrote their letter in 1780, coastal Africans had been trading with visiting Europeans for three and a half centuries. Although Europeans dealt with a plethora of people before 1700, they largely concentrated their trade at regions where Africans allowed them to build forts ashore, typically at the terminus of trade routes along which gold and tropical commodities flowed. During the fifteenth century, the Portuguese constructed forts at Arguin, in modern-day Mauritania; Bissau and Cacheo in Upper Guinea; São Jorge da Mina, in modern-day Ghana; and in the Kingdom of Kongo. In 1576, the Portuguese concentrated their presence in West-Central Africa by founding a colony at Luanda, in modern-day Angola; thirty years later, they constructed another post at nearby Benguela. The entry of northern European joint-stock companies to the African trade during the seventeenth century significantly increased the number of permanent coastal facilities. England, Holland, France, Sweden, Denmark, and Brandenburg all chartered companies that constructed forts to protect their purported monopolies from domestic and foreign interlopers. France and England's companies erected forts on the Senegal and Gambia Rivers to access the trade in gum Arabic, an important dyeing agent. The English, Dutch, Danes, and Swedes built forts along the Gold Coast to break into the lucrative gold trade; by the end of the seventeenth century, twenty-five "factories" lined the region's beaches. In the late seventeenth century, the English, Dutch, and French also built trading posts at Whydah, in the Bight of Benin, all within cannon shot of a station that the Portuguese had erected in 1580—rare coastal facilities constructed specifically for the slave trade. Before 1700, the European presence in Africa expanded considerably, but it remained disproportionately concentrated in areas of the coast with permanent facilities ashore, principally Senegambia, the Gold Coast, the Bight of Benin, and Portuguese Angola.[4]

The geography of the early slave trade was largely shaped by the locations of forts, as Europeans used the same trade routes through which they had purchased commodities to purchase captives. More than half of the 2.1 million people embarked before 1700 were carried from West-Central Africa, the overwhelming majority of whom were taken from the Portuguese settlements south of the Congo River. The next-largest areas of departure were Senegambia, the sites of the French and English forts, and the Bight of Benin, where the Portuguese, Dutch, French, and English possessed "lodges" at Whydah; a nascent slave trade from the forts on the Sierra Leone River and the Gold Coast also began in the late seventeenth century.

While European captains did purchase captives direct from African brokers in areas without onshore facilities—the Bight of Biafra, the Windward Coast, the Loango Coast, and Southeast Africa—departures from these regions made up just 11 percent of the total traffic. The pre-eighteenth-century slave trade was hence largely synonymous with the "fort trade" in which land-based European agents purchased captives from African brokers, imprisoned them in the dungeons of coastal facilities, and then embarked them on ships.[5]

The dissolution of the exclusive rights of the English Royal African Company (RAC) was crucial to the increase in the volume of the slave trade, and a dramatic reorientation of its African geography. Parliament founded the RAC in 1672 with a monopoly on England's trade with Africa, and within a decade the company was annually carrying more than five thousand Africans and controlled 80 percent of England's slave trade. Even so, the RAC consistently failed to obtain the increasing numbers of captives demanded by American planters, a demand that interlopers from London and Bristol sought to meet. These private traders formed a powerful political lobby that successfully championed the right of Englishmen to trade freely in enslaved people. Parliament responded by terminating the RAC's monopoly in 1698, leaving the slave trade open to private British merchants for a 10 percent tax on exports; in 1712, the 10 percent impost ended. The debt-ridden RAC finally abandoned slaving in 1731, and in 1750 Parliament closed the company and vested its forts in the hands of the Company of Merchants Trading to Africa, a non-monopoly holding company tasked with assisting private merchants but not slave trading itself. From 1698, then, the slave trade was open to British merchants who traded alongside the moribund RAC; after 1731, the trade was entirely the preserve of private merchants.[6]

Private merchants rushed to invest in the African trade after 1698, almost doubling the volume of England's slave trade within twenty years. Londoners initially dominated, largely because they inherited expertise and commercial networks from the London-based RAC. Outport merchants also flocked to the trade, led by Bristolians. Bristol's rise in the trade was rapid: from 1700 to 1732, the number of slave ships annually departing the port increased from two to fifty; in 1728, Bristol outpaced London as the leading British slaving port.

Liverpool did not seriously enter the business until the 1730s, but the northern town soon overtook both Bristol and London, largely because of the dislocations caused by the War of Austrian Succession (1740–1748). Liverpool held its lead until abolition, by which point it had a near monopoly on Britain's trade.[7] Bristol and especially Liverpool were unlikely candidates to wrest control of Britain's slave trade from London. Both ports were tiny compared to London, which was home to around six hundred thousand people by 1700. Liverpool was then inhabited by just five thousand people, and even Bristol—the "metropolis of the West"—had a population of twenty thousand. In addition to their small size, the outports had environs that were rustic in character. The roads out of Liverpool wended through Lancashire and Cheshire, rural counties populated by farmers and weavers. Southwest England had been an important area for the flour and woolen trade since the Middle Ages, but the region was still underdeveloped compared to London's hinterland of busy roads and market towns.[8]

Although the outports' surroundings appeared backward, they underwent profound changes at the turn of the eighteenth century. The population of England grew by an anemic 10 percent between 1650 and 1750, from 5.5 million to 6.1 million, a figure that masked explosive expansion in the countryside around Bristol and Liverpool. Between 1630 and 1750, the combined population of Lancashire and Cheshire increased from 309,000 to 457,000; southwest Lancashire—the area immediately adjacent to Liverpool—accounted for much of this growth. And in the same period, the population of the three counties surrounding Bristol grew from 482,000 to 626,000. As the authors of one history of Lancashire note, this growth was "not so much an urban increase as a thickening of the population over the countryside," with agricultural improvement and falling mortality enabling the sustained growth of families in rural villages. Bustling country settlements provided a constant stream of ambitious young migrants to the nearby port cities: Liverpool's population increased sixteenfold between 1700 and 1800, from five thousand to eighty thousand; three-fourths of this growth derived from in-migration. Bristol more than tripled in size during the same period.[9]

Country people possessed of capital and ambition migrated to the port cities to try and make their fortunes in the new trades in

*Figure 1.1. Principal British slave-trading ports, c. 1700–1808.
Based on data from Slavevoyages.org.*

slave-grown tobacco and sugar. British tobacco imports increased exponentially in the seventeenth century: from half a million pounds in 1630 to almost forty million by the end of the century. Sugar imports from the Caribbean followed a similar trajectory, from almost zero in 1640 to fifty million pounds a year by 1700. Both trades continued their expansion at a slower pace throughout the eighteenth century. American planters imported consumables and manufactures, resulting in a parallel surge in exports to the colonies. And the collection of goods in port prior to their export, and then the distribution of sugar and tobacco throughout Britain and Europe, caused a blossoming in coastal trades. The Atlantic trades were thus dynamic motors of growth in the otherwise stagnant English economy during the seventeenth century.[10]

Expanding Atlantic markets presented opportunities to migrants that were unavailable in the more established trades to Europe and the Indian Ocean—both of which continued to be largely controlled by London-based merchant societies. Those societies dispatched factors to permanent trading posts; these agents received carefully selected exports such as woolens and manufactures. The factors bartered these items for enumerated goods depending on the location of trade, such as wine and oils, which their companies then distributed throughout England along well-regulated channels. Admission to the societies was carefully guarded, preventing newcomers from entering without the permission of existing members. Moreover, interlopers struggled to subvert the societies' stranglehold on trade because they did not possess factories in key ports and there were few new areas where trade could be opened. The Atlantic trades, by contrast, were largely open. Unlike picky factors, colonists in the Caribbean and North America required a wide variety of goods, both durables and consumables, to establish and maintain plantations. Colonists exchanged imported goods almost exclusively for sugar and tobacco, rather than the enumerated items that returned from European ports. And the rapid expansion of plantation agriculture in the Americas offered a growing number of trading locations to which merchants could dispatch their vessels. In the early seventeenth century, ambitious "new men" flocked to London to seize the opportunities presented by the Atlantic trades, forming a body of merchants that was interlinked through partnership, patronage, and kinship. At the end of the century, though, migrants instead began to look to the outports, where burgeoning Atlantic trades offered "the chance to use their capital and their contacts to become merchants," a profession that had been previously closed off.[11]

Outport merchants elbowed their way into the London-dominated Atlantic trades by aggressively trading at the margins. In the second half of the seventeenth century, tobacco planters in Maryland found it increasingly difficult to obtain indentured servants from London because of the booming demand for bound workers in more affluent Virginia. Liverpool's tobacco traders—mere minnows compared to London's leviathans—obliged the Maryland planters by recruiting servants from Lancashire's populous villages and nearby Irish ports, with which Liverpool had traded for centuries. Liverpudlians likewise pushed into the sugar trade by shipping Irish servants and foodstuffs to the marginal eastern Caribbean islands. Extra profits were obtained by aggressively cutting shipping expenses, purchasing poor-quality sugar and tobacco at low prices, and smuggling. Bristol merchants pursued similar strategies. Londoners imported four-fifths of their sugar from Barbados and Jamaica in 1686; Bristolians sourced more than half from the more marginal islands of Antigua, Montserrat, and Nevis. In the Chesapeake, Bristol traders established trading posts on the York River to avoid competition from Londoners on the wealthy James River. These strategies provided a wedge into the London-controlled tobacco and sugar trades that merchants in the outports pried open in the eighteenth century.[12]

Once a merchant had grown his capital in the Atlantic trades, investing in the slave trade was an enticing proposition because it was potentially profitable, albeit perilous. The slave trade was uniquely risky because it involved trading people; captives fought back or perished, threatening their enslavers' investments. Voyages to Africa, then the Americas, and back to Britain were also lengthy—often lasting a year or more—and thus hazardous. Unlike the other Atlantic trades, in which merchants typically rented out space on their vessels, slave traders owned both the ship and the cargo, further increasing risk. Merchants who could manage these risks stood to make substantial gains, though. Data on the early slave trade's profitability is lacking, but studies of the mid-to-late eighteenth-century trade have discovered that returns averaged about 10 percent per annum—a healthy return given that annual interest rates hovered around 4 percent. But the average conceals enormous volatility: returns on individual voyages ranged from more than one hundred percent—so-called Golden Voyages—to catastrophic losses; the slave trade was, as one Liverpool captain aptly described it, a "lottery." It was precisely this potential for great gains that drew many merchants to the slave trade; as the same captain noted, "every adventurer" in the lottery "hoped to gain a prize." This was especially true of the outport merchants, ambitious migrants who had already usually risked their capital in the sugar and tobacco trades. In-migration from the countryside provided a stream of newcomers who could replace those who crashed out of the hazardous slave trade.[13]

Examining the backgrounds of the ten largest British slaving families demonstrates the importance of migration and the Atlantic trades to the community of merchants that dominated the slave trade during the eighteenth century. Of the ten families, seven had recent ancestors who migrated to a port city; the remaining three families originated in the ports themselves. The migrants all hailed from the proximity of Liverpool, except for the Laroche family, who moved to Bristol as Huguenot refugees from France in the early eighteenth century. Analyzing the occupations of the first non-merchant male member of the ten leading slave trading dynasties illustrates the families' humble origins: eight of the ten had a tradesman or farmer as their ancestor. All the families are remarkable for the rapidity with which they joined the merchant elite, highlighting the prospects for advancement through Atlantic trade, the slave trade in particular: each family member who first invested in the slave trade was also the first member of his family to trade as a merchant. Seven of the first investors founded multigenerational slaving businesses, sometimes involving both their sons and their grandsons. Analyzing the community of Bristol slave traders reveals that these ten leading families were representative of wider trends: of 196 individuals for whom a birthplace is known (out of a total investor cohort of 568), half (ninety-eight people) hailed from Bristol and the remainder migrated to the city, principally from the adjacent counties of Gloucestershire (twenty-three) and Somerset (twenty-six). Most of the Bristol traders were sons of either a tradesman or a farmer;

Table 1.2. The ten largest British slave-trading families and their origins

	Family name	Port of investment	First year of investment	Last year of investment	# of years invested	# of voyages financed	# of people enslaved	First investor in the slave trade	First investor's father's occupation	Family origin
1	Gregson	Liverpool	1744	1801	58	213	73,748	William (1735–1809)	Porter	Liverpool
2	Backhouse	Liverpool	1745	1807	63	212	64,504	John (1717–1776)	Gentleman	Milnthorpe, Westmoreland
3	Aspinall	Liverpool	1766	1808	43	193	61,957	James (1729–1788)	Mariner	Liverpool
4	Case	Liverpool	1763	1808	45	193	58,594	George (1747–1836)	Mercer	Prescot, Lancashire
5	Boats	Liverpool	1753	1795	43	155	54,273	William (1716–1794)	Barber	Liverpool
6	Tarleton	Liverpool	1716	1802	87	184	52,674	Thomas (1680–1731)	Surgeon	Aigburth, Lancashire
7	Earle	Liverpool	1699	1804	105	176	49,703	John (1674–1749)	Brewer	Warrington, Lancashire
8	Dawson	Liverpool	1760	1799	40	118	47,935	John (?–1812)	Yeoman	Cumberland
9	Laroche	Bristol	1727	1768	42	135	41,965	James (1703–1770)	Servant	Bordeaux, France
10	Davenport	Liverpool	1748	1786	39	159	40,151	William (1725–1797)	Lawyer	Capesthorne, Cheshire

Source: The largest family members have been ascertained by analyzing the "vessel owner" field for British ships in *SV.* The occupations and origins of the family members are principally drawn from David Pope, "The Wealth and Social Aspirations of Liverpool's Slave Merchants of the Second Half of the Eighteenth Century," in *Liverpool and Transatlantic Slavery*, ed. David Richardson, Anthony Tibbles, and Suzanne Schwarz (Liverpool: Liverpool University Press, 2007), 164–226. For the Laroche family, see "LAROCHE, James (1734–1804), of Over, nr. Bristol, Glos.," in *The History of Parliament: The House of Commons 1754–1790*, ed. Lewis Namier and John Brooke (London: Boydell and Brewer, 1964). For the Davenport family, see David Richardson, "Davenport, William (1725–1797)," *Oxford Dictionary of National Biography* (Oxford: Oxford University Press, 2004).

few were descended from merchants or gentlemen. As historian Melinda Elder has rightly observed, provincial slave traders were "marginal" men.[14]

John Earle (1674–1749), the progenitor of the most long-lived of Britain's slaving families, exemplifies the striving migrants who drove the expansion of the slave trade. The Earle family members trace their origins to Stockton, a small village up the Mersey River from Liverpool. Robert Earle (d. 1615) moved from the family farm to nearby Warrington sometime around 1600, likely to take advantage of the opportunities offered in the growing market town. By the second half of the seventeenth century, Robert's grandson John (1627–1709) possessed the largest house in the town, was active in politics, and carried on a thriving business as a brewer. In 1688, John sent his fourteen-year-old son, John Junior, to apprentice in the Liverpool tobacco house of William Clayton (1651–1715), himself a migrant to Liverpool from rural Lancashire. After completing his apprenticeship, the younger Earle fitted out four slave ships with Clayton, marking the beginning of his family's three-generation connection to the slave trade; by the time of abolition, ships financed by the Earle family had carried almost fifty thousand people from Africa. This slaving dynasty of more a than century—perhaps the longest-standing in British history—began with the ambitious descendant of farmers and brewers.[15]

The backgrounds of outport merchants such as John Earle are clearly humble compared to the backgrounds of their London competitors. The RAC's directors and investors were "powerful and wealthy" London residents, most of whom were tied to other chartered companies trading with Europe and the East Indies. Director Edward Colston (1636–1721), for example, was born into Bristol's elite via his father, who was one of the town's largest wine and sugar merchants. Rather than remaining in the provinces, Colston apprenticed with London's Mercer's Company and then launched his own successful business as a merchant trading with Europe and the Mediterranean, a career that secured him an RAC directorship in 1680. The London merchants who supplanted RAC men such as Colston "emerged . . . overwhelmingly from the community of Atlantic traders." Although this community had itself originated with ambitious and socially middling "new men," many of them provincials like

*Figure 1.2. Portrait of the London slave
trader Humphry Morice (1679–1731),
painted by Godfrey Kneller, c. 1700. © Bank
of England. Reproduced with permission of
the Bank of England Museum, London.*

Colston, it had by the end of the century become an established elite: half of London's seventeenth-century colonial traders were the sons of merchants, and a sixth were the sons of gentlemen. Only a third mirrored John Earle and his fellow outport merchants in being the sons of artisans or yeomen. Humphry Morice Junior (1679–1731) embodies these merchant princes who headed London's slaving community before 1750 (Figure 1.2). Morice's father, Humphry Senior (1640–1696), was a successful London merchant trading with Europe and the Americas whose path to success had been smoothed by his own father, a baronet who owned an eleven-thousand-acre manor in southwest England. Humphry Junior had a privileged upbringing on the family's country estate before apprenticing to a London merchant house trading with Europe. Soon after completing his apprenticeship, Morice began to invest in the slave trade, using the skills that he had learned in the European trade. By the 1720s, Morice had emerged as the "greatest" slave trader in England and an influential politician, owing to his success campaigning for the liberalization of the slave trade and his governorship of the Bank of England. Londoners like Morice—the son of a merchant and a noblewoman—were many rungs above provisional upstarts such as John Earle on the social ladder.[16]

John Earle and his fellow outport merchants—the descendants of provincial tradesmen and farmers—wrested control of Britain's slave trade from merchant princes such as Humphry Morice by seeking out markets where they could purchase captives direct from African brokers at low prices. At the turn of the eighteenth century, Londoners such as Morice had developed a well-worn pattern for their slaving voyages: ships touched first at Sierra Leone and along the Windward Coast to purchase wood, water, and rice; ran down the Gold Coast buying gold and enslaved people in small numbers; and then embarked hundreds of captives in the war-torn Bight of Benin. Prices for enslaved people steadily rose on the Gold Coast and in the Bight of Benin under the pressure of this expanding trade: in 1675, a person could be bought in Benin for, on average, £3; by 1700, prices had tripled; slave prices followed a similar trajectory on the Gold Coast. Outside this three-hundred-mile stretch of coast, though, the prices of people remained low: at the turn of the eighteenth century, captives could still be purchased in the Bight of Biafra, the Loango Coast, and the Windward Coast for as little as £3 to £5 a person (Figure 1.3).[17]

The low prices for enslaved people at these less developed African markets were offset by considerable risks. Europeans had been settled on the Gold Coast and in the Bight of Benin for several hundred years, and so well-regulated methods of trade had developed that enabled visiting captains to quickly purchase enslaved people. When the London ship *Hannibal* traded at Whydah in 1694, for example, its captain bought seven hundred people in just two months by daily picking captives out of a squalid prison that was established and regulated by the king; the RAC's lodge facilitated the transfer of the prisoners to the anchored ship. At less busy markets, by contrast, captains had to negotiate directly with African merchants who were

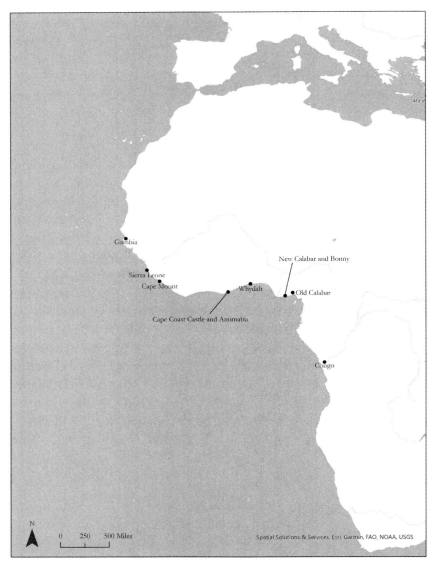

Figure 1.3. Principal African ports engaged in the slave trade with Britons, c. 1700–1808. Based on data from Slavevoyages.org.

often wary of European visitors, sparking violence. Along much of the Windward Coast, for example, Africans refused to board European vessels or guardedly transacted business from their canoes; whites seldom went ashore except in armed boats. Many ports were closed to the slave trade, either temporarily or permanently, as violence between coastal people and visiting whites spiraled. When Britons and Africans did settle their differences, the sporadic supply chains that fed enslaved people to the coast made acquiring hundreds of people a potentially drawn-out process: for example, captives were so scarce on the Windward Coast and in Sierra Leone that only a handful of ships exclusively loaded there before 1700. The deadliness of the West African climate also made acquiring people over a long period particularly dangerous for crewmen and captives. Collectively, these hazards dissuaded many London merchants from dispatching their vessels to less established African slaving markets.[18]

Outport merchants, by contrast, deliberately sought out marginal African markets because they offered a potentially lucrative entry point into the slave trade that bypassed London competition. Because outfitting voyages to less developed markets cost less, merchants with meager capital were able to take larger shares in the vessels. African merchants in those ports also demanded smaller bundles of imported goods for captives, making it easier for provincial merchants to assemble cargoes from their limited commercial hinterlands. In 1700, for example, enslaved people could be purchased at Calabar with a cargo that mostly (70 percent of the value) comprised metal bars and pewter vessels that could be procured either in England—especially near Bristol—or in Europe. In the same year, acquiring people at Whydah required a much more complex cargo, more than half of which was made up of cowry shells and cloths sourced from the Indian Ocean via the London- or Amsterdam-based East India Companies. The same populous hinterlands that furnished outport merchants with their limited trading cargoes provided ambitious men who could captain slaving vessels to potentially deadly African ports as well as desperate country people who could be forced to crew the ships.[19]

The first generation of outport merchants, who traded in the period 1700–1725, identified these low-priced, but risky, African markets by conducting multiport expeditions over large areas of the

African coast. In August 1700, Richard Norris, one of Liverpool's leading sugar and tobacco traders, instructed Captain Thomas Brownbill of the ship *Blessing* to make "ye best of yr way to ye coast of Guinea," where he was "not limited . . . to any place." Instead, he was to sail along almost two thousand miles of coastline searching for slaving markets, touching first at the "Windermost p[ar]t of ye gold coast"—that is, the Windward Coast. With no forts and few other ships, Norris expected Brownbill to have "opportunity of ye whole [Windward] coast to trade." Only if he found no "Encouragement" there was Brownbill to proceed to the busy slaving port of Whydah. If competition at Whydah was stiff, Brownbill was to bear south and trade on the Loango Coast—a region seldom visited by English vessels. Sixteen years later, the owners of the Liverpool ship *Two Brothers* pursued a similar strategy: they instructed their captain to run along the coast and "try all places to purchase healthful slaves." The ship was not to trade on the Gold Coast, because the captives would "be so dear" there. By scouring the African coast for ports where their vessels could obtain people at the lowest possible prices, outport merchants thus traded at the margins, just as they had when they pried their way into the other Atlantic trades.[20]

As British merchants searched the African coast for captives, they opened myriad new ports to the slave trade. In the 1730s, Liverpool merchants began to fill their vessels with people in Sierra Leone and along the Windward Coast, turning both regions into major slaving markets. In the 1750s, Liverpool merchants opened the slave trade at the Cameroon River; in the 1760s, Lancaster men built private slaving forts hundreds of miles up the Gambia River and at the Îles de Los on the Windward Coast. In the same period, a coterie of Scottish émigrés to London purchased the RAC's abandoned Bance Island factory in the Sierra Leone River and reopened it; and in the 1780s and '90s, Liverpool ships sailed up the Congo River to trade for enslaved people, while simultaneously pioneering the slave trade at lagoon-side sites in the Bight of Benin. Only abolition halted the search for new African slaving markets.[21]

The career of Liverpool trader William Davenport (1725–1797) reveals the motivations that drove merchants' hunt for markets. Davenport moved to Liverpool from his native Cheshire in 1740 to make his fortune as an apprentice to a slaving merchant who had himself migrated from rural Lancashire. After completing his apprenticeship, Davenport financed vessels to a variety of busy slaving ports, especially the Gambia River and Old Calabar, but his profits from the ventures were disappointing. He looked to the Cameroon River, a port just one hundred miles to the south of Calabar, as a potential alternative market. Although the Dutch had been purchasing ivory from the Duala people of the Cameroon River since the mid-seventeenth century, it remained largely unknown to British merchants. Suspecting that low-priced captives and ivory could be obtained there, Davenport sent the *Racoon*, a tiny sloop, to the river in September 1756. Davenport ordered the *Racoon*'s captain to send a list of the specific goods that the Duala people demanded for slaves—information that would be essential to the success of future voyages to the river. The captain fulfilled his instructions by purchasing eighty-three people and securing intelligence on trade with the Duala, information that Davenport likely tried to keep secret from Liverpool rivals who sought commercial intelligence on African ports "so unknown."[22]

Davenport subsequently reaped substantial rewards by his opening of Cameroon to the slave trade. Between 1758 and 1785, he and his partners dispatched forty-one slave ships to Cameroon, which carried off more than half of the 17,341 people sold from that port in that period. Davenport reaped, on average, a 28 percent return on these voyages—profits that far exceeded those he earned from his numerous ventures to other, more competitive, African markets. He enriched himself via the Cameroon slave trade because his captains possessed information on the specific demands of Duala brokers and traded in cooperation with each other to drive down the prices of enslaved people. This strategy was the root of Davenport's success in the slave trade and eventual fortune. After Davenport retired in 1786, numerous merchants in Liverpool and London dispatched slaving vessels to Cameroon, making it an important source of captives in the eastern Bight of Biafra. The collective results of the actions of ambitious merchants such as Davenport was thus an expansion in the geography of the slave trade in Africa.[23]

Outport merchants successfully traded with these myriad African ports by developing the infrastructure through which complex assortments of goods could be sourced to meet the specific, and often shifting, demands of African consumers. As one English visitor explained, the "Windward and Leeward Parts of the Coast are as opposite in their Demands, as is their distance." Moreover, the brokers' whims changed so rapidly that a commodity that sold well on one voyage might be "rejected" on the next. British merchants sought to anticipate and shape African consumer habits by establishing manufactories of Guinea goods. Davenport, for example, founded a company with several other Liverpool slavers that sourced beads and cowries from Europe and the Indian Ocean—goods that constituted a third of his trading cargoes to Cameroon. He also dealt in iron bars and gunpowder, both key items in West African markets. Other outport merchants made or distributed textiles, metalwares, guns, and gunpowder. Manufacturers supplied their own vessels with these goods, reducing the amount of cash they had to put into their ventures; they also sold their wares to other slaving partnerships. By thus vertically integrating their companies, outport merchants reduced the risk that their cargoes would be rejected by picky African slave sellers while simultaneously increasing profits.[24]

Ship owners received lengthy credits when buying Guinea goods, considerably reducing the entry costs of their violent business. Ships were out at sea for, on average, between six months and a year, and so would-be investors had a long wait before they received returns that could offset their outfitting costs. Receiving credits for outward cargoes that extended as long as—and sometimes longer than—a voyage therefore enabled merchants to enter the business by, in essence, borrowing goods and then repaying their cost with the proceeds of American slave sales; losses were covered from capital. These credits were secured on a merchant's reputation, which was generated within a tight-knit community of fellow traders. Many merchants shared common origins in rural towns and villages and were therefore willing to vouch for one another; common religious affiliations and marriages also cemented ties and increased trust. Shared participation within the outport's oligarchic political structures further secured reputations and credits.[25]

As outport merchants founded new companies to source trading cargoes, they helped to develop the hinterlands of their new homes into manufacturing centers for the slave trade. Take, for example, the making of gunpowder—a commodity that became increasingly important for acquiring captives as firearms were introduced into West Africa during the early eighteenth century. Throughout the seventeenth century, England's gunpowder industry had been centered in the counties adjacent to London, enabling powdermakers to simultaneously supply the army, the navy, and the capital's merchant community, slave traders included. As the slave trade expanded beyond London in the early eighteenth century, outport merchants were forced to source powder either from these southeast powdermakers or from Holland—a potentially dangerous and expensive undertaking given powder's volatility. Slaving merchants solved this problem by establishing five new powder works in the proximity of Bristol (1722; 1749) and Liverpool (1757; 1764; 1798) that almost solely produced "African" gunpowder for the slave trade. Gun making likewise shifted away from London as makers in Birmingham—working in partnership with Bristol and Liverpool slave traders—successfully produced low-priced guns that appealed to African consumers, especially those in emerging markets such as the Bight of Biafra and the Loango Coast. As these complex manufacturing chains developed over the eighteenth century, provincial merchants could increasingly source Guinea goods from their own environs rather than from London or abroad.[26]

Moving goods from manufactories aboard slave ships also became more efficient as provincial merchants worked to improve their home ports' primitive physical infrastructure. At the opening of the eighteenth century, Bristol and Liverpool's ports were little more than the muddy banks of tidal rivers where ships were loaded by laboriously hoisting the cargo aboard. These delays increased the costs of shipping and made it difficult to compete with Londoners, who traded from the capacious Thames. In the early eighteenth century, provincial merchants sank substantial capital into the building of stone quays, the dredging and marking of rivers, and the digging of enclosed locks. Liverpool's construction of the Old Dock in 1715—Britain's first commercial wet dock—was particularly crucial in spurring the town's trade. The town's common council, which was dominated by Atlantic merchants, mortgaged Liverpool's communal property to finance the construction of the spacious stone basin, which was surrounded by a new custom house, warehouses, and a quayside. In the same period, Bristol's burghers dredged and marked the Avon River and constructed quays where hundreds of ships could safely tie up. By 1725, slave ships could anchor at Bristol or Liverpool and quickly load and unload their cargoes, substantially increasing the speed at which ships could be fitted out, while also reducing costs. Goods flowed to slave ships aboard small coasting vessels that likewise put in at the new docks; wagons and boats brought other commodities along recently turnpiked roads and newly dug canals. Through these strategies outport merchants thus developed the physical infrastructure that enabled them to meet the demands of their African partners and seize control of Britain's slave trade.[27]

For African merchants, participation in the slave trade promised access to the coveted goods brought by Britons through their increasingly complex supply chains: alluring textiles, powerful weaponry, exotic manufactures, and useful metals, all produced to meet their exacting demands. Coastal Africans could gain further goods by charging port dues for permission to trade (so-called *comey*) and by demanding gifts (*dashes*). Imports were useful in themselves, but they also enabled Africans to earn "wealth in people"—the primary form of capital in Atlantic Africa—by establishing tributary relationships with dependents or through the purchase of enslaved people. But securing wealth via the export slave trade was difficult when visiting whites could sail on to another port if they found taxes and prices too high, especially when neighboring African people could deliberately attempt to draw ships away by slashing their charges. To reap the slave trade's profits, coastal brokers hence needed to transform their homes into efficient slaving markets while simultaneously preventing their competing neighbors from doing the same.[28]

The Fante of the Gold Coast were one of the first African people to vault from marginality to preeminence via Britain's slave trade in the early eighteenth century. The Fante originated in the heavily forested interior of modern-day Ghana, where they formed a confederacy that was bound by common matrilineal descent and a shared language. In the fourteenth century, the Fante migrated to the coast, where they erected two settlements, Kwaman, and their capital, Mankessim, five miles north of the sea. To trade gold with visiting Portuguese captains, Fante settlers established new

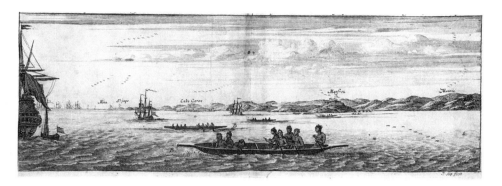

Figure 1.4. The Gold Coast from El Mina to Moree, c. 1680. From Thomas
Astley, ed., A New General Collection of Voyages and Travels *(London,*
1745–1747), vol. 2, facing p. 589. This image is based on a description of the
Gold Coast given by Jean Barbot, who traded along the African coast c. 1678–
1682. At the time of Barbot's voyages, the gold and slave trades were centered
on Cape Coast Castle and El Mina, both of which can be seen to the left, with
numerous ships at anchor nearby. Barbot's image pointedly ends at Mouri—the
border with Fante lands to the east. Reproduced from www.slaveryimages.org.

coastal towns at Kormantse, Anomabu, and Tantumquerry, forming
a roughly rectangular polity that stretched twenty-five miles along
the coast and twenty miles into the interior. In the mid-seventeenth
century, the Dutch and English erected a fort at Anomabu and Kormantse, respectively, enabling the Fante to attract caravans bringing
gold to the forts and to trade European goods with other groups
on the coast and in the interior. Fanteland was, however, just one
of a plethora of tiny states on the Gold Coast; in 1629, there were
thirty-four polities in the proximity of the coast. And as late as 1670,
a Dutch visitor emphasized that the "chiefest place of Trade" on
the Gold Coast was to the west, at El Mina—a Dutch fort under the
sovereignty of the Mina people. Few would have then guessed that
the Fante would soon emerge as the principal slave traders on the
Gold Coast.[29]

The introduction of firearms transformed the Gold Coast
into what one European observer described as a "complete Slave
Coast" and enabled the Fante's rise. Before the late seventeenth
century, warfare between the fragmented people of the Gold Coast

was endemic and bloody, as armies fought each other with swords, lances, and bows. After the defeated warriors were slaughtered or captured, the victors rounded up women and children. Prisoners were retained as slaves or sold into the interior, where they were forced to dig gold or hack back the dense forest to make way for agriculture; coastal people also *purchased* enslaved people from Europeans, bolstering this nascent slave trade. Small-scale conflicts seldom resulted in the complete conquest of a polity, though, as defeated rulers typically agreed on a truce by pledging reparations and ransoming prisoners. The introduction of reliable flintlock muskets via the gold trade, beginning in the mid-seventeenth century, shattered this balance of power. Coastal rulers, the Fante included, abandoned heavy infantry and archers in favor of lightly armed warriors supported by teams of trained musket men. The flow of firearms up-country sparked an even more significant "gunpowder revolution" in the interior. Denkyira and Akwamu, two forest states to the northwest and northeast of Fanteland, adopted the new weapons to best effect and won a series of crushing victories over their neighbors. Both states enslaved their vanquished enemies and either kept the prisoners or sold them to Europeans, turning the Gold Coast into a major exporter of enslaved people in the closing years of the seventeenth century.[30]

The stream of captives leaving the Gold Coast became a flood in the eighteenth century after the rise of Asante, a militarized slave-trading empire in the interior. As a vassal of Denkyira, Asante had resented the annual levy it had to pay to its overlord, and it launched a successful war of independence in 1701. Asante next embarked on a series of expansionary wars that lasted until 1752 and subjugated an area stretching three hundred miles from the sea. Asante's conquests supercharged the Gold Coast slave trade: between 1700 and 1750, almost half a million people were carried from the region—five times the number of people enslaved before 1700. Asante sustained its slave trade after 1750 by demanding an annual tribute of captives from its vassals and enslaving recalcitrant subjects. To meet Asante's demands, rulers either seized their own people via corrupted legal codes or raided neighboring states, wracking the frontiers of the growing Asante empire with violence. Kidnappings of individuals such as Ottobah Cugoano, coupled with debt bondage and domestic slave sales, generated smaller streams of captives, a portion of whom were forced toward the coast.[31]

The Fante sought to make themselves the leading middlemen for the sale of the growing numbers of people enslaved by Asante by conquering competing trading states on the coast. Although Fanteland was geographically constricted, the small polity was, like rural Lancashire, "heavily populated," a French visitor observed in 1679, making it "one of the most considerable [polities] on the Gold Coast." The Fante army was accordingly one of the largest on the Gold Coast and would, a Dutchman opined in 1705, soon invade the "circumjacent Countries." A year later, this prediction came true: armed with guns procured from the English, the Fante attacked neighboring Asebu, burning villages, killing the king, and vassalizing the surviving people. In 1708, Fante turned to Fetu, kidnapping the king and forcing him into a tributary relationship that ceded control of Cape Coast Castle—a large British fort where Asante merchants principally sold captives. Having knocked out their coastal competitors, the Fante turned inland and crushed Cabesterra, a state that sat astride the main route from the Asante capital of Kumasi to the coast. In the 1720s, the Fante took control of two states to the east and smashed polities to the north through which captives passed on their way to the coast. By 1730—just twenty-five years after beginning their campaigns of conquest—the Fante had eliminated their neighboring competitors in the slave trade. As historian James Sanders surmises, the Fante's motivation for their conquests was to become "exclusive middlemen who brought down the Asante trade."[32]

The Asante and Fante next developed the physical infrastructure through which enslaved people could be swiftly brought down from the interior. In 1728, a Great Road from Kumasi, the capital of Asante, was opened leading to El Mina and the adjacent Fante slave markets. The completed road was well maintained and lined with rest stops and markets, enabling Asante merchants to march captives from Kumasi to the sea in just ten days. To ensure that the Fante did not monopolize their trade with Europeans, Asante built two other Great Roads in the mid-eighteenth century: one to the Danish forts at Accra on the eastern Gold Coast and another to a small Dutch fort at Cape Lahou on the western coast—the road to Cape Lahou bypassed coastal middlemen entirely. Both routes proved too lengthy or perilous to compete with the Kumasi–El Mina road, though. Fante statesmen further reinforced their position as the key middlemen for the Asante slave trade when they agreed to the opening of a more direct road from Kumasi to Anomabu. The road from Kumasi to El Mina as well as the road from Kumasi to Anomabu had major slave markets at the frontier between Asante and Fante territory, approximately two days' march from the coast, beyond which Asante merchants were forbidden to proceed. It would be this system of roads and markets—established as early as 1728—that most enslaved people would pass along on their way to Atlantic slavery on the Gold Coast.[33]

While they secured the supply of captives from Asante, the Fante converted Anomabu from a fishing town into one of the largest slaving ports on the West African coast. During the seventeenth century, European vessels anchored beyond the surf in the town's "road" to purchase gold, either direct from the Fante, who numbered approximately six thousand by 1680, or from the officers of small Dutch and English forts. Fante merchants began developing Anomabu as a major slaving port at the close of the century when interloping captains arrived in considerable numbers to purchase people. To prevent the fort officers meddling with this lucrative trade, the Fante stripped, beat, and ejected the RAC's governor in 1686; his two successors likewise left their posts ignominiously. When the company's officers tried to drive off interlopers, the Fante broke into the fort, set it alight, and fired guns at the walls; at the start of the eighteenth century both the RAC's agents and their Dutch counterparts despaired that they had lost the trade at Anomabu because of the influx of private traders. Tensions between the Fante and the fort officers continued throughout the early eighteenth century, and in 1730 the RAC finally abandoned its Anomabu factory; the Fante razed it shortly thereafter. The Fante did accede to the construction of an expensive new British fort at Anomabu in 1753 in exchange for lavish gifts; Richard Brew (d. 1776), a private British merchant, also established a nearby "castle" soon thereafter. Both structures, however, were largely insignificant to a slave trade that was primarily conducted on the adjacent beaches between ship captains and Fante merchants.[34]

Although marginal to the operation of Anomabu's slave trade, the forts served an important role in cementing cross-cultural bonds between Fante merchants and visiting British captains. The mixed-race offspring of fort officers and Fante women were often apprenticed within the forts as clerks and scribes, enabling them to become key cross-cultural brokers. Fort officers and their mixed-race children also became important go-betweens for defusing tensions between the Fante and British visitors. For example, Richard Brew married the daughter of John Currantee (d. 1764), the head of the Fante at Anomabu, positioning Brew and his children as key agents in local and international politics. Fante merchants also provided their sons and daughters as hostages to ship captains in exchange for trade goods, with the proviso that these "pawns" could be enslaved if the trader did not return with captives after a specified period. In addition to underpinning credit relations, pawnship cemented long-standing commercial relationships between Fante and Britons because the people who served as "pawns" lived alongside Europeans on the ships for long periods. The sons of African traders also learned European languages and cultures, which helped them when they later entered the slave trade as brokers themselves. Fante headmen furthered their commercial partnerships by sending their sons to be educated in Britain. As early as 1750, Fante children could be found in Liverpool, whose merchants were then successfully elbowing their Bristol rivals out of the Gold Coast markets; by 1788, when Liverpool merchants were the leading slave traders on the Gold Coast, there were "about fifty" children of African merchants in Liverpool, "chiefly from the Windward and Gold Coasts." The Fante thus intertwined family and commercial networks to bolster their connections with British slave traders, both on the coast and in Britain itself.[35]

In addition to the ready availability of captives, British ships were drawn to Anomabu because of the abundance of maize (corn)—a key foodstuff for feeding enslaved people on the ships. By trading directly with Africans, private British merchants considerably extended the amount of time that their vessels would be anchored on the coast—a period when the captives aboard needed to be fed. Once at sea, enslaved people also required feeding at least twice a day, and so ship captains had to purchase large quantities of provisions before they left the coast. Britons brought some of this food with them from England in the form of dried flour and beans. But relying solely on dried European food was potentially dangerous, as it could spoil in the hold; slave traders believed that captives would also refuse to eat a monotonous and unfamiliar diet. Fante brokers sought to meet visiting whites' demand for foodstuffs by planting maize, a calorific crop first introduced by the Portuguese that thrived in the coastal environment. Anomabu was particularly rich in the grain; in 1689 a fort officer described the port as the "principal granary" for the entire Gold Coast. Maize was so important to the slave trade at Anomabu that its labor requirements shaped the movement of enslaved people: captives were likely forced to plant it in the rainy seasons in April and May and harvest the crop between September and December. They were then sold away to the coast—carrying the harvested maize—and sold to visiting Britons. The availability of both enslaved people and the maize that would feed them during their imprisonment thus made Anomabu a one-stop shop for the slave trade.[36]

Anomabu's efficiency drew British vessels in the eighteenth century, especially ships from Liverpool and Bristol that sought a trading location where fort officers and Londoners could not interfere. Interloping vessels initially resorted to Anomabu as one of many ports while sailing down the Gold Coast, purchasing gold and small groups of captives at each location. By the early eighteenth century, Anomabu had become a key slaving port as Bristol and London captains purchased people there at the conclusion of multi-port voyages along the coast. Once the Fante had eliminated neighboring ports and secured supply lines to the interior after 1729, Anomabu became the key slaving port on the Gold Coast, and Bristol and Liverpool vessels began purchasing entire shiploads of captives there. When the Bristol ship *Black Prince* sailed to the Gold Coast in 1762 and 1763, for example, it anchored at Anomabu for four months while the captain purchased 438 people. By the second half of the eighteenth century, outport merchants dominated at Anomabu; London vessels typically steered for the forts that lined the coast, where ship owners possessed stronger commercial ties with the resident officers. Fante merchants thus ensured that captives enslaved on the Gold Coast were typically forced-marched along roads that led from Asante's expanding empire, through Fante territory, and then into the dank holds of British slave ships.[37]

In the early eighteenth century, British merchants looked to the Bight of Biafra as a region where they could purchase enslaved people at lower prices than at the increasingly busy Gold Coast and Bight of Benin. Located six hundred miles to the east of the Gold Coast's beaches in what is now Nigeria, the Bight is a maze of swampy inlets and creeks formed by the deltas of the mighty Niger and Cross Rivers. The delta formed natural boundaries between the myriad Ijo- and Ibibio-speaking people who inhabited the western and eastern portions of the Bight, respectively. Eighty miles north of the sea, the land rises sharply to a wide plain inhabited by millions of Igbo-speaking people. The Igbo were, in the seventeenth century, organized into small patrilineal villages, some of which were linked by alliances and kinship ties into larger "village republics," albeit ones that never grew into kingdoms or empires akin to Asante. Small-scale warfare, raiding, and trade between these various fragmented people produced captives that Portuguese, Dutch, and English traders began purchasing during the early seventeenth century. By the third quarter of the seventeenth century, this trade had grown so large that Biafra had emerged as one of the largest slaving regions in Africa.[38]

In the closing years of the seventeenth century, though, the Biafran slave trade stagnated as Europeans left the unhealthy region in favor of the growing markets on the Gold Coast, Bight of Benin, and West-Central Africa. Unlike on the Gold Coast and in Benin, where ships typically anchored offshore away from mosquitoes and pathogens, vessels trading in Biafra anchored up pestilential rivers that were deadly to captives and crewmen. In 1679, for example, a ship left Biafra with two hundred captives having already "thrown more than 100 who had died into the sea, and its crew was so weak that it had no more than five men to run the ship," as French slave ship captain Jean Barbot (1655–1712) observed after encountering the vessel at sea. Ships continued to visit Biafran ports in the closing years of the century, but, as Barbot warned, their captains had to "pray for a quick passage," or else they would not arrive in the Americas "alive and in health." Barbot opined that the sickly vessel he encountered would lose a further hundred people before reaching the Americas and that other vessels had likewise "lost, some half, and others two thirds" of their prisoners on the Middle Passage. When the ships from Biafra arrived in the Americas, many of the survivors "died there, as soon as landed, or else turn'd to a very bad market." American planters began to associate "byte slaves" with poor health, especially compared to the supposedly robust people taken from the Gold Coast and the Bight of Benin. The Dutch all but ceased dispatching vessels to Biafran ports after 1671 because of the "malignity of the air"; Londoners followed suit twenty years later. The Biafran slave trade was consequently overshadowed by supposedly healthier growing markets to the west; in the first quarter of the eighteenth century, far more captives were taken from the Gold Coast (229,239 people) than from Biafra (66,833 people).[39]

Like the Gold Coast, the Bight of Biafra was transformed into a major slaving region through the growth of a polity in the interior: the Aro. The Aro ("the spear") were an ethnically diverse group who migrated over the Cross River early in the seventeenth century and founded Arochukwu ("the spear of God"), a town atop a strategic escarpment that bordered densely populated Ibibio- and Igbo-speaking lands. Aro settlers encouraged these neighboring people to join their households, swelling the small population of initial migrants via an assimilative process known as "human proliferation." Striving Aro family members trekked out into the populous Igbo lands, where they hoped to make their fortune through trade by establishing outposts. These outposts became villages, villages grew into towns, and towns bloomed into colonies. Trade routes connected these settlements to Arochukwu, along which large caravans of merchants carried a variety of goods procured both locally and from the coast. As their trading diaspora expanded, the Aro bought increasingly large numbers of captives from the Igbo, many of them people charged with purported crimes. The Igbo, like Europeans, punished criminals via fines, corporal punishment, exile, and execution; sale into slavery was seldom used, except for the most serious of crimes. After the arrival of the Aro, the Igbo imposed enslavement—and sale to the Aro—as a punishment for a growing number of offenses, including theft, arson, witchcraft, and kidnapping. The Aro trade network also provided a means for Igbo husbands to send away supposedly unfaithful wives, masters to dispose of un-ruly captives, politicians to banish their opponents, the superstitious to banish the cursed, and kidnappers to sell their victims. A case of an enslaved Biafran man interviewed by a Danish missionary in the Caribbean illustrates how this process worked. Because of his "contentious disposition" and the "constant brawls that he had with his fellows," the man had been "ambushed" by his fellow villagers, who sold him into slavery. Taken together, these numerous means of enslavement—all of them small-scale, individual actions, rather than the organized warfare that plagued the Gold Coast—produced a growing number of captives whom the Aro purchased using goods obtained through their blossoming trade network.[40]

Like the Fante, the Aro developed the physical infrastructure that enabled enslaved people to be moved to the coast in enormous numbers. The Aro retained skilled adults, young boys, and captives born near Arochukwu and sold other people at two fairs at Bende and Uburu—Igbo towns to the north and west of Arochukwu, re-spectively. The Aro timed the two four-day-long fairs so that each opened twenty-four days after the other, providing time for some-times thousands of captives to be gathered at the markets. Aro in-termediaries bought and sold captives within a specialized section of the market and then marched those destined for sale to Euro-peans to riverside markets. Coastal brokers met the Aro there and exchanged European imports for the captives, who were bound and pushed into canoes for the journey to the coast and sale to the an-chored slave ships. When this sophisticated system went into oper-ation is difficult to ascertain, but apparently it was functioning by 1699 when John Grazilhier purchased people aboard the English ship *Albion Frigate* and saw "above forty great canoes" go "up the river, to purchase slaves inland." These captives came, according to the captain of Grazilhier's ship, from the "Hackbous Country"—a corruption of Igbo—where the coastal people "fetch all their sub-sistence." As the extent and sophistication of this slaving network grew, the flow of captives to the sea exploded: by the conclusion of the eighteenth century, more than twenty thousand people—fifty a day—arrived at the coast in the busiest years.[41]

Myriad groups of coastal Africans in the late seventeenth cen-tury purchased the captives who were pushed down from the Aro markets, preventing any one port from dominating the business. In the Rio Real delta in the western Bight, three main groups of brokers participated in the slave trade: the Kalabari of New Calabar, the Ibani of Bonny, and the Andoni of Andoni. European ships anchored at one of these ports and then dispatched boats to the other ports to purchase captives; canoes also brought enslaved people to the anchored ships from other ports in the delta. In 1699, for example, the *Albion Frigate* anchored at Bonny and then sent a sloop "to and fro" between New Calabar, "Dony," and "circumjacent trading places" to purchase 648 people. No one location monopolized the slave trade in the eastern Bight either. Within the Cross River delta, Old Calabar was not a single port but instead a collection of villages, each controlled by a different group: Effiat people at the entrance to the Cross River; Ibibio speakers on the western bank; Efik people within a creek feeding the river; and Qua people in the surrounding lands. People on the Santo Domingo River and Rio Del Rey also participated in the export slave trade, further dividing the business.[42]

The Efik sought to aggrandize the expanding slave trade at Old Calabar in the early eighteenth century. The Efik had migrated from east of the Cross River sometime in the sixteenth century and settled at Creek Town—a fishing village perched up a narrow and defensible channel that linked the Cross and Calabar Rivers. Within Creek Town, the Efik divided themselves into distinct "wards"—patrilineal households that each constituted a separate compound within the town; subgroups existed within each family, each of which could tie itself back to the ward's founder. By the late seventeenth century, at least three major wards existed within Creek Town: Duke, Robin John, and Ambo, all of whom were active in the slave trade. Even so, the Efik remained small players in the export slave trade throughout the seventeenth century. Creek Town was a poor location for trading with Europeans, whose large vessels could not anchor in the shallow creek. English ships instead anchored nearer the sea and then sent longboats to purchase captives upriver at Creek Town and downriver from Qua people. Whites "drove their trade" with "villages and hamlets all about" along the Cross River, Jean Barbot observed at the end of the seventeenth century.[43]

The Efik positioned themselves as the key middlemen on the Cross River by eliminating their competitors in the slave trade. Efik warriors first sought to prevent the English from trading with Qua people by intercepting longboats returning from upriver. In November 1681, for example, three canoes, assisted by more than three hundred armed men ashore, fell upon the longboat of the RAC slave ship *Vine* as it returned from the Akwa River with eleven people purchased from the Qua. The Efik drowned one of the crewmen and held the others prisoner at Creek Town until the *Vine*'s captain agreed to trade with them at their agreed prices. Creek Town's strategic position also helped the Efik secure control of the traffic. Although poorly sited for receiving European ships, the channel upon which Creek Town sat connected the Calabar River, where ships dropped anchor, to the Cross River, which led to the Aro's riverside slaving markets. The Efik consequently had better access to the growing flow of captives from the interior and could therefore block non-Efik canoes seeking to travel upriver to the Aro. The Efik also stopped people bringing captives downriver to the European ships. Akpa people had, for example, brought prisoners of war from the lands north of Old Calabar to Dutch ships anchored in the Rio del Rey in the first half of the seventeenth century. The Efik prohibited this trade, effectively closing the Rio del Rey as a slaving port; the Akpa abandoned the slave trade and instead joined the Aro as mercenaries. By 1720, the Efik had, via these numerous strategies, successfully secured a monopoly on the slave trade from the Cross River.[44]

The Efik rise was also facilitated via strategic partnerships with British outport merchants. Bristolians eclipsed Londoners as the largest group at Calabar circa 1720—precisely when the Efik secured control of the slave trade in the Cross River. Bristolians likely dominated at Calabar by forging close ties with King Ambo, the head of Creek Town's Ambo ward; the ship *King Amboe* was named to flatter Bristol's key trading partner. After Ambo's death in 1729, Bristol merchants tied themselves to the members of the Robin John ward, a partnership that maintained Bristol's position until 1750. Liverpool merchants elbowed aside their southern neighbors by instead tying themselves to members of the ambitious Duke ward, which was led by Duke Ephraim (d. 1786). William Davenport, for example, successfully traded at Old Calabar for almost forty years by partnering with former slave ship captains who had formed close bonds with Efik traders during their numerous voyages. These captains assembled the outward cargoes—especially fine textiles—for Davenport's ships to ensure they met the Efik's specific desires. Davenport also employed captains who, over careers of several decades, developed personal ties to Duke traders and who could also introduce junior officers to the Efik, perpetuating multigenerational links between British officers and African merchants. To further cement these ties, Duke headmen sent their offspring to be taught English in Liverpool, where they lived in the households of merchants such as Davenport. Upon returning to Calabar, Efik merchants gifted enslaved children and prized ivory tusks to favored merchants and captains and kept up a regular correspondence that provided valuable commercial information to their "friends" in Liverpool.[45]

Fearing eclipse at the hands of the upstart Duke ward, the Robin John family sought to seize control of the Calabar slave trade in the 1760s. Historians have assumed that the two Efik wards had split from Creek Town and founded their own towns downriver sometime in the seventeenth century. There is, however, no evidence of this break in the reports of returning Europeans or in maps of Old Calabar. Rather, both wards had likely inhabited Creek Town together until 1763. In that year, Ephraim Robin John, the head of the ward, left Creek Town with his family and dependents and founded a new settlement on the left bank of the Calabar River at Old Town (*obutong*). The new settlement was situated to control the slave trade: Old Town overlooked a narrow bend in the river that Europeans had to round to reach Creek Town. Robin John sought to command the trade by aiming two cannons seized from a Liverpool ship at the river. The Duke ward members, who remained at Creek Town, responded by stopping the Old Town merchants' canoes from traveling up the river to the Aro markets; Robin John seized Duke vessels in turn. By 1767, the animosity between the two wards had all but halted the Calabar slave trade. British captains connived with the Duke ward to bring a bloody resolution to the impasse. The Duke leaders invited the Robin John men to a meeting aboard a Bristol slave ship—ostensibly neutral territory—and, at a prearranged signal, killed or enslaved them. The survivors limped back to Old Town with their market power crushed. The Duke ward cemented its own power by moving from Creek Town to Duke Town—a new site a mile downriver from Old Town, where British ships could anchor without fear of "being Stopt by the Old Town people." Within Duke Town, members of Duke Ephraim's family used accusations of witchcraft to eliminate pretenders to the deceased Duke's titles after 1786, ensuring that his biological sons remained the leading traders in the port. By first knocking out nearby non-Efik and then purging internal competition, a single Efik household thus concentrated the Cross River slave trade in its hands.[46]

As the Efik emerged as the largest group of slaving brokers in the eastern Bight in the mid-eighteenth century, they were eclipsed by the Ibani of Bonny, ninety miles to the west in the Rio Real. Established on a swampy and low-lying island at the mouth of the Rio Real, Bonny gave few indications in the seventeenth century that it would soon become the largest slaving port in West Africa. Dutch visitors in the 1660s described Bonny as a "pretty large Town" but contrasted it unfavorably to adjacent New Calabar, "the chiefest Place of Trade" in the Rio Real. English captains, who began visiting the estuary later in the century, likewise preferred to trade at New Calabar because its brokers "g[o]t slaves much faster than at Bandy [Bonny]." The Kalabari were "two or three days out and home" from the slaving markets to the north, whereas the Ibani took "eight or ten days" because they had to paddle up the Imo River for sixty miles—a route lined with potential rivals, including the Andoni people, who themselves participated in the slave trade. Bonny was also poorly placed to access Aro markets compared to Old Calabar, which connected directly via the Cross River. A combination of unfavorable geography and the power of local rivals therefore made the Ibani minor players in the slave trade before 1700; as one Londoner aptly observed in that year, "The people att New Callebarr are much greater than the people of Bandy."[47]

The Ibani overcame these locational disadvantages by adapting their society to meet the needs of both the African and the export slave trades. The Ibani were headed by a king (*amanyanabo*), a tradition that the Ibani people brought with them when they first settled on Bonny Island sometime around the year 1000. King Asimini, who received the first Portuguese visitors to Bonny in the late fifteenth century, purportedly sacrificed his daughter to the sea gods to make the river accessible to European ships and sent one of his sons to be

Figure 1.5. Bonny, c. 1820. The anchorage off the Town of Bonny-
river sixteen miles from the entrance, *by P. M. G, c. 1820. The
image shows British vessels loading palm oil, but it nonetheless captures
how the slave trade at Bonny operated before 1807. Reproduced with
permission of the National Maritime Museum, Greenwich.*

educated in Portugal. Asimini demanded comey (port dues) from
Portuguese mariners to increase the Crown's wealth, and he formed
a "supreme judicial body" that met once every four days. Asimini's
daughter or perhaps granddaughter Queen Kambasa further solidi-
fied the Crown's power by using wealth derived through European
trade to form a royal bodyguard and introduce orders and ranks.
The security provided by Bonny's powerful monarchy encouraged
Europeans to trust large quantities of trade goods to Ibani merchants. Those brokers carried the borrowed goods upriver and lent
them to their Aro partners, whose own dependents traveled to the
fairs at Bende and Uburu to purchase enslaved people. The movement of captives back to the coast canceled out this chain of debts.
The Ibani strengthened this chain by adopting the Aro's religious
beliefs. The Aro worshipped Chukwu, a deity whose will could be
divined by an oracle located at Arochukwu—a town named after the
god. The Ibani consulted the oracle on the succession of kings and
the change of priests and had a shrine dedicated to the oracle in the
town; the Kalabari likewise made pilgrimages to Arochukwu. The
Efik, by contrast, put little stock in the oracle because they resorted

instead to the collective decisions of a secret society known as Ekpe. The Ibani belief in the Aro oracle and centralized political economy therefore helped to make Bonny a conduit through which borrowed imports could flow into the interior and be traded for people.[48]

Violence was equally important to the rise of the Ibani. They secured their routes to the Aro fairs by destroying towns that could potentially block their fleets of canoes. In Queen Kambasa's reign, Bonny fought the Ogani people, who resided on the opposite banks of the Imo River to the Aro's main trading sites and who had acted as middlemen between the coast and the interior for centuries. After capturing a key Ogani town, the Ibani established a colony at Kala-oko, nearby at a strategic site on the Imo River that would serve as a rest stop for fleets of canoes traveling upriver. King Ama-kiri, one of Kambasa's direct descendants, conquered the Andoni town of Asarama, which controlled a narrow bend in the Imo River that Ibani canoes passed en route to the Aro fairs. Other villagers fled the riverbanks to avoid being conquered and enslaved by the well-armed fleets of Ibani canoes. The Ibani also crushed the competing ports of New Calabar and Andoni. Both New Calabar and Andoni had deep anchorages for European ships, security for credit transactions via a powerful central ruler, access to rivers leading to the Aro, and—in the case of New Calabar—a larger trade in people. The Kalabari and Doni people therefore viewed the rise of the Ibani with alarm and attempted to crush the upstarts sometime in the early eighteenth century. The war initially went poorly for the Ibani, and the reigning King Halliday abdicated in favor of his general, Perekule, a descendant of Queen Kambasa, who used the "great wealth" he had accumulated through slave trading to finance the war. Under Perekule's leadership the Ibani defeated New Calabar and Andoni—confirming Bonny as the premier slaving port of the Rio Real. The war also further increased royal power at Bonny: after centuries in which the crown changed hands between aspiring families, it now remained within the Perekule family, with Perekule crowned as King Pepple I. Warfare therefore knocked out Bonny's competitors in the Rio Real and strengthened the king's ability to borrow goods that could be used to buy slaves.[49]

The Ibani extended their commercial advantage by securing a supply of yams from the interior—the key foodstuff used by Britons to feed Biafran captives aboard the ships. Within Igbo society, yams were revered as the "king of crops" because they provided a bountiful harvest that underpinned the diet. Yams were "a man's crop," leaving women a subsidiary role that largely revolved around the planting of less important "women's crops" such as beans and cassava. Igbo and Aro slaveholders forced men to harvest yams prior to their sale: exports of captives from Biafran ports increased after the yam harvest, when male agricultural workers became surplus. The retention of men also resulted in significantly higher numbers of enslaved women being shipped off from Biafran ports versus other African regions. Bonny thus emerged, like Anomabu, as a key slaving port because Britons were able to simultaneously purchase thousands of enslaved people and the foodstuffs that would sustain them on the ships.[50]

The elimination of coastal competitors, the securing of supply lines for captives and yams, and strategic partnerships with the Aro all combined to transform Bonny from a bit player in the slave trade into West Africa's "wholesale market for slaves." Beginning in the 1720s, British—especially Liverpudlian and Bristolian—ships anchored at a port where captains knew that they could fill their vessels with captives arriving from the Aro fairs much faster than at competing ports such as Old Calabar. Although the Efik purchased slaves from the Aro, they did not link their slave trade to the schedule of the fairs in the same way. Instead, Efik brokers went up-country in small groups of canoes and brought back handfuls of prisoners from a "vast commercial network covering some 30,000 square miles," which included both Aro and non-Aro sellers. It consequently took twice as long to buy human cargo at Calabar versus Bonny. Bonny's comparative advantage enabled the Ibani to outpace their eastern rivals in 1741 and emerge as the largest slave traders north of the Congo River—a position that they maintained until abolition.[51]

Broteer Furro (c. 1729–1805), the eight-year-old son of his people's ruler, was playing in his natal home, hundreds of miles from the sea, when news arrived that would forever change his life. Broteer's father, Saungm Furro, heard that an army had invaded a neighboring state and "laid waste [the] country"; the army was now "speedily" coming to conquer his own nation. Broteer and his fellow villagers beat a swift retreat, but the advancing army forced the men into battle and quickly defeated them. The women and children had hidden among reeds, but they were soon found by the invaders, who gave Broteer a "violent blow on the head" and seized him. A soldier then tied a rope around his neck and put him in a coffle with the women and his father, who had surrendered along with the other warriors. Marched to a nearby camp, Broteer looked on helplessly while his father was beaten to death. The soldiers pushed Broteer and the other prisoners toward the sea but were themselves con- quered by another army; Broteer was "taken a second time." When his new captors finally reached Anamabo, they sold him to the slave ship *Charming Susanna;* his mother was likely sold to a different ship or retained as a slave in the interior. Renamed Venture Smith by the ship's steward, Broteer began a new life traumatized and alone as an American slave. Five hundred miles from Anomabu, Olaudah Equiano (c. 1745–1797), aged eleven, also suffered the ordeal of en- slavement. Olaudah grew up in the Igbo-speaking lands adjoining the Bight of Biafra, the son of the ruler of a small village republic. While he was playing with his young sister alone in a yard, three kidnappers scaled the walls of his village compound and seized them both. Olaudah was bound, gagged, and hurried away to a nearby wood until night, when the kidnappers forced the children to quickly march away from their home. When they rested, Olaudah and his sister found solace from the terror of being taken from their parents by, he recounted in his autobiography, "bathing each other with our tears." Olaudah lost this "small comfort" when his sister was, in his words, "torn from me and immediately carried away," leaving him to "cr[y] and "griev[e] continually" for days. He spent several months trudging toward the coast, during which time he was enslaved by numerous masters, before he was eventually sold to a British slave ship, likely at Bonny.[52]

Olaudah and Broteer—two of the millions of people shipped off from Africa in the eighteenth century—were enslaved by a vast machine that was built by equally ambitious British and African merchants. Britons hailing from the rural hinterlands of Liverpool and Bristol sought their fortune by seeking out African markets where captives could be bought at low prices, such as those in the Bight of Biafra. By simultaneously developing the manufacturing hinterlands of their homes, these outport merchants successfully met the demands of African consumers for imports, enabling them to outpace their rivals in London. The introduction of those imports across the West African coast facilitated the emergence of powerful new slaving states like Asante and the Aro. As these groups rapidly expanded, they enslaved millions of people. Because of the strategic partnerships formed by the Fante, Efik, and Ibani with their British partners, enslaved people were principally force-marched to a handful of major slaving ports, such as Anomabu, Bonny, and Old Calabar. The bonds between Britons and key groups of coastal people ensured that the two boys would be shipped to the British Americas, and not the Portuguese, French, or Dutch colonies. Enslaved people like Furro and Equiano paid the price of merchants' ambitions to elevate themselves from marginality to preeminence via the slave trade.

CHAPTER TWO

Cross-Cultural Trade and the Sale of Enslaved People in Atlantic Africa

I
N APRIL 1702, A CAPTAIN in the employ of the Royal African
Company wrote from Old Calabar to complain of the chaos
that had accompanied the slave trade's explosive growth. Just
four years after the liberalization of England's slave trade,
private slave ships had come to the river "one on the back of another." These newcomers had kidnapped men, women, and children; "robbed Cannoes [sic] on the Water"; taken merchants and
their families as hostages; and even shot dead some brokers. The
Efik retaliated by abducting white crewmen until their relatives
were released; killing whites; and refusing to sell people to offend-
ing captains. The slave trade almost came to a halt in the Cross
River; the RAC captain complained that the "actions" of the other
Englishmen had "been the occasion of my so long lying here." Such
scenes threatened to play out along the West African coast as private British merchants flocked to the slave trade during the early
eighteenth century. Freed from the strictures of a single monopoly
company, private traders openly competed against one another in
Africa to try and quickly obtain enslaved people at the lowest prices.
English captains had few qualms about extorting and enslaving Africans with whom they had not developed long-term commercial
relations. African merchants simultaneously competed to attract the

business of potentially duplicitous and violent English newcomers, while trying to fend off potential rivals. Competition between Africans and whites—and among Britons—therefore threatened to derail the expansion of the slave trade before it could begin.[1]

Traders in men knew that they could not allow mutual animosity to halt their deadly business. Coastal Africans, such as the Efik, relied on the trade for their livelihood and so could ill afford to let conflict hinder slaving for extended periods. Britons likewise knew that drawn-out disputes would prevent them from purchasing people and cause the deaths of people already imprisoned on the ships. A "long stay" in Africa was, a Liverpool consortium reminded their captain, "always attended with great mortality among both Blacks and Europeans." Ship owners also knew that enslaved people would fight for their liberty while imprisoned in sight of land, especially as their numbers grew while their captors sickened and died. Captives could drive the ship ashore and leap to freedom if they were able to overcome the weakened crew, an opportunity that would be lost once the vessel departed for the Americas. Merchants believed that such insurrections would "inevitably ruin the Voyage" because it would lead to "either the total loss of the Ship" or the "kill[ing] or wound[ing]" of "a great number of the Slaves." To minimize the risks of insurrection and mortality—risks that increased every day the ship was at anchor—ship owners urged their captains to complete their purchases in Africa quickly; "dispatch is the life of a Guinea voyage" was a common aphorism. African slave traders understood this grim logic well; one Efik merchant pointedly reminded a group of Liverpool merchants that it was in their interest to send a "good cargo" because their ship would then "no stand long before shee full [of captives] for go away"—a key concern for Britons trading at the Cross River.[2]

If slaving ports like Old Calabar were to be transformed into major hubs for Britain's slave trade, merchants thus needed to develop a set of market practices that would enable thousands of enslaved people to be violently forced aboard myriad ships with minimal friction between brokers and captains. Considerable energy has been devoted to uncovering the complex mechanisms that facilitated such cross-cultural trade. Historians have found that slave traders adapted indigenous systems of pawnship and kingship to secure credit transactions; developed Atlantic creole languages and customs that bridged the yawning divide between African and European cultures; and intermeshed family and commercial networks to increase trust. Yet our understanding of the actual process of selling enslaved people remains slight. Scholars have largely assumed that Britons purchased anyone presented to them because they wanted to get off the African coast as quickly as possible. Recent scholarship has indirectly buttressed this position by emphasizing the agency of African middlemen; Europeans could do little to compel powerful African merchants to sell them only particular people, given their lack of military power and the constant risk of death and disease in the tropics. Britons' purchasing strategies were apparently unimportant because captives were forced directly from the interior aboard the ships, regardless of their condition. Our knowledge of how enslaved people were priced and exchanged for goods is also poor, especially compared to the robust literature on the pricing of people within the domestic U.S. slave trade. Neither do we understand how slave traders divided captives among the numerous ships that anchored at the busiest African slaving ports—decisions that would powerfully shape enslaved people's ultimate fates.[3]

By drawing on the accounts of slave traders on the West African coast, including those of non-Britons, this chapter demonstrates that British and African merchants devised a brutally effective set of practices for trading people in Africa. They sifted and sorted captives to obtain only those people who might survive the Middle Passage and satisfy British American colonists' stringent demands for healthy workers. Enslavers simultaneously melded their differing economic philosophies to produce hybrid trading methods through which enslaved people and complicated assortments of imported goods could be priced and exchanged for each other. Traders in men also agreed on a sequence through which enslaved people would be embarked on the ships: captains who had recently arrived on the coast principally loaded low-priced children and women, who ostensibly posed little threat to the crew; those nearing departure embarked higher-priced adults—especially men—who then had less time to rebel or perish aboard the deadly ships. The adoption of these new trading techniques turned ports like Old Calabar into booming slaving markets because they reduced the friction of the cross-cultural trade in people. But those practices—which were de-signed to reduce violence between merchants—were predicated on violence toward enslaved people: slave traders subjected captives to invasive bodily inspections; tore family members from each other; and imprisoned people in deadly ships anchored on the coast, often for months.

The millions of captives who were forced-marched to the African coast during the eighteenth century—people like Broteer Furro and Olaudah Equiano—ranged considerably in age and health. Africans enslaved people, as one Briton observed, "of all ages, from a month, to sixty years and upwards." Powerful African slaveholders in pop-ulous societies such as Asante and the Aro—not visiting Britons—largely determined who would be moved to the coast and who would remain enslaved in the interior. In no African port could Britons purchase only healthy adult men; they were always also offered, as one observer noted, "old people, women, & children." These diverse people arrived at the sea in varied states of health, depending on the length of their route and the arduousness of their trek to the coast. Most captives were force-marched to the sea in large caravans with potentially rebellious men slaves shackled, tied with rope, or pushed along with a wooden trunk locked at the neck. Unshackled captives, even adolescents, had to carry foodstuffs, equipment, and trade goods, sometimes weighing as much as fifty pounds. Captives drawn from deep in the interior spent months trudging to the coast carrying such heavy loads and arrived "very meagre in consequence of the fatigue experienced by them in their long journey from the interior," as a Briton noted; many people arrived, another observed, with "Sores from travelling through the Woods." As many as half of captives perished on these arduous forced marches to the coast; their bodies were cast into the "bad bush" to rot or be devoured by wild animals. Still others who hailed from near the coast, such as Ottobah Cugoano, arrived at the ships in good health, having spent as little as a day being force-marched from their homes. As one ex-perienced slave ship officer explained, captives for sale were "very different, sometimes in good Order, sometimes in bad."[4]

    Far from viewing these diverse captives as "equally suitable for exchange on the Atlantic market," Britons instead sought only those people who met strict criteria of age and health—as the instructions that ship owners issued their captains to guide their slave purchases reveal (see Appendix A). Some instructions were quite vague: many merchants simply exhorted their captains to purchase "Slaves" or captives "suitable for the Westindia Markett." But others stipulated specific criteria of age and health that captains were meant to observe when selecting people. Purchase "Prime healthy young Men and women," the owners of the Bristol ship *Molly* ordered. The *Dispatch*'s owners went further and provided instructions on the ages of people that the captain should buy: "none but ye healthy & strong & of a convenient age—none to exceed ye years of 25 or under 10 if possible, among wch so many men; & stout men boys as can be had." The captain of the *Experiment* was similarly ordered to purchase "well grown people free from spot or Blemish none to be older in appearance than twenty five years." As the owners of the London vessel *Africa Galley* summarized in their 1700 orders, British slave traders generally sought people under "Thirty years of Age," all of whom were meant to be "clear from any distemper" as well as "healthy sound and clear limbed"—so-called "prime slaves" in the trade's macabre lexicon.[5]

British merchants ordered their captains to obtain "prime slaves" in response to the demands of American colonists and because they knew that sickly people would perish aboard their ships. As we will see, the largest colonial planters refused to purchase unhealthy, elderly, or adolescent captives, and they paid premiums to obtain the healthiest Africans; as the *Dispatch*'s owners reminded their captain, adult men and teenage boys (so-called men boys) were the "most Valluable at ye Plantations." British merchants therefore wanted to ship only people who would yield the most from their sale in the Americas, especially given that the cost of feeding and imprisoning people on the Middle Passage was largely the same regardless of a person's age and health. Slave traders also sought Africans who could "stand the Passage"—that is, people healthy enough to survive the arduous voyage. As Dutch surgeon Pieter Gallandat described in his uniquely detailed guide to selecting captives on the coast, captains sought "young, strong, unmarred healthy slaves" because it was "very difficult to heal sick slaves on board a ship" and "there is much less profit to be made from the sale of old, sick or deficient slaves in

[the] West Indi[es]." Slave traders were simultaneously cognizant of the horrific conditions they created for captives on their own ships and their own profits when they ordered their captains to purchase healthy people in Africa.[6]

Captains, assisted by a ship surgeon, subjected people to a lengthy, humiliating, and invasive bodily inspection to identify those who met these strict purchasing criteria. Captains aimed to first sort people into four categories of age and gender: men, women, boys, and girls—a typology used throughout the Atlantic world. Most children could be identified, wrote Gallandat, "at first glance." But the difference between a teenager and an adult was less clear. Captains consequently utilized height as proxy for age, using a ruler accurate to half an inch or notches on a ship's mast to measure people. They deemed males more than four feet and four inches in height and females more than four feet to be adults, even, as a Danish observer wrote, "if they are not more than 12 years of age"; captives beneath these heights were categorized as children. Whites next sought to identify the elderly by washing captives' heads to search for gray hairs painted over by the brokers; prying open their mouths and looking for decaying or missing teeth; peering closely at their skin looking for wrinkles, scars, or "blemishes"; and paying particular "attention to the slackness of [women's] breasts." According to two separate witnesses, British captains licked the faces of males, both to test for the faint traces of beard, indicating manhood, and to taste the sweat for indications of illness (Figure 2.1).[7]

Whites next sought to detect people with injuries or illnesses. A captive had to have "no wounds, fractures, stiff limbs, hidden ailments, or any injuries," wrote Gallandat, and ship captains did not buy people who had "fevers, chest maladies, jaundice, scurvy" or liver disease. The doctor also gauged a captive's sensory capacities by covering each of the person's eyes in turn with one hand and then jabbing toward the other eye with a finger. He ordered the African broker to speak to captives to ensure that they could hear; throughout the inspection, buyers listened carefully to see if the broker had to raise his voice, indicating deafness. He next "carefully examine[d] the [African's] entire body," by making the person jump and flail his or her arms, while also paying particular attention to feet and hands, since missing toes or fingers would hamper field labor. A person's

Figure 2.1. An enslaved man being inspected by an English captain,
c. 1784. Slave Market (Marché d'esclaves), 1783. From Auguste Chambon,
Traité général du commerce de l'Amérique . . . *(Amsterdam: Marc-Michel*
Rey, 1783), vol. 2, between pp. 400 and 401. Reproduced with permission
of the John Carter Brown Library, Providence, RI.

genitals even came under scrutiny for evidence of venereal disease. Such inspections could be extremely drawn out—lasting up to "four hours," according to one experienced slave trader.[8]

Enslaved people found these examinations to be terrifying, invasive, and humiliating. Former slaves rarely mentioned inspections, likely because they were too traumatic; Equiano was one of the few to describe the experience when he euphemistically wrote that he was "handled, and tossed up to see if [he] were sound." Captives had good reason to forget such an experience. According to Gallandat, surgeons needed to be careful to distinguish between those who were ill and those who were taken with "severe anxiety," behaving as if they "had a heavy fever" from the "fear" of being "killed and eaten by the white men"—an impression that was no doubt confirmed when potential European buyers tasted their skin and inspected them like "Beasts" in a livestock market. When a Swedish botanist and doctor took the pulses of slaves in Senegambia, they "trembled with Fear, thinking he was a Purchaser, and would send them to the Islands, which they dread." Africans were so fearful of being purchased that they deliberately "cut off their fingers, or toes or ears" to make themselves unsalable. While examinations were petrifying for everyone, women particularly suffered at the hands of the "often very brutal" surgeons; a Dane on the Gold Coast saw numerous young women "crying, and broken-hearted" after invasive inspections. Some African merchants were aghast at such treatment; when an English vessel traded on the Congo River in 1700, the "king and his attendants were so much ashamed" at the examinations that he required the captain "for decency sake, to do it in a private place."[9]

At the conclusion of the medical examination, slave ship captains decided whether to barter for the captives or reject them. According to numerous witnesses, captains immediately offered to purchase any slave that was healthy and within the accepted age range. A British captain recalled, for example, that he tried to purchase people "judged saleable . . . without a Discrimination." Another experienced officer stated that he "never knew an Instance in the Course of my Trade" where a "good . . . slave was refused." A group of three Liverpool captains likewise told Parliament, "[We] generally purchase every saleable Slave that offers of either Sex." As a Danish officer bluntly stated, "When they are young we buy them."[10]

Whites simultaneously rejected myriad people because they deemed them too young. Captains knew that infants would sell for little in the Americas and occupy room that could be taken by healthy adult slaves. Some ship owners even ordered their captains not to be, as one Bristol merchant callously wrote, "imposed on with . . . Little Children." Many slave ship captains even arrived on the coast with a minimum age for slaves in mind. Four feet was the most common minimum because, as one former British slave trader wrote, that was "the lowest Size required for the West Indies." According to the same witness, this size requirement resulted in the rejection of people younger than fourteen years old. Children below four feet in height were consequently "seldom purchased." The account books of Richard Miles (d. 1818), a Briton who officered numerous Gold Coast forts between 1765 and 1780, are particularly revealing. Miles's accounts—the largest and most complete record of a British merchant's trade on the African coast—detail his purchase of 2,461 enslaved people between 1771 and 1780, of whom just 171 were children (7 percent). Miles rarely purchased very young children: of the sixty-nine children whose height he recorded, just nine were shorter than four feet; he clearly sought older children and teenagers, likely because he was responding to the demands of the captains to whom he later resold his prisoners. Trading accounts kept by slave ship captains reveal that they likewise purchased few young children. John Newton (1725–1802), who helmed the Liverpool ship *Duke of Argyle* in 1750 and 1751, recorded in his logbook the acquisition of sixty-seven enslaved children, most of whom were taller than three feet and ten inches. Newton's officers purchased younger children when trading up rivers in longboats, but he sought to end this practice by giving them "positive orders to buy none under 4 foot." Prior to leaving Africa, Newton also swapped three of his "small boys" for a much older girl and a woman from another ship. The surviving accounts of the *Duke of Buccleugh, Eliza, Daniel,* and *Tom,* which record the heights of purchased children, evince the same patterns: the captains did buy adolescents, but they formed a very small proportion of the human cargo—just 6 percent of captives, on average. Captains thus took, one Bristol slave trader testified, "as few" prepubescent children "as possible."[11]

Whites were particularly reluctant to purchase children accompanied by their mothers. According to a Danish observer, captains did not want mothers and children, because "small children [would] nearly always die on the journey to the West Indies." Captains would dislike purchasing a pregnant woman, he added, because she "could easily lose her life in childbirth" aboard the ship. The tragic case of one pregnant woman embarked on a British ship in 1787 is particularly illustrative: the woman was "reduced to a mere skeleton" because the ship "afford[ed] few, or rather no, comforts," and she then died giving birth; her infant was "fed with flour" and perished two days later. Another witness wrote that captains avoided buying women with babies because they "[take] up thrice as much room as a single slave" on the ship; and a captain wrote that his fellow traders did not like to buy women with infants "at the breast," because the children cried and defecated on both their mothers and the women between decks, leading to "endless arguments." Crewmen were also aggravated by crying children on the ships; one Liverpool officer "threw" a one-year-old overboard to its death because its crying had "disturbed his sleep." Trading accounts confirm that captains had a clear preference for women without children: of 404 women embarked on six vessels for which detailed accounts survive, just twenty-seven were accompanied by infants. "It is," a former British slave ship sailor remembered, "a very rare matter for any captains of Guineamen that they ever buy women with children."[12]

The most callous captains even turned away children who did accompany their mothers for sale to ensure that they were not "plagued with a Child on board." Miles was twice as likely to purchase a child alone than an adult, implying that he may have separated mothers from their children; other captives were, like Equiano and Furro, torn from their parents within the African slave trade. As one experienced former officer testified, enslaved children almost "always came [aboard] without any relations." On one of the rare occasions when Miles did resell to a ship a mother with her child he had purchased, the captain complained that the woman was a "very good one" but "her having a child" was a "very great objection." He appears to have sent both mother and child back ashore.[13] Some officers even refused to accept mothers with infants. The commander of the *Ruby*, which traded at Bimbia Island in 1787 and 1788, rejected a woman who was brought aboard "with a Child in her Arms." The woman was brought back to the ship the next day without her child and "in great Sorrow" because the coastal traders had, the ship's surgeon later testified, killed the child "in the Night to accommodate us in the Sale." A Danish trader wrote that he had witnessed numerous captains take an infant "from the mother's back and throw it onto the beach, pushing the mother into the boat, and sailing away with her." He added that the Fante also presented mothers for sale without their children and then, once the deal had been closed, revealed the infant, forcing captains to take the child for free. This tale—which the Dane meant to illustrate the perfidy of the Fante—therefore reveals much about slave ship captains' heartless attitudes toward infants, whom they routinely turned away.[14]

Europeans also rejected the elderly, because they believed they would, as one Liverpool consortium callously stated, "sell for little & often die." A Dutch captain wrote that whites at Whydah turned away anyone who was "above five and thirty Years old" and those who were "grey-haired." Newton likewise recorded in his logbook that he rejected numerous enslaved men for being "old"; he turned down several women who were, he wrote, "long breasted," apparently an indication of age. Another captain trading on the Gold Coast sent back men who were, he wrote, "by no means merchantable" as they were "old, Dropsical and with swell'd testicles." Britons also sent back captives with teeth that showed evidence of decay and any with gray hair and beards. As with the young, captains cared little if they tore elderly people from friends or relatives, even if it resulted in the death of the rejected person. The mate of a vessel at Benin in the 1760s, for example, was presented with three people kidnapped by a local pirate named Captain Lemma Lemma. The mate purchased the young man and woman, but he thought the other man to be "too old, and he refused to buy him." Lemma Lemma "chopped off" the elderly man's head and had him "immediately thrown overboard." Britons "so invariably rejected" the elderly, one former slave ship officer told Parliament, "that [African merchants] seldom brought them" for sale.[15]

Captains seldom rejected enslaved people because of their ethnicity. So long as they belonged to one of the myriad ethnic groups that planters believed were enslaved in the region where they traded, the captains accepted them. If, however, the slaves were clearly from another part of the coast—something that would be indicated by a person's language, physical characteristics, and scarification—the captain would reject them for fear that the planters would query the origin of the entire human cargo and potentially pay lower prices as a result. In 1773, for example, a captain rejected a woman on the Gold Coast because he wanted a "prime asante woman as the coast can afourd." Another captain was more explicit: he had received a woman from Richard Miles and complained that she was "a Benin Slave," whom he could not "think of Keeping," explaining: "It may prove to be a great detriment to my average [sale price] in the West Indies, In case she was taken notice of." These instances were rare, however. Miles's voluminous papers, for example, contain no other cases where captains rejected slaves on the grounds of their origin.[16]

The sickly were the most apt to be rejected because whites knew that unhealthy people's conditions would deteriorate on the unhygienic ships, and they feared the spread of disease. Surgeon

Alexander Falconbridge (d. 1792) reported that in his experience of purchasing more than a thousand people there were a multitude of "defects" that disqualified people from being embarked. "If they are afflicted with any infirmity, or are deformed," he wrote, "they are rejected." Another captain said that his "greatest care of all is to buy none that are pox'd, lest they should infect the rest aboard." Captains wanted to avoid, above all, "fluxes" and "fevers" that could decimate an entire human cargo. As a captain who sent back two women "ill of the flux" told a British fort officer, he would not "have the ship infected with them." "No sickly Slave," one surgeon remembered, "[was] ever purchased" in the three slaving voyages he made. As another experienced slave ship officer concluded, "All that are sickly are refused. . . . All such as are healthy . . . are purchased."[17]

Britons thus turned away very large numbers of people offered to them on the African coast. Miles noted in his correspondence with ship captains between 1773 and 1776 the sale of 179 captives, of whom captains sent back fifty-one, or just more than a quarter. Miles himself must have rejected the unwell and the elderly when he first purchased captives from the Fante. Testifying before Parliament, Miles's colleague John Fountain admitted as much: "Even in the cause of humanity," he told them, he would not "purchase what would be by me unsaleable, and by such repeated purchases make myself a beggar." Newton's exceptionally detailed logbooks for two voyages that he commanded in the 1750s shows that he likewise rejected a quarter of the captives whom he viewed. These are low estimates, however, because Miles was reselling captives who he had himself already inspected; Newton's officers trading in a longboat purchased many of the captives, and so the numbers of people whom they rejected do not appear in his logbooks. Captains trading directly with African brokers rejected much larger numbers of people. Captain Richard Rogers, who traded at Old Calabar in 1788, told his Bristol employers that he had seen "6 & 7 hundr[e]d Slaves," of whom he had bought only one hundred. Another captain on the Gold Coast told Miles, "[I have] only purchased thirty two & have seen three hundred," who were mostly "Old Men & Women or young Children." Surgeon James Arnold, who helped purchase several hundred captives aboard the *Ruby*, told Parliament that he rejected "full as many [slaves] as they bought." And when Captain James Fraser (d. 1798) bought captives at Ambriz, a small port near the Congo River, he rejected "twice the number . . . more than [he] purchased." Fraser subsequently sailed to Bonny on numerous voyages and purchased more than a thousand enslaved people there; his surgeon, Falconbridge, reported that he also rejected large numbers of people. Although there is variety in these estimates, Britons clearly turned away at least one in four of the captives offered to them, and often many more, as they sought to obtain only enslaved people who met their strict standards of age and health. By thus rejecting large numbers of people, Britons successfully maximized their potential profits from their American sales and reduced the risk that their human cargo would be infected by sickly people being brought aboard. Enslaved people consequently suffered through protracted and traumatizing inspections to determine their health and age and were brutally torn from each other on the African coast.[18]

Britons sifted and sorted captives to obtain individuals who could be profitably resold in the Americas, but also to price people so that they could be exchanged for goods—a complex process that underwent considerable adaption to accommodate the slave trade's expansion. Unlike Europeans, who typically valued things according to abstract monetary units such as gold or silver coins, Atlantic Africans exchanged items at fixed ratios, such as 1:1, 2:1, or 3:1. These "systematic equivalences," as historian Philip Curtin has labeled them, were determined by regional communities and fixed for long periods of time, regardless of fluctuations in supply and demand. The purposes of systematic equivalences were to create, as Curtin notes, "comparative values that linked food, labor, and social values." Africans hence valued enslaved people who conformed to specific standards of age and health in terms of their exchangeability at fixed ratios with goods. In sixteenth-century West-Central Africa, a "standard adult male slave" was a healthy person between fifteen and eighteen years of age whose exchange value was the amount of labor that he could perform during his lifetime—equivalent to a single piece of luxury cloth. When the Portuguese began purchasing slaves in Angola during the 1500s, they consequently exchanged captives for "pieces" of Indian cloth on a one-to-one basis, and a healthy adult male captive became known as a *peça da India*. Whites continued to buy enslaved people in Africa through a process of simple barter during much of the seventeenth century. In Senegambia, Europeans exchanged iron bars for a captive, also labeled peça da India—a "young male slave in good health, no more than twenty-five years of age." When the Portuguese arrived in the Bight of Biafra, they found that Africans exchanged "slaves, cows, goats and sheep . . . for copper bracelets," for eight or ten of which "one slave" could be obtained. In the Bight of Benin, the Portuguese purchased captives with cowry shells imported from the Indian Ocean; by the mid-seventeenth century, "a slave" could be bought for a hundred pounds of shells. In the slave trade's early years, Europeans thus conformed to African methods of pricing enslaved people according to their interchangeability with single categories of goods.[19]

The slave trade's growth in the second half of the seventeenth century placed inflationary pressure on this exchange mechanism, which caused widespread social and political disruption. The acquisition of valuable imports had initially proved beneficial to African states, as European goods like metals and shells were often used as currencies; imports increased the money supply. In Benin, for example, the burgeoning supply of cowries enabled markets to grow and improved the state's ability to collect taxes and tolls, underpinning the construction of palaces and the raising of a large army. The influx of cloth, iron bars, and copper bracelets to other areas of the coast had similarly deleterious effects. But as Europeans poured commodities into Atlantic Africa, the value of currencies plunged, threatening the stability of the indigenous economies and societies: vibrant cloth-making industries declined; tax bases dried up; and prices for goods rose, angering consumers. States that had formerly thrived through slave trading found their power and legitimacy threatened by inflation.[20]

In the late seventeenth century, African merchants sought to curtail inflation by insisting that Europeans bring an "assortment" of goods instead of currencies. Commodity money such as cowries and metals would still be exchanged for captives but made up a shrinking share of a bundle of goods that included an array of items. In the Bight of Benin, for example, cowries went from being the sole item exchanged for enslaved people in 1600 to a third of imports by value in 1670 and less than 20 percent by 1700. Historians have struggled to pinpoint precisely when "sorting" was introduced to the various parts of the African coast but have found that it was clearly entrenched across Atlantic Africa by the mid-eighteenth century. The invoices of goods shipped to Africa by the Royal African Company circa 1673–1733 reveal that the spread of assortment was an evolutionary, rather than revolutionary, process. In the 1670s, almost every African region was importing fewer than half a dozen goods, with a handful of commodities making up most cargo. Thus, RAC ships brought just four items to Old and New Calabar in that period: iron bars, copper bars, manillas, and beads; the metalwares composed 98 percent of the cargo, indicating that they were the principal exchange for captives. Vessels sailing to Whydah in the same period carried a more complex cargo of cowries, iron bars, manillas, and various cloths, but cowries (35 percent of the cargo by value) and iron bars (20 percent) predominated. Brokers in the Bights of Benin and Biafra had thus already moved away from the exchange of single items for enslaved people by the 1670s but were still conducting a trade somewhere between assortment and barter. On the Gold Coast, by contrast, African merchants were importing much more complex cargoes consisting of more than a dozen different goods, implying that they had already embraced a form of sorting. By 1700, though, the size, cost, and complexity of trading cargoes had increased to every region of the African coast; ships to Old Calabar were now carrying ten different commodities, of which metalware constituted just 61 percent of the total value. Assortment was hence adopted gradually across Atlantic Africa as the slave trade expanded at the turn of the eighteenth century.[21]

Assortment was a key innovation that both paralleled and facilitated the slave trade's growth. A slave trade based upon the exchange of enslaved people for currencies was unsustainable because it rapidly destabilized African societies through runaway inflation. Assortment opened a bottleneck by enabling African merchants to acquire currencies in manageable quantities, as well as a cornucopia of goods sourced by their European partners. The increasing use of assortment was, however, potentially fraught for the African polities who sought to regulate and control the slave trade. The previous method of trading enslaved people for single items, while inflationary, was straightforward: so long as imports met basic standards of quality and size, they could be swapped at simple ratios for captives who themselves had to conform to specific standards, without recourse to abstract units of account. Conducting, regulating, and taxing such a trade was not difficult for African merchants and rulers—most of whom did not rely upon paper accounts and records. Assortment introduced a dizzying amount of complexity: Africans had to decide which imports would be included in the assortment; what standards of quality and size those goods had to meet; and how various commodities should be valued versus one another and enslaved people. Each of these considerations was further complicated by the participation of numerous African merchants in every port, each of whom transacted business with a plethora of whites. At the minor Gold Coast slaving port of Tantumquerry, for example, Richard Miles purchased 957 enslaved people from 192 different Fante merchants; on the Loango Coast, a merchant community of almost six hundred individuals was engaged in the slave trade in the second half of the eighteenth century. African merchants needed to establish a common set of market practices that applied to these potentially competing actors if their homes were to become efficient slaving markets.[22]

Africans solved the problem of price by introducing imaginary units of account for valuing both people and goods. Rather than price goods and slaves in European currencies—pounds sterling, Spanish dollars, and so forth—Africans insisted that they utilize their own "trade currencies" as units, which typically originated from the commodity money that had been used to purchase slaves, such as cowries, metals, and cloths. Over the course of the seventeenth century, each coastal region developed its own trade currency, the value of which was then used to price slaves and the goods that were used to purchase them. Thus, Upper Guinean brokers typically employed iron bars; merchants on the Gold Coast used gold ounces; from Benin through the western Bight of Biafra, commodities were also priced in iron bars; the Efik, uniquely, used copper bars; and the people of the Loango Coast valued in pieces of cloth. Europeans acceded to the use of these diverse currencies because it enabled the better calculation of profits; captains could compare the prices that they traded goods for in Africa, called the coast price, against the prices of the goods in Europe, the prime cost; the difference revealed which goods were profitable and which unprofitable.

African statesmen imposed order by stabilizing the price of imports in these trade currencies for long periods, ensuring that merchants did not have to haggle over the values of goods within every transaction. At Bonny, for example, the prices of twelve commodities that were commonly traded for enslaved people remained largely the same across the eighteenth century. On the Gold Coast, eight of twelve different commodities did shift in value between 1728 and 1800 but then only by a small sum. Importantly, these shifts were neither sudden nor common, allowing Britons and Fante brokers to daily transact business without fear that prices would suddenly rise or fall. Extant account books detailing the acquisition of captives in Africa also confirm that neither African nor British merchants sought to undercut each other by offering goods for prices lower than the commonly agreed sum (see Appendix B). Richard Miles, for example, usually sold goods at the same prices across his barters even when purchasing enslaved people from different sellers; he only altered his prices when a broader shift occurred along the coast. Powerful social, cultural, and criminal sanctions apparently ensured that both African and British merchants adhered to customary prices.[23]

Because the prices of goods were fixed for long periods, imported commodities needed to be of specific volumes, dimensions, or weights to be acceptable in trade. Britons had to bring textiles printed in particular colors and patterns and cut those fabrics to exact yardages; to string bunches containing a precise number of beads; to sort hats and knives into dozens; and to measure out gunpowder and liquor into thousands of identically sized kegs. Some vessels even had "shops" aboard where Africans could peruse samples of these wares to ensure they conformed to their standards. African sellers examined goods carefully before accepting them: they held cloth out "between themselves and the light," looking for the smallest "hole or tear"; tasted liquor for "bite"; and fired unloaded muskets to ensure that they would "strike fire well." They rejected any item that did not meet their standards, even for the smallest fault. On both the Gold Coast and the Loango Coast, for example, Africans insisted that guns had to have three screws holding the trigger guard and lock in place and rejected those with two screws. As one captain observed, "If the Europeans are exact in inspecting their captives, [the Africans] are equally so in inspecting their goods."[24]

Although enslavers seldom disputed the prices of goods, they did haggle over the prices of people—a process that occurred when Britons first arrived in port and "broke trade." "Breaking trade" varied in its exact form between ports, but it typically involved the payment of taxes, the giving of presents, and a drawn-out discussion over slave prices. A day after anchoring at Bonny in 1699, for example, Captain James Barbot Sr. (d. 1706) of the ship *Albion Frigate* visited the Ibani king ashore, showed samples of his goods, and made an initial proposal for the price of captives. The king insisted that Barbot pay an assortment worth thirteen iron bars for a healthy adult man, an increase on previous prices "because of the many ships that had exported vast quantities [of slaves]." The heated meeting lasted from three in the afternoon "until night, without any result." After a week of negotiation, Barbot finally reached an agreement with the king, whereupon the "king order'd the publick cryer to proclaim the permission of trade with us." Trading at Bonny almost a century later, Captain James Fraser likewise agreed on slave prices with the king when he first arrived in the port. The king then sold Fraser a single male slave at a price that the other Ibani merchants had to adhere to in their own dealings.[25]

The setting of prices took place at all the major slaving ports visited by Britons. When Captain James Barbot Jr. (d. 1730) sailed to the Congo River in 1700, he was told that there would be "no likelihood of any trade until we had adjusted with the prince the price of slaves, and the standard of our merchandizes." A week after his arrival, Barbot "agreed with the prince about the trade of slaves," setting a price equivalent to eight pieces of cloth for healthy adult men. On the nearby Loango Coast, the prices of slaves were set "at the beginning" of trade through negotiation with the *mafouk*, a royal appointee who acted as the primary point of contact between Europeans and the merchant community. On the Gold Coast a different method operated. As one historian writes, "Trade was broken anew every day by the first captain and black merchant to reach terms" by agreeing the "price of a prime male slave." This "price was [usually] the same as the day before," he adds. At Whydah, captains "attended" the king upon their arrival to show "samples of [their] goods" and to make "agreement about the [slave] prices." After setting the prices and paying customs, "the bell was order'd to go about to give notice to all people to bring their slaves." As with the prices of goods, slave prices agreed on when "breaking trade" acted as a guide price that other African brokers conformed to when initially transacting business with the captain. As one Gold Coast officer observed, coastal traders and Europeans knew in advance "at which price each [slave] is valued" before they transacted business.[26]

When undertaking these negotiations, Britons agreed on the price of "prime" men and then used that value to also price healthy enslaved women and children. The exact amount that they deducted from the price of a male slave varied depending on when and where they traded, but it was almost always below the price of an equivalent man. When James Barbot Sr. traded at Bonny, for example, he agreed to pay thirteen iron bars for men and nine iron bars for women; trading at the same port almost sixty years later, the captain of the *Molly* began his trade by paying five bars less for women than men. On the Gold Coast, Richard Miles consistently paid two ounces less for women than men. "Boys and girls" were valued, Barbot noted at Bonny, "proportionally . . . according to their ages." Paul Isert (1756–1789), a Dane who visited the Gold Coast in the 1780s, reported that the price of a prime slave was reduced by a fixed amount for every inch that a person was beneath four feet and four inches—the supposed height of an adult. Miles's purchasing records show that Britons on the Gold Coast did price enslaved children according to their age, but not by height alone. Miles always paid less for children than adults, and less for girls than boys of the same height. But the variability in the prices he paid for children of the same height indicates that he made assumptions about a person's age and health that were not based strictly on stature. Nonetheless, children were seldom valued more than a prime adult captive of the same gender, implying that captains still priced enslaved children using healthy adults as a benchmark.[27]

Captains also used a healthy adult person to price captives who had what one British fort officer called "defects." "The loss of a tooth . . . a blemish in the eye" or "the loss of a toe or finger" would, the officer noted, make a person "objectionable, as a prime Slave."

But the captive "would not be refused for any of those defects, altho'
the price would not be the same given for him as if he was a prime
Slave." On the Gold Coast, British and Danish slave buyers used a
fixed system of deductions for such injuries. Miles, for example, paid
discounted prices for captives missing toes, teeth, and fingers, as well
as those he deemed "ordinary" or "indifferent." Although captains
were willing to purchase injured people, they formed a tiny frac-
tion of the enslaved people boarding the ships. Of the 2,461 people
whom Miles purchased, just sixty-two had what he considered to be
bodily defects. Slave ship captains were similarly selective: the trading accounts of numerous ships show few captives being purchased
at discounts.[28]

   With the prices of captives already established, the purchasing
process consisted of a debate between the captain and the African
broker over the composition of the assortment. American mariner
Nathaniel Cutting (d. 1824) observed such a transaction when he
saw John Knox, captain of the Liverpool slave ship *Hercules*, purchasing a man from Robin Gray, an African merchant of Cape
Mount, a slaving port near Sierra Leone, in January 1790. Cutting
describes Knox giving Gray cowry shells equal to the "previously
agreed" price in iron bars, and Gray then "mentions the article
which he wants & lays down then a number of Cowries equal to
the number of Bars at which it is currently sold." If Knox agreed to
include the item in the assortment, he wrote "down the articles" on
a slate, "affixing against it the number of Bars." When that round of
bartering had been completed, an "assistant" cleared the shells, and
Gray proceeded to name the next article he desired until "the whole
number of Cowries [were] returned." Over the course of several
rounds, the trading assortment was formed. Paul Isert described an
identical process on the Gold Coast and added that African sellers
would "pick and choose" for "hours." Once the composition of the
assortment had been agreed on, an officer took the slate to the ship's
hold and drew out the listed goods, which he gave to the African
broker; that middleman then handed the bundle, minus his fees, to
the slave seller. Captains marked the completion of the barter by
giving the broker several dashes, usually knives, tobacco, and liquor.
The captain then took formal possession of the purchased person.
English, Dutch, American, and French visitors to different parts of

the coast all described a similar purchasing process, indicating that it was common in Atlantic Africa.[29]

At first glance, the process of assembling the assortment appears chaotic, as captains were at the whim of African merchants such as Gray, who could demand any goods they desired in any order. But spotlighting the purchase of a man and a woman on the Gold Coast in the 1780s illuminates the logic that underpinned assortment bargaining in Atlantic Africa. The transactions were observed by Isert for "a young, grown man . . . and for a young woman who has no blemishes"— a "prime" man and woman, in the trade's dehumanizing typology—for prices agreed on "without any further discussion" at 160 Danish thaler for the man and 128 for the woman. For both people, the African seller initially demanded muskets and gunpowder; in a subsequent round, he requested four dozen knives. The seller then named a variety of different goods that fluctuated in price, from as little as a single thaler for some cowries to as many as sixteen thalers for a keg of brandy. The composition of the goods within these subsidiary rounds changed, according to Isert, between slave barters, depending on the whim of the seller.[30]

These sample transactions—out of millions made in Atlantic Africa during the eighteenth century—highlight three key features of assortment that brought order to a potentially anarchic marketplace. First, although the exact items included in each round for both the man and woman were often different, barters followed a similar pattern, with the same category of goods being included in roughly the same order. Accounts recording the acquisition of captives indicate that this remained true across multiple transactions: captains typically purchased people with assortments constructed by a similar sequence of rounds, with the same categories of goods in each round. Second, expensive and inexpensive goods both had to be included within the bundles, and so there were broadly two types of commodities within the assortment: a small number of high-priced items and a larger number of lower-priced items. Europeans understood these two categories well; French slave traders distinguished between *grandes merchandises* and *petites merchandises* in their *assortiments*; Britons labeled the grandes merchandises "heads of goods" or "commanding articles." Whites who could not include even a single commanding article within their assortment became,

Table 2.1. Goods exchanged for an enslaved man and woman, Gold Coast, 1784

Round #	Type of good	Quantity and type of goods exchanged for man	Value of goods (thalers)	Quantity and type of goods exchanged for woman	Value of goods (thalers)
1	**Firearms**	**5 muskets**	**30**	**5 muskets**	**30**
2	**Gunpowder**	**80 lbs. gunpowder**	**40**	**60 lbs. gunpowder**	**30**
3	Metalware 1	2 iron rods	6	[none]	—
4	Brandy	1 anker	16	1 crate	12
5	**Knives**	**4 dozen**	**4**	**4 dozen**	**4**
6	Beads	[none]	—	"various"	12
7	Hardware 1	2 tin basins	2	2 brass kettles	8
8	Textile 1	1 flowered cotton	10	1 neganepaut	10
9	Textile 2	1 chelloe	10	1 niccanee	10
10	Textile 3	1 bejutapant	10	1 half say	10
11	Textile 4	½ taffeta	10	[none]	—
12	Textile 5	1 East India kerchief	12	[none]	—
13	Metalware 2	1 brass basin	4	[none]	—
14	Metalware 3	3 copper rods	3	[none]	—
15	Metalware 4	2 lead rods	2	[none]	—
16	Cowries	[none]	—	Cowries	1
	"To the Guard"	[not detailed]	1	[not detailed]	1
		Total (14 rounds)	160	*Total (10 rounds)*	128

Source: Isert, *Letters,* 113–14. The *grandes merchandises* are highlighted in bold. For two similar transactions on the Gold Coast circa 1776, see Clarkson, *Substance,* 4.

in the parlance of the trade, "unsorted" or "dissorted," preventing them from purchasing captives. In Isert's example, guns, powder, and knives were the heads of goods; Isert considers them commodities that "must always be included" in the transaction "or the trader will not sell them [the captives] to you." Two of these goods—guns and powder—were also the most valuable in the assortment, making up almost half of the price of the man and the woman. The numerous lower-priced goods in the subsidiary rounds observed by Isert were the petites merchandises.[31]

The third key feature of assortment is that men, women, and children were purchased for different bundles of goods. Because men typically sold for more than women, they were exchanged for a larger bundle composed of more rounds: in Isert's example, the man was purchased with an assortment agreed on after fourteen rounds, versus ten for the woman. With the exception of the grandes merchandises, which were almost identical for both men and women, the goods exchanged within the subsidiary rounds of petites merchandises consisted of different types and quantities of commodities. Thus, the woman was bought with a crate of brandy, rather than an anker of brandy; with brass kettles instead of tin basins; and with three different types of Indian textiles—a thaler's worth of cowries was paid for the woman but not for the man. Although Isert did not describe a sample barter for enslaved children, they were purchased with much smaller bundles than the equivalent for an adult of the same gender. Writing in 1700, the owners of the *Africa Galley* advised that at Bonny there would be "no certainty for Boys and Girls of any sort of goods but as you can agree and have to spare"—meaning that the captain would not have to trade the same assortment he paid for enslaved adults. The merchant added that the captain should consequently "put off . . . those goods that are not much desired . . . for Boys and Girles." Enslaved children themselves vividly recalled being purchased with small assortments. Broteer Furro was, for example, sold for just "four gallons of rum, and a piece of calico"—a tiny quantity of goods compared to the large bundles that Europeans paid for enslaved adults. Negotiating the composition of assortments when purchasing people was guided by an underlying set of rules that was understood well by both Britons and Africans.[32]

The development of these market rules was crucial to the slave trade's expansion because it reduced the chaos and friction that was inherent in cross-cultural trade, especially in the growing slaving ports where African merchants transacted business directly with British ship captains. These market practices also enabled, through a near-alchemical process, diverse people to be reduced to the status of a commodity. After being inspected, sifted, and sorted, enslaved people became goods in the eyes of their captors: a "prime" woman, an "ordinary" man, an "undersized" child—just some of the trade's degrading categories. Thus commodified, enslaved people could be priced and sold through a procedure that enabled African merchants to obtain commodities sourced from across the globe, and Britons to acquire the healthy captives they desired.

Although captains sought to purchase captives from African sellers without European competition, the concentration of the slave trade meant that there were almost always multiple vessels trading at the major African slaving ports. Few enslaved people passed through small ports whose infrastructure could fill one vessel at a time; markets where captives could be obtained at low prices were soon overrun by other ships. Most merchants hence deliberately dispatched their vessels to busy markets such as Bonny and Anomabu, where they knew that their captains would face competition from other ships. Seasonality made it more likely that these vessels would trade alongside one another, as outfitters sought to time the arrival and departure of their ships around African crop cycles. More than a dozen vessels often anchored at the busiest African ports during eighteenth-century peace years, all of them embarking captives at the same time. Competition between Britons was thus the norm in the eighteenth-century slave trade; "it is not to be Expected from the Great Number of Ships in the African Trade that it shoud be otherways," observed one Liverpool merchant in 1761.[33]

Britons and Africans developed a set of practices to ensure that each of these competing vessels could be filled with enslaved people. When a ship first arrived at the coast, the risks of mortality and insurrection were minimal, and the costs of food, fuel, and water low. Merchants therefore urged their captains to strike hard bargains to ensure that initial slave prices were low. When the *Earl of*

Liverpool sailed to Bonny in 1797, for example, the ship owner ordered the captain to "propose to the leading Traders very low Bars to Begin with"—offer the lowest possible prices. If the Ibani disputed the offer, then the captain was to "shew them a disposition to go to New Calabar" instead. A guide to the slave trade likewise informed readers that the "key" to success in the trade was to "put a moderate price on the first [prime]" slaves purchased because that price "regulated all those the ship [subsequently traded]." The same guide advised captains to achieve this by offering goods that were "in greater quantity or of least value" in the initial assortment. In this way, captains would pay fewer grandes merchandises in their early barters, lowering prices while reducing the risk that the captain would exhaust the supply of the most essential trade goods. After enumerating the "commanding" goods needed in every slave barter, the owners of the ship *Blaydes* also told their captain, "[Do not] part with too many of those articles at the beginning of yr trade" because it "[will] dissort your cargo."[34]

For their part, African slave traders sought to drive up the initial price of captives and refused to trade with vessels that did not meet their terms. As Captain Peter Potter related, when he arrived at the Cameroon River in June 1775 and offered prices beneath those of competing captains, "[the Duala took] oaths that they would not sell me one slave if I did not give them the same as the others." Only after further heated bargaining did Potter reach an agreement and open his trade. On Potter's subsequent voyage in the following year, the Duala refused to trade with him for "a whole Month" because he had refused to pay their prices; any merchant who traded with Potter would have his goods confiscated, his house pulled down, and his plantain trees "distroy[ed]." African merchants also disputed what goods would be included in the assortment for captives, as well as their quality. When James Barbot Sr. traded at Bonny in 1700, for example, the Ibani insisted that he pay a bar more for slaves—the same amount as another ship—and "objected much against our basons, tankards, yellow beads, and some other merchandize, as of little or no demand there at the time." If a captain did manage to drive down prices, African merchants sometimes acquiesced, knowing that they were then under no obligation to trade with that captain and could direct their business to other ships. Potter, for example, eventually got the Duala to agree to his prices, but, he related, they were "very careless whether the[y] sell me any slaves or not" because they knew that other ships were coming. Initial prices agreed on for enslaved people were thus a compromise between equally hard-dealing Africans and Europeans.[35]

Captains purchased small numbers of enslaved people— especially women and children—at these low prices before stepping up their offers to speed their departure. Merchants urged their captains to increase prices once their vessels held large numbers of prisoners because, cautioned the owners of a Bristol ship, the "Risque of Sickness & Mortality then becomes great." Captains were meant to significantly boost prices when their vessel was "half slaved"—when the ship held half the predetermined number of enslaved people that the ship was meant to carry from Africa. The acceleration of prices was also dependent on the actions of other whites: if a captain suddenly offered higher prices to hasten his departure, captains at a similar stage in the buying process followed suit. At that point, captains offered greater quantities of goods in their assortments or revealed desirable commodities that they had hidden. The captain of the *Bristol Merchant*, for example, was explicitly ordered: "Keep some of the goods you find most in Demand to the Last," to "command your trade when you come near finishing your purchase." Captains consequently increased the prices they offered over the course of their trade, sometimes significantly. The captain of the *Molly*, which took 286 people from Bonny in April 1759, almost doubled the prices he paid for enslaved people over three months, with a significant increase around the middle of his time on the coast. When he increased the price for an enslaved man by ten bars he added two kegs of powder and two extra Indian fabrics—all grandes merchandises—and introduced a brass pan that he had not included in earlier assortments.[36]

As an experienced captain noted, African ports were filled with captains offering differing prices: "The ships that have been longest in the River, and preparing to sail, pay a higher price than the vessels lately arrived." Although the captain was describing his numerous visits to Bonny, his statement was equally true for the other major African slaving ports. Writing from Old Calabar in 1768, for example, a British captain reported the staggered prices that the commanders of five other ships were paying, with those nearing their departure offering 40 percent more than the newcomers. This practice was so entrenched that a captain thought of his vessel as occupying a place in an orderly line of ships, awaiting his "turn" to purchase people; the few captains who tried to leap the queue by offering higher prices early raised the ire of their fellow mariners and risked exhausting their cargo or "disorting" themselves. As vessels periodically departed filled with enslaved people, captains moved up the line by increasing their offers; meanwhile other ships arrived and joined the back of the queue, maintaining the cycle.[37]

The importance of these market practices for shaping the movement of enslaved people aboard the ships is best illustrated by focusing on Bonny—the busiest eighteenth-century West African slaving port. Depending on his "opulence," each Ibani merchant bought, according to the surgeon Alexander Falconbridge, "forty to two hundred" slaves at the Aro fairs. The merchants returned in canoe fleets holding between four hundred and two thousand prisoners. They imprisoned their captives in cells within their canoe houses, where they were "oiled, fed, and made up for Sale." In a typical year there would be approximately ten vessels—most of them British— waiting to forcibly embark these captives, each paying a different price depending on the timing of its arrival. In April 1791, for example, thirteen vessels waited for the Ibani fleet to return from the fairs in twenty days' time. A captain of one of the recently arrived vessels wrote that seven of the ships would sail once the canoes arrived from the fair because their captains would "pay very high to sail." Seeking the highest prices, Bonny merchants invited the captains who had "been longest in the river" to have "the first choice" of the captives. According to one officer who purchased people at Bonny, the enslaved were "drawn up in regular lines" within the brokers' houses. Captains arrived in the early evening, paced along these lines of prisoners, and carefully picked out people in groups of ten or less who met their standards of age and health, before paying the previously agreed-on price for them.[38]

Given that the captains nearing their departure were paying a larger assortment that included more grandes merchandises, they principally purchased enslaved adults; those captains ignored enslaved children. When the *Molly*'s captain neared his departure, for example, he purchased 122 adults (sixty-four men and fifty-eight women) and just two children (one boy and one girl). The captain of the *Trelawny* likewise bought just one boy after augmenting the prices he offered, having previously purchased sixteen children. The canoes first pulling away from the Ibani brokers' houses thus principally carried enslaved adults to ships that were nearing their departure. Captains proposing lower prices—those who had arrived most recently—next proceeded to the brokers' houses to sift through the people who remained. Whites sought to identify any healthy person whom the previous group of captains had not selected by subjecting them to particularly thorough and humiliating inspections. Once they found a healthy captive, they sought to purchase him or her using smaller assortments of goods that contained fewer grandes merchandises. When adults were not available, captains purchased women and children. The *Molly*'s captain, for example, purchased forty-five enslaved children before increasing his prices, along with 103 men and women.[39]

After several groups of captains had picked out the healthy captives from the brokers' house, there remained only "the refuse"—those whom whites believed to be too young, old, or sickly to be worthy of purchase. Falconbridge saw these people "cruelly beaten" by the Ibani merchants and, he alleged, murdered at New Calabar. Captain James Fraser told Parliament, though, that the "youngest" rejected captives were "kept by the Bonny people in their houses," as canoe boys, porters, servants, or wives. The Ibani "sent back" the "old or unsaleable" to the Aro, he added, along with the "goods that ha[d] been paid for the Slaves that ha[d] been sold." James Morley, who officered six slaving voyages between 1758 and 1775, likewise believed that some of the "refused" captives were "sent from one part of the coast to another for sale," while "others remain[ed] and work[ed] in plantations." Morley had seen such people working in the fields "who [were] very old; their hair [was] quite white." These elderly captives likely served out the remainder of their lives as African slaves, while their sickly and adolescent counterparts may later have been returned to the coast and offered for sale to Europeans again or retained as captives in the interior.[40]

The process of sale illuminated by focusing on Bonny occurred in the other major African slaving ports. A recent study of thirty-nine

Dutch slaving voyages conducted between 1751 and 1797 trading at numerous African ports found that captains purchased varying proportions of men, women, or children, depending on the length of time that they had been on the coast. There was, the authors of the study write, "a bias towards purchasing children and females at the start of loading and towards men in the final weeks." They suggested that the Dutch captains used this strategy to preserve the health of enslaved men, who suffered higher mortality rates than women and children aboard the ships. Reconstructing the purchasing process in Africa reveals, however, that Dutch captains were, like their British counterparts, equally motivated by their desire to obtain healthy slaves in the face of competition from other captains. A French captain trading on the Loango Coast in the 1780s observed that the captains of newly arrived vessels would see only "the refuse of others" (le rebut des autres) until they raised their prices late in their purchase negotiations. A month after another French captain arrived in the same region, he purchased seventy-four people, of whom just eleven were men and women; the rest were "little boys and girls." He believed his "turn [would] come" to purchase more enslaved adults once he increased his prices to hasten his departure. The remarkable parity between the British practices revealed here and those in the French and Dutch trades thus implies that Europeans employed identical slave purchasing strategies wherever they traded in Africa.[41]

These methods had crucial implications for the length of time that enslaved people spent on a slave ship anchored on the coast. When healthy enslaved men arrived on the coast they were typically moved almost immediately aboard a ship that was nearing its departure, as captains sought to limit the amount of time that potentially rebellious men would be imprisoned on the ship. Healthy women or children, by contrast, might be purchased by a recent arrival to the port, and they would consequently be imprisoned on a slave ship for many months before they departed the coast. The youngest, sickliest, and oldest slaves endured inspections and sales for the longest periods, as those who were "refused by one captain," Morley observed, were "offered to another at a lower price." Some captives were consequently rowed back and forth between ship and shore in search of buyers. In 1775, for example, a fort officer on the Gold

Coast sent seven women and five men "rejected by [Captain] Champlin & [Captain] Cazneau" to another fort officer, who was then to offer them to a third captain. Another fort commander offered to a fellow officer five women, a man, and five boys who were "very maugre" from "long confinement & irregular feeding." The commander had already presented the group to a slave ship officer, but he had "objected to them." The same commander complained that he would no longer send captives thirty-five miles up the coast to Anomabu to have them "approved" at the ships lying there, presumably because so many of them were subsequently returned. Richard Miles sometimes inadvertently sent the same slaves back to captains who had already rejected them: in 1776 a captain returned four captives, among them a woman and a boy whom he had "had ye refusall of some time since." African brokers likewise offered returned slaves to another captain after they had been rejected. When a British slave trader rejected someone he described as a "very bad man slave," the Fante merchant took the man and offered him to the ships along with three other captives. Enslaved people thus suffered through multiple inspections, sales, separations, and terrifying sea journeys on the African coast—a direct result of the mechanisms devised by slave traders to efficiently sort enslaved people and funnel them aboard the ships.[42]

In June 1774, an enslaved woman and her child were forced aboard a boat on the Gold Coast to begin the journey from African to Atlantic slavery. The woman came from the small coastal town of Lagoe and had been kidnapped along with her child by the neighboring Akron people. The Akron sold her to Thomas Westgate, the commander of Winnebah Fort, who locked the woman in the fort's cells. Three weeks later, Westgate sold the woman and her child along with several other captives to the ship *Juno*, which was anchored at Anomabu, thirty-five miles down the coast. As the *Juno*'s longboat passed along the coast, the woman would have seen her home at Lagoe and numerous slave ships anchored offshore, with boats and canoes ferrying captives back and forth—a familiar sight for the coastal woman. Even so, the "apprehensions" she felt at being sent to the ships overcame her; she was "in fits" by the time she arrived at the *Juno* and had to be "carried" aboard the vessel. "It is very well known," Westgate laconically observed, that the "dread some slaves have of going on b[oard] a Ship has driven them out of their Senses." For "3 or 4 days" after she boarded the *Juno*, the woman had been "in fits." She was eventually "sent on shore" along with her child, where she was likely reimprisoned and then offered for sale to another ship captain by Richard Brew, the fort's commander. If the woman had indeed gone insane, Brew would have found it impossible to sell her to another captain and instead given her away to a Fante slaveholder; Westgate implied as much when he wrote that he would "stand to the loss" of the woman's price. Meanwhile, more than three hundred other men, women, and children—including the people who had been on the boat with the woman and her child—were carried away on the *Juno* in November 1774, and eventually sold in Barbados.[43]

The case of the woman from Lagoe powerfully illustrates how slave traders shaped the divergent fates of enslaved people on the African coast. Captains did not purchase every enslaved person offered to them, because they wanted to buy Africans who were healthy enough to survive the Atlantic crossing and the correct age to be salable to planters. They therefore forced enslaved Africans to undergo a humiliating bodily inspection and then ruthlessly rejected any person who did not meet their criteria. Hence, a remarkably large number of people were, like the woman from Lagoe, rejected by captains and either offered to another captain or retained in Africa as a slave. The process by which enslaved people were commodified on the African coast was thus much more ruthless—and much more sophisticated—than historians have appreciated; slave traders "separated" enslaved people, former captain John Newton remembered, "as sheep and lambs are separated by the butcher." This violent process was essential to the successful operation of Britain's slave trade as it expanded during the eighteenth century, because it enabled both white and African merchants to gain from cross-cultural trade: Britons were able to acquire the healthy captives who, they hoped, would be able to survive the horrors of the Middle Passage while also expediting their departure from the pestilential coast; Africans could vend enslaved people to European buyers at different price points and receive in return a growing array of goods. The victims of these merchants typically arrived aboard ships "without a friend or any means to procure one," a former slave poignantly remembered, having been pulled away from family members, fellow villagers, and even people with whom they had arrived on the coast.[44]

CHAPTER THREE

Merchants and the Creation
of the Floating Dungeon

WRITING IN 1700, London merchant Thomas Starke (c. 1649–1705) cautioned the captain of his ship *Africa Galley*, who was departing for the Bight of Biafra to purchase 450 people: "The whole benefitt of the Voyage lyes in your care in Preserving the Negroes lives." To achieve that end, Starke ordered his captain to follow a strict routine on the Atlantic crossing: he was to bring the captives on deck during the day, wash their sleeping spaces belowdecks with vinegar to increase hygiene, and serve foods that were meant to fortify people's bodies. Starke also warned his captain to keep a "continuall Century [*sic*]" over the Africans to prevent them from "riseing" to seize the ship. The *Africa Galley* was duly loaded with a panoply of equipment to control the restive prisoners: wooden planks to be converted into barriers between the slaves and the crew; cannons to train on the prisoners when they were on deck; small "Armes" for the crew; and "handcuffs" to imprison men slaves.[1] Starke's orders capture the two key risks that slaving merchants sought to mitigate when they forcibly transported enslaved people across the Atlantic: mortality and resistance. Slave traders such as Starke understood that their vessels were pestilential dungeons that would weaken and kill their enslaved prisoners every moment that they were trapped aboard. They also knew that Africans would resist their captivity at every opportunity, through both small-scale acts such as hunger strikes and full-blown insurrections that sought to seize the ship. Historians have found that slave traders sought to mitigate these twin risks by converting their vessels into "floating dungeons": marine prisons designed to crush resistance while also "Preserving" the lives of as many of the captives as possible—all of whom would be sold once the ship reached the Americas. By the time it put to sea with its enslaved prisoners aboard, a slave ship was, Marcus Rediker insightfully notes, a "strange and potent combination of war machine, mobile prison, and factory."[2]

While we now know a great deal about how slave ships operated thanks to the works of scholars like Rediker, the origins of the floating dungeon nonetheless remain a mystery. Little attention has been devoted to discerning how shipping practices in the slave trade changed over time, which has given the misleading impression that the methods employed in the late eighteenth century—when abolitionists publicized them—were the same as those employed in the seventeenth century. By studying how merchants organized their ventures across time, this chapter reveals that the methods for forcibly transporting people were, in fact, transformed to facilitate the expansion of Britain's slave trade. At the turn of the eighteenth century, English merchants formulated a new shipboard regime that both decreased the periods that enslaved people were trapped in the deadly holds of the ships and made it almost impossible for Africans to seize the vessel. The standardization of these techniques was crucial to the enlargement of Britain's slave trade because it substantially reduced the risks inherent in forcibly transporting people across the Atlantic Ocean—making the trade a more attractive investment to merchants like Starke. Confident that captives would struggle to rebel and that mortality was at an acceptable level, slaving merchants elected to maximize their profits by tightly packing their ships with people. Slave traders selected vessels that were purposely designed to hold differing proportions of men, women, and children, and they carefully calculated the minuscule spaces into which those captives could be squeezed on the voyage. As a result, Africans were typically forced to lie on their sides for sixteen hours in sweltering, dark, and dirty rooms alongside hundreds of other people during the night and were pressed together into a seething crowd above deck in the day. Four hundred thousand Africans perished in these dreadful conditions aboard British ships during the eighteenth century. And one-fifth of surviving Africans left the ships in the Americas in various states of ill health, with some on the verge of death or driven out of their senses. British merchants thus fixed on a profitable new method for shipping people that was premised on killing and maiming Africans.

When English merchants entered the slave trade in the mid-seventeenth century, Iberian traders had already devised a set of techniques for forcibly transporting enslaved people around the Atlantic world. Although sources for the earliest Portuguese slaving voyages c. 1450–1650 are sparse, a 1550 report on the slave trade from West Africa to the Cape Verde islands provides a glimpse of these methods. In the words of an anonymous Portuguese pilot, "The men are separated from the women, the former being made to stay below decks and the latter above" in the various rooms and cabins that constituted the caravels' distinctive castles; both groups of captives are as "naked as when they were born." Writing of a slaving voyage he undertook from Cape Verde to Cartagena in 1594, an Italian merchant also observed the separation of the sexes: the men slaves were "below decks" and the women "lodged after their own fashion on deck." According to the Portuguese pilot, Africans were segregated by sex because the men would "not do anything except stare at them [the women]" during the voyage, by which he presumably meant that the Africans would have sexual relations. Moreover, the separation of the sexes was meant to isolate ostensibly rebellious enslaved men and place enslaved women among the crewmen—making them more prone to sexual assault. This enforced separation of the sexes would become a staple of the Middle Passage across the trade's long history.[3]

Portuguese mariners sought to reduce enslaved people's ability to rebel by imprisoning them belowdecks for the duration of the voyage. An account by the Spanish priest Alonso de Sandoval (1576–1652), who interviewed Africans arriving in Cartagena in the mid-seventeenth century, reads: "The captives are closed off from the outside so that they cannot see the sun and the moon" and are "shackled at the neck along a chain of six-by-six slaves, or two-by-two, fettered at the ankle." The crew allowed Africans above deck in small groups just once a day to eat, wash, and defecate. Locking people belowdecks for the duration of the voyage was effective for preventing revolts: captives could seize the ship only if they broke out of their shackles and then pried their way out of the locked hold; small groups of shackled prisoners brought above deck needed to coordinate an attack on the more numerous crew, something that was difficult to achieve given the isolation of potential allies. Portuguese slave traders were consequently adept at preventing resistance: of 464 recorded insurrections across the trade's history, just six occurred on ships flying the Portuguese flag. Precautions taken by Portuguese enslavers to prevent revolts took a terrible toll on the health of enslaved people, though. Urine, excrement, vomit, and blood accumulated to a horrifying degree below decks, making the space a breeding ground for diseases. "Even staying down there for an hour," Sandoval writes in his account, "runs the risk of serious illness, so powerful is the stench, the cramped space, and the misery of it." He does not exaggerate: prior to 1700, more than a quarter of embarked captives perished in these conditions, while the survivors arrived in the Americas "looking like skeletons" and afflicted with hernias, sores, swollen limbs, gastroenteritis, and blindness.[4]

Although the Portuguese techniques had catastrophic effects on the health of enslaved Africans, English merchants adopted these methods with few adaptions in the mid-seventeenth century for fear that enslaved people would otherwise seize the ships. On the *Friendship*, an English vessel destined for the Gambia in 1651, the commander was told to be "veary careful to keepe them under" so as to ensure that the captives did not "ryse" on the crew, demonstrating that men, and possibly women, were kept below decks. As late as 1679, Royal African Company captains still locked enslaved people below throughout the voyage; officers knew how many Africans were aboard only by counting them above deck once every two weeks. Jean Barbot, who sailed along the African coast twice between 1678 and 1682 as a commercial agent on French slave ships before emigrating to England, where he wrote an important multivolume description of Atlantic Africa, reported that French and English captains were further emulating the Portuguese by separating the sexes, albeit with both groups now locked below in separate prisons below decks labeled the "men's" and "women's" rooms. The men were, Barbot wrote, "placed in the forepart beyond the main mast, and the women towards the stern." At some point in the early eighteenth century, British merchants added another division below decks that began at the mainmast and finished at the wall to the men's room, to create a "boy's room"; girls remained with the women or were forced into storerooms at the aft of the ship. Africans were, one observer noted in 1684, "suffocated, stewed and parboiled altogether in a Crowd" within these segregated cells, which were perpetually damp from seawater sloshing in and condensed sweat. "Great numbers" of Africans died in these wretched conditions, Barbot observed, with "two, three, and even four hundred" people perishing "out of five hundred shipp'd in Guinea." Barbot accurately captured the catastrophic mortality rates on seventeenth-century English ventures: on average, one in four people were killed, with some vessels losing as many captives as Barbot estimated.[5]

Barbot proposed a new set of shipboard regimes that would "save the lives of many thousands" of Africans and so "render the voyages much more advantageous to the [ship] owners." Following the example of the Dutch, he recommended that English and French slave traders should increase the height between decks, cut "air-ports" into the side of the vessel, and incorporate "gratings and scuttles" within the main deck—increasing air flow to the captives trapped below. Captains were also meant to increase rations of food and water. On early Portuguese voyages, Africans had been fed once a day with millet cooked down into a starchy slop, accompanied by a small cup of water, causing malnourishment and dehydration. To prevent enslaved people wasting away, Barbot recommended that they be fed twice a day, with a breakfast of beans cooked in lard brought from Europe and a dinner of maize or manioc, seasoned with palm oil and pepper, purchased in Africa. Offering African foodstuffs was intended to provide a familiar meal that was suited to enslaved people's constitutions, ostensibly reducing their propensity to rebel. Beans and palm oil supplied protein and fat; Barbot noted that beans were "proper fattening food for captives." After each of the two meals, crewmen were to serve the captives "a full coco-nut shell of water" (approximately half a pint), far from the quantity of fluids needed to stave off dehydration but an increase on earlier water allowances. Between meals, enslaved people were to be offered "a handful" of wheat or manioc, brandy, and tobacco pipes.[6]

Barbot advised that enslaved people should be allowed above deck during daylight hours to consume these meals as a means of further reducing sickness. On his two voyages, captives were all brought on deck "twice a-day, at fix'd hours": ten in the morning and five in the afternoon (Figure 3.1). After coming above, the Africans on Barbot's ship were grouped into "a mess of ten" people—a practice derived from the organization of white crews—with each group given a large tub of food that they ate with their hands or a wooden spoon. At the conclusion of each meal, the crew sent the captives belowdecks again, with water served to them as they reentered the hold. While the Africans were all on deck, crewmen cleaned accumulated filth from the rooms below; "thrice a week" the rooms were also fumigated with vinegar. Barbot permitted women above deck "as they pleas'd" between meals and some men "by turns, successively," in small groups. At such moments, crewmen allowed captives to "divert themselves on deck," something that was meant to lift the Africans' spirits while also preventing the muscular atrophy that resulted from sleeping in the crowded spaces below deck. Rather than shackling all the men, Barbot chained only people who threatened the crew or other prisoners. Thomas Phillips (c. 1664–1713), who commanded an English slaving voyage in 1694, reported precisely the same regime, as did Barbot's nephew James Jr., who served as a commercial agent on an English ship in 1700, indicating that some captains had adopted Barbot's methods by the end of the seventeenth century.[7]

Barbot warned captains who wanted to allow their prisoners the "liberty" of being on deck that they also needed to "deprive them of all the means whereby they could raise a revolt." He cautioned commanders: "Have as many of your crew as you can sleeping at the rear of the vessel, and keep all your weapons, fire-arms and others, in your cabin, with a sentinel on guard." Phillips followed Barbot's advice and kept his men armed with "loaded and prim'd" weapons behind the main mast. The door that led to the crew quarters beneath the quarterdeck was "always kept shut, and well barr'd," with two loaded cannons pointing out of portholes on either side and

Figure 3.1. A depiction of 311 enslaved people eating a meal aboard the Nantes slave ship Marie-Séraphique, *c. 1771. Jean-René L'Hermite and Jean-Baptist Fautrel-Gaugy [?],* Vue du Navire La Marie Séraphique de Nantes au Moment du Repas des Captifs, *2nd Voyage à Loangue, 1771. A colorized version of a photograph of a now lost image. Reproduced with permission of the Château des ducs de Bretagne, Musée d'histoire de Nantes.*

two other guns trained on the men from above. At mealtimes Phillips had crewmen armed with muskets watch the captives; other crewmen stood at the cannons that "yaun[ed] upon" the main deck with lighted matches held just above the touch hole, so that they could blast the men the moment they rebelled. The development of reliable and deadly firearms was thus crucial to the institution of the new shipboard routine, because they allowed small numbers of whites to guard numerically superior Africans above deck. Only when the captives were sent below after each meal were the matches extinguished, and the men stood down. Even so, Phillips stationed guards over the locked hatches to ensure the Africans could not break out.[8]

Despite these precautions, bloody insurrections remained common aboard ships—especially when captives were permitted above deck. Phillips reported that Africans had "surpriz'd and butcher'd" the crews of numerous ships sailing at the end of the seventeenth century; insurrections occurred on both of the voyages undertaken

by Dutch slave trader Willem Bosman (1672–1703) in the same period. On James Barbot Jr.'s ship, the captives rose up while being
led below after one of their meals because the crew naively assumed
they would not rebel. Using knives, pieces of iron pried from a door,
and their broken shackles, they fell upon the crewmen, killing and
wounding several. Firing from the raised quarterdeck, the other
crewmen quelled the revolt, after which "about thirty of the ring-
leaders" were "severely whipt." Only by closely guarding the men
slaves throughout their time on deck, James Barbot's uncle Jean
opined, would slave traders "not hear of so many revolts as have
happen'd." Jean Barbot added that terror was an important strategy for quelling revolts. He took the view that "chopping parts off
a living man with blows from an axe and presenting the separated
parts to the others" was an ideal way to "terrify the others and keep
them obedient." On the *Florida*, which sailed to Calabar in 1714, the
captain used just such a strategy: he "order'd the Carpenter to cut
off ye head of a dead Negro with his ax, & fix it on a Pole made fast
to ye Ships side, & to throw ye limbs about ye Deck" to terrorize his
rebellious prisoners.[9]

Fearful of the threat posed by hundreds of restive Africans,
many captains continued to keep enslaved people locked belowdecks throughout the Middle Passage. Jean Barbot noted that he
was exceptional in permitting the captives on deck during the two
voyages that he conducted in the 1680s. "We allow'd them much
more liberty . . . than most other Europeans would think prudent to
do," he writes. "Some commanders, of a morose and peevish temper,
will not suffer any [Africans] upon deck but when unavoidable ne-
cessity to ease themselves does require"—that is, to defecate. These
captains imprisoned Africans below because they thought their
presence on deck, continues Barbot, "hinders the work of the ship
and sailors, and . . . they are troublesome by their nasty nauseous
stench or their noise." Barbot does not need to mention that locking
hundreds of people belowdecks reduced their ability to rebel, particularly as captains recognized that the time enslaved people were
"all on deck" was when they were "aptest to mutiny." By the end
of the seventeenth century, captains thus understood that imprisoning people belowdecks for the duration of their voyages—several months on the African coast followed by around ten weeks at

sea—would injure or kill a significant proportion of them, reducing their employers' venture profits. But they also knew that bringing captives above to preserve their health considerably increased the risk that the Africans would stage a successful revolt.[10]

At the turn of the eighteenth century, British slave traders introduced new security techniques drawn from ships of war that substantially reduced Africans' chances of successfully rebelling— decisively shifting captains toward employing Barbot's methods. Hundreds of men-of-war and privateer vessels sailed the Atlantic during the Nine Years' War (1688–1697) and the War of the Spanish Succession (1701–1714); pirates preyed on shipping throughout the Golden Age of piracy (c. 1650–1730). Slave ship captains hence organized their crew into well-drilled "quarters" with "Great Guns and small Armes . . . Loaded and in readiness" to repel these numerous "Enemies" at sea, as Humphry Morice noted in his orders to the *Judith*'s captain in 1728. Having the crew "on guard and defence," Morice added, "may likewise be useful to you should hereafter an Insurrection happen or be attempted amongst your Negroes." Slavers borrowed other devices from warships to quell resistance. Each section of a man-of-war was sealed off by bulkheads pierced with loopholes through which cannons could be fired "to clear the Decks fore and aft." Commanders of slave ships, such as Barbot and Phillips, employed the same devices to control captives massed above deck at mealtimes.[11]

Slave traders amalgamated bulkheads with barricades—another feature on warships—to create another formidable obstacle to revolt. On men-of-war, the barricade was, as a marine dictionary explained, "a strong wooden rail, supported by several little pillars or stanchions, and extending, as a fence across the foremost part of the quarter-deck." The barricade was topped with a net locked in place with iron beams above to prevent boarders scaling the obstacle, and the space behind the "fence" was filled with cork and old ropes, forming a barrier that would "intercept and prevent the execution of small-shot." Seeing the benefit of having an impassable barrier that could prevent the men slaves on the main deck from reaching the crew on the quarterdeck, slave traders first installed barricades on their ships in the opening years of the eighteenth century. But they modified the naval "barricade" into what they called the "barricado"—a structure that was designed to repel unarmed slaves rather than musket-armed boarders. The barricado was a smooth wooden wall, nine or ten feet high, extending over the sides by three or four feet, and with a single door that was guarded whenever the slaves were on the deck. Slavers swapped the netting on top of the barricade for spikes and removed the intervening stuffing, knowing that unarmed African men slaves would fire few shots into the structure. Carrying forward techniques from late seventeenth-century slave ships, they installed swivel guns above the barricado and "pierced" it with loopholes. Crewmen stationed atop the barricado kept arms trained on men slaves all day; on one ship, they periodically fired warning shots over the heads of African men at mealtimes. All but three members of the crew remained behind the wall, ensuring that the men slaves would take out few of their warders if they rose up and that a sizable body of whites remained ready to respond to an insurrection.[12]

Two other innovations made it difficult for captives to reach the barricado or escape over the ship's sides while on deck. The first were long "deck chains" that stretched the length of the main deck, which were anchored in place on the other side of the barricado. Crewmen locked enslaved men into the chains the moment they were brought on deck, effectively immobilizing them; as one crewman observed, men slaves "cannot stand up with out permission, nor can they move from the spot." Whites also strung up netting around the ship's sides. Like the barricado, "quarter-netting" was originally designed to keep boarders out of warships and deflect enemy shot, and so it was filled with hammocks, old sails, and cork. By removing the padding, slave traders converted netting from a device to keep boarders out into a cage to keep enslaved people in. With bulwarks, netting, chains, a vigilant crew, and a barricado, slave ships became true marine prisons.[13]

As one slave sailor observed after describing this formidable array of security apparatus, "the poor slaves would have no chance of success whatever in rising." Insurrections certainly remained common and may even have increased in frequency after the implementation of the new shipboard regime; historians estimate that full-scale rebellions occurred on perhaps one in ten slaving voyages—a testament to enslaved people's desire for freedom in the face of insurmountable odds. "Successful rebellions were," however, "quite rare," and "the great majority of revolts were suppressed with the vessel remaining under the control of the original owner." The 1722 case of the *Ferrers* typifies why it was so hard for enslaved people to capture the ship. Ten days out from the African coast, the male captives rose up at the evening mealtime, attacking the crew with their dinner bowls and murdering the captain, who had foolishly gone in front of the barricado to help distribute the food. The men quickly captured the entirety of the main deck and must have assumed that the *Ferrers* would soon be theirs. But they were thwarted by the barricado, behind which the armed crew mustered with muskets and pikes. Unable to scale the wall, the men fruitlessly tried to pry the door open. Eventually, the crew fired a cannon into their midst, which "occasioned a terrible Destruction": eighty men were killed either by the shot or by drowning when they leaped overboard to escape the blast. A similar chain of events happened time and again throughout the eighteenth century, dooming enslaved people's attempts to gain their freedom (Figure 3.2). Given the minuscule odds of success, it should not be surprising that insurrections did *not* happen on nine out of ten slaving voyages, leaving the captives to pursue other forms of resistance, such as hunger strikes and suicide.[14]

Confident that their new security regime could thwart revolts, British slave traders adopted a rigid new daily schedule in which enslaved people would be on deck throughout the day, rather than just at mealtimes as Barbot had originally proposed. At approximately nine in the morning, the crew unlocked the hatches and brought the captives above, the unshackled females going up one hatch to the quarterdeck and the shackled men to the main deck. As pairs of men came on deck, crewmen checked their leg shackles to make sure that they had not been tampered with; two armed crewmen stood atop the barricado watching for signs of resistance. The pairs of men were then led to the deck chain and locked in place. Meanwhile, the ship's cook, often assisted by enslaved women, prepared the captives' breakfast. Once the men had been locked into the chains, the officers ordered the Africans to form into their "messes" and then distributed bowls of food to each group; a crewman or an enslaved boy distributed water to the messes from a bucket. At the conclusion of the first meal, the captives were then forced to "dance"—

Figure 3.2. An insurrection aboard a British slave ship thwarted by the barricado, c. 1789. From William Fox, A Brief History of the Wesleyan Missions on the West Coast of Africa *(London: Aylott and Jones, 1851), facing p. 116. A colorized version of an image originally published in Carl B. Wadstrom,* An Essay on Colonization, particularly applied to the Western coast of Africa . . . in Two Parts *(London: Darton and Harvey, 1794). Reproduced from www.slaveryimages.org.*

humiliating forced exercise—after which they sat on the deck until the next meal, which commenced around four in the afternoon; another round of forced activity followed dinner. As soon as the sun began its descent around six in the evening, the Africans were forced belowdecks. The female captives were sent to the rooms beneath the quarterdeck, while the deck chain was unreeved and the men taken off in pairs and sent below, after having their shackles inspected again. Once all the captives were below, the crew locked the hatches. The Africans remained belowdecks for another sixteen hours until the next day, when, if the weather was good, they were brought up again and forced to undergo the same routine—a regime that began while the ship was anchored in Africa and ended the day before the captives were sold in the Americas.[15]

British merchants embraced this new shipboard regime at the opening of the eighteenth century. In the 1680s, most captains were still locking captives below decks for the duration of the voyage, Barbot and a few others excepted, with the men and women divided by a "strong partition at the main mast"—presumably a belowdecks bulkhead rather than a barricado. By 1694, English captains, such as Phillips and Barbot's nephew James Jr., followed Jean Barbot in allowing captives on deck only during mealtimes, with the ship fortified by locking the doors that led from the main deck to the crew's quarters; six years later, Starke ordered the captain of the *Africa Galley* to allow the Africans on deck "as much as you cann," with the men and women separated by a "Bulkhead upon Deck" that had four pointing cannons through it. From 1704, the Royal African Company instructed its captains: "Prevent the Mortality of ye Negroes" by "wash[ing] yor Decks with vinegar and divert[ing] them as much as you can with some sort of musick and Play," indicating that the captains were likewise allowing Africans on deck for at least some of the day. Both the "Baracado" and netting are first mentioned in the 1720s; a naval officer who witnessed numerous English slave ships in the same period wrote several "Rule[s]" for the trade that included keeping the crew "on a barricado'd Quarter-deck," the chaining of men slaves, and the feeding of the captives twice a day. From then on, surviving firsthand accounts and logbooks of British slave ships describe a similar system in which captives were above deck during the day and below at night, with men and women separated by bulkheads below and a barricado above. By century's end, this system was so ubiquitous that slaving merchants described it as the "usual Manner of treating the Negroes during the Voyage."[16]

The institution of this new regime in the early eighteenth century substantially reduced mortality on the Middle Passage. In the second half of the seventeenth century—when most English captains still imprisoned Africans belowdecks—almost a quarter of Africans died at sea (22 percent). During the eighteenth century— when Britons began bringing captives above deck throughout the day and providing greater quantities of food and water—one in six people (16 percent) perished on the crossing. The length of the voyage fell by only a week between these periods, from seventy-seven to seventy days, and so voyage length likely had little bearing on this trend. Insurrections remained common in both periods, but almost none met with success. Through careful experimentation, British merchants thus created the floating dungeon, a vehicle that would forcibly transport millions of people across the Atlantic.[17]

In 1729, experienced slave ship surgeon Thomas Aubrey penned a guide that advocated a series of additional reforms to the increasingly ubiquitous shipboard regime on British slave ships that was intended to further reduce shipboard mortality. Over his 135-page volume, Aubrey described the myriad diseases that afflicted whites and blacks in Africa, as well as his supposedly successful treatments. He concluded by advising that surgeons should take extra care to ensure that sickly captives were not purchased; the quality and quantity of rations should be further improved; and the killing of Africans by crewmen had to be prohibited. Missing from Aubrey's plan were reforms that would address the root causes of sickness among enslaved people: the spread of germs, viruses, and bacteria. Germ theories of diseases would not be confirmed until the mid-nineteenth century, leaving physicians like Aubrey to guess at the causes of enslaved people's illnesses. Aubrey held to common medical orthodoxy that people fell ill when their particular "Nature and Constitution" was corrupted by external stimuli. Thus, he believed that Africans suffered "fluxes"—gastroenteritis—not because they encountered bacteria or consumed amoebas in tainted water, as modern medicine has discovered, but rather because of the sudden transition from a diet of "raw Flesh, Fish, and Fruits" to salty ship provisions or because of the "Relicks" of venereal diseases. Aubrey also shared the common belief that deadly diseases spread via the "evil Quality of the Air" in belowdecks prisons. The transformation in shipboard management techniques detailed above had been driven in part by these medical theories, as slave traders sought to withdraw enslaved people from lower decks where "bad air" ostensibly collected during the day; serving Africans with familiar foodstuffs was likewise meant to fortify their constitutions. The partial reduction in mortality brought about by these changes appeared to confirm the veracity of contemporary medical thinking. In reality, the new regime was effective only because it took captives out of breeding grounds for germs and bacteria for a period of the day, while simultaneously increasing the body's ability to fight infection through increased allowances of water and food.[18]

Because slave traders did not understand the fundamental medical causes of illnesses, the continued deaths of their prisoners perplexed them. The seeming randomness of mortality on ships that had the same shipboard management regime was particularly puzzling: on some voyages, large proportions of the Africans perished; on others, none of them. This variety stemmed from the fact that infectious diseases introduced to the ships were the primary killers of captives: while crowded ships sailing in the tropics were ideal vectors for transmittable diseases, there was no guarantee that those diseases would enter the ship in the first place. The length of the Middle Passage was also a crucial determinant of slave mortality because the chances of a disease breaking out and spreading through the human cargo increased over time. Mortality rates hence correlated closely, but not uniformly, with the duration of the voyage, which was itself closely connected to the region of Africa from which the ship departed. People carried from the Bight of Biafra typically suffered significantly higher mortality rates than those taken from Upper Guinea, for example. While death stalked every slave ship, mortality rates were much higher on those vessels that spent longer at sea and varied because of chance.[19]

Contemporaries understood the importance of time at sea well, but they were at a loss to explain why captive Africans perished. Captain Phillips, for example, complained that his seven hundred prisoners on the *Hannibal* suffered "great sickness and mortality" even though his crew brought the Africans above deck to eat and exercise, cleaned the decks daily, and offered his prisoners supposedly ample rations of food and water. "To think that we should undergo so much misery," he complained after 328 people died on the crossing to Barbados, "and take so much pains to so little purpose." One of Aubrey's commanders captured the profound ignorance about the causes of enslaved people's deaths in slave traders' typically callous fashion: "What a Devil makes these plaguy Toads dye so fast?" With medical thinkers such as Aubrey offering few solutions, merchants came to consider the deaths of many of their prisoners to be a regrettable reality of their business. The financial loss springing from the loss of some people would be covered by the returns from selling their surviving shipmates. Moreover, if the seemingly capricious nature of disease meant that the ship reached the Americas with few, or no, deaths, the ship owners received a boost in their returns by selling more living people. In short, merchants deemed a trade in which a sixth of purchased people perished a business that was worth pursuing. Attempts to reduce mortality through further modifications to shipboard practices accordingly ground to a halt after the 1720s; significant reforms to shipping techniques did not occur again until 1789, when Parliament placed restrictions on how many captives could be carried on the vessels and further increased rations of food and water in response to abolitionist campaigning.[20]

Having settled on this murderous business model, merchants tried to maximize their profits by packing their vessels with enslaved people. Slave ships had, from the beginning of the trade's history, usually been thronged with people. A witness reported that in the earliest Portuguese voyages, for example, the men slaves were "pressed and squeezed together one against the other in such a way that they had great difficulty in turning from one side to the other when they wanted to"; another witness described the captives on another Portuguese vessel as being "pressed together like herrings in a barrel." Northern European enslavers, the English included, followed the Portuguese by crowding enslaved people on their vessels: Barbot described the captives on the ships of numerous nations as being "as close together as they can be crouded." Slave traders understood that imprisoning large numbers of people in such enclosed spaces would cause sickness; Barbot, for example, wrote that captives being "so crouded in a low place . . . occasions many distempers." But those illnesses stemmed, according to medical orthodoxy, not from the density at which people were packed together but rather from sickly people corrupting the trapped air in an enclosed space and so infecting others. The density at which people were imprisoned thus had, according to the thinking of enslavers, little bearing on mortality. Cramming Africans into ships consequently remained a key business strategy for slave traders; as Captain John Newton observed of the mid-century Liverpool trade, "With our ships, the great object, is to be full"—a statement that remained true of Britain's slave trade across the eighteenth century.[21]

Ship owners carefully planned their ventures in Britain to ensure that their vessels were "full" of people, beginning with the selection of the ship. Although systematic data on slave ships is sparse for much of the eighteenth century, the registers of Liverpool shipping detail the dimensions and construction of 762 ships that conducted 2,206 slaving voyages between 1767 and 1808. The registers reveal that merchants typically purchased used vessels and converted them into slave ships; less than a third of ships were purpose built for the trade. Regardless of a ship's origin, merchants selected vessels to hold differing numbers of people, who would be forced aboard the ship at specific African markets. For riverine regions—especially those in Upper Guinea—merchants purchased smaller shallow-drafted vessels, measuring on average seventy-five feet long and twenty-two feet wide, because they knew that few captives would be embarked, averaging two hundred per vessel. Merchants purchased larger vessels—averaging ninety feet in length by twenty-five feet across—for voyages to deepwater African ports in Lower Guinea, where they knew that enslaved people would be embarked in greater numbers. Merchants adapted their vessels to the slave trade by employing carpenters to cut a system of gratings into the decks that would draw air into the between decks: a single rectangular grating ran down the center of the main deck; two smaller parallel gratings were at the front of the deck; and a smaller hatch drew air in at the aft. Ventilation ports pierced either side of the vessels at regular intervals, each six by six inches, covered with hatches that could be closed in bad weather.[22]

Ship owners adjusted the layouts of their vessels to imprison the specific groups of Africans whom they expected their captains to purchase in particular markets. The average height of space between decks on Liverpool ships was five feet and two inches but ranged considerably: on 329 of the 2,047 voyages (16 percent) for which the deck height is recorded, the space measured less than four feet and four inches—ostensibly the height of enslaved adults. On such vessels, the owner knew that most captives would be unable to "stand up without stooping almost double," related a visitor to the Liverpool ship *Spitfire*, a vessel with a between-deck height of just four feet. By contrast, 165 vessels (8 percent) had decks of six feet or more apart, and so Africans would have been able to stand to full height when below. Despite this variety, merchants clearly adapted their vessels according to the height of their intended prisoners: ships

sailing to Senegambia, the Gold Coast, and the Bight of Benin—
where Britons expected to purchase taller captives—had decks, on
average, three to four inches higher than those of ships sailing for
Sierra Leone and the Windward Coast, where more children and
teenagers were acquired.[23]

Merchants likewise adjusted the configuration of the slaves' belowdecks prisons depending on how many men, women, or children
they expected their captain to buy—something that was likewise
shaped by the African port to which their ship intended to sail. A
detailed survey of nine Liverpool ships taken by Parliament in 1788
shows that the rooms for the men and boys on most of the vessels collectively occupied around two-thirds of the between-decks
space—mirroring the proportion of male captives that Britons usually purchased. But three of the four vessels that were dispatched to
the Bight of Biafra, where Britons purchased "a great Proportion
of . . . Women slaves," had proportionally larger women's rooms.
Ship owners also added or removed "platforms"—wooden shelves
raised approximately two feet above the deck and extending out six
feet on either side of the slaves' prisons—to particular rooms, depending on the vessel's destination. The *Venus*, a ship destined for
New Calabar, had platforms only in the women's room to increase
the holding capacity for female prisoners. By contrast, both of the
vessels fitted out for the Windward Coast, where captains bought
more "small slaves," especially enslaved boys and teenagers, had platforms in the men's and boys' room but not in the women's room.[24]

Merchants also computed how many people would fit into each
of the rooms aboard the modified ships—and hence how much
space each person would be squeezed into. Ship owners calculated
the number of people their captain would purchase—a ship's so-
called complement—to maximize their ship's carrying capacity and
to determine the composition of the trading cargo and the size
of the crew. They therefore carefully measured the spaces below
deck and made chilling assumptions about the amount of room
that each enslaved person required. Bristolian slave trader James
Jones (c. 1745–1795) provided the only detailed description of how
merchants would "judge of the Number of Slaves to be carried"
when he appeared before Parliament in June 1788. Jones testified
that the "general Rule" was that the "Merchant, with the Captain,

surveys the Ship, to see how many may be carried properly." The two men would first measure the width of the vessel to gauge "how many Slaves can lay crosswise," as Jones described it, by dividing the breadth by the presumed height of enslaved people. He testified that in a ship twenty-four feet wide (the average breadth of a slave ship according to the Liverpool Registers), there would be room for "Four Slaves to lie crosswise," implying that each person was expected to occupy six feet of horizontal space across the ship. When pressed further, he admitted that different numbers of people would be forced into lines across the ship depending on their heights: merchants expected four men, five women, or six children to occupy the horizontal space in a twenty-four-foot-wide vessel, for example. Having computed how many people would lie across the ship horizontally, Jones and the captain would then "judge, from the Length of the Ship's Lower Deck, how many [slaves] she [would] conveniently carry" by dividing the length of the ship by the assumed breadth of a person. Jones thought that adult men could lie in a space sixteen inches wide, and that children needed a single foot, an opinion corroborated by Liverpool merchants at the same hearing. Although he did not state it explicitly, Jones perhaps allocated women around fourteen inches of horizontal space. Slaving merchants thus envisaged the "rooms" on their ships as rectangles that would be filled with a grid-like pattern of enslaved people.[25]

The famous diagram of the Liverpool slave ship *Brooks* captures how merchants anticipated their vessels would appear once packed with people. The diagram was designed by the Society for Effecting the Abolition of the Slave Trade to show, as abolitionist Thomas Clarkson (1760–1846) explained, "how many persons" of particular heights and breadths could be hypothetically imprisoned in the ship "without trespassing upon the room allotted to the rest." The abolitionist draughtsman who sketched the *Brooks* using Parliament's measurements of the vessel drew the Africans lined in a grid-like pattern, with people arrayed in rows and columns within separate rooms—exactly how slave traders like Jones planned their vessels to be filled. Enslaved men were shown occupying spaces measuring six feet by sixteen inches; women, five feet by sixteen inches; boys, five feet by fourteen inches; and girls, four feet six inches by twelve inches—almost the dimensions given by Jones and other slave

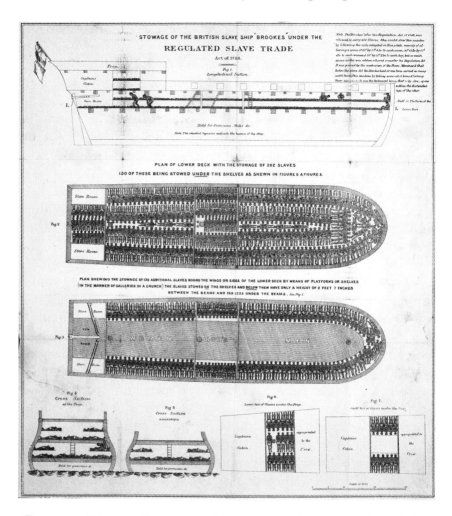

Figure 3.3. Diagram of the Liverpool slave ship Brooks, *c. 1789. From Society for Effecting the Abolition of the Slave Trade,* Description of a Slave Ship *(London: James Philips, 1789). Reproduced from https://upload.wikimedia.org/ wikipedia/commons/8/82/Slaveshipposter.jpg.*

traders in their testimony. The resulting image showed 470 enslaved people (190 men, 183 women, 70 boys, and 27 girls) trapped aboard the *Brooks* (Figure 3.3).[26]

In reality, merchants assumed that Africans should be imprisoned in much smaller spaces than the *Brooks* image depicted and

Jones had claimed. The *Brooks* had never carried 470 Africans on any of the four voyages it conducted between 1782 and 1787. Instead, its Liverpool owners had expected the captain to purchase between six hundred and seven hundred captives, and so the owners must have assumed that each person needed no more than twelve inches of horizontal room in which to lie belowdecks. The ship's captain had fulfilled—and exceeded—the owners' expectations on its four voyages: the ship carried 650 people in 1782, 619 in 1784, 740 in 1785, and 609 in 1787. Data from Liverpool's custom records confirm that the *Brooks* was unexceptional in being so crowded. The 470 captives depicted in the *Brooks* diagram each had an average of seven feet two inches square of horizontal space. By comparison, the median level of crowding on 251 voyages before 1789 (when Parliament began regulating the trade) was six feet four inches square; on only sixty-eight (27 percent) of those voyages were the captives less crowded than the diagram showed. On 114 of the 251 voyages (45 percent), captives were crammed into spaces measuring less than six square feet per person—"tight packing," in the trade's macabre lexicon. These 114 voyages included all four of the *Brooks*'s voyages.[27]

An image of the French slaver *Marie-Séraphique* on its voyage of 1772 and 1773 accurately captures the horrible realities behind these dry statistics. Unlike the depiction of the *Brooks*, which was produced by abolitionists, the skilled rendering of the *Marie-Séraphique* was painted by two officers serving aboard the vessel (Figure 3.4). Although the ship was French, the 307 captives are shown to occupy just six feet three inches square per person—within a square inch of the average crowding on voyages from Liverpool between 1782 and 1788. The rooms are thronged with people: most of the captives lie in parallel rows—as the ship owners would have planned—but individuals are also crammed into the small intervening spaces, such as around the capstan, on the edges of walls, and even atop ledges. Most of the Africans have been forced to lie painfully on their sides jammed up against their neighbors, with their right arm pinioned beneath the adjacent person and their left arm stretched above their head or draped across their chest. Though in rows, they look like people in a crowded prison, with their legs, arms, and heads tangled together and their bodies stretched uncomfortably across wooden beams or crammed into corners. The male slaves are completely

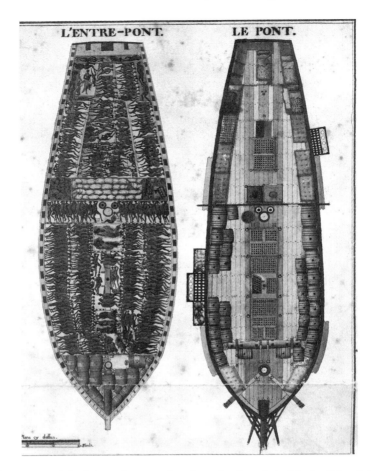

Figure 3.4. A depiction of 307 enslaved people aboard the Marie-Séraphique
*on its Middle Passage, c. 1770. Jean-René L'Hermite and Jean-Baptist
Fautrel-Gaugy [?], Plan, Profile et Distribution du Navire La
Marie Séraphique . . ." [1770?]. Reproduced with permission of the Château
des ducs de Bretagne, Musée d'histoire de Nantes.*

naked, their right leg joined to the left leg of another man by a bar-
like shackle, whereas the women wear checkered blue loincloths and
no shackles. Such was the reality of the Middle Passage for most
enslaved people.[28]

Evidence from sailors and captains vividly captures the suffering of captive Africans in these typically terrible conditions. Newton
wrote that captives on his ships were forced to lie in "rows, one

above the other" and "close to each other, like books upon a shelf." Another former officer testified of the Africans aboard the two ships he served on in the 1760s: "[They] lie exceedingly crowded, and in a manner one upon another, and can neither lie on their backs nor at full length, nor change their posture with ease." Experienced crewman James Morley likewise testified that the Africans had "scarcely room to do more than lie upon their sides" because they seldom had "12 inch or more in breadth" to lie in—the typical degree of crowding before the passage of Parliamentary regulations in 1789. Crewmen achieved this shocking level of crowding through violence. As the Africans came belowdecks, they were met by three crewmen who were employed in "stowing and packing them together" by "adjusting their arms and legs, and prescribing a fixed place for each." Morley performed this task himself and ensured that the slaves were, he related, "as close as possible that I could put them"—"spoonways," in the trade's jargon. "Those which did not get quickly into their places" were, one ship surgeon remembered, "compelled by the cat [whip]."[29]

The Africans would have been equally crowded on the deck during the day. A view of the *Marie-Séraphique*'s upper decks shows that it was filled with tackle, yards, ropes, wheels, furnaces, toilets, and numerous water barrels—significantly shrinking the amount of room in which the male captives could stand (Figure 3.4). Goats and chickens were kept in cages off the *Marie-Séraphique*'s side, but on other slaving vessels pens for pigs, goats, cattle, and even big cats consumed further deck space. Although the quarterdeck had less clutter, the female captives trapped there would have been hemmed in by the crew of forty-one men, almost all of whom stayed behind the barricado. Enslaved people were therefore packed together above deck into a crowd that must have swayed and surged with the rolling of the vessel. A mate on a slave ship was perhaps correct when he said that he was "almost Melted" in the "Midst" of the Africans on deck.[30]

When Africans could be obtained "at a very moderate price," captains further reduced the already meager space allocated to their prisoners. During the closing years of the American Revolutionary War (1775–1783), for example, captives purchased for low prices and in high numbers were held in truly nightmarish conditions aboard the ships. In June 1782, the captain of the Liverpool ship *Mosley Hill* purchased 797 people at Bonny because he found slaves "remarkably cheap from the dullness of trade." There was "no interval of room between their bodies," and they "suffered so much" that there was "nothing but shrieks and yelling the whole night" belowdecks. A year later, the *Juba*'s captain bought 735 people at Bonny in less than a month, fifty-three of whom were eventually left ashore because they could not be crammed aboard the ship. The 682 people who boarded the vessel were so crowded that they were "even obliged to lie one upon another." Two hundred people perished on the Middle Passage, but, one Liverpool firm wrote enviously, the ship's owners "yet [got] money" by selling the survivors at a huge profit. The numerous instances (one in four) when captains purchased *more* people than they had hoped to indicates that these voyages were not unusual, especially in periods when competition was light on the African coast.[31]

   Enslaved people suffered in these terrible conditions because of the careful decisions taken by their enslavers in distant Britain. Even before a slave ship left for Africa, merchants had planned their voyage to ensure that people would be packed together so tightly that there would be, as one crewman observed, "not room to put down the point of a stick between one another." Stooping in the cramped belowdecks of their vessel while it was anchored in Britain, they envisaged their African prisoners—men, women, and children of differing heights and builds—and then measured out the smallest possible spaces within which those people could survive. Through such "tight packing," merchants hoped that their vessels would hold a sufficient number of people for the deaths of some to be more than offset by the sale of the survivors. Merchants were thus intimately engaged in the violent business of slaving, even if they never left Britain.[32]

On the voyage from Britain to Africa, ship crews put merchants' careful plans into action by constructing the cells within which enslaved people would be held. When a ship neared the Canary Islands or Cape Verde, the carpenter first "raised the gratings" by cutting holes into the main deck and then constructing ventilation ports. The captain next had the area between decks cleared of timber, ropes, and barrels so that the carpenter could build the bulkheads and platforms that would form the slave prisons. On the *Duke of Argyll's* 1750 voyage to Sierra Leone, for example, Captain Newton "mark'd off the Slaves' rooms," presumably by drawing chalk lines across the deck based on the calculations made before his departure from Liverpool in collaboration with the ship's owner. The ship's carpenter then "began to build the bulkheads" that would form the walls of the "rooms." Once these partitions had been constructed—a task that took at least a week—the carpenter spent several weeks erecting the barricado. The crew rolled two carriage guns through the completed barricado and affixed "swivel blunderbusses" to the top, as Newton described. As the carpenter hammered the barricado together, the crew manufactured the nets that would be locked around the vessel's sides to form the jail walls.[33]

The women and children who were typically purchased first once the ship anchored entered the ship while this work was still under way and were often forced to assist the crew. When the first thirty captives arrived on the ship *Hudibras*, which traded at Old Calabar in 1786, they were put to work "cleaning the decks, both above and below," under the supervision of a boy sailor. A "number of boys and girls" worked aboard a ship anchored at Bonny, "hand[ing] up firewood and yams and assist[ing] the cook in peeling them." As many as a dozen women also assisted cooks by "pounding, washing, and boiling rice." Captives arriving first on the ships slept belowdecks in rooms that were often filled with ropes, sails, barrels, lumber, and even chests of arms, and enclosed by half-finished partitions and platforms. Once the captain had bought several adult African men, however, a strict disciplinary regime commenced. Thirty-one days after the *Duke of Argyll* anchored at Sierra Leone, for example, Newton had purchased thirty-two enslaved people: ten men, ten boys, four women, and eight girls. On December 17, 1750, Newton bought three more men, and the next day he ordered that the crew begin "with Chains and Sentrys," because he feared that the men were sufficiently numerous to stage an insurrection against his crew of thirty. The crew now locked each man to another by the wrist and ankle with heavy shackles; odd numbers of captives had both of their legs and hands linked together. The "Chains" that Newton referred to were the "deck chains" into which pairs of enslaved men were locked whenever they were on deck.[34]

Enslaved people were held in prisons that were also floating markets, as the ships usually served as the trading platforms for the buying of slaves. The captain of a Liverpool ship at Sierra Leone, for example, spent his days seated under an awning on the quarter-deck "eating, drinking, laughing, squabbling or talking defamation, lies or blasphemy" with "ten or dozen traders" from whom he purchased captives. The numerous enslaved women imprisoned around this scene could see this raucous activity but could not speak to the traders because "All communication" was "prevented betwixt the Slaves aboard of ship, and the traders and canoe-men who c[a]me to sell Slaves." Enslaved men likewise could not interact with visiting African merchants or most of the crew because they were isolated from the quarterdeck—where trade took place—by the barricado. Captives also could not gaze at the shore because a five-foot-high wooden "breast work" surrounded the ships, which made it diffi-cult to see over the side without standing at the edge of the deck—something that few men could do because they were locked in place by the deck chains; crewmen whipped unchained men who tried to "look over the ship's side." Women had a clear view of the shore but could see nothing of the men imprisoned on the other side of the barricado. Beyond mealtimes and forced "dances," Africans conse-quently sat on the deck and tried to occupy themselves in conversa-tion or by playing with beads and dice given to them by the crew.[35]

Purchased captives were thrust among the other prisoners on the deck on an almost daily basis. If the purchased person was a male, then he was made to stoop through the small barricado door onto the main deck; each adult man was immediately shackled to another man and locked into the deck chain. Women and girls as-cended a small set of stairs to the quarterdeck. The detailed trading accounts of the Liverpool ship *Golden Age* reveals how the arrival of captives steadily reduced the space available to each person on the ship. The *Golden Age* anchored at Whydah, in the Bight of Benin, on August 15, 1792, and just over a month later the first captives—two men and three women—were forced aboard. By the end of 1792, the captain had purchased 152 males and 94 females, at which point each person likely had sufficient room to sleep flat on his or her back without intruding on neighbors and enough space above deck to move freely. Over the next four months, a further 161 men and 85 women were forced aboard the vessel, drastically reducing the available room. For two months before the *Golden Age* left the coast, the Africans slept in conditions akin to those depicted in the image of the *Marie-Séraphique*, with individuals jammed up against their neighbors belowdecks at night and thronged above during the day. Crowding became especially acute two weeks before the *Golden Age*'s departure, because the captain tried to "shove in" groups of captives to reach his "complement"—the precalculated number of people the ship was to carry. These new arrivals caused bitter arguments and even fights between the Africans trapped in the already heaving rooms belowdecks. When a "boat-load of captives" were brought to a Liverpool vessel off Benin, for example, Africans who had already been "packed together to a degree of pain" for several weeks found their meager space further reduced, and "much noise ensued."[36]

Crewmen sought to free up space by moving children out of the rooms belowdecks. On the *Ranger*, for example, the captain purchased just fifteen enslaved boys, and so some of the men, who numbered over a hundred, slept in the boys' room. When there were "full-grown Men Slaves enough" to occupy both the men's and boy's rooms, related Liverpool Captain Robert Norris, the boys were "moved" out of their room, and that "Space [was] given to the Men." Crewmen likewise moved girls out of the women's room into the gun room, a space that was made claustrophobic and dangerous by the rudder, which swung back and forth across the room. When there were a "sufficient Number of grown Slaves on Board to occupy" the rooms belowdecks, continued Norris, the crew moved all the children above deck, where they slept under a sail; on rainy days, the children went "down into the Cabin." Norris had fifty children in the cabin on his voyages, and a passenger on a slave ship from the Windward Coast at the end of the eighteenth century slept above twenty-five "little girls" in the cabin. Twenty-nine boys slept under the adjacent half deck—a covered space that ran from the end of the captain's cabin to near the main mast—alongside the surgeon and the first mate. Archibald Monteith (d. 1854), an enslaved boy who was taken away from Old Calabar in the 1800s, described the relative liberty he enjoyed by being taken out of the rooms below. He was put in the captain's cabin with eleven other boys, where, he remembered, he had room to move about as well as food from the officers' table. The fate of the adults was terrible by comparison: at night Monteith could hear their "heartrending cries of anguish" from the sweltering rooms belowdecks.[37]

Children also slept on temporary structures above deck. Norris's ships had a platform built for the boys by placing boards between two parallel spare masts that were suspended six feet above the deck, creating a temporary deck upon which "a double Range" of "small boys" slept. Other children lodged in the ship's boat, which was either suspended over the deck or hung off the side of the ship. On the *Nightingale*, for example, "30 of the boys" slept and ate in the longboat because there was "not room below for them." Captains sometimes tried to purchase children as they neared the completion of their purchase precisely because they could be forced into these ancillary spaces. Captain James Charles of the *Africa* told Richard Miles, for example, that his ship "fill[ed] fast" and he still had 140 people to "stuff" into his ship to reach his "complement" of six hundred captives. Even so, he still wanted to purchase forty boys from Miles just before the ship weighed anchor, as they would be put in the boat suspended above the deck. Moving the children into the boat would ensure, Captain Charles claimed, that the adults would not be packed "like herrings in a cask" and "sweated to death" below. In reality, moving children above enabled him to purchase more people.[38]

Enslaved women were also sometimes moved into the cabins, where they suffered sexual abuse at the hands of the crewmen. According to one witness, the "Captain, officers, and passengers" selected the most "handsome young women" and took them into their cabins; common sailors also shared their "hammock and [their] allowance" with their "Favourites." The women were expected to wait on the officers in the cabin and assist in the running of the ship by helping the cook and washing clothes, in exchange for which they escaped from the steaming prisons. Falconbridge noted that the officers on ships were "permitted to indulge their passions among [the enslaved women] at pleasure." Common sailors were also "allowed to have intercourse" with women who provided consent—but consent was an impossibility given the uneven power dynamics between captives and crew. Crewmen had little empathy for their victims: on one vessel, an officer bet another "a double case of wine" that their four "Cabin girls"—all of whom were renamed, unlike the rest of the female slaves—would fetch more than 350 dollars when they were sold in the Americas.[39]

Slave ships were sites of feverish activity before they left Africa. A captain would indicate to the traders that his ship was ready to depart by daily hoisting a flag and firing a cannon, while brokers came and went to collect goods, bring captives, and redeem pawns. Meanwhile the crew hoisted in water, provisions, and livestock; put up the sails and rigging; and took down temporary awnings from the deck. The rigid routine continued aboard the ship, but the captives must have known that they would soon be taken from Africa, given the changing pace of activity. On the day of departure, captains ordered the anchor hauled up and then waited for the first strong breeze to push the ship off—something that might happen when the captives were above deck. When the *Bruce Grove* sailed from the Gold Coast at three in the afternoon on July 20, 1802, for example, its 325 prisoners, who were above deck and could plainly see the land drawing away, were crying and "wringing their hands and rattling their chains." When they came on deck again the next day, the realization that they had departed from Africa and were now on the open ocean caused "fresh lamentations," and many people "refused to eat" because their "spirits" were "much depressed." Once the ship was at sea, the routine did not appreciably change. The Africans were still brought on deck in the morning, fed the same foods at the same times of day, and then locked below at night. Some captains believed that their prisoners were unlikely to rebel—especially those from supposedly peaceful "nations," such as "Congos" (KiKongo speakers)—once out of the sight of land and so removed the men slaves' handcuffs and dispensed with the deck chains. The monotony of shipboard life increased, as there now was, a boy sailor remembered, "nothing to be seen but sea and sky" except the "sun blazing out of the mighty deep, and sinking deep into it as if to be for ever extinguished."[40]

Enslaved people's health deteriorated rapidly as the crowded vessel pressed out to sea. The day the *Isabella* pulled out of the Gambia River in 1798 the slaves were "all bad with sea sickness" and could "eat nothing"; three days out, they could still stomach nothing but bread. Only on the fourth day did the Africans "eat hearty of their mess"; on the same day the crew "washed out" the rooms, presumably to remove the accumulated vomit. Africans also began to contract "flux" from water that became "black as ink" with a "shockingly bad" smell as insects, amoebas, and bacteria bred in the stagnant barrels. Once a person drank the water, amoebas entered the body and caused abdominal swelling, weight loss, dehydration, and violent diarrhea; cysts within bloody stools further spread the infection, especially via unwashed hands plunged into communal eating bowls. Belowdecks, tightly packed captives contracted dysentery from their neighbors, especially when the infected could not reach toilet tubs by climbing over the packed bodies and had, instead, to "ease themselves as they [lay]." Toilet tubs overflowed, flooding the sleeping places with infectious excrement, so that the deck resembled "a slaughter-house." Captives had few opportunities to wash away the infectious filth from their bodies: extant logbooks show that crewmen typically allowed Africans to clean themselves just once every week, and frequently only once every fortnight.[41]

Africans suffered from a plethora of other infectious diseases that caused them to break out in pox, sores, and ulcers. Smallpox and measles ran like wildfire through the tightly packed prisoners, potentially killing hundreds if it was not arrested through inoculation or by quarantining the infected; survivors had their skin blistered and often lost their sight. Yaws, an ulcerous disease native to Africa, also infected large numbers of people because it was transmitted through contact with infected lesions. Enslaved people's skin was chaffed by rough wooden planks, stung by salt air, and rubbed away by crudely forged shackles; Falconbridge recalled that particularly emaciated people had their "flesh" entirely removed from the "shoulder, elbows, and hips," revealing the bones underneath. Inactivity also wasted people. For the sixteen hours that captives were locked below they could barely move from their painful sleeping position, causing cramps, numbness, and eventually muscular atrophy. On one ship, the captives' legs were "so cramped" that the surgeon had to bathe them in "warm water before they cou'd walk." Coming above deck in the day allowed captives to stretch out their painful limbs but did not allow them to move freely, because the deck was so "fully occupied by the slaves . . . as to render it difficult to move." Although Africans were usually forced to continue "dancing" twice a day, people were so closely packed that the women were "driven in amongst themselves," while the men could "only jump up and rattle their Chains." On especially crowded ships, captains gave up forced "dancing" entirely. When the *Brooks* crossed to Jamaica in 1784 packed with 619 people the "custom of dancing . . . was not practiced till it was too late to be of service."[42]

Hot and cold weather at sea compounded enslaved people's miseries. The heat belowdecks increased to dangerous levels, and so captives were "bathed in sweat" within "rooms . . . as wet as if water had been thrown over them." Ships becalmed in the doldrums—vast marine deserts—became blazing infernos above deck too; one sailor noted that the unshaded planks were like a "hot iron." Conversely, when cold weather whipped across the deck, enslaved people were forced below. Seventeen days after the Liverpool ship *African* left the coast in May 1753, for example, the air was "very sharp & cold," and the naked slaves could not be "upon deck in ye day time" because the temperature had dropped to seventy-four Fahrenheit—versus a hundred degrees when the ship had been on the coast. Temperatures remained low for another two weeks, and so the Africans were kept below; those who were able to come above huddled in the cold. Bad weather likewise kept the *Black Prince*'s prisoners below for almost an entire month on the Middle Passage; the prisoners were not able to wash for two months. The rooms became particularly hellish at such moments because the slaves had to eat, drink, and defecate in spaces that were "always wett" from water sloshing in. "The heat and smell of these rooms when the weather will not admit of the Slaves being brought upon deck," wrote John Newton, was "insupportable." Once the Africans were finally able to come above, they were, a passenger on a slave ship recalled, "extremely dispirited" and "sickly."[43]

People trapped in crowded rooms belowdecks suffered particularly from high temperatures and a lack of air. To prevent the ship from filling with water during downpours, the crew covered the gratings that fed air into the rooms with tarpaulins. The closing off of light and air caused mass panic. When the crew of the *Brooks* sealed the hatches in a storm, for example, the terrified captives tried to "heave" the hatches up and cried out "We are dying." When the covers were taken off, the Africans flew "to the hatchway with all the signs of terror and dread of suffocation"; many others were "in a dying state." Even in good weather captives struggled to breathe in the crowded prisons below. One officer recalled that the women on his ship desperately hauled themselves up to the gratings to try and "breathe more freely." Fearing that they would "take the air from the other slaves," the crew mercilessly drove them back. On the *Royal George*, the slaves made a "universal shriek" at midnight, a sailor on the vessel remembered. The crew asked what "ailed them," and they replied with "wild confusion of mind" that the "devil was among them" as forty people perished from a lack of air.[44]

Although water rations increased aboard slave ships in the eighteenth century, Africans were further debilitated by constant dehydration. Captains allocated their prisoners half a gallon of water a day, but that included the water to boil their provisions, leaving approximately half a pint of water to drink after each of the two daily meals. This meager ration scarcely replaced the fluids lost by constantly sweating in the steaming rooms below deck and did little to rehydrate people drained of water by dysentery. As the voyage wore on, Africans consequently suffered increasingly painful headaches, weakness, dizziness, and muscle cramps. In the worst cases, dehydration caused anorexia and made it difficult to digest food, further wasting the captives' bodies. As Africans withdrew into themselves and refused food, crewmen assumed that the captives were suffering from "fixed melancholy"—ostensibly a sign of rebelliousness. In reality, the person was in the terminal stages of dehydration, when the body began to shut down to conserve remaining fluids; death soon followed.[45]

During the eighteenth century, four hundred thousand men, women, and children perished from this deadly matrix of diseases and ill treatment aboard British slave ships. But what of their shipmates who were maimed by the voyage but survived? Historians have devoted scant attention to these survivors, largely because they have accessed the records of slave traders who recorded when enslaved people died but not when they sickened and lived. Switching the focus from mortality to morbidity reveals that the dreadful conditions aboard slave ships seriously wounded a significant propor-

tion of the enslaved people who were embarked in Africa—with crucial consequences for the subsequent fates of those wounded people
in the Americas.

The uniquely detailed medical log of a voyage of the Liverpool
slave ship *Lord Stanley* offers a microcosm of the Middle Passage's
impact on the health of captive Africans. The *Lord Stanley* dropped
anchor at Angola in March 1792, and over the next three months
the captain purchased 389 men, women, and children. When the
ship reached Grenada in June 1792 with 372 survivors, Christopher
Bowes, the ship's surgeon, submitted his journal to the customs
house in conformity with Parliamentary regulations. Bowes's journal included his detailed daily notations on his patients, beginning
with their initial symptoms and ending with their discharge from
his care or their deaths. It reveals that more Africans contracted illnesses but subsequently recovered than died on the Middle Passage:
of the 389 captives embarked, thirty-eight fell ill (one in ten people),
sixteen of whom (4 percent of those embarked) died and twenty-two
of whom survived (6 percent). There were no apparent differences
in the illnesses contracted by those who lived and those who died:
thirty-three people had diarrhea ("flux"), of whom thirteen perished,
usually within a week of contracting the illness. Africans who survived the flux spent around two weeks recuperating, sometimes as
long as a month. By the end of that near-death experience they were
"mere skeletons," as the ship surgeon Thomas Aubrey observed. Another person died of chest pains, one of head pains (perhaps the
result of dehydration), and one of "tremors"; two people who had
chest pains survived. Although less detailed than Bowes's journal,
the logbooks of the *Eliza* and the *Swift* show a similar pattern: more
captives fell ill during the voyage than perished.[46]

The invoices of British American slave sales confirm that significant numbers of enslaved people were debilitated by the Middle Passage. As we will see, American slave traders separated sickly
and healthy captives at their sales, and they noted in their resulting
invoices how many people fell into each category. There are 260
such records that survive for the period 1700–1808, detailing the
sales of almost sixty thousand people (see Appendix E), of whom
19 percent were sickly when they arrived in the Americas—slightly
more people than perished on the Middle Passage (13 percent of

embarked captives). This figure tallies closely with the informed estimate by the abolitionist James Ramsay (1733–1789), who attended numerous sales in Saint Kitts during the 1760s and 1770s, that "a Fifth Part" of all captives arriving in the Americas were sickly. Remarkably, morbidity remained almost constant across the period 1700–1808, at approximately 19 percent of the people who survived the Middle Passage. Mortality, by contrast, fell from 16 percent of embarked captives circa 1700–1788 to 7 percent on average before abolition. Reforms to shipboard management regimes therefore increased the numbers of people who reached the Americas alive, but the reforms did not reduce the numbers of captives who sickened on the voyage. In other words, those who would have perished instead arrived in ill health.[47]

Unhealthy captives varied considerably in the severity of their condition. The sickliest were on the verge of death and considered beyond saving by the crew, often after a bout of dysentery. Next were those who would live but who had been maimed: the blinded, those missing limbs, and people driven mad by the horrors of the slave ship. The first two groups were often labeled the "refuse" by slave traders. Numerous other people were ill but would likely recover, such as weak and emaciated people making a recovery from smallpox, "fluxes," "fevers," and other diseases. These Africans were often labeled "ordinary." Alongside these sickly captives were their ostensibly healthy shipmates. In reality, their bodies would have atrophied from inactivity and thirst, their skin galled by chains and sleeping on wooden boards, and their minds traumatized by mistreatment, the deaths of friends, and the terror of being imprisoned in a crowded marine prison.[48]

The proportion of people who fell into these macabre categories varied wildly between voyages. "In healthy voyages," a former slave ship captain observed, "there may be about ten in an hundred that are sickly." In "unhealthy" voyages, by contrast, he thought there was "no rule" as to the number. Ramsay accurately observed that the "Proportion of refuse Slaves" varied so wildly because of a variety of factors: "the Size of the Ship . . . the Length of the Passage and the Breaking-out of any epidemic Disorder among them." Apparently, morbidity was driven by some of the same factors that made mortality so variable. Even so, there were several key differences. There was no connection between the proportions of sickly people and the African region from which they had departed: vessels leaving Upper Guinea and West-Central Africa arrived in the Americas with proportions of sickly captives equal to those on ships from Lower Guinea (19 percent of those arriving)—even though it took ships from Upper Guinea typically two to four weeks less time to complete the crossing. There was also little connection between the numbers of captives who sickened on a voyage and those who died; large numbers of people might perish, but that did not mean that their surviving shipmates would arrive in the Americas unwell. By the same token, voyages with little mortality often had high proportions of sickly prisoners. The timing of sickness breaking out on the vessels likely explains these trends: when diseases emerged soon after a ship left Africa, it quickly killed large numbers of people but left a long period for the survivors to recover; when illness broke out near the Americas, by contrast, the ship disembarked large numbers of living, but sickly and dying, prisoners.[49]

In February 1787, the slave ship *Hudibras* arrived at Barbados, apparently ending the Middle Passage for the ship's 290 scarred, emaciated, and exhausted captive Africans. The *Hudibras* had left Old Calabar two months earlier packed with 340 men, women, and children. Several days after leaving the coast, the enslaved men staged what William Butterworth (1769–1834), a boy sailor on the ship, called a "fierce" insurrection that was thwarted by the slave traders' security apparatus. As the men slaves attempted to scale the barricado, the crew doused them with boiling water, shot several, and stabbed others; many of the survivors drowned themselves in the aftermath. Several days later, the Africans planned a "simultaneous rising of both sexes" that was prevented when a black interpreter revealed the plot; the captain "flogged most severely" the two leading insurrectionists "without the trouble of a trial" and then doused them with "a strong pickle . . . consisting of cayenne pepper, salt, and beef brine." Thwarted, the captives continued on the sweltering voyage across the Atlantic, crammed together, as on most British slave ships, in unsanitary prisons belowdecks at night. In the thronged men's room, fights broke out between the captives who "resented" any intrusion on their meager space by other people crossing the deck to reach the toilet tubs. Dysentery soon "raged amongst the slaves to an alarming degree," killing "two or three" people a day and enervating others. The appearance of Bridgetown, Barbados, on the horizon was therefore a miraculous sight that promised escape from the deadly ship.[50]

Like the overwhelming majority of British slave ships sailing in the eighteenth century, the *Hudibras* thus successfully completed its voyage by reaching the Americas with most of the captives that had been embarked in Africa still living, enabling the ship's owners to profit from the venture. That so many British ships completed the Middle Passage is remarkable, given enslaved people's constant attempts to escape their bondage, even when the odds of success were slim. These attempts at liberty were almost always defeated because slave trading merchants had devised, through a careful process of experimentation at the turn of the eighteenth century, a malevolently effective system for preventing rebellion. This system had proved so successful that it was embraced by British merchants as a standardized method for shipping enslaved people; by the era of the *Hudibras*, every slave ship featured a barricado, shackles, chains, and a well-armed crew. Slave traders packed these floating jails with enslaved people to maximize their potential earnings, knowing well that one in six of their prisoners—and often many more—would perish and be cast into the sea. The deaths of fifty people on the *Hudibras*'s typically dreadful Middle Passage would, for example, have been met without surprise by its owners when they received a report of the vessel's arrival in the Americas. The use of this particularly brutal and violent new regime was what enabled British slaving merchants to ship 2.4 million people across the Atlantic Ocean during the eighteenth century. But it also led directly to the deaths of almost half a million people and maimed an equal number of the survivors—most of whom faced another tortuous voyage aboard the slave ship within the waters of the Americas.[51]

CHAPTER FOUR

Guinea Factors and the Forced Migrations of Enslaved People within the Americas

W HEN THE *HUDIBRAS*'S captives glimpsed Barbados, they assumed that they would finally escape from the ship and "evinced their joy by singing an occasional song." Three hours after dropping anchor, their hopes were dashed when the captain returned aboard. He had learned that Barbados was "glutted with slaves" and so gave orders to set sail again. For the next few days, the *Hudibras* ran between numerous Caribbean islands, seeking a profitable slave market; on February 26, 1787, the ship finally reached Grenada, where the survivors of a typically deadly Middle Passage were soon sold. The captives' forced transportation through the British Americas in search of slaving markets was a consequence of the slave trade's expansion. Had the *Hudibras* sailed a hundred years earlier, its captain would almost certainly have landed his prisoners in Barbados—then the preeminent English American slaving market. By the time the *Hudibras* arrived in the Americas in 1787, though, British slave ships landed enslaved people at more than a dozen different locales. For Britain's slave trade to operate effectively, slave traders thus needed to devise ways to distribute thousands of enslaved people arriving on myriad ships to these various colonies. This chapter demonstrates how such a distribution system was created by focusing on American slave traders—or Guinea factors as they were contemporaneously known. These merchants sought profits by obtaining consignments of slave ships from Britons and then selling captives into the plantation complex. In addition to organizing slave sales, factors each fed market information to British merchants, and so slave ship captains were armed with intelligence that enabled them to make calculated decisions about when and where to land enslaved people in the Americas. Transatlantic links between British and American slaving merchants hence transformed the vastness of the British Americas into a series of interlinked slaving markets through which slave ships such as the *Hudibras* were able to move after the Middle Passage.[1]

This chapter therefore emphasizes that the first sight of land did not typically mark the end of the Middle Passage for enslaved people. Most were, like the prisoners aboard the *Hudibras*, forcibly transported within American waters to often-distant markets. Reaching these markets strained the health of exhausted people who had been trapped aboard a crowded slave ship on the Atlantic crossing; many perished in American waters who could have been saved had they been landed at a ship's first port of arrival. American voyages also enabled surviving Africans to gain an understanding of the alien new lands to which they had been dragged, beginning the process of acclimatization even before they left the ship. Remarkably little attention has been devoted to these voyages prior to enslaved people's arrival at their final destination; historians have instead focused on the intra-American trade that as many as one in four Africans were moved into *after* their sale in the British Americas. The slave trade within the Americas was, these studies have found, enormous, clearly structured, and crucial for shaping the lives of enslaved people who were shifted to often-distant colonies. This chapter demonstrates that the majority of Africans were forced through an equally well-organized American slave trade before disembarking, with equally momentous effects on their lives.[2]

At the opening of the eighteenth century, England possessed a vast American empire, within which were four principal markets for arriving slave ships (see Figure 4.1). Barbados, the first of these markets, remained the most economically important plantation colony in 1700 owing to a brutally productive form of plantation slavery

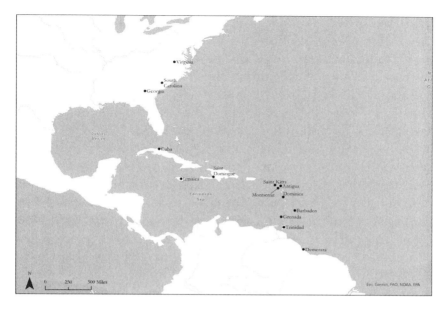

Figure 4.1. Principal British American slave markets, c. 1700–1808.
Based on data from Slavevoyages.org.

that the island's colonists had pioneered in the mid-seventeenth century. To establish and expand the plantation complex, English slave ships had landed almost 180,000 captives on Barbados during the seventeenth century—making the island by far the largest seventeenth-century slave market. Three hundred miles to the north were the Leeward Islands, the second principal area for the English slave trade. English settlers had flocked to Saint Kitts, Nevis, Montserrat, Antigua, and Barbuda in the first half of the seventeenth century and sought to convert the islands to plantation colonies on the Barbadian model. Periodic invasions from the neighboring foreign islands hindered this project, and so the slave trade to the Leewards was small before 1700: for every captive landed, five were taken to Barbados. Even so, the germ of slave societies had been planted in each of the Leewards by 1700, which British merchants sought to nurture by directing their slave ships to the islands. Jamaica—the largest of England's Caribbean colonies—lay more than a thousand miles to the west of Barbados and the Leewards. After capturing the island from Spain in 1655, English buccaneers had used Jamaica as a base to raid and trade with Spain's American possessions. Jamaica's pirates-cum-planters used their booty to purchase almost ninety thousand people through England's slave trade, forcing them to transform the island's fertile lands to sugar fields. Ample lands still remained available for plantation agriculture in 1700, and so Jamaica was poised to vault ahead of the Leewards and Barbados as the principal English American slave market.[3]

Although the mainland North American colonies—the fourth zone—were much larger than Jamaica, they were nonetheless marginal to England's slave trade. In the late seventeenth century, fourteen thousand Africans had been taken to six of the twelve North American colonies (Rhode Island, Massachusetts, New York, New Jersey, Maryland, and Virginia); an intercolonial slave trade carried Africans to the remaining mainland colonies. Most captives were taken to the Chesapeake—especially Virginia—where tobacco planters had begun replacing white indentured laborers with enslaved Africans in the closing years of the seventeenth century. Caribbean sugar planters nonetheless dwarfed Virginia's tobacco lords, and thus few slave ships made the long trip to the mainland: more captives were taken to the tiny sugar island of Montserrat than to English North America before 1700. Even so, the North American colonies represented distant, though still important, markets of last resort for English slave ships.[4]

The number of slaving markets expanded considerably in the eighteenth century as the plantation frontier expanded and Britain seized new American territory. Across the century, Jamaican colonists opened the island's sparsely populated eastern, western, and northern parishes to sugar agriculture and established new port towns that soon became hubs of the slave trade; British ships disembarked Africans at thirteen Jamaican ports during the eighteenth century, versus three before 1700. The expansion of tobacco cultivation in the Chesapeake and North Carolina simultaneously opened new North American ports to the slave trade. While Africans were hacking out the sugar and tobacco frontier, South Carolinian colonists adopted, in the 1720s, rice as a lucrative tropical staple, turning Charleston into a key market for British slave traders. After 1766, the "rice revolution"—and the slave trade—spread into Georgia, adding Savannah to British slave ships' itineraries. Conquest added further slaving markets to Britain's American empire. During the Seven Years' War (1756–1763), Britain obtained Dominica, Saint Vincent, Grenada, and Tobago, all of which would quickly emerge as key slave markets. The acquisition of Demerara, Essequibo, and Surinam in 1796, followed the next year by the seizure of Trinidad during the French Revolutionary Wars (1793–1802), further expanded Britain's slaving empire. Through these conquests, Britain doubled the number of its Caribbean colonies from seven in 1700 to fourteen by 1797; the temporary seizure of colonies, coupled with the opening of ports to British ships by foreign powers, provided British merchants with sporadic access to numerous other markets throughout the eighteenth century.[5]

British American slave markets also opened and closed with the waxing and waning of the colonists' demand for captive laborers. During the first half of the eighteenth century, the numbers of enslaved people shipped to the Chesapeake exploded as tobacco planters expanded cultivation and abandoned white servitude. After mid-century, though, natural increase reduced the colonists' reliance on the slave trade, driving slave ships away. The slave trade to the Leewards and Barbados likewise plummeted after 1750, thanks to the growth of resident slave populations and those colonies' economic decline relative to larger and more productive colonies such as Jamaica. Colonial policy also closed markets to slave ships. South Carolina's Assembly, for example, halted the colony's slave trade between 1740 and 1748, and again between 1787 and 1801; several newly independent American states likewise halted the slave trade after the Revolution. No Caribbean legislature prohibited the trade, but individual assemblies did mirror their North American counterparts in imposing duties on slave imports that were designed to drive slave ships away. Conquest by foreign powers, or the fear of invasion, likewise periodically closed British American colonies to arriving slave ships. The archipelago of British American slaving markets was thus vast but also ever shifting during the eighteenth century.[6]

Guinea factors enabled ships to navigate this extensive, diverse, and often changing constellation of markets. The practice of employing factors to sell captives had originated with England's chartered slaving companies during the seventeenth century. The Royal African Company, for example, had employed agents for the sales of arriving Africans in Barbados, Nevis, Jamaica, and Virginia. Each factor received a commission of 5 percent of the value of every person he sold, as well as 7 percent of the remittances to the RAC; before 1670, factors also received a salary. These potential earnings made selling people a "sought-after employment" that usually drew applications from the colonial elite; two of the RAC's factors served as governors of Jamaica and Barbados, for example. Factors served an important dual role: they communicated with the company to ascertain when ships might arrive and then organized sales of enslaved people. By reporting sales results to London, agents kept the company abreast of fluctuations in demand for captives within their colony. The RAC's directors collected this information from each of its factors, compiled it with news from African agents, and used it to decide when and where to dispatch their ships in the future. The RAC thus possessed an intelligence network centered on London that ensured its vessels did not sail blindly searching for Atlantic slaving markets.[7]

The RAC's strategy of directly employing American factors contributed to its downfall, however. The company extended sizable credits to colonial slave buyers—a model that had been employed by the RAC's predecessor joint-stock firms. Colonists repaid their debts by delivering crops such as sugar and tobacco or by remitting bills of exchange via the RAC's agents. But many buyers proved unable or unwilling to pay on time, leaving the company with mounting debts; by 1690, colonists owed £170,000—two-thirds of the company's capital. The RAC's inability to collect its debts starved it of the liquidity that it needed to fit out ships and maintain its African forts, limiting its ability to compete with interlopers. The RAC's failure therefore demonstrated the considerable risks of trying to operate a vertically integrated company that bought enslaved people in Africa and sold them in the Americas. If thousands of private merchants were to successfully operate in the slave trade, they consequently needed to find a different way to sell enslaved people in the Americas that did not entail shouldering the sorts of colonial debts that had doomed the RAC.[8]

Private Guinea factoring firms emerged in response to British merchants' demands. Unlike the RAC's directly employed agents, these new firms would be independent entities; no contract or salary bound them to British slave traders. Private agents continued to organize the sales of shiploads of captives consigned to them and then remitted the proceeds of the sale, minus their commission, back to the ship owner. Factors typically remitted barrels of crops such as sugar or tobacco in the hold of the returning slave ship; in the second half of the eighteenth century, they increasingly issued bills of exchange drawn on a British "guarantor"—usually a merchant-banker engaged in the bilateral colonial trade in tropical commodities. In both cases, slave ship owners did not, like the RAC, usually take colonial debts onto their books; the factor instead assumed those debts. The hazards of the slave trade were thus divided under this new model: the British merchant house forcibly transported captive Africans to the Americas and therefore assumed the risk that enslaved people would rebel or perish on the voyage; Guinea factors sold those Africans and accepted the risk of colonial default. Those risks remained considerable, however. Factors extended credit to each purchasing colonist for the value of the people he or she bought, creating a string of debts that the factor hoped to recoup before his own debts with the slave ship owner became due. If colonists defaulted, agents would not be able to honor their own obligations, sometimes bringing about their collapse. As one Bristol merchant noted, "Loss by remittances is the Rock more Guinea houses have splitt upon than any other."[9]

The risks of Guinea factoring were offset by the large sums that could be made by selling people. Like the RAC's factors, agents received a 5 percent commission on sales and a further 5 percent on remittances. The risk of bad debts was offset by a hefty interest of 8 percent on loans, which was, one Saint Kitts firm wrote in 1763, "no inconsiderable part of the factors profit." Selling a single shipload of captives could therefore reap significant profits. The same Saint Kitts firm boasted that it could make "at least a thousand pounds profit" by selling three hundred people arriving on a single slave ship: £450 in commission; £400 on remittances; and £228 interest on debts. Because colonists typically purchased Africans on credit, factors could time transactions so that they earned these sums without having to draw on their own, often limited, capital stock; a merchant established himself as a slave factor in Charleston, South Carolina, in 1772 with just £1,500 as capital, for example, a sum that would underpin slave sales amounting to more than £4,000. Moreover, factoring's commission-based returns were much more constant than the wildly fluctuating profits from investments in slave ships. Selling people was, as one British merchant observed to a Jamaican factor in 1761, "the only way to enrich you & make you close your days in England."[10]

The potential rewards of the American slave trade drew thousands of ambitious fortune hunters to the business. Records are not sufficiently complete to determine the total number of individuals who engaged in the factoring business, but approximately a thousand merchants organized the sales of 2,396 British voyages circa 1673–1808 for which the factor can be identified. Somewhere around five thousand people might therefore have worked as Guinea factors across the history of Britain's slave trade. These individuals typically organized themselves into firms consisting of two or three partners to spread risk and reduce the trade's entry costs. Sole traders were less common, given the business's hazards, but they stood to make greater sums than partnerships. The men who entered Guinea factoring were overwhelmingly drawn from the existing community of colonial merchants engaged in the bilateral trade in commodities and British manufactures; few individuals migrated to the Americas specifically to engage in the slave trade. Scottish merchants were overrepresented in the American slave trade; having been largely excluded from investing in slave ships by English competition, they instead sold people in the Americas. John Tailyour (1755–1816), for example, was born in Montrose, Scotland, and entered Guinea factoring in Kingston, Jamaica, after first serving an apprenticeship as a tobacco factor in Virginia on behalf of a Glasgow merchant house. Would-be Guinea factors tended not to be the largest merchants in their respective colonies before entering the slave trade, though. Major merchant houses eschewed the slave trade because they already engaged in much less risky bilateral trade with Britain; in late eighteenth-century Jamaica, for example, more than two-thirds of Kingston's merchant houses did not engage in the slave trade, in-

cluding the largest sugar houses. As in Britain, slave trading was left
to marginal men who were willing to take risks in the pursuit of
potentially large profits.[11]

So many merchants entered the American slave trade that numerous firms usually operated in each port, especially in periods
when importations of captives surged. In Charleston, South Carolina, for example, thirteen different firms sold people between 1733
and 1740, the opening years of the colony's slave trade. When the
slave trade increased between 1749 and 1774, fifty-four companies were in operation. Myriad factors likewise operated in British
Caribbean ports. In Kingston, Jamaica, eleven different firms sold
slaves in 1752 and 1753, when an official report provides a rare
glimpse of the factors operating on the island. Barbados and Grenada, for which snapshots are extant for 1730–1733 and 1784–1787,
respectively, show a similar pattern: thirteen companies operated on
Barbados, six on Grenada. The prevalence of firms ensured that the
failure of one company—a frequent event given the precariousness
of the business—would not imperil the slave trade as a whole, because other factors quickly absorbed the collapsed firm's business.
The decentralized nature of Guinea factoring during the eighteenth
century thus made the slave trade much less susceptible to the sort
of systematic failure that ruined the RAC.[12]

The many firms that engaged in Guinea factoring each needed
to develop two networks if they were to succeed in the business:
one of British slave traders and another of colonial slave buyers.
A typical slave ship was worth approximately £8,000 by the mid-
eighteenth century—a sum that had more than doubled by the
time of abolition. British merchants therefore dispatched their
valuable vessels only to factors whom they knew; as one Jamaican
agent wrote, "Every Guinea Ship that arrives here is particularly addressed to some house." Factors secured consignments of ships by
visiting Britain to personally establish their reputations; others had
their characters vouched for by British correspondents. Charleston
factor Henry Laurens (1724–1792), for example, entered the slave
trade by first traveling to London, Bristol, Liverpool, and Lancaster
to secure consignments of slave ships. Two years later, Laurens, in
partnership with English émigré George Austin (1709–1774), sold
106 Africans in Charleston from the *Orrel*, a ship owned by his new

Liverpool contacts—the commencement of a lucrative thirteen-year career during which Laurens sold 7,233 people. Familial links were also key: brothers, cousins, and in-laws of British slave traders partnered with American agents to establish factoring firms and then received ships from their family members. American slave traders had to simultaneously develop what one Jamaican factor called their "country interest"—a parallel network of customers to whom the factor would sell arriving Africans on credit. Most developed their "country interest" by selling low-priced plantation stores on short credits, enabling them to discover who among the colonists might later be sold enslaved people at higher prices and on longer credits. For example, Thomas Hibbert Sr. (1710–1780)—Jamaica's largest slave trader at mid-century—initially imported dry goods from his native Manchester; only after a decade in that business did he shift into slave trading. Through these strategies, factors aimed to develop a base of customers who would give them "the preference when they purchase[d] Negroes" as soon as a slave ship arrived to them from their British correspondents.[13]

The example of the Jamaican firm Rainford, Blundell and Rainford illustrates the complexity and size of Guinea factors' dual networks. The firm was founded by Samuel Rainford (d. 1798), a former ship captain who had traded with the Caribbean as a Liverpool merchant before migrating to Kingston, Jamaica, in 1774. Rainford partnered with his brother Robert (d. 1804), who likewise migrated to Kingston, and Jonathan Blundell Jr. (1758–1800), who remained in Liverpool, to form the slave factoring firm Rainford, Blundell and Rainford. The three men maintained their connection to Liverpool's slavers via Blundell Jr. and his father, Jonathan Blundell Sr. (1723–1800), whose own father, Bryan (1674–1756), had pioneered the town's slave trade. As a detailed network analysis has shown, Blundell secured consignments of slave ships from a dozen key merchants who themselves possessed "sub-nets" of investors. Blundell had particularly strong ties to slaving magnate William Boats (1716–1794) via the "young females" of the Boats and Blundell families. These merchants dispatched, between 1779 and 1795, 17,229 Africans to Rainford, Blundell and Rainford aboard fifty-one different ships. The Rainford brothers sold these captives to a network of "over three hundred and fifty customers," who were identified through their earlier trade in lower-priced imports, such as fish and lumber. The brothers' residence in Kingston also allowed them to chase down their debtors once captives had been sold. Guinea factors such as the Rainfords were hence the key nexus between British slave traders and American slave buyers.[14]

Each factoring firm developed its own network of British merchant firms from whom it received consignments of captives, and so Guinea factors tended not to compete. Kingston factor John Tailyour, for example, repeatedly insisted that he would not undercut the terms of credit offered by the other "respectable established Houses" to pluck business from other factors' networks. Factors could undercut each other by offering more generous credits to British ship owners, but this was a "folly," as Tailyour put it, that could lead to bankruptcy given the constant threat of planter default. An analysis of credits issued by factors to slave ship owners for 330 sales in the period 1750–1807 confirms that most factors shared Tailyour's opinion: credits in the same port and period rarely varied from one another, even when different firms organized sales. Neither did factors offer lower commissions to attract business; rates remained constant regardless of when and where a sale took place. Uncompetitive and difficult to enter, Guinea factoring was therefore an oligopoly. In Kingston during the 1780s and 90s, five firms controlled more than half of the Jamaican slave trade, a pattern that was comparable elsewhere: in Charleston, five firms handled 45 percent of slave sales during the period 1755–1775; in Barbados from 1751 to 1755, five houses controlled 63 percent of the trade; and in Grenada from 1784 to 1788, a single firm handled the sales of 57 percent of arriving Africans. The uncompetitive nature of Guinea factoring was such that a small number of well-capitalized firms controlled the business, leaving more numerous smaller companies to take sporadic shipments of people.[15]

The thousands of merchants who traded as Guinea factors during the eighteenth century—both the leviathans and the minnows—integrated British American slaving markets. Through their connections to select British merchants, factors drew slave ships to their colonies where the factors had a readymade network of colonial customers waiting to purchase the captives. With numerous agents operating in each slaving port, these transatlantic networks collectively formed a vast web that stitched myriad slaving markets into a cohesive whole. This web was created not by a single company, as the RAC had attempted. Instead, it was, as David Hancock has perceptively described when analyzing the Madeira wine trade, a decentralized network that was self-organized by its participants—a model that proved insidiously effective for accommodating the expansion of Britain's slave trade. These participants were men who each sought, as Hancock wrote of the wine traders, to "further their own commercial and social goals in the context of their local situation." In the case of Guinea factors, their "goals" were to make a profit on every person whom they sold into slavery.[16]

The importance of Guinea factors' networks for determining enslaved people's fates becomes evident through analyzing the decisions made by slave ship captains when seeking American markets. To the ship owner, this stage of the voyage was the most crucial because the outcome of American slave sales could make the difference between profit, loss, and—in the most extreme cases—bankruptcy. As Liverpool merchant Edgar Corrie explained in 1788, investors in the slave trade faced "four risques," each of which could "overset the best planned voyage." Purchasing fewer captives in Africa, the deaths of those people on the Middle Passage, and falling slave prices in the West Indies—the first three "risques"—each reduced the profitability of voyages. But "the remittance" from American slave sales was existential because it "involve[d] the entire capital of the Merchant." Ship owners feared that factors would issue bills of exchange as returns from slave sales that would later be "protested" by a factor's British banker, locking up the merchant's investment in potentially worthless credit instruments, potentially for years. If factoring firms collapsed into bankruptcy during that period, they could bring down their British slave-ship-owning creditors with them.[17]

Acutely conscious of these threats, merchants furnished their captains with detailed instructions on where and to whom they should sell their captives in the Americas. When the *Jason Galley* sailed from Bristol in August 1743, for example, its owners wrote a thirteen-hundred-word set of orders, more than half of which provided guidance on seeking American markets. Six months later, the owners sent updated orders to factors in Saint Kitts, Jamaica, South

Carolina, and Virginia in case the *Jason Galley* put in there. The contents of these orders contained similar information regardless of which firm wrote them: they detailed the colonies to which the ship should sail and the names of the factors to whom the captives should be consigned. Personal connections with Guinea factors were crucial to the creation of the itineraries of American markets outlined within these orders; slaving merchants rarely ordered their ship to a market where they did not possess links to at least one factoring house. The *Jason Galley*'s prisoners, for example, were eventually sold in Kingston, Jamaica, by DuCommon and Becher, a factoring firm linked to the ship's owners via Michael Becher (1704–1758), one of the vessel's investors. A slave ship's American destination was shaped from the outset by British merchants' ties to factors.[18]

Merchants also considered the geography of the Atlantic world when outlining the American markets where their captains were meant to steer the ships. Prevailing winds and currents in the Atlantic blew British ships from Africa first to the eastern Caribbean islands, and so captains could not sail directly for markets further downwind, such as Virginia and Jamaica. Ship owners thus usually ordered their captains to stop at multiple American markets: the seventy-nine extant sets of instructions ordered captains to visit between two (twenty-seven orders) and more than five (four) markets; the average was three. Captains were typically ordered to stop first at an eastern Caribbean island before proceeding to other markets downwind, such as Jamaica or South Carolina. Of the seventy-nine orders, twenty-seven (33 percent) directed the captain to visit Barbados, from which every other British American slaving market could be reached by following the prevailing winds and currents downwind. Large numbers of slave ships (25 percent of orders) were also ordered to one of the Leeward Islands, which sit athwart rapid currents that flow northwest to the shores of North America and southwest to Jamaica. If the schedule stretched to three or more locations, the captain was expected to visit several eastern Caribbean islands before then going to either Jamaica or North America.[19]

Captains stopped first at an eastern Caribbean island to gain intelligence on American slave markets. Given the time lag between the departure of a slave ship from Britain and its arrival in the Caribbean, ship owners had ample time to deposit letters in the eastern Caribbean islands with new information on where to steer the vessel. Such instructions were so crucial that the owners of the Liverpool ship *Lottery* told their captain in 1802, "The want of our Instructions [in Barbados] woud probably be the Ruin of the Adventure." Factors elsewhere in the Americas also sent letters to eastern Caribbean markets to provide arriving captains with intelligence that they could use to decide where to proceed. One Grenada firm, for example, had a sister "Barbados Establishment" that provided, in its words, "Capt[ain]s that may call there the best information with respect to the Markets in the different Islands." Given that the eastern Caribbean islands were themselves plantation economies, captains also stopped there first to assess whether they should sell their captives rather than proceed elsewhere. The demand for captives in Barbados, the Leewards (especially Saint Kitts), and the Windwards (especially Dominica) was further boosted by merchants who sought to purchase captives arriving from Africa and reexport them to adjacent French and Spanish colonies. The reexport slave trade, coupled with continuing planter demand for new workers, accordingly induced captains to test eastern Caribbean markets before proceeding on their voyages to the west.[20]

Ship owners provided their captains with what they termed "limits" to guide them as they assessed market conditions upon their arrival in the Caribbean: minimum slave prices that the captain was expected to receive from the sale of the Africans; from the 1770s onward, ship owners also frequently detailed the lengths of credits they expected from sales. Slave traders knew that slave prices and terms of credit varied considerably between colonies and were consistently higher in the markets most distant from Africa. For example, in 1765–1774, a stable peacetime period, slavers could obtain £38 for a healthy enslaved man at Barbados and the Leeward Islands and realize their returns within seven months. Alternatively, they could obtain £42 for a male slave at the Windward Islands, albeit with on average a four-month-longer wait for the proceeds. At Jamaica, captives sold for £47 a person, but this price was offset by credit terms of fourteen months—the highest in the British Americas. This pattern repeats in 1783–1792, with higher slave prices at Jamaica, but much longer credit terms. In both periods, North American factors sold people for high prices, a result of the long voyage needed to reach those colonies from the Caribbean and duties on slave imports.[21]

Prevailing east-to-west winds meant that it was hard for captains to double back to markets once they had passed them, making the decision to seek higher slave prices downwind often irreversible. British merchants labeled Jamaica and the North American colonies "ultimate market[s]," because ships could not seek further markets without beating back against the wind. Such voyages could take up to a month, almost certainly crippling and killing a large number of a ship's enslaved prisoners. By contrast, stops at markets in the Windward or Leeward Islands could be undertaken, one Barbadian factor noted, "without any material prejudice" because the captain could still subsequently follow the prevailing winds to markets to the west if he could not sell his captives at the ship owner's limits. Captains consequently visited British American markets in a sequence that sought to take advantage of the prevailing winds. In 1803, for example, London slavers Thomas Lumley and Company ordered the captain of their ship *Bedford* to steer first for Surinam—then the most easterly British American market—and subsequently run through eleven other American markets, beginning with the Windward Islands, then the Leeward Islands, and finally Jamaica or Cuba. Seasonality also guided merchants when deciding where to order their vessels. In winter, planter demand for enslaved labor in the North American colonies dropped; it also became hazardous to forcibly transport hundreds of naked captives north. Ship owners consequently ordered captains to steer for North America only if they could reach those markets "at a proper Season"—early September for Virginia and Maryland, late October for more temperate Carolina. Captains were also told to sell their prisoners at the first viable market that they reached in the eastern Caribbean, rather than undertaking perilous voyages to distant markets during the hurricane season between June and November.[22]

Although seasonality and geography were important, the health of enslaved people was the principal criterion that captains used when they decided whether to sail to other markets. Guinea factors priced captives according to their health, with the fittest Africans sold for as much as thirty times the value of their maimed shipmates. Given the wretched conditions aboard the ships, captives' health, and therefore value at sale, would deteriorate further if they had to make additional voyages of even a few days. As one Saint Vincent factoring firm observed, Africans suffered "some mortality" from "lengthning the Voyage" by heading to other markets rather than selling the captives on the island. Merchants consequently ordered their captains to make for markets elsewhere in the Americas "provided the [human] cargo be healthy," as one Liverpool consortium instructed. Conversely, if the Africans were "sickly" merchants cautioned commanders to "make the best" sale they could in the first market they reached, which was usually one of the eastern Caribbean islands, "for fear of mortality." This grim logic was incorporated into the pricing of captives within the Americas: colonists in markets farthest from Africa paid more for people in part to induce ships to undertake lengthy voyages that were likely to kill or maim some people.[23]

Captains consequently made chilling calculations whether higher slave prices would cover the financial losses if Africans sickened on extra voyages. If a ship arrived in the eastern Caribbean with ill captives and its captain found prices sufficiently high to meet his "limits," then he sold the Africans. In June 1753, for example, John Newton landed his captive cargo in Saint Kitts because the captives would "drop fast had we another passage to make," to "Jamaica or America." Two years later, the *Molly* was likewise obliged to "sett down" in Saint Kitts rather than proceeding to Maryland because the captain had "buried one third of his Negroes with a swelling in the stomach & other disorders." A Barbadian factor sold 187 people from the *Pearl* in March 1793—"all that could be Kept alive"—because the captain would have "buryed the most of them" if he had "proceeded to Jama[ica]," as intended. A year earlier, a Grenadian factoring firm had sold the survivors of the *Fame*'s deadly voyage because of what it called the "cruelty of sending the slaves off in the state they were in to Jamaica." South Carolina and Georgia's strict quarantine laws also induced British captains to land unhealthy people in the Caribbean rather than sailing on to North America. Laurens told one ship captain arriving at Saint Kitts that if his prisoners "shou'd have the Small pox or any disorder that shall much reduce" them, the captain would "do much better in the West Indias" than in South Carolina.[24]

Ultimately, though, captains were motivated by the profits of their voyage—something that they had an interest in, given that they were paid a commission on the value of the people whom they sold—not enslaved people's well-being when electing where to steer their ships. When slave prices were sufficiently high at faraway markets to cover the death and debilitation of Africans, the captain hauled up anchor and forced his prisoners to undergo extra voyages. Newton, for example, only decided to land his "worn out" captives in Saint Kitts in 1753 after examining the ship owners' "orders" as well as "intelligence" from other markets. Had his employers ordered the ship to Jamaica, and prices for captives there been sufficiently high, Newton would no doubt have weighed anchor; as he wrote in his logbook, Saint Kitts was "as good a market as any of the neighboring islands." Enslavers like Newton made these calculating decisions individually, but their collective effects on the slave trade's geography are most obvious during the military and economic credit crises of the 1770s and 1780s. In 1772, for example, a speculative bubble burst within the Glasgow tobacco trade, precipitating a financial panic that quickly spread to the indebted colonies in the eastern Caribbean. Within a year of the outbreak of the crisis, Jamaica's slave trade had almost doubled in volume compared to 1772 as captains steered away from the credit-starved eastern Caribbean islands. South Carolina saw a similar expansion, with slave imports almost doubling between 1772 and 1773. A fall in planter demand in the eastern Caribbean stemming from a distant credit crisis thus caused captains who would otherwise have landed their captives in the eastern Caribbean to instead seek more lucrative markets to leeward—with dire consequences for the captives' health.[25]

The credit crisis of 1772 and 1773 was a harbinger of much larger reconfigurations in the forced migrations of enslaved people within the British Americas during the American Revolutionary War. By 1775, the strain from the 1772 credit crisis had not eased, and British merchants were complaining about the lengths of credits being issued for slave sales and about falling slave prices. The onset of the war drove up the cost of freight and insurance, and imperiled overstretched Guinea factors' standing with their metropolitan guarantors. In the war's opening years, slave ship captains made for Jamaica, seeking factoring firms that could sell people on sound credit and for high prices. The entry of the French into the war in January 1778 decimated Britain's slave trade; by 1781, just Barbados, recently captured Saint Lucia, and Jamaica remained as markets for the few slave ships still engaged in the trade. But Barbados had been ravaged by hurricanes, drought, and the collapse in planter credit since 1772, and Saint Lucia was threatened with recapture. Almost every British ship consequently headed for Jamaica, including those packed with sickly captives who would have been disembarked in the eastern Caribbean islands during peacetime. The shifting geography of Britain's slave trade during the 1770s thus powerfully illustrates how slave ship captains conceived of captive Africans as perishable commodities that could be forced to undertake harrowing voyages within the Americas if such journeys resulted in higher profits. When distant markets offered prices high enough to cover the financial loss stemming from the killing of people, captains made the extra voyage. By contrast, commanders landed sickly slaves in the eastern Caribbean only when they calculated that they could obtain more revenue by selling their prisoners there. Calculations made by British merchants, American factors, and slave ship captains were thus crucial in shaping the fates of enslaved people in the Americas.[26]

For enslaved people, voyages in American waters were not merely a continuation of the Middle Passage but rather a distinct stage in the long process of enslavement. This phase began when the ship first arrived in a Caribbean port, where fresh provisions and water were usually brought aboard as "refreshments" for the Africans. When the *Hudibras* arrived at Barbados, for example, a boat immediately pulled alongside and delivered "oranges, limes, guavas, and plantains," a welcome relief from a monotonous diet at sea of starches and salt provisions. Citrus also provided much needed vitamin C to scorbutic captives who had been trapped on a ship for months, potentially saving enslaved people from a painful death. Half of the six hundred people imprisoned on the infamous *Brooks*, for example, were stricken with scurvy by the time they reached Antigua in 1784—a disease that had already killed forty people on the Middle Passage. After dropping anchor, the crew rushed ashore to procure a variety of fruit and vegetables, including lemons and limes, which quickly cured the scurvy. Had the *Brooks* continued to Jamaica without the fruit, the sickly Africans "must have perished," the ship's surgeon later wrote. Captains also purchased livestock, such as chickens, goats, and sheep, after first dropping anchor in the Americas, providing protein to Africans who had usually not tasted meat for months.[27]

Arrival in an American port also enabled captives to slake their raging thirst, sometimes saving entire human cargoes from death through dehydration. While the London ship *Spy* was still two weeks' sail from the Americas with 468 African prisoners in May 1794 the crew found that the remaining stock of water was dangerously low. The captain served the captives bread instead of boiled provisions once a day to "save water for cooking" and gave out brandy instead of water. Twelve days later, the cook abandoned "boiling beans for the slaves[,] the water being very short," and so the Africans had only bread and brandy as rations. Tempers frayed among the dehydrated crew: one of the crewmen beat the men slaves in the room below; another sailor attacked the hen keeper because he would not let him drink the chickens' water. In desperation, the crew began consuming saltwater, and they "induced the slaves to do it likewise," further exacerbating dehydration. Miraculously, the small Caribbean island of Margarita came into sight the next day, and the crew rushed ashore to get water; within two days the Africans were said to be "getting better." The *Spy* continued on to Kingston, Jamaica, where the captives were sold. Captains steering up the long North American coast also put into ports to replenish their exhausted supplies of water. Unlike the black, stinking, and parasite-infested water that the captives drank on the Middle Passage, water loaded in the Americas was drawn from springs ashore and so must have been refreshingly clear.[28]

Africans trapped aboard vessels that did not replenish their water supplies ashore faced catastrophe. The small size of the Caribbean islands, coupled with the poor navigation skills of some officers, meant that slave ships sometimes overshot their destinations. During wartime, ship owners also advised their captains to avoid stopping in the Caribbean islands for fear of privateers. In the most infamous incident, in November 1781 the British captain of the captured Dutch slave ship *Zong* bypassed Tobago, where he could have stopped to refill his water barrels. Ten days later, the *Zong* arrived off the coast of Jamaica—the ship's destination—but the inept crew assumed that they were off French Saint-Domingue. Steering west to reach what the crew assumed would be Jamaica, the *Zong* followed the prevailing winds instead into the open ocean. With four days of water remaining, and a voyage of ten to fourteen days back against the prevailing winds to reach Jamaica, the crew decided to murder their enslaved prisoners to conserve fresh water; the *Zong*'s Liverpool owners would claim back the massacred captives' value from the ship's insurers. Between November 29 and December 1, the crew hurled 142 live Africans overboard. The survivors were sold in Jamaica three weeks later, and the crewmen were never charged with murder. The *Zong* case was no aberration: a naval captain encountered the Liverpool slave ships *Rose* and *Spy*, which sailed together for Jamaica in the same period, "in great Distress both in point of Provisions and Water" because the captains had not replenished their water supplies. The naval captain provided both ships with water but asked what the captains would have done if they had not encountered him. They replied that they would have made their captive Africans "walk the plank" and claim on the insurance. The cases of these three ships are only those that abolitionists could document, and they are likely representative of tens, or even hundreds, of other ships that sailed through the Americas with their water supplies exhausted, or at least so low that the captives were, as on the *Spy*, reduced to dangerously low allowances.[29]

Ships remained in port only to load provisions and collect market intelligence, but these few hours provided a crucial opportunity for the Africans to examine the new land to which they had been carried. Many captives believed that they were not being taken to islands to work but would remain at sea until the white crew killed and ate them. The boy sailor William Butterworth related that when he was belowdecks on the *Hudibras* during the Atlantic crossing, the captives were "very inquisitive about their future destination, and asked, if we always lived on the water?" and insisted that the whites had "procured them for the purpose of killing and eating them!" Interisland voyages helped to ease these fears. Africans continued to be mustered on the deck while anchored in port, and so they could see the first evidence that their fate would be different from what they initially feared. When the *Hudibras*'s prisoners arrived at Bridgetown, Barbados, they "eagerly surveyed it from the deck" and were "lost in astonishment" when "they saw men on horseback, carts moving in different directions, the shipping in the bay, and immense numbers of people," most of them enslaved.[30]

Some Africans also got the first inkling of the brutal and humiliating process of sales to which they would be subject when they reached their final destination. The day after the *Britannia* arrived at Tobago in January 1777, a factor "came on board to view" the ship's 454 prisoners. The captain then had the captives "Oyld" to make them appear healthy before the "many Gentlemen" who "Came on Board to view the Slaves." After two further days of negotiation with these potential buyers, the captain must have decided that his prisoners would not fetch high enough prices in Tobago, because he hauled up the anchor and made for Jamaica instead, where the captives were again subjected to the humiliation of being "Oyld," before being sold. In the early eighteenth century, Bristol captains routinely sold the sickliest captives in the eastern Caribbean before forcing their healthier shipmates on voyages to the most distant North American and Jamaican markets. The *Greyhound*'s commander, for example, sold "25 Mawger slaves" in Barbados in 1723; after the ship was under sail for Virginia, he had a further eight sickly captives rowed ashore and sold. Writing to the ship's owners at the conclusion of the sale in Virginia, the captain implausibly claimed that the remaining Africans had approved of his depositing their sickly shipmates in Barbados. More likely, they faced wrenching separations from people they would never see again.[31]

When ships did weigh anchor, the remaining prisoners endured the misery of seeing the land recede as they began another voyage into the unknown. Having witnessed the abject condition of enslaved people ashore, Africans cannot have been eager to be sold in the colonies from which they were departing. Yet they almost certainly wanted to escape from the ship; as Newton wrote of his prisoners in 1753, "[They have been] so long on b[oar]d that their patience is just worn out." Moreover, Africans would not have known how long they would spend making voyages to American markets; so far as they knew, they might have been making a brief stop at an island before proceeding on another voyage of several months. For many captives, these ideas would have been confirmed by previous stops at the Atlantic islands of São Tomé and Principe for wood, water, and provisions *before* undertaking the Middle Passage. Spending another long period at sea was a horrifying proposition for people who had only just survived the Atlantic crossing. When the *Hudibras* pulled away from Barbados, for example, one of the crew cruelly told the enslaved prisoners that the ship would be "out at sea still for two moons [months], without seeing land." The rumor ran through the ship "like a train of gunpowder" and almost ignited a third slave revolt, before the captain publicly disavowed the rumor. Laurens was perhaps correct when he wrote that enslaved people "grow dispirited and pine away for knowing the reasons why" the ships "turn[ed] their back on the Islands."[32]

Once back at sea, the monotonous daily shipboard routine resumed, but the Africans usually had an opportunity to see land and continue the process of adjustment because ships navigated through American waters by hugging landmarks ashore. When the *Hudibras* ran past Saint Vincent and Grenada, their "fertile fields presented to view numerous groups of slaves at work." According to Butterworth, this was the moment when the Africans realized that they would be "engaged in the same employment" and not be eaten by the crew. People trapped aboard vessels making for Jamaica were likewise able to learn of their fate because ships ran along the island's southern coast, which was lined with plantations. On ships making their way ten to thirty miles up narrow "creeks" within the Chesapeake Bay, Africans could most clearly see the fate that awaited them because the ships closely passed numerous tobacco plantations and towns. Beyond plantation slaves, captives would have seen enslaved sailors and fishermen on the numerous vessels that plied American waters and on the boats that brought provisions to the ships. Given the numerical prevalence of enslaved people in the islands, waters, and colonies that slave ships passed through, captive Africans would immediately have seen that they had not arrived in a "white man's country."[33]

The periods that enslaved people spent moving through American waters varied considerably depending on the ship's destination. Vessels leaving Antigua could reach the other English Leeward Islands in less than a day, given that they were within a hundred miles

of each other. Sailing from Barbados down to the other eastern Caribbean islands was likewise a relatively short voyage, usually four or
five days. Reaching Jamaica or the North American colonies from
the eastern Caribbean islands entailed being longer at sea. Vessels
leaving the Leeward Islands for Jamaica followed the winds and
currents on a route that took them beneath Puerto Rico and then
Hispaniola—a journey of six to seven days. Ships going from Barbados or the Windward Islands to Jamaica, by contrast, cut diagonally
across a thousand miles of open ocean, aiming for Cape Tiburon,
the western tip of Hispaniola, or the Morant Keys, Jamaica's eastern
cape, which took seven to ten days. Voyages to North America were
even more protracted. To reach South Carolina from the Leewards,
ships had to steer north of Puerto Rico and then up through the Bahamas before following the coast of Florida to Charleston, an eight-
day journey. Following the coast for another four hundred miles to
the Chesapeake added at least another week to the Middle Passage,
sometimes much longer; the journey from Barbados to Virginia was
around thirty days. Voyages within the Americas evidently ranged
from a few hours to as long as a month.[34]

Although short compared to the typical fifty-nine-day passage
from Africa to the eastern Caribbean, voyages within the Americas were miserable in the extreme because enslaved people were already emaciated, sickly, and dehydrated from the Atlantic crossing.
On March 11, 1791, for example, the *Pearl* limped into Barbados
"in great Distress" after 104 Africans perished on the ship's two-
month passage from Old Calabar. The 368 survivors, many of them
"in a dangerous state" of health, must have looked at Barbados and
thought their ordeal had ended. But the *Pearl*'s captain forced his
prisoners to endure a ten-day voyage to Saint Vincent and then Jamaica, seeking higher profits. By the time the *Pearl* arrived in Kingston, supplies of food and water were two days away from running
out, and twelve other Africans had perished; seventy-three others were maimed. Seventeen years later, the Liverpool ship *Kitty's
Amelia* arrived in the Caribbean after a "toilsome passage" across
the Atlantic during which both enslaved people and crewmen died
"daily." Rather than put in at Trinidad, the commander "r[a]n with all
speed" for Kingston, Jamaica, pursuing profits. The Africans faced a
deadly voyage; fifty people perished on the eight-week voyage from

Bonny to Kingston, most of them in American waters. The captain of the *Flora*, which carried seventy-three people in 1793, wrote that his twenty-day passage from Dominica to Jamaica was "the worst" aspect of the ocean voyage because he "could mess [feed] the Slaves on Deck one day during the whole time." For nineteen days, the *Flora*'s captives were hence locked belowdecks, where they would have fed surrounded by their own excrement. On the *Gambia*'s 1771 voyage to Charleston, the winds were so strong that for four days the crew could not provide any food or water to the captives, who were locked below the whole time. Twenty captives "Sufficated," and their shipmates were "mutch impeaird."[35]

Contrary winds further extended these already wretched voyages, especially on ships heading to North America. Unlike the Caribbean, where the trade winds blow steadily from east to west, strong land winds blow off the North American continent, keeping slave ships from entering ports. In 1756, the Bristol ship *Concord* was "buffeted" 140 miles off the coast of South Carolina for "five weeks . . . with Contrary winds," wrote Laurens. The vessel limped into Charleston harbor with just forty-nine captives alive, the remnants of seventy-one people who had embarked in Africa. A decade later, thirty enslaved people likewise perished during the sixteen days that the *Britannia* battled strong winds off Charleston bar. After making for Tybee, Georgia, to purchase new anchors and provisions, the *Britannia* returned to Charleston, where the surviving Africans were then sold. Some vessels were forced away from the Carolina coast entirely by these strong winds. In 1755, for example, the ship *Emperor* reached Charleston but was stuck off the bar for eight days by a strong gust of wind that, according to Laurens, "destroy'd him a good many Slaves." The *Emperor* instead sailed to Jamaica, where the ship's 270 surviving prisoners were sold. The *Republican* likewise spent twenty-five days trying to fight her way into Charleston harbor in 1804 before giving up and making for Havana, via the Bahamas.[36]

On voyages within both the Caribbean and North American waters, captives also risked being drowned if their floating prison struck land or was blown over in hurricane winds. On September 18, 1805, the *Eliza* was tacking along the Guyana coast searching for the entrance to the Demerara River with 157 enslaved people aboard when, at three in the afternoon, it "took the ground" near the Berbice River. The crew worked the pumps and lightened the ship by throwing barrels over the side, which got it off and a "little out to sea." The next day, at 7 A.M., though, the *Eliza* struck the ground again and almost had her keel knocked off, which would have quickly sent the ship to the bottom along with its prisoners. After two more days of fruitlessly trying to get the beached vessel out to sea, the crew disembarked the presumably terrified captives into smaller vessels and rowed to Demerara, where they were sold. Even ships that reached harbors were not safe from the elements. In 1722, a hurricane lashed Jamaica and battered the numerous vessels anchored in Kingston harbor—including many slave ships. Although most rode out the storm, some with the Africans still aboard, at least one of the slavers sank, taking with it "most of the Men and Negroes." Another hurricane blew the Bristol ship *Emilia* ashore in Kingston harbor in 1785 with 360 people still aboard. A hundred of the Africans perished through a "scarcity of water, and a total want of country provisions" before their sale.[37]

Captives faced human hazards within American waters, which were often infested by pirates and privateers. Given the frequency of warfare in the eighteenth century capture was a very real risk for enslaved people; pirates preyed on shipping in peacetime. Privateers and pirates specifically sought valuable slave ships because they tended to arrive in the Americas alone, unlike the well-guarded convoys of sugar ships. Moreover, slavers plied predictable routes to eastern Caribbean islands—especially Barbados—making the waters on either side off those islands hunting grounds for privateers. Yet, slave ships were also formidable opponents, thanks to their large crews and heavy armaments, and hence their captains often chose to fight off attackers. When the *Will* arrived east of Tobago in 1800, for example, a French privateer swooped. Rather than strike her colors, the *Will*'s crew fought a four-and-a-half-hour cannon battle in which the privateer crewmen repeatedly tried to board the vessel. After receiving a battering, the French privateer fled. The *Will*'s 405 prisoners were locked belowdecks throughout the fight, where they must have been terrified by the sound of booming cannons, rattling muskets, bellowed commands, and the clash of sword blades. At one point a cannon ball blasted through the men's room, which "wounded twelve blacks, two of whom died in consequence next day, and two others had their thigh bones broken." Some of these battles were so fierce that the slave ship sank, taking its enslaved prisoners to the bottom. In 1747, for example, a Spanish privateer sank the *Ogden*, killing all of the crew and 370 enslaved people, with the exception of "one man, five boys, and nine negroes."[38]

Some African men were made to serve as armed marines in these sea battles. Their selection and training occurred while the ship was still in the Atlantic: six days before the *Spy* arrived at Margarita in May 1794, the captain had "a number of the slaves at the great guns and small arms," while the crew worked the cannons on the ship's other side. Once slave ships arrived in the Americas, the addition of armed slaves to the crew made Guineamen even more formidable opponents. When an American corsair chased the *Brooks* down near Saint Vincent in April 1777, the slaver captain had to decide to "fight or be taken." He elected to fight: "[I had] fifty of our stoutest slaves armed" with muskets who, alongside the crew, "killed a great number on board the privateer." An hour after the bloody engagement, the stricken privateer sank, while the *Brooks* sailed on to Jamaica, where the enslaved men—who had "fought with exceeding great spirit"—were sold along with their shipmates. Numerous enslaved men similarly served "very well" on the *Rose* when she was attacked by a French privateer off Saint-Domingue in April 1781. As the French crew were about to hurl a flaming grenade onto the *Rose*'s deck, one of the Africans "shot it away with his musket." The French privateer had to sheer off—but only after setting the *Rose*'s deck ablaze; the fire "hurt" the enslaved men because they were not wearing "trowsers," the captain reported. The *Rose* also proceeded to Jamaica, and the Africans—including the marines—were sold.[39]

Africans fought not through affinity for their captors but rather because the crew promised them rewards. As the ship *Mary* neared American waters in November 1806, Captain Hugh Crow (1765–1829) "selected several of the finest of the black men" to join the crew in exercising with muskets, passing gunpowder to the cannons, "and in other minor duties." Crow rewarded the Africans with "a pair of light trowsers, a shirt, and a cap"; he gifted captives who could strike a moving bottle with a musket shot with a "dram" of alcohol and a new cap. The enslaved men "were very proud of this preferment," Crow wrote, something he might have been correct about given that it might have allowed the men to escape the crowded rooms belowdecks and marginally improve their rations. Crow's "preferment" did not, however, save the men from being sold when the *Mary* reached Jamaica. The captain of the *Bedford* went further than Crow by offering enslaved men freedom if they fought with the crew. The ship had arrived east of Barbados in 1803 and was "harassed" by numerous privateers, one of which struck. After fortifying the ship with leftover trade goods, the captain "chose out a few of the slaves" that could "best use" muskets and "encouraged them by half promising their freedom in case we succeeded." Other captives assisted the crew by bringing in the sails in anticipation of the coming fight. The crewmen and armed slaves soon beat off the privateer. Later that day, though, another privateer fell on the ship, and the captain "knocked all the slaves out of Irons" and turned their shackle bolts into shot for the cannons. After quickly defeating the second privateer with cannonades and "three cheers," the *Bedford* proceeded to Barbados and then Demerara, where all the Africans were sold—including those who had fought alongside the white crew and been offered their freedom.[40]

While slave ships, unlike most merchantmen, could fend off small privateers, they were frequently seized by much larger predators in American waters. Prize crews usually boarded the captured slaver and sailed it to the nearest slave market, where the human cargo would be sold. The Liverpool sloop *Mary* with ninety African captives, for example, was captured by a French privateer near Saint Vincent on February 24, 1777. The French crew "carried her to St Lucia, where they sold the Sloop & Negroes." Capturing vessels sometimes selected only the healthiest adult captives and left their sickly shipmates on the slave ship, which then sailed to a British colony. When a Spanish privateer captured the *John and Mary* off Virginia, for instance, the Spaniards picked out only "38 of the choicest Slaves, all men," and sailed away with them; their 137 shipmates were taken to Virginia aboard the *John and Mary*. During wars, French, Spanish, and Dutch islands consequently became entrepôts for the sale of enslaved people captured from British ships. In the American Revolutionary War, French and American privateers sold so many enslaved people in Martinique that they were said to be "cheaper there than in Africa."[41]

Although enslaved people were sometimes armed and were tantalizingly close to land, they were able to stage remarkably few insurrections: of 413 documented revolts circa 1700–1808, just twelve (3 percent) occurred in American waters. The lack of revolts was perhaps a result of the difficulty of assimilating the fact that they were surrounded by islands peopled by whites as well as thousands of enslaved people. The presence of so many other vessels armed and manned by whites also dissuaded captives from attempting rebellion, and further reduced the already minuscule chance of a successful insurrection. When the *Ferrers* was anchored at Kingston, Jamaica, in 1722, for example, the captives—who had already murdered the ship's captain in Africa and staged a hunger strike on the Middle Passage—"attempted twice to mutiny, before the Sale of them began." Both revolts were quickly crushed. The lack of full-scale revolts does not mean that captives did not resist their enslavement by other means, though. Through their defiance, the Africans on the *Ferrers* dissuaded Jamaica's planters from purchasing them, causing the ship's owners to lose substantial sums. Fifteen years later, one hundred African men on the Bristol slaver *Prince of Orange* jumped overboard while the ship was anchored at Saint Kitts. Thirty-three of the men "resolv'd to die and sunk directly down"; their sixty-seven companions were pulled back aboard "almost drowned" and sold; many of them subsequently perished from "the Injury the Salt Water had done them." This mass suicide attempt thwarted the captain's plan of "proceeding to Virginia" to sell his prisoners. Proximity to land might have enabled the men to leap overboard: some captains unshackled the men slaves once within sight of land in the Americas on the assumption that the crew then had little to fear from the prisoners. Even captives who remained shackled could use their last moments together to plot mass resistance. A Barbadian planter was "credibly informed that a whole Cargo of Negroes . . . had made a resolution, rather to die, than be compelled to work" before their sale on the island. They subsequently killed themselves "through different modes of suicide."[42]

Within days of departing Barbados, the *Hudibras* arrived in Saint George's Bay, Grenada. Soon after the ship dropped anchor, young

William Butterworth took "a number of females and young boys" ashore "for the purpose of washing." The Africans were, Butterworth later wrote, "ready to kiss the ground on which they landed, and examined . . . every herb and bit of grass that presented themselves to their astonished view." Four years later, a sailor who led a hundred African men from the *Spy* to wash ashore in Jamaica—having stopped first at Barbados—wrote that his prisoners were likewise "glad to have their feet on shore again." When the *Spy*'s captives saw the pond to bathe in, "they gave a shout" and then "ran into it." Free from their shackles, the Africans began to "plunge and jump and shout, quite delighted, and tumbling one over the other like a set of wild men." The "transient feeling of joy" shown by the Africans from the *Hudibras* and *Spy* at reaching land was not a figment of their captors' imagination. They had survived not just the Middle Passage but also an arduous and enervating additional voyage within the Americas. While typically short—lasting less than a week in the case of the *Hudibras* and ten days for the *Spy*—these voyages were crucial components of the captives' experience. Moving through the Americas even for a few days enabled enslaved people to begin to acclimatize to the strange new world they found themselves in. This was not the "Land of the Dead" that they had so feared in Africa and during the Atlantic crossing, a netherworld where they would be kept on the slave ships until they were consumed by their white captors. But neither was it, as Butterworth ironically described it, "the land of promise." It was, instead, a place where they would, as their own eyes revealed to them from the decks of the ships, toil in the fields under the eyes of brutal whites—a world not dissimilar to the slave ship.[43]

Voyages within the Americas would also have important physical effects on enslaved people. Africans typically arrived in the Americas sickly, thirsty, emaciated, and dispirited after spending months trapped aboard the ships. The first sight of land must thus have been an incredible sight, especially for people who had been trapped aboard the vessel for the longest periods or were near death. But slave traders' business strategies meant that most Africans arriving in the British Americas would have their hopes of escaping the vessel cruelly dashed. While they would not have known it, Africans were forced through the Americas on migratory pathways that had been carefully constructed by profit-seeking Guinea factors in collaboration with distant British merchants. Most people therefore spent days and even months on forced migrations through American waters—a gauntlet of privateers, pirates, poor weather, and privation, which collectively killed the weakest enslaved people and crippled others. Africans who stepped ashore at their final American destinations, like the captives from the *Hudibras* and the *Spy*, were thus right to celebrate that they had reached the end of a deadly and extended Middle Passage. But enslaved people's joy at surviving the Atlantic crossing was, as one former slave ship captain grimly observed, "short-lived indeed"; within days, slave traders would subject them to traumatizing sale.[44]

CHAPTER FIVE

Many Middle Passages

Merchants, Planters, and the American Slave Trade

"THE FIRST OBJECT which struck" sugar planter William FitzHerbert (1748–1791) when he arrived in Bridgetown, Barbados, in December 1770 "was a Guinea ship [a slave ship] laden with Negroes to be sold." The "miserable" Africans were "all upon Deck Stark naked, & Dancing their country Dance to the beat of a kind of Drum." Three years later, English mercenary John Gabriel Stedman (1744–1797) was likewise "strongly attracted" by the sight of Africans "to be sold for slaves" in Surinam. "They were a drove of newly-imported negroes . . . who were just landed from on board a Guinea ship that lay at anchor in the roads." The sixty Africans resembled "walking skeletons covered over with a piece of tanned leather." Two whip-bearing sailors drove the emaciated captives toward a sales yard, while the ship's dog "worr[ied]" anyone who fell behind.[1] FitzHerbert and Stedman witnessed the fate that awaited the 2.4 million Africans who survived the Atlantic crossing to the British Americas: imprisonment in port, followed by sale to colonists. Given that every African was subjected to this brutal process, historians have usually viewed sale—and the subsequent forced dispersal of people into the colonies—as a shared experience. Yet, Africans arriving aboard slave ships were remarkably diverse. The purchasing strategies of Britons in Africa meant

Figure 5.1. Enslaved people landed ashore from a slave ship in Surinam, c. 1773. From John Gabriel Stedman, Narrative of a Five Years' Expedition, against the Revolted Negroes of Surinam . . . *(London: J. Johnson, 1806), vol. 1, facing p. 209. Reproduced with permission of the John Carter Brown Library, Providence, RI.*

that ships carried, as Stedman observed, "men and women, with a few children." Large numbers of these people arrived in the Americas maimed and wracked with illnesses after the Middle Passage. The Africans that Stedman saw appeared as if they had "risen from the grave," but the fact that they could walk implies that they were some of the healthier prisoners; many of their shipmates could not climb from their sick beds, let alone walk.[2]

This chapter demonstrates that enslaved people's physical condition was a powerful determinant of their experiences and fates in the Americas because of the ways that slave traders organized sales. As in Africa, slave traders devised a standardized process of sale in the late seventeenth century, which was then adopted by merchants across the British Americas to facilitate the slave trade's expansion. This new process was designed to sort people according to their physical characteristics and then distribute them to different American buyers: affluent planters typically acquired healthy adult Africans at high prices, leaving the unhealthy and adolescents to be selected by merchants, middling colonists, and speculators for smaller sums. American slave sales were therefore the mirror image of those conducted in Africa, with the healthiest enslaved people, especially men, being taken from the ships first, and women, children, and the sickly languishing on the vessels for longer periods. This chapter also shows that American sales were much more drawn out than has been assumed. The average sale was completed in almost four weeks, but rapidly shifting colonial demand for captives meant that some sales were completed in less than an hour—so-called scramble sales—while others dragged on for months. Regardless of their length, the operation of sales was premised on the assumption that captives could be sorted like goods and separated from each other—regardless of people's ties. As a result, enslaved people were usually violently torn from most of their shipmates before facing often-divergent fates. While healthy adult Africans were quickly marched to plantations—sometimes within two weeks of arrival in the colonies—their sickly shipmates were forced into other slave trades within which they could be trapped for months. For many Africans, sale in the Americas therefore marked the commencement of another Middle Passage that could be just as traumatic and deadly as the first.

American merchants sold enslaved people within an environment that was remarkably free of regulation, especially when compared to the highly controlled marketplace in early modern England. Legislation confined economic activity in England to specific locations, such as markets; prevented sellers from marking up goods above "fair" prices; and forbade speculators to snap up goods cheaply and then retail them at a profit. These various laws sought to preserve the "common good" by protecting consumer rights and preventing the "rich" from "act[ing] as they pleased in the marketplace." Few of these regulations were incorporated into marketplaces within England's American empire, though. Without designated spaces in major towns and cities, colonists transacted business wherever they met, be it a wharf, a street corner, a shop, or a counting house. Few rules governed how market actors interacted in these locales, beyond customary expectations of fair bargaining. Accordingly, prices were set by agreement between buyers and sellers; auctions were particularly popular in the Americas precisely because they allowed buyers to efficiently negotiate prices. In the absence of regulation, there was little to prevent affluent colonists from using their power to snap up sought-after goods, leaving the poor with whatever the rich had refused. The trade in people was no different: almost without exception Guinea factors were left to conduct their sales however and wherever they chose. Some laws did govern the American slave trade, but those ordinances typically sought to prevent the spread of infectious diseases and to raise taxes from the valuable trade in people. Legislatures also left it to Guinea factors to decide to whom they wanted to sell enslaved people, and at what prices. The American slave trade was hence almost completely unregulated; African rulers imposed far more restrictions.[3]

Absent rules governing their businesses, English American slave traders hence devised their own sale methods. These techniques in all likelihood initially grew from the convict and servant trade that provided English American planters with a captive workforce during the colonies' formative years, circa 1607–1650. Bound white laborers, like captive Africans, were typically single male adults who were expected to perform heavy work on sugar, cotton, and tobacco plantations. Indentured laborers were also imported into islands in unsanitary, overcrowded vessels, often resulting in death and debilitation. As one historian states, when servants arrived in the Americas they were "displayed on deck, the planters came on board to inspect them, and they were 'set over' [sold] to the highest bidder." Buyers and sellers in the servant market developed a dehumanizing language that they would later apply to enslaved Africans. Using a phrase that would not be amiss in a slave trader's letters, the seller of a group of Irish convicts in 1636 judged them to be "very lustye and strong Boddied," and he therefore hoped to "[sell them] to the best Advantidg" in Barbados. Planters also grew accustomed to attaching a price to humans depending on their physical condition: when a shipload of convicts arrived in Barbados in May 1656, they were sold for prices that varied "according to their working faculties." The planters ascertained the health of laborers, as a convict shipped to Virginia in the mid-seventeenth century recalled, through a callous and dehumanizing inspection: they examined "our limbs," he wrote, "made us walk to see if we were compleat," and "view'd our teeth to see if they were good." Even before Africans were forcibly shipped to the English Caribbean in large numbers, English American colonists had already begun viewing humans as commodities to which they could attach a price based on their physique.[4]

When colonists began to purchase Africans in large numbers after 1650, factors made important modifications to sales methods. Whereas English-speaking servants were able to ask to be sold alongside their shipmates, colonists viewed Africans as alien and savage people who could be separated from each other with impunity— even relatives. Africans were also commodified to a much greater degree: unlike servants, who were sold clothed, Africans were stripped naked, shaved, and polished with oil. Factors were nonetheless eager to ensure equal access to enslaved people for all colonists, regardless of their economic stature. They consequently grouped captives into uniformly sized "Lotts" that included a mixture of adults and children, the healthy, and the sickly. Each person within the group was sold at the same price regardless of age, gender, or health, ensuring that affluent colonists could not use their superior market power to pick out the healthiest captives at high prices. Colonists who wanted to purchase more people had instead to select multiple "Lotts," but they were unable to alter who was included within them; they arrived at the ship, plantation, or warehouse on an agreed date and received their captives, who were usually purchased with sugar, to-bacco, or bills of exchange. This sales method was so prevalent by 1662 that it was, according to the directors of England's principal chartered slaving company, "customary" in Barbados—then almost the sole English American slave market.[5]

As Barbados became increasingly socially stratified in the 1670s, the Royal African Company's factors embraced a new method for selling people that was designed to enable the richest sugar planters to obtain the healthiest Africans. By 1673—when the Royal African Company's detailed sales records commence—Barbadian society was becoming increasingly dominated by a small cadre of elite planters who owned the majority of enslaved people and the most productive lands, and who controlled politics; the remaining whites earned a marginal living on the fringes. Under pressure from this powerful group, the RAC's Barbadian agents organized their sales, accord-ing to historian David Galenson, to "accommodate the wealthier and more important planters." When a ship arrived at Bridgetown, the RAC's agents "divided" the Africans by separating the healthy from the ill, males from females, and adults from children. All but the sickliest people were then distributed in their assigned groups around the upper deck of the ship—the most common location for the RAC's sales. On the opening day, the Barbadian plantocracy boarded the ship, where they found food and alcohol laid out to greet them. Rather than purchasing preformed "Lotts" of people, buyers instead fanned out through the "croud" of captives and formed their own lots, before negotiating a price that was typically fixed for all the people within the group. When planter William Bulley picked out eighteen men and eight women aboard the *London Merchant* in March 1673, for example, he paid £20 10s. (twenty pounds ten shillings) for each person, regardless of sex. Another buyer later se-lected six men and a woman from the same vessel but negotiated a price of £17 10s. for each. Because the richest colonists entered the sale first, they were able to pick out the strongest adults—especially men; women were "2.5 times more likely to be sold" later in the sale than men. This process continued until the affluent planters had completed their purchases, leaving the sickly, elderly, and young to be acquired at lower prices by merchants, speculators, and middling whites. The RAC's Barbadian sales, writes Galenson, thus proceeded in "roughly descending order of planters' wealth."[6]

The RAC's Jamaican agents, by contrast, continued to sell slaves in lots because the island remained, in the 1670s and 1680s, comparatively flat socially. As in Barbados, the factors sorted the slaves into groups that varied in size and composition, depending on the health and age of the human cargo, but always included adult men and women, some healthy and some ill. The mortally ill, as well as children, were typically not included in lots, however. During the first sale conducted by the RAC's Jamaican factors in November 1674, for example, 302 of the 410 Africans from the *William* were sorted into lots, each of which contained three men and two women, with each group selling for £115, or £23 per person. Colonists arrived at the ship and chose how many lots of captives they desired, with the largest buyers purchasing, in the case of the *William*, six lots of people and the smallest buyers just one. There was little negotiation between individual sellers and the factors because the "lotted" captives were always sold at fixed prices; buyers had, instead, to collectively drive down the prices. Once the lotted Africans were sold—which usually included most of the adults—children were the next to be presented for sale. During the sale of the *Henry and William*'s captives in May 1680, for example, the "lotted" adults were sold on the first day and the children were sold afterward, but to a different set of buyers. As in Barbados, the very sickliest Africans were sold either in bulk to merchants or at auction to close the sale. The RAC's sales methods hence reflected, and reinforced, the particular social structures of the colonies within which the company's agents operated.[7]

In 1690, the RAC sought to experiment with the auction to allow colonists throughout the Americas fairer access to enslaved labor. In 1689, the company had received myriad complaints that the "best" captives had been "putt aside for Private friends" who were offered generous terms of credit by the company as well as discounted prices. The RAC responded by mandating that enslaved people would henceforth be sold by "Inch of Candle"—another term for an auction. The factors were to "publish a day of sale" that allowed sufficient time for "all Buyers to come in." Rather than being sold in groups formed by the buyers or in prearranged lots, each captive was to be sold either individually or, at most, with one other person. Africans were to go under the hammer one after another, with buyers making offers until a candle had burned down an inch, at which point the auctioneer called the sale for the highest bidder. In this way, the captives would be "openly sold" for prices that reflected a person's supposed market value rather than a privately agreed-on price. The experiment with this new sales method was short lived: the RAC's factors immediately complained that selling hundreds of people by auction would take too long; that the method of sale was "strange" to the colonists; and that interlopers organized their own sales by more "advantageous" means. In December 1692, the company abandoned the auction after only a single sale: factors would again be allowed to organize their sales however they chose.[8]

Soon after the abandonment of auctions, RAC factors across the English Americas adopted the Barbadian methods of allowing buyers to select Africans before negotiating prices with the factor. In Jamaica, the growing class of elite planters were allowed to seize the healthiest adults, especially men, early in the sale, leaving the other colonists to select from the remaining Africans. When the *African* landed 364 captives in Jamaica in June 1694, for example, just seven buyers selected 111 people—all but seven of them men—on the first day of the sale. The RAC's agents in the Leeward Islands of Nevis, Montserrat, and Antigua almost without exception employed the Barbadian methods. Factors in Virginia, by contrast, continued to "lott" arriving Africans at least as late as 1686, after which they embraced the models employed by their Caribbean counterparts. By the early eighteenth century, the RAC's agents thus employed a similar sales process, regardless of where they operated in the Americas: they allowed the richest colonists entry to the sales first to purchase the healthiest Africans at the highest prices, leaving less affluent buyers to acquire the remaining prisoners at lower rates.[9]

Private Guinea factors adopted the same techniques with few modifications during the eighteenth century. Many of the RAC's factors worked for the company and then, as it declined, shifted into private trade, taking their methods with them. Moreover, the RAC's techniques had likely become customary practice in many colonies by century's end; alternatively, the RAC may have based its own methods on those practiced by competing factors. Regardless of how the RAC's sales methods were transmitted to private traders, they were evidently in wide use throughout the eighteenth century: extant invoices for 260 sales conducted in a variety of British American colonies between 1700 and 1808 show Guinea factors employing a version of the process first pioneered by the RAC's Barbadian agents in the 1670s (see my Appendix E). Descriptions of sales methods in the French and Danish Caribbean indicates that non-British factors likewise utilized the same process, presumably having witnessed it in the British islands. When the missionary Christian Oldendorp (1721–1787) visited Saint Croix in the 1760s, for example, he wrote that the "strong and healthy" Africans were sold first, followed by the "sick and weak." In Saint-Domingue, French Guinea factors sorted (*alloti*) arriving captives into groups according to their "age, strength, and vigor," as one French historian has written, and sold the healthy adult captives first, leaving the "tail of the cargo" (*queue de cargaison*) to be sold later. Through a process of experimentation, American slave traders—be they British, French, or Danish—fixed upon an efficient and standardized technique for selling shiploads of people during the seventeenth century.[10]

Reconstructing how those sales operated demonstrates how Guinea factors shaped the forced migration of enslaved people within the Americas, as well as the experiences of captive Africans. Like the RAC's factors, private merchants boarded arriving ships, viewed the captives to assess their health and age, and elected whether they wanted to organize the sale. If they agreed, they first decided whether to vend the Africans through a private sale or advertise publicly. If the factor opted for a private sale, the captives were usually quickly sold to a select group of buyers, usually merchant houses engaged in the intra-American slave trade. Merchant buyers typically bought all the captives at a fixed rate, with both the healthy and the unhealthy included; only the very sickliest Africans were excluded. Ten days after the *Madam Pookata* arrived in Dominica in March 1787, for example, a "French Merchant" purchased all but two of the 164 captives in just fifteen minutes. Over the next two days, the captives were embarked on sloops and schooners in groups, likely to undertake the short voyage to neighboring Martinique or Guadeloupe; their two shipmates were sold on Dominica.

Through such sales, Guinea factors quickly sold entire shiploads of people at wholesale prices, enabling the captain to return the vessel to Britain without delay. British slaving merchants tended to dislike private sales, though, because they feared that factors were in ca-hoots with some "friend or intimate" who would purchase the cap-tives for lower prices than could be achieved through a public sale. Viewed across the eighteenth century, private sales were therefore rare: of 260 sales for which accounts are extant, just fifty (19 percent) were private sales, most of which occurred in the island entrepôts of the eastern Caribbean during the second half of the eighteenth cen-tury. Enslaved Africans arriving in the British Americas were thus typically sold through what contemporaries called a "country sale," which was advertised publicly and was ostensibly open to all.[11]

When conducting a "country sale," the Guinea factor first chose a day on which the sale would open. The RAC had commenced its seventeenth-century sales soon after a slave ship's arrival: typically, within three days in the eastern Caribbean and a week in Jamaica. The expansion of settlement during the eighteenth century meant that factors typically opened sales after longer periods to allow "ev-ery person in the country who wishes to purchase . . . time to come to the sale," as one Jamaican agent described. Slavers also took Afri-cans' health into account when selecting an open day. For example, another Jamaican factor weighed up whether "a long or a short day would be most advantageous" for the sale of the *African Queen*'s 214 captives, who were "dying daily" when they arrived in January 1793. By a "short day," the merchant meant the sale proceeds would be maximized by selling healthy Africans "in as few days as possible." A "long day" meant waiting for a longer period so that unhealthy people could be given "a good Feeding in the interim"—restoring as many captives to health as possible. The factor elected for a "long day" and imprisoned the *African Queen*'s captives for sixteen days before the sale opened. Most agents waited a similar period: the average time between the arrival of 620 ships and the sale opening was twelve days; few (55 of 620) captives were held for less than a week. A significant number of people (127 of 620) spent longer than two weeks imprisoned in port, and some (25 of 620) were trapped for more than three weeks. In rare cases where Africans suffered from smallpox or other infectious diseases, people spent as long as a month recovering before their captors offered them for sale. Sales began on every day except Sunday, with Tuesday and Wednesday the most common opening day, presumably to leave the most time before and after the Sabbath.[12]

Factors next publicized the coming sale by posting advertisements in colonial newspapers. Such adverts were initially crude. For example, the 1718 Jamaican advertisement for the *Margaret*—the earliest extant slave sale advertisement in the British Caribbean— consisted of a twenty-seven-word block of text, all the same font size, that was buried in a column of notices. In the second half of the eighteenth century, advertisements became much more visually striking. Although the amount of text barely changed from the *Margaret*'s notice, printers used different font sizes to make the advertisements easier to read and more eye catching, while also adding accompanying images. The word "NEGROES" or "SLAVES" spelled out in the largest block capitals was designed to initially draw the reader's eyes. The text that followed differed between publications, but a unifying feature was an emphasis on the Africans' purported health and youth. In the 794 extant advertisements drawn from newspapers published across the British Americas circa 1718–1808 (see Appendix D), the most common descriptor is "choice" (in 342 of 794 advertisements), a word presumably selected to emphasize the captain's careful purchasing strategies in Africa. "Young" (in 330 notices), "Healthy" (218), and "Prime" (217) were the next most common adjectives, often in combination, such as "prime and young." Factors also explained that Africans had previously "had the smallpox" and so were now immune; "were all inoculated"; or had arrived "after a short passage" (sometimes specifying the number of days). Accompanying images of stocky grass-skirted captives, or enslaved women holding the hands of accompanying infants, sought to reinforce these ideas of happy and healthy Africans available for sale. The grouping of numerous advertisements made such commercials an unmissable segment of colonial newspapers and ensured that readers would have had no difficulty learning of impending sales.[13]

Florid newspaper advertisements bore no relation to the traumatized and dying people who remained trapped on the ships. For example, in 1755 Henry Laurens advertised the *Fortune*'s 180 captives as being "all in very good health" but privately described the same Africans as a "scabby Flock" and "the most mangey Creatures that ever were seen." A year later, he wrote that 150 Africans on the *Gambia* were "very low in flesh," whereas the advertisement pictured thickset African men and stated that the captives were "in good health." In a 1793 advertisement a Jamaican firm described the survivors of the *Rodney's* hellish voyage as "Healthy." Yet, twenty-one of them would die before the sale was completed, and fifty-four of their shipmates were in a "Meagre emaciated state." The uniformity with which factors vaunted the health of arriving Africans within their advertisements was clearly an intentional strategy to ensure that prospective buyers could discover the true condition of captives only by attending the sales.[14]

Factors also detailed the African origins of enslaved people within their notices: of the 794 notices, all but twenty-six detailed where the ship had sailed from, the "ethnicity" of the captive Africans, or both. Factors particularly vaunted the origins of people desired by colonists for their supposedly positive "national" characteristics. Charleston merchants, for example, were extremely specific in detailing the origins of enslaved people from Upper Guinea—whom South Carolina's rice planters preferred. Charleston factors even occasionally (in 16 of 258 notices) tried to entice rice planters by noting that Africans from Sierra Leone and the Windward Coast came from the "Rice Coast" or "Rice Country." Conversely, factors knew that South Carolina planters had prejudices against enslaved people from the Bight of Biafra, and so they euphemistically described Biafran slaves as being from "Africa" or "Guiney." Jamaican sugar planters, by contrast, sought "Coromantee" (Akan-speaking) and "Ebo" (Igbo-speaking) people because of their purported ability to cultivate sugar. Kingston slave traders therefore prominently advertised the origins of enslaved people carried from the Gold Coast and the Bight of Biafra, sometimes by specifying the numerous ethnicities of captives from a single ship. People from the Windward Coast and Sierra Leone—who were less liked by Jamaican colonists—were typically marketed without any ethnic designator by factors. As with the captives' health, factors thus vaunted enslaved people's origins only when doing so would encourage potential buyers to attend a sale.[15]

Advertisements were circulated widely to draw customers. Merchants published them in "several Newspapers"; "past[ed] up" poster-sized copies around port cities; and had extra copies "dispers[ed] . . . thro' the country by special messengers on horse back." Slaving merchants appended handwritten letters to notices sent to the most favored customers in their networks. When John Tailyour sent an advertisement for the sale of the *Alert*'s 266 Africans to his sugar-planter cousin in January 1789, he wrote that "the cargo is a pritty good one" and therefore "hop[ed]" his cousin could attend; "if not," Tailyour added, "that you will send down people to choose [captives] for you." In the smaller Caribbean islands, factors hired vessels to "intimate the sale in the neighboring Islands." Some agents resorted to another particularly chilling advertising technique: they had the healthiest enslaved men marched through town "with the intent of letting the planters see what fine slaves we had got." On the morning of the sale's opening, an enslaved boy also went through the streets ringing a bell and distributing notices to any potential buyers who somehow might have missed this blizzard of advertising.[16]

The purpose of this advertising campaign was to draw as many colonists as possible because, as Laurens put it, the "success of a Sale much depends on the Numbers that attend." Factors understood that a large crowd would bid up the price of slaves—and hence their own commission. Or, as Laurens wrote in 1756, the arrival of a large slave ship "draws down the People from every Part of the Province & one bids upon the other." Many buyers would travel "70 to 80 Miles" from the "remote parts of the Country" to attend sales. For example, Nathaniel Phillips (1733–1813), a Jamaican sugar planter, spent two days traveling thirty miles on the island's infamously poor roads to reach Kingston slave sales in June 1781. Once in town, Phillips lodged in a tavern and purchased enslaved people from two different ships before returning home—a twelve-day journey in total. Attending slave sales in the smaller Caribbean islands also entailed extended travel. In 1776, for example, Barbadian planter Joseph Senhouse (1743–1829) traveled along the west coast of Dominica, a route that buyers would have taken when attending slave sales, on what he called an "exorable bad road, or more properly along no [road] at all." The land was "full of huge rocks, & loose stones"; in some places the road "led up steep & slippery hills," and in other places through "deep muddy soil" into which he sank "up to the knees." Colonists did not want to undertake such journeys to reach slave sales only to come away without purchasing anyone.[17]

While potential buyers made their way to ports, the Africans remained imprisoned aboard the anchored ship, allowing them to continue the process of acclimatization that had commenced when they arrived in American waters. The monotonous routine that had begun in Africa continued: enslaved people were brought up in the morning, fed twice, forced to "dance," and then returned below as the sun went down. The routine was broken by visits from merchants, customs inspectors, doctors, potential buyers, and curious visitors. When Olaudah Equiano arrived in Bridgetown in 1755, for example, "Many merchants and planters" came on board the ship who "put us in separate parcels, and examined us attentively." The same whites "pointed to land, signifying we were to go there." The strange visitors' gestures did little to calm Equiano's fears that "we should be eaten by these ugly men." The next day, though, the factors sent "some old slaves from the land to pacify us," who told Equiano and his shipmates that they "were not to be eaten, but to work," a "report" that "eased" the captive Africans "much." Stepping ashore to wash or be driven to a sales space allowed captives to glean further information about their impending fate. When Equiano was taken ashore, he wrote, "Every object was new to me" and "filled me with surprise," especially the brick houses and people on horseback. By conversing with Africans ashore, Equiano and his shipmates soon began to learn about the strange land to which they had been taken.[18]

Living conditions aboard the ships marginally improved while in port, at least compared to the miseries of the Middle Passage. Captains who had kept enslaved people in chains while coasting through the Americas finally "Nockt the hand cuffs of the Sleaves" in port, as the captain of the *Maria* wrote in the logbook two days after arriving in Jamaica in 1773. Factors also delivered "clouts" to the slaves—small loin cloths that concealed the Africans' genitals after months of nakedness. Fresh food was brought regularly from shore, most of it starches, such as potatoes, plantains, yams, and corn, which captives were forced to eat in large quantities. When the *Gregson* anchored in Kingston in January 1793, for example, the 334 captives consumed ten thousand plantains in the nine days before the sale commenced—three per person per day—in addition to various "vegetables" and oranges. Captives finally received protein, as their jailors brought them offal, such as a cow's head, tripe, or "pluck" (the heart, liver, and lungs)—a relief from the diet of dried starches at sea. Water was also no longer rationed and was drawn from springs ashore, finally alleviating enslaved people's perpetual thirst. This increase in food and water, coupled with the relaxing of security measures, had one goal: to revive emaciated Africans prior to the start of the sale. "I am Indivering to get them up, till the day of sale," the captain of the *Fame* wrote from Grenada, with "as much as Meat & Drink will do."[19]

This marginal improvement in diet did little to save the sickliest captives. On average, 4 percent of Africans arriving in the Americas perished either before or during the sale (see Appendix E). To prevent rumors of the Africans' sickness spreading among the colonists and therefore "hurt[ing] the sale," "the dead bodies" were "concealed in the hold until night" and then thrown into the harbor. The disposal of bodies from slave ships was so common that it sometimes caused public health crises. Residents of Kingston were warned in 1785 not to bathe in the harbor because sharks had come into the shallow water to consume the bodies of Africans. So many bodies washed ashore in Charleston in 1807 that the city council outlawed the "inhuman and brutal custom" of "throw[ing]" deceased captives into the river "to save the expense of burial." Such laws were apparently ineffective: a young sailor who was tasked with burying an enslaved man ashore in Kingston in 1801 instead tied the body to a bush, leaving it "floating in the water." The numerous decomposing bodies that littered American slaving ports were gruesome reminders that Guinea factors' advertisements were facades that masked the miseries experienced by enslaved people aboard the ships.[20]

As the opening day of sales neared, Guinea factors prepared to vend their prisoners. They first selected a sales space. Less than half (282 of 794) of extant advertisements described the location of sales, indicating that they were sufficiently well known to buyers or that purchasers would be directed to the space by criers on the day. The

more detailed notices reveal that Africans were sold in any place that
could hold hundreds of captives and potential buyers, including tav-
erns, houses, plantations, sail lofts, and even "a butcher's slaughter-
house" on a Jamaican beach. By far the most common locations (123
of 282) were the ships themselves, which would be anchored either
at a wharf, in the harbor, or up a creek. Slave ships were purpose
built to imprison hundreds of captives, and they could be adapted
into a sales platform by clearing obstacles from the deck and removing accumulated filth. Surrounding water also made it difficult for
enslaved people to flee either before or during the sale—although
Africans did occasionally escape when ships were tied up at wharves.
A "store" or "yard" was the second most common location (60 of
282), which would either be owned by the factor or be rented just
for the sale. These "Guinea-yards," as one Jamaican colonist called
them, were likely warehouses or high-walled yards, with a single
large gate or door that could be "thrown open" at the commencement of the sale.[21]

Factors priced Africans imprisoned within these spaces using
a system that was remarkably similar to that employed in Africa.
Healthy males aged between eighteen and thirty were, as in Africa,
deemed to be "prime slaves" and assigned a price that was, according
to Tailyour, "fixed." These prices, Laurens advised one slave ship
captain, were "wholly influenc'd by the value of our Staples." As a
result, when prices of sugar, tobacco, and rice rose or fell, so did
the prices of people. Factors used the price of a prime man to value
healthy women and children as well: healthy adult women were typically valued at 5 to 10 percent less than their male counterparts;
children were sold, as on the African coast, at prices that varied according to their age and height, with four feet and four inches once
again the cutoff between adolescence and adulthood. Sickly or elderly captives, by contrast, were valued according to their "goodness
& the demand at the time of the sale," Tailyour explained. People
with minor wounds and diseases from which they could recover
might be priced at a discount from a "prime" slave, whereas the ter-
minally ill might be valued at as little as a single pound, or even be
offered for nothing. By the conclusion of this process, the Africans
would be, a former Charleston factor stated, "ranged in order for

sale"—positioned with captives who were deemed to be of a similar age, gender, and health, each group of whom had an assigned price.[22]

Slave traders mercilessly separated Africans to place them in these groups and then humiliated them by forcing them to appear as uniform as possible to the buyers. One Grenadian factor "laughed at" a captain who tried to group Africans with their favored ship-mates because, the merchant said, "it was his and their business to sell them to the best advantage." Once pulled apart from their shipmates, Africans were forced to wash and shave, while surgeons simultaneously treated their wounds and sores using abrasives and "astringents." Captives were then smeared with a combination of "blacking and palm oil," making people within each price category apparently indistinguishable from each other. "They shave the Men So Close & gloss them over So much," one Jamaican slaveholder complained, "that a person Cannot be Certain he does not buy old Negroes." Factors next reduced the light in the sales space to fur-ther blur distinctions between people. Crewmen draped spare sails around and over the decks of ships and closed the shutters in rooms ashore so that sale spaces were "dark" even at midday. Darkening, shaving, and glossing collectively made the captives appear as ge-neric commodities who were meant to be indistinguishable except for their sex and height.[23]

The unhealthiest Africans—those who could barely rise, let alone stand in a sales room—were separated from their healthy shipmates during this process of sorting and pricing. Factors be-lieved that placing captives who were on the verge of death along-side their shipmates would shatter the carefully crafted illusion of health. In the Windward Islands, factors were so reticent to sell sickly people alongside supposedly healthy people that they had them rowed ashore and sold before the sale began. Elsewhere in the Americas, the unhealthy were typically pulled aside from their shipmates and sold at the end of the sale. When the *Fanny*'s 230 Af-ricans were sold in Kingston in January 1793, for example, its agent reported that eight "diseased" people and two "mere infants" whose mothers had presumably perished on the voyage "could not pos-sibly be brought forward in our Sales." Every other prisoner from the *Fanny*—including children, the elderly, and those weakened by

the voyage—were offered for sale together. Factors thus separated
out only those people whose physical condition was so visibly poor
that they might make buyers think the entire shipload of captives
was unwell.[24]

   While factors violently sorted the Africans within the sales
space, the buyers gathered outside. On average, thirty-eight people
bought captives at sales for which invoices are extant. In some cases,
though, just a single person bought entire human cargoes, and in
others, such as aboard particularly large vessels, there were more
than a hundred purchasers. These estimates undercount the number
of colonists who attended sales because they do not include people who left empty handed; assistants, both enslaved and free, also
accompanied buyers to help choose captives. "Great Croudes" of
people hence typically gathered at sales; one Jamaican planter noted
that there were "200 people at least in a Small room," when he tried
to purchase Africans in July 1776. The gathering of so many people
made slave sales "quite a holyday, or a kind of public fair," wrote a
witness to a 1795 Demerara sale. Colonists arrived with their wives,
children, and slaves, all of whom were "arrayed in their gayest ap-
parel." Factors actively cultivated a festive atmosphere by hiring a
"fife & drum" to literally drum up the sale and provided ample food
and alcohol. As the witness noticed, colonists thought slave sales "a
day of feasting and hilarity." For the "poor Africans" it was instead a
"period of heavy grief and affliction."[25]

   Immediately before the opening of the sale, the factor announced the prices of people to the assembled buyers. He likely
called out the prices of "prime" enslaved men and women, from
which the buyers could compute the prices of enslaved children. If
a large enough number of buyers objected to the price, they could
try to beat the price down. In July 1756, for example, Laurens wrote
that he had a "tollerable Shew of People," at the sale of 150 captives from the *Carlisle*, "but it Soon appear'd they would not buy
without a Considerable abatement from the former prices." "With
much to do," he continued, "we got them to give £235 [South Carolinian pounds] for about 20 of the best men, then were Obliged
to lower to £225, & so by degrees down to 200." Conversely, when
large numbers of buyers were desperate to buy, the factor could,
as Laurens smugly wrote, "choose his Chaps" and "make them

pay what price he pleas'd." Meanwhile, others turned away—as
an interaction recorded by Jamaican planter Thomas Thistlewood
(1721–1786) in his diary shows. At ten o'clock in the morning on
Monday, August 12, 1776, he boarded the slave ship *True Briton* in
Savanna-la-Mar harbor with several other planters. He had hoped
to pay 55 Jamaican pounds for "prime" captives, but the factor would
not "abate off £59," and so Thistlewood and "about a dozen" other
purchasers left the sale, though "others Staid & [the factor] Sold a
good many [people]." Given that most colonists purchased Africans
with credit, factors also needed to know potential buyers, and so
they turned away strangers unless they could pay cash.[26]

With the buyers pruned to only those who could afford to purchase people, the factor announced the opening of the sale, which
usually commenced around 10 A.M. As the chosen hour approached,
drummers likely began a tattoo that steadily rose in tempo, increasing the tension among the gathered buyers. Within the darkened
sales space, the captives would fearfully have listened to the excited
noises of the band, the shouting factor, and the gathered buyers. As
the town clock or ship's bell chimed the hour, the factor fired a pistol
or a cannon—a sound that would have been clearly audible to the
Africans—and called out: "The sale is opened!"[27]

Once sales had opened, they typically proceeded in three phases. In
the first stage, the "healthy, well assorted or prime slaves" were sold
for what abolitionist James Ramsay called a "certain average"—that
is, for the prices that the factor had determined before the sale. The
factor admitted only buyers who were creditworthy and could afford
the set prices for captives, ensuring that only the richest colonists—
especially those with connections to the factors—entered the sale
first. These buyers tended to be planters who sought healthy adults
who could work from sunup to sundown growing tropical commodities such as sugar and rice. Planters knew well that sickly captives
forced to undertake such labor would quickly die. Whites were also
loath to integrate young children into the plantation community—a
long and deadly process. As one Jamaican attorney candidly wrote
to an absentee sugar planter considering buying Africans, "mere
Children" would have to be "housed for 5 or 6 years, & if they live
in the course of 10 years may be useful." He added that "not 3 in

10 will live without the greatest care" and therefore advised buying
"young men from 18 to 22 or 23," even though they would cost almost twice as much as "Meagre Children." Plantation owners also
avoided purchasing people older than thirty because they would
have few working years before they joined the ranks of the elderly;
as Laurens advised a slaving merchant, Africans on the "Wrong Side
30 years of Age wont move at all." Guinea factors hence understood
well that elite planters demanded only "prime slaves" and would reject captives who did not meet their preferences. As Laurens noted
of Carolina's rice and indigo planters, "Whilst prime People can be
had our Planters will not touch such as are not so." Writing from
Jamaica thirty years later, Tailyour expressed almost the same sentiments about sugar planters: "No man in good circumstances wishes
to buy any other than prime slaves." He added in the same year,
"Planters in great Credit buy none but Prime Slaves."[28]

Planters used a variety of techniques to ruthlessly sort through
the gathered enslaved people and obtain the "prime" slaves they demanded. When sugar planter Simon Taylor (1739–1813) boarded a
slave ship to purchase twenty-four African men in Jamaica in 1765,
for example, he brought five white assistants who fanned out through
the ship and selected as many "fine [African] Men as they each could."
The assistants reunited with Taylor, and they then "ch[o]se the best
out of them" by seizing the healthiest captives and roughly shoving aside anyone they deemed not "fine" enough. Other colonists
employed enslaved men as aides for the same purpose. While some
colonists worked through the ship separately, others stayed together
and, using ropes or interlinked handkerchiefs, "encircled with these
as many [captives] as they were able," before likewise "pick[ing] and
cull[ing]" the people within the group. Individual buyers also hung
cardboard "tallies" around their chosen Africans' necks, or grabbed
captives and hauled them away from other buyers. Once colonists
had selected Africans, they "hurried out of the yard" with their prisoners, who "cr[ied] and beg[ged] that . . . their friend or relation . . .
might be bought and sent with them, wherever they were going."
Whites usually ignored these cries, not wanting to be burdened
with sickly, elderly, or young slaves. This ruthless process of seizing enslaved people continued until the most affluent buyers had
completed their purchases; other buyers left the sale empty handed.

Figure 5.2. The sale of 333 enslaved people from the Marie-Séraphique, *Saint-Domingue, c. 1773. From Jean-René L'Hermite and Jean-Baptist Fautrel-Gaugy [?],* Vue du Cap Français et Du Navire La Marie Séraphique de Nantes Capitaine Gaugy Le Jour de l'Ouverture de sa Vente Troisième Voyage D'Angole 1772, 1773. *Reproduced with permission of the Château des ducs de Bretagne, Musée d'histoire de Nantes.*

During the sale of the *Lovely Lass*'s captives in 1789, for example, Tailyour wrote to the ship's owner that he had sold 321 Africans but had 77 remaining, despite having had "purchasers enough for 7 or 800 slaves" on the opening day. "Had there been that number of prime people on board," he continued, "all would have been sold."[29]

A painting of the sale of 333 people from the *Marie-Séraphique* at Cap Français, Saint-Domingue, on January 14, 1773, depicts how these opening stages of American sales occurred (Figure 5.2). Buyers are being ferried out to the vessel from shore and are ascending a set of stairs leading to the main deck. The ship is still divided in two by the barricado, with men slaves on the main deck and women on the quarterdeck, where the factor and captain are stationed beneath an awning. Numerous male colonists are shown carefully selecting from the naked male captives on the main deck: buyers can be seen approaching individuals, touching their faces, making them raise their arms in the air, and holding their hands—clearly inspecting them closely. On the other side of the barricado, female colonists—including women of color—are simultaneously examining enslaved women. Groups of Africans chosen from the deck are seated by the side of a table laid out with a lavish meal while their purchasers negotiate with the captain and factors over prices and terms of credit. A boat in the foreground rows a group of purchased Africans away from their shipmates; their new master is shielded from the sun by a large parasol. This unique image thus powerfully captures the African experience of sale in the Americas: humiliating inspection by large numbers of white colonists followed by forced separations from most shipmates.[30]

In the sale's second stage, middling planters, town dwellers, and merchants entered the sale to purchase what Ramsay called the "second days slaves"—the elderly, sickly, and adolescent captives left after the richest planters had made their purchases. Although Ramsay's grim label suggests that this phase occurred on the second day, it actually took place whenever the healthiest captives had been sold, and often at the same time. When Thomas Thistlewood tried to enter a slave sale on its first day in August 1776, for example, he was accompanied by Mary Cope (b. 1736), the wife of his employer, who sought a "girl, about 12 years of age," who could be trained as a seamstress and gifted to her daughter Peggy. As this account reveals, healthy children were particularly apt to be sold at this stage, as colonists sought young people who could be apprenticed in a trade or put into domestic service. Planters sometimes sought teenage boys in this stage of the sale, as they could work for the remainder of their adult lives, often in skilled positions. When the managers of a Jamaican sugar estate wanted people trained for the "Carpenters Business" in 1785, for example, they purchased "three very likely" boys, who were then apprenticed to a white carpenter for five years. Some colonists knowingly bought sickly Africans in this second stage of the sale for low prices, in the hopes that they could restore their prisoners to health. In August 1756, Patrick Hinds (1719–1798), a Charleston shoemaker, purchased a teenage boy—in all likelihood to apprentice him in his trade—from Laurens knowing that the boy was "very Mauger" and "full of sores" with the view to curing him through the "application of Proper Remedys & kitchin Physick."[31]

With the first two groups of captives sold, there remained in the sale's third and final stage only the "refuse slaves": Africans who had "fallen sick and [were] become emaciated during the passage," as

Ramsay described them. Merchants first picked out large groups of captives who met a minimum criterion of health, leaving the remaining Africans—usually the sickliest, youngest, and oldest people—literally "Carr[ied]" to auction and sold for small sums to close the sale. "Every person employed about the streets betwixt the wharves and vendue stores," Jamaican planter Hercules Ross (1745–1816) told Parliament, "had almost daily opportunities of observing" Africans being "landed in a very weak and wretched condition to be sold at vendue." Auctions began at ten in the morning, and each captive was carried out to the block, where they must have lain or sat given their weakened state. As the captives were desperately ill, it was not unusual for Africans to be landed "in the agonies of death" and then to perish "in the piazza of the vendue master," Ross stated. The fall of the auctioneer's hammer typically marked the end of the sale of a human cargo, after which the factor began the process of preparing the ship for its departure to Britain.[32]

The voyage of the London slave ship *Comte du Norde*, from which 571 enslaved people were disembarked at Charleston in 1784, best illustrates how this three-phase sales process shaped Africans' subsequent fates in the Americas. In 1781 and 1782, British merchants had obtained people in Africa for low prices, crammed them aboard ships, and sold the survivors in the Americas at spectacular profits. In June 1783, London merchants Samuel Hartley (1739–1816) and Miles Barber (1733–c. 1791) hoped to seize these gains by purchasing HMS *Oiseau*, a decommissioned naval frigate, and outfitting it as one of the largest slave ships in British history. Barber and Hartley renamed the ship *Comte du Norde* and ordered its captain, James Penny (d. 1799), to sail for Malembo in Angola and purchase a thousand people. When the *Comte du Norde* dropped anchor at Malembo on December 3, 1783, Penny found to his horror that sixteen French captains were all competing to purchase captives. Captains nearing their departure were paying between fifteen and sixteen pieces for a healthy male captive, while the "new arrivals" were paying twelve pieces; Penny had originally hoped to pay seven pieces for "prime slaves." To avoid buying sickly people, he raised his offer to nine pieces and bought captives who had been "refused by the other" French captains, especially "little boys and girls" who would eventually make up just more than half of his human cargo. As he neared his departure from the coast, Penny increased his prices again and began purchasing more young adults. On May 30, 1784, the *Comte du Norde* put out for the Americas with 674 people aboard, most of them teenagers and children; twenty-three people had perished while the ship was on the African coast.[33]

People began to sicken and die in large numbers soon after the *Comte du Norde*'s departure. A day out a young boy died of "flux," and over the next ten days eight other people perished from the same disease. Seventeen days into the voyage, measles infected three hundred of the Africans, killing "six & seven slaves per day," Penny told Barber. By the time the vessel reached Saint Kitts after just thirty-three days at sea, seventy people had died. Although the *Comte du Norde*'s emaciated and maimed prisoners could see land, the Middle Passage had not ended: Penny rowed ashore and found a letter from Barber advising him to seize the "truely great" slave prices at Charleston, South Carolina. Eight days later the *Comte du Norde* arrived off Charleston bar but was kept out by contrary winds. With the assistance of enslaved boys at the sails, the ship dropped anchor in Charleston harbor on July 21, 1784, seventeen days after first arriving in the Americas. The additional voyage to Charleston—half the time it took to cross the Atlantic—cost the lives of thirty-five people. Immediately after learning of the *Comte du Norde*'s arrival, Charleston slave factors Ball, Jennings and Company advertised the sale of the 571 remaining captives, which would commence on August 3, 1784. The advertisement, like others, vaunted the health of the captives and their "short passage" from Angola, making no mention of diseases that had decimated the Africans. Prior to the opening of the sale, another eight people would die from the "dreadful disorders" that had infected the ship on its voyage.[34]

The 563 surviving Africans—165 men, 81 women, 208 boys, and 109 girls—were sold via the three-stage process employed by factors throughout the British Americas. Prior to opening the sale, Ball and Jennings sorted the Africans into groups and priced the healthiest adults: they valued men at £70; women at £60; and children at prices that varied according to their age, with boys ranging from £45 to £65 and girls from £45 to £55. In the first stage of the sale, which lasted three days, 119 individuals purchased 355 Africans, typically in groups of five or more. Adults were mostly sold in this first stage of the sale: of the 246 adults who survived the voyage, 129 were taken away on the first day and 62 on the second—three-quarters of the total. Less than a third of the children were sold in the same period. In the second stage, which stretched for eleven days, fifty-six buyers selected groups of ten people or less, most of them children (123 of the 159 people sold). In the third stage—the last two days of the sale—four men bought the remaining captives, all but one of them a child, to close the sale. These last buyers paid half as much for their prisoners as for the adults who were sold on the first day.[35]

Adults and children were marched away from the *Comte du Norde* to different destinations. Planters purchased most of the adults and took them into the countryside, sometimes far from Charleston: sixty-two people went to the plantation parishes of Prince William, Saint Bartholomew, and Saint Helena—more than forty miles from the city. Captives typically marched these long distances with their shipmates, as planters tended not to buy individual Africans; planter Joseph Woodruff (1735–1799), for example, bought six men and four women and likely took them to his estate in Saint Andrews Parish, Georgia—a journey of more than a hundred miles. Charleston residents, by contrast, bought very few adults: just thirty-five, or 15 percent of the total; given Penny's purchasing strategies at Malembo, these Africans may have been teenagers rather than adults. City dwellers instead purchased large numbers of children, most often individually or in small groups of no more than five. Carpenters, bricklayers, butchers, grocers, shipwrights, shoemakers, shopkeepers, and vintners all bought adolescents, presumably to train them as apprentices or put them to work as servants. These Africans would have disembarked at wharves from the *Comte du Norde* and marched through the city streets to their new homes within the populous commercial center of the town. The forty-nine sickly children who were sold to close the sale were, by contrast, bought by merchants from Lancaster, South Carolina, a frontier town almost one hundred and fifty miles from Charleston, and by a partnership from equally distant Georgia. These merchants likely imprisoned their captives in Lancaster and Savannah and then sought to retail the survivors singly or in small groups to buyers who could not attend Charleston slave sales.[36]

The case of the *Comte du Norde* illustrates in microcosm how Africans who survived the Middle Passage faced very different fates because of how factors organized their sales. Planters principally marched healthy adult Africans to distant plantations in groups, while children principally remained in cities or were taken to other towns to work as apprentices or servants. Their sickly shipmates— many of whom had been crippled by the Middle Passage and voyages in American waters—were taken the farthest, despite being the least able to move. Slave sales were thus crossroads at which slave traders forced enslaved people to take divergent paths into American slavery according to their age and health.

Although sales such as that aboard the *Comte du Norde* were broadly consistent in proceeding in three stages, they varied in length. Historians have tended to emphasize the speed and violence of sales, usually by drawing on abolitionist tracts that described all American sales as frenetic single-day "scrambles." The invoices for 260 British American slave sales conducted in a variety of colonies between 1700 and 1808 reveals, though, that sales were much longer than has been thought. Scrambles did take place, but only rarely: fifty-seven sales (22 percent) were completed in a single day. The average length of a sale—defined as the number of days between the sale of the first and the last captive—was twenty-seven days (see Appendix E). When we add to this figure the almost two weeks that captives were usually imprisoned before their sale, the last Africans to be sold were imprisoned in port in the Americas for just over half the time it took to complete the Middle Passage, on average. The typical slave sale was evidently much more drawn out than a scramble.[37]

Although sales were usually drawn out, their length nonetheless fluctuated wildly. The RAC's sales had been completed within five days, on average, between 1674 and 1697. But between 1698 and 1725 they extended to a month. Sales were usually completed over similarly longer periods at mid-century but then shortened dramatically in the years before the American Revolutionary War; one Jamaican factor wrote in 1772 that at a recent slave sale he "really expected one half of the white people on board would have been trod to Death by the other half" in their rush to grab Africans. The lengths of sales after the 1783 peace varied so much over place and time that it is difficult to generalize. Between 1789 and 1793, for example, many Africans were "pick'd up with great scrambling" in Jamaica; in January 1793, an entire shipload was sold on the island "in the short space of four hours." After the outbreak of war with France in February 1793, though, the average lengths of sales stretched to well over a month. The lengths of sales occurring simultaneously, but in different colonies, also varied considerably. In 1805, for example, a human cargo was sold in "one hour" in Jamaica, while 350 other Africans were sold over an eight-month period in the Bahamas. Africans spent very different periods trapped within sale spaces, depending on when and where they were taken in the Americas.[38]

The varying lengths of sales can be explained by focusing on Jamaica and South Carolina during the 1750s, when account books for Kingston factors Case and Southworth and Charleston merchants Austin and Laurens are extant for an overlapping period (see Appendix E). These records show that, in 1754 and 1755, the five sales organized by Case and Southworth took forty-nine days to complete; in the same period, Austin and Laurens sold human cargoes within just three days, on average.[39] Case and Southworth sold people over long periods because the Jamaican demand for captive workers had then waned as sugar prices tumbled. The price of sugar on the London market had surged during the late 1730s and again in the late 1740s, and so Jamaican planters sought large numbers of Africans; the *asiento*, which had granted British merchants a legal monopoly on the reexport of Africans to the Spanish colonies, also further boosted demand. But the price of sugar had collapsed after the peace in 1749, from forty-two shillings per hundredweight in 1747, to just twenty-seven shillings in 1750. Although the price recovered and stabilized at around thirty-five shillings over the course of the 1750s, it remained low enough to make planters reticent to purchase Africans or expand cultivation; the cancellation of the asiento in 1749 also substantially reduced the reexport slave trade. With weak demand from planters and merchants, Jamaican slave factors found it difficult to sell people quickly.[40]

South Carolinian planters bought Africans at scramble sales in the same period, by contrast, because they received high prices for their staples on world markets. While sugar tumbled, rice soared from 3.25 shillings per hundredweight in the late 1740s to more than seven shillings by the mid-1750s. In the late 1740s, South Carolinian colonists had also started growing indigo in substantial quantities as "[a]n excellent colleague Commodity with Rice," a shift that was subsidized by a parliamentary bounty. Between 1750 and 1755, the price of indigo steadily increased; exports from Charleston grew fivefold over the same period. Calculating planters knew that if they could obtain Africans, they could grow more crops and profit by the commodity boom. Colonists therefore flocked to buy imported Africans: at the sale of the *Pearl*'s 243 captives, Laurens reported that he could have sold twice as many Africans to the buyers present had the ship carried them; when the *Prince George*'s 260 captives arrived a month later, Laurens excitedly wrote that there had been enough colonists present to purchase a thousand people. Between 1753 and 1755, Laurens sold seven shiploads of Africans to these hordes of buyers, who literally fought each other to obtain workers.[41]

The onset of the Seven Years' War (1756–1763) dampened South Carolinian colonists' demand and stretched sales. As Laurens wrote, in wartime "the demand for Slaves cannot be half so great with us as in times of Peace" because commodity prices would plunge, while shipping costs increased. His predictions proved correct: after the outbreak of war with France in May 1756, the price of rice fell by almost 20 percent and of indigo by 10 percent. When Laurens opened the *Carlisle*'s sale on July 8, 1756—the same day that word of war being declared reached Charleston—the news "entirely discourag'd numbers from buying [captives]." At another sale in that month, Laurens told the ship's owner, "The planters wont come near us unless they are mearly haul'd along." The average length of the eleven sales that Laurens organized between 1756 and 1758 hence stretched to twenty-three days, on average. In the war-torn Caribbean, sales extended to fifty-seven days in the same period. Lurches in the prices of commodities or political changes in distant European capitals thus fundamentally changed the time that Africans spent trapped in American sales.[42]

Beyond determining the periods that captives spent imprisoned in American ports, these shifts altered the African experience of sale. When colonial demand for enslaved labor was high, captives faced the violence and terror of the scramble. The "crowd" of buyers "rush[ed] down upon the terrified Africans" the moment the sale opened; if the barricado was still in place, buyers scaled it, with others clinging to them. The captives were "instantly struck with the most dreadful apprehensions": some "f[e]ll prostrate upon their faces," while others "embrac[ed] their companions, expecting immediate death." Many Africans "shriek[ed] through excess of terror," creating "a general cry, and a noise through the whole ship"—a sound that must have been audible throughout port towns whenever such sales took place. Buyers roughly seized hold of the terrified captives while simultaneously trying to fend off other colonists. When two buyers seized the same person, each began "pulling & hauling" to try and pry the African away from the other. Colonists who lost the struggle to obtain the "good Slaves . . . came to collaring & very nearly to Blows"; one man was killed in a duel conducted after such a brawl in Jamaica. Many Africans tried to escape the ferocious buyers by "climb[ing] over the walls of the court yard, and r[unning] wild about the town," or leapt into the sea.[43]

In more drawn-out sales, by contrast, Africans suffered humiliating bodily inspections by potential buyers. When Mary Cope sought an African girl to train as a seamstress, for example, she looked at their hands to see if they had "long Small taper[ed] Fingers" that could perform fine needlework. Cope must have moved through the ship seizing hold of young girls and carefully inspecting their hands, roughly shoving aside any girls she thought unsuitable. At the sale of the *Concord*'s Africans in August 1756, South Carolinian planters likewise refused to purchase many people because they inspected them closely and found them to be "full of defects." White buyers subjected captives to such invasive and intimate inspections for weeks, sometimes for months. When eighty-one people were disembarked from the *Venus* at Kingston, Jamaica, in March 1757, for example, the factors could find few buyers, and so dispatched the vessel two weeks later to Savanna-la-Mar, a small port town to the west. Finding little demand there, the captain had the Africans force-marched to two other towns on the north of the island led by a "negro guide"—a thirty-five-mile journey over poor roads and rough terrain. By August, all the captives had been sold, but only after a five-month odyssey around Jamaica during which they were constantly examined by potential buyers; seven of the Africans perished along the way. A person's experience of sale thus differed remarkably depending on when and where he or she landed in the Americas.[44]

Captives' experiences—and subsequent fates—also differed enormously according to their age, gender, and health. Healthy adult captives, especially men, were usually bought quickly, even in sales that crawled on for weeks or months, and were then marched toward the plantations; enslaved people bought at 10 A.M. would often be on the road by midday. The distances that enslaved people subsequently marched to their new prisons varied greatly: some would reach plantations on the day of their sale, others spent up to a week traveling on foot or in boats. Given that adult men were typically embarked shortly before a slave ship's departure from Africa and spent the least time within American sales, they spent the shortest periods imprisoned within the ships. Healthy adult women spent longer periods aboard the ships, on average, but nonetheless departed the ships in the Americas soon after the sale opened and faced equally long marches to plantations. Enslaved children, who were usually embarked first in Africa, spent some of the longest periods aboard the ships but then traveled the shortest distances from sales, given that they were often taken to work in port cities. Half of the children sold from the *Comte du Norde*, for example, walked a few hundred yards from the ship to the homes of their new masters in Charleston; most of the adults sold from the same vessel marched more than forty miles—and in some cases more than a hundred miles—toward the plantation districts.[45]

Unhealthy people, who made up, on average, one in five arriving Africans, faced very different fates. While their shipmates trudged away from the ship, they remained trapped aboard, usually for the duration of the sale. Because planters would not purchase these Africans, factors sought to close sales by forcing the remaining captives into subsidiary slave trades that were designed to extract value from their damaged bodies. Hundreds of thousands of people were moved through these trades, which operated in every American slave colony. Yet, with the exception of the seaborn intra-American trade, historians have devoted little attention to how this business operated. Moreover, plantation papers (the principal source base for studying the lives of Africans after they left the ships) shed little light on the fates of unhealthy captives because planters did not purchase them. By weaving together various sources from late eighteenth-century Jamaica, I have been able to sketch the contours of the large, sophisticated—and exceptionally deadly—American slave trade for the first time.

Enslaved people's entry into the American slave trade usually began when they were bought by colonial merchants from the ships. Guinea factors thought it "dangerous to keep the remains of any cargo long on hand" because they knew that "weakly slaves would . . . soon have died." They hence invited merchants who "speculated in the purchase of the Slaves left after the first day's sale" to come and inspect the remaining Africans once their healthy shipmates had been sold. Some of the largest such buyers in Jamaica were Sephardic Jews, who likely engaged in the slave trade because it complemented their business of retailing to the island's colonists and trading with the neighboring Spanish colonies. British merchants were also involved, especially Guinea factors. Regardless of their background, these merchants sought Africans who met a minimum standard of age and health. According to Falconbridge, who witnessed several slave sales in Jamaica in the 1780s, merchants would enter the sale space and "examine" the remaining Africans by making them "stand up, in order to see if there be any discharge" that might indicate that the captives suffered from "flux." "When they do not perceive this appearance," Falconbridge continues, "they consider it a symptom of recovery" and purchase the Africans. Merchants paid the same prices for the captives that passed this test, indicating that health was their most important purchasing criterion. When Kingston merchant David Henriques purchased sixteen men, twelve women, twenty boys, and ten girls on the second day of the *Ruby*'s sale in December 1789, for example, he paid £48 in Jamaican currency for each person regardless of age and sex; captives sold on the first day were priced at £68, £66, £64, and £62, respectively, for men, women, boys, and girls. Buyers nonetheless also assessed Africans' age: on October 2, 1771, for example, Thomas Thistlewood inspected "the Rem[ain]d[e]r of the New Negroes brought ashore" the day after their shipmates had been sold. Thistlewood examined a "little Boy, and girl" but deemed them to be "a poor Choice, so bought none." Jamaica's slave traders thus purchased emaciated and weakly people rejected by affluent planters, but not the unhealthiest or youngest captives.[46]

The sickliest Africans were taken to auction where they were bought by the "poorer sort of people," who "ma[d]e a trade in purchasing refuse Slaves" at heavy discounts, healing them, and then reselling them. The buyers of "refuse slaves" were diverse: Jewish merchants, surgeons, planters, tradesmen, and shopkeepers all engaged in the business. Women were especially apt to buy sickly Africans, particularly compared to the overwhelmingly male buyers who entered a slave sale at its opening. When 262 people were sold from the *Alert* in Kingston in February 1789, for example, men bought 203 individuals in the first two days. The fifty-nine sickly and adolescent Africans who remained were then sold over a five-day period to nine buyers, five of whom were women, for prices that were, in some cases, half of what prevailed on the opening day. At other auctions, colonists bought "dying" Africans for as little as a single dollar and agreed to take orphaned infants for nothing. Africans acquired for these small sums were carried or stretchered back to the homes of their buyers and offered rudimentary medicine. Those who survived faced two fates: their captors either resold them for a substantial profit or kept them to enter the ranks of slaveholding society. When purchasers found that enslaved people's health was the "contrary of their expectations," though, or found that healing the slaves would cost "more than they gave for them," they turned their prisoners out onto the streets. James Morley saw people lying about "the beech [*sic*] . . . in the market place, and in the different parts of the town" who had been sold from his ship "in a very bad condition, and apparently nobody to take care of them."[47]

Merchants imprisoned larger groups of Africans—sometimes numbering more than a hundred people—in stores, yards, and livestock pens, where they "fatten[ed]" people before reselling them at a profit. An archaeological analysis of the Hibbert House, the Kingston residence of Guinea factor Thomas Hibbert, reveals the dank spaces where Africans were imprisoned after being purchased from the ships. The house's extensive basement included a "slave cellar" where Africans would have been imprisoned: a "barrel-vaulted cell" accessible only via a "single strong door" that was "illuminated through a single barred window opening." Africans would have recuperated within the dungeon before being sold within an enclosed courtyard at the rear of the building. Enslaved people spent weeks, sometimes months, imprisoned in such spaces. In March 1790, for example, four African men fled from the house of Abraham Bernal (d. 1790) and Moses Henriques (1740–1826), a partnership that engaged in the internal slave trade, six weeks after their sale from a slave ship. Other Africans spent even longer periods imprisoned after their sale from the ships. Hibbert's nephew Robert (1750–1835), for example, purchased several "refuse Negroes" from the *Russell* on June 21, 1774, in partnership with a Kingston doctor. The captives were initially taken to a "Mrs Denton," who was charged with "look[ing] after" them before they were sent to recuperate in a livestock pen on the island's north side. Four months later, the Africans were still imprisoned there, where they were likely put to work until their sale. On February 2, 1793, a consortium of four Jamaican merchants purchased seventy unhealthy Africans on the third and final day of the *African Queen*'s sale for £40 each, leaving twelve "sick & very Meagre" people to be sold at auction for £140, closing the sale. The merchants who purchased the seventy captives could not "boast of their bargain," wrote one of the factors who had sold them: they had found buyers for only twenty-five people by March 10, and ten of the captives had perished. Two months after arriving in Jamaica, most of the surviving Africans thus remained incarcerated in port.[48]

As Africans recovered within these prisons, their captors sought to either "retail them out singly" to Jamaican colonists or sell them wholesale to "Foreigners," John Tailyour explained. Because Jamaica's slave traders elected to shunt captive Africans in either of these directions, there was a close relationship between Jamaica's domestic and overseas slave trades: when Jamaican demand for slaves was low, merchants shipped Africans away from the island; when demand was high on the island, merchants principally resold captives locally. This relationship is especially evident in a detailed report of 83,357 captives brought into Kingston and 11,694 captives who were shipped off again between 1793 and 1799. In 1793, Jamaican demand for enslaved people was high owing to robust sugar prices and fear that Parliament might abolish the slave trade. As a result, merchants pushed Africans into Jamaica's internal slave trade; just 1 percent were taken from the island. By 1795, though, the onset of war coupled with rising shipping costs had reduced the domestic demand for enslaved labor to such an extent that almost a third of all arriving Africans were shipped off. With the easing of military pressure in 1798, Jamaican buyers reentered the market, and Africans were once again resold within the island. Economic forces thus largely determined the direction into which merchants forced enslaved Africans within the intra-American trades, be they domestic or foreign, just as they determined sales lengths.[49]

Recuperated captives pushed into the export slave trade faced arduous sea voyages to distant markets, often alongside healthy captives whom merchants had acquired in the opening stages of slave sales. Africans typically arrived in Jamaica, the 1793–1799 report shows, aboard large ships, each of which carried around 267 people. They were then embarked—after passing through the dungeons of merchants like Hibbert—onto small sloops and schooners, in groups consisting of twenty-seven people, on average; shipments of more than one hundred people and fewer than ten people were also common. Larger groups of Africans were likely squeezed aboard dedicated interisland slave ships; smaller groups shared space with cargo. Most captives (8,259 of 11,694) were carried either to Cuba or to ports in western Saint-Domingue, then occupied by the British Army, both of which could be reached in less than a week. Beyond these major markets, Jamaican merchants dispatched people to modern-day Colombia, Venezuela, Honduras, Louisiana, and Georgia, reaching all of which entailed voyages of several weeks; almost nine hundred people were forced on an almost thousand-mile journey against the prevailing winds to recently conquered Trinidad. The 628 Africans who were sent to the Cayman Isles and Saint Thomas likely faced a third intra-American voyage, given that both markets were island entrepôts rather than plantation colonies. Regardless of their destination, these often-lengthy sea journeys must have been arduous for sickly captives who had only recently endured the Middle Passage and imprisonment in Jamaican ports.[50]

Africans who were retained in Jamaica faced equally grueling journeys into bondage. Merchants purchased large groups of captives from the ships and then took them to towns across the island, making enslaved people available for purchase away from the port towns where the ships typically anchored. For example, merchant

Robert Jones (d. c. 1834) purchased groups of Africans at Kingston slave sales and then brought them to Runaway Bay, a sleepy port town in the sparsely settled Saint Ann's parish on Jamaica's north-eastern coast. On November 2, 1792, he advertised "25 Choice Young Eboe" slaves who had been "Imported from Bonny," likely on the *Thomas*, whose sale opened in Kingston on October 19, 1792. The *Thomas* sale was concluded in three days, and so the twenty-five Africans likely spent eleven days traveling to Runaway Bay—a forty-mile journey, either on foot over mountainous terrain or on small boats around the coast—before being offered for sale from Jones's store. Captives sold from port towns like Kingston and Montego Bay marched much shorter distances from the anchored ships into prisons such as the Hibbert House, but then faced sometimes equally lengthy marches to the homes of their buyers. Such journeys were particularly taxing for sickly Africans who were, as Falconbridge described, "unable to stand but for a very short time."[51]

"Retailers" like Jones did not vend their prisoners to Jamaica's wealthiest planters, because those buyers instead purchased adult Africans direct from the slave ships at premium prices. Instead, slave traders catered to middling whites—tradesmen, doctors, plantation overseers, and penkeepers—who sought only small numbers of Africans or lacked the capital and contacts to attend slave sales. Although these men and women are, by their nature, difficult to study, the uniquely detailed papers of Dr. Alexander Johnston (1739–1786) reveal the fates of Africans who were resold within Jamaica's slave trade. In 1763 Johnston emigrated from his native Scotland to Saint Ann's, Jamaica, where he established himself as a plantation doctor. Like other middling whites, Johnston sought to make his fortune by purchasing enslaved people and either hiring them out or forcing them to grow provisions on his small plantation. In 1766, he bought three African women from Aaron Baruh Lousada (1706–1768), a Sephardic merchant who, like Jones, purchased Africans in Kingston and resold them in Saint Ann's. Johnston also purchased four other Africans from local "retailers." In July 1770, he bought a woman he renamed Betty, another woman he renamed Sally, and Sally's child, Little Polly, who was "about 1 year old," from the merchants James Draper and James Holden. A month later he bought a teenager, whom he renamed Junius, from Benjamin Grimes, "a man who bo[ugh]t New Negroes" in Kingston. Between 1765 and 1770, Johnston thus bought seven Africans from three different slave traders: five women, a girl, and a boy.[52]

Johnston purchased twenty-four other slaves from numerous other people. Sometime before 1767, he visited Kingston and purchased at least five teenage boys from a slave ship—his only visit to the ships before October 1775. He obtained the rest of his prisoners from middling whites in Saint Ann's: he bought three people from the marshal, who was likely liquidating a local planter's estate; thirteen individuals from seven other planters; and a woman and her two children from James Draper, who would later sell him Africans. Jamaican colonists evidently traded large numbers of enslaved Africans with one another. Johnston himself sold people: four months after he obtained a woman who had been renamed Betty for just ten shillings as part of a judgment against a neighbor's estate in November 1767, he resold her for £15 in Jamaican currency. In October 1770 he sold a boy renamed Romeo, whom he had purchased from another planter just nine months earlier. While eminent planters typically purchased groups of healthy adults directly from slave ships, middling whites like Johnston thus opportunistically bought individual enslaved people who ranged in age from newborns all the way up to thirty-five-year-old men and women. The "retailing" of Africans by merchants was therefore part of a much larger internal slave trade through which enslaved people—both Africans and Creoles—were bought and sold in large numbers.[53]

Johnston paid high prices for the Africans whom he purchased from merchants, and so he must have assumed that they were in good health. When he bought the three women from Lousada, for example, he paid £160 in Jamaican currency for them, or £53 each, around the price of a "prime" slave sold from the ships. Presumably, Lousada had imprisoned the captives long enough for them to appear healthy to a doctor like Johnston. Within a year of Johnston's purchasing the three Africans, however, one of the women hanged herself, and another died "of a Dropsy," leaving just one woman, Mary, alive. Johnston fulminated in his diary that, as an "inexperienced" recent arrival on the island, he had been duped by Lousada into buying mentally and physically unwell people. Johnston paid equally high prices for the three Africans from Draper and Holden;

but two perished within three months of their purchase through diseases they may have contracted on the ships: Sally died from flux, and Little Polly of Guinea worms. Of the seven Africans Johnston purchased from retailers, then, just three survived their seasoning, indicating that sickly captives continued to die in large numbers after their resale in the Americas.[54]

Johnston briefly entered the deadly business of slave trading himself in 1776. Between 1771 and 1774 he settled his captives on a plantation and stopped buying people. In 1775 and 1776, though, he expanded his slaveholding by buying fifty-six people (fourteen men, two teenage boys, twenty-nine women, and eleven girls) direct from at least four different ships; Johnston paid high prices for the Africans, indicating that he had joined the plantocracy in acquiring healthy captives at the beginning of slave sales. As part of this plan, he bought thirteen men, two teenage boys, and a woman from the ship *Gregson* at Montego Bay on October 17, 1776, and paid £348 in Jamaican currency for them—£56 per person. On the same day, he purchased four "sickly" people for just £15 each from the same ship: three girls, whom he renamed Lucy, Polly, and Sally, and a man he renamed—perhaps with a macabre sense of humor—Chance. All four died soon thereafter: Lucy on October 24, just one week after the sale; Polly on October 29; Chance on November 4; and Sally on November 25. By comparison, just one of the Africans whom Johnston purchased earlier at the *Gregson*'s sale perished in the same period.[55]

The example of Alexander Johnston illuminates a large and well-organized slave trade internal to the Americas within which enormous numbers of unhealthy Africans perished. During Johnston's brief experience in the trade every single one of the unwell people he purchased aboard ship died shortly after; most of the Africans he purchased from slave retailers likewise quickly perished. A rare contemporary estimate indicates that Johnston's example reflects the deadliness of the American slave trade. Based on his experience witnessing the slave trade on Saint Kitts, James Ramsay estimated that "not more than one in three" of the "refuse" slaves remained alive after three years in the Americas, a loss of 66 percent, adding: "[After some refuse sales] almost all die before they become useful." By contrast, historians have found that between 10 and 25 percent of Africans purchased by planters from slave ships died within three years. The human toll of the slave trade within the Americas was thus much higher than has been appreciated. British ships disembarked 2.4 million people in the Americas during the eighteenth century, of whom 4 percent (96,000) died before or during sales. A fifth of the 2.3 million survivors—460,000 people—were sold into subsidiary slave trades but remained in ill health. If two-thirds of those people subsequently perished, as Johnston's example and Ramsay's estimate indicate, then approximately four hundred thousand Africans died either aboard the ships in American ports or soon after their sale. Almost as many people died within the American slave trade as on the Middle Passage.[56]

An "uncommon scene" occurred in "many of the streets" of Kingston, Jamaica, on June 24, 1790. A "great number" of enslaved people, likely some three hundred, had been landed ashore from the slave ship *Duke of Buccleugh* and were being marched to a yard in town, where they were to be sold the next day. Instead of trudging through the town in bewilderment and terror, as the mercenary John Gabriel Stedman had seen, the captives instead "paraded about for some time" while wearing "a sort of rustic crown" they had manufactured during imprisonment aboard the ship. One "very stout" woman wore a "chintz wrapper" and was accompanied by "two females who appeared to pay her particular attention." The Africans "danc[ed], together with every outward exhibition of festivity," something that the Kingston newspaper took to be "signs of happiness" and "ea[se] under the novelty of their situation." The captives' dancing was certainly not a sign of their "happiness." Rather, it was a defiant gesture that showed the Africans' individuality while simultaneously asserting the strong bonds that had formed between shipmates—three hundred men, women, and children who had survived the Middle Passage together. Despite their defiance, the sale opened the day after the Africans' "parade." Although people had previously sold quickly in Kingston—often in a single day—this sale extended to almost a month after the island's governor laid a snap embargo on shipping. The ban made "foreigners . . . afraid to buy" and also prevented those who "wish[ed] to purchase to send [people] to the distant part of this Island" from buying. As a result, many of the Africans were imprisoned in a sale yard for a month, where they were subjected to constant inspections by white buyers; the factor eventually closed the sale by selling "a considerable number" of the captives "at vendue for low prices."[57]

The *Duke of Buccleugh*'s captives thus suffered the same fate as millions of other enslaved people who were shipped to the British Americas in the eighteenth century: not a "scramble" but instead a drawn-out multistage process that was intended to vend every African, from the healthiest "prime" adult to the sickliest "refuse" slaves, to diverse colonial buyers. Because different classes of buyers were admitted at each of the three stages of this process, colonists from across the social spectrum—from the most affluent planters to the poorest speculators—could purchase enslaved people, widening access to slave ownership in the colonies. By employing these sales methods, Guinea factors were also able to profit through the sale of every African, regardless of those people's physical condition, and hasten the departure of ships. But the operation of American slave sales, just like those in Africa, was premised on the notion that enslaved people were commodities that could be sorted and divided according to their "quality." As a result, shipmates who had formed powerful bonds—such as the Africans aboard the *Duke of Buccleugh*—were mercilessly separated and forced to take very different routes into American slavery. Slave sales were thus traumatic and often drawn-out experiences that powerfully molded enslaved people's divergent fates.

Epilogue

Traders in Men during the Age of Revolutions, circa 1775–1808

B Y 1775, TRADERS in men had constructed an Atlantic-wide system that enslaved tens of thousands of people every year, forcibly transported them to the Americas, and shifted the survivors into the plantation complex and subsidiary slave trades. This system appeared self-sustaining: the exploitation of new African markets provided a growing supply of captive workers; a spreading American frontier drove demand for enslaved people. The products that captive Africans were forced to grow on plantations financed the American slave sales that enabled British merchants to outfit further slaving vessels—keeping "the wheel in motion." The smooth functioning of this insidious machine was enabled by slaving merchants' employment of an interlinked set of standardized techniques developed over the previous hundred years. By the late eighteenth century, Britons dispatched vessels to the African coast confident that their captains would be able to quickly embark hundreds of healthy enslaved people by ruthlessly rejecting the sickly, the elderly, and adolescents. The risk of rebellion and death at sea had been mitigated through the application of strict shipboard discipline and a rigid daily regime. Once in the Americas, slaving vessels sought out the most lucrative slaving markets by tapping into the sophisticated information network established by Guinea factors. And those factors utilized sales methods that enabled them to sell shiploads of enslaved people to a plethora of colonial buyers. After a century of almost continual growth, Britain's slave trade thus appeared to be enjoying a Golden Age.[1]

The onset of the Age of Revolutions in 1775 ultimately spelled doom for Britain's booming trade in people. Although the trade's morality had always been attacked, especially by enslaved people and Quakers, organized antislavery societies emerged only in the Revolutionary era. After the outbreak of the American Revolutionary War, several newly independent northern states outlawed the slave trade. With the onset of peace in 1783, Quakers on either side of the Atlantic petitioned to immediately abolish the business; both the British and the American legislatures refused to consider the motions. These early strikes provided the impetus for twelve evangelical Britons, influenced by Enlightenment ideals, to organize, on May 22, 1787, the Society for Effecting the Abolition of the Slave Trade. SEAST brought slaving merchants' brutal business practices to public attention and pressured Parliament into debating the abolition of the trade for the first time in February 1788. After a drawn-out campaign, abolition passed both houses of Parliament by a landslide in March 1807; a year later the last British slave ship crossed the Atlantic. Given the impetus that it gave to abolition, the Age of Revolutions was apparently a disaster for slaving merchants. Slave trading, which many had previously viewed as "genteel employment," increasingly fell out of the bounds of civilized behavior in Britain. Abolitionism also ended slaving merchants' long-cherished liberty to organize their businesses as they saw fit, as Parliament began passing increasingly strict regulations in July 1788. Unlike British slave owners, who received massive compensation payments at emancipation in 1838 for the loss of their human property, slave traders received nothing at the ending of their business in 1807.[2]

Scholars have debated at length whether abolition terminated a business that was in "decline" or was an act of "econocide"—the strangulation of a vibrant and expanding trade. Examining Atlantic slaving merchants' businesses between 1775 and 1808 offers new perspectives on this important debate. Merchants' businesses were indeed in decline after the American Revolution (1775–1783), following the catastrophic loss of the North American colonies and the stagnation of the British Caribbean colonies. This chapter argues that the chaos sparked by revolutions and abolition was— ironically—what staved off decline and drove Britain's slave trade to new heights. The chapter further contends that the twilight years of Britain's slave trade proved to be some of the riskiest, but also the most lucrative, in its long history. Guinea factors' returns increased because they drew commissions on selling people in an era of rapidly rising slave prices. But the risk of catastrophic failure also increased in this tumultuous era. Economic uncertainty likewise drove many British merchants out of the business, including some of the largest firms in the trade's history. Surviving firms nonetheless enjoyed a near monopoly on the slave trade after the elimination of French competition in 1793, enabling them to earn sizable profits. African brokers gained more too, as they demanded increasingly large bundles of trade goods in exchange for enslaved people and charged higher taxes on visiting Britons. Traders in men who could navigate the turbulence of the Age of Revolutions consequently exited their bloody business with immense fortunes that dwarfed those earned by enslavers of previous eras.[3]

On June 27, 1787, abolitionist Thomas Clarkson cantered toward Bristol to collect evidence against Britain's slave traders. As he came in sight of the city, Clarkson was filled, he related, "[with a] melancholy for which I could not account." "Trembling," he suddenly realized what an "arduous task" he and his fellow abolitionists had begun. SEAST, an organization of just twelve people, sought to demolish a business that remitted, in the year of Clarkson's journey, more than a million pounds to the British economy. Clarkson entered a bastion of the industry thanks to Bristol's lucrative, century-long involvement in the Atlantic trades. As someone who sought to "subvert one of the branches of commerce of the great place," he feared the "persecution" of the city's slaving merchants and worried if he would "even get out of it alive." Although Britain's slave trade appeared formidable, it had serious weaknesses in 1787, owing to the dislocations caused by the aftermath of the American Revolutionary War. After reaching a heady peak in 1775—the year of Thomas Paine's screed—Britain's overinflated slave trade had collapsed during the war. After the 1783 peace, merchants rushed back into slaving in the hopes of seizing the profits to be made from buying enslaved people cheaply in Africa, cramming them aboard ships, and then vending them to American colonists eager to once again purchase captive laborers; by 1784, the trade had reached its prewar level. The boom did not last. African merchants pushed slave prices above their prewar levels by 1785; Parliament's closure of Britain's Caribbean colonies to American ships, coupled with a series of devastating hurricanes, simultaneously eroded planter profits and drove down slave prices in the Americas. Between 1784 and 1789, Britain's slave trade declined and then stagnated at a level far below its prewar heights.[4]

French competition compounded British slaving merchants' woes. Prior to the American Revolutionary War, the British had squeezed the French out of most West African markets, confining French ships principally to markets in West-Central Africa and the Bight of Benin. In the Americas the French trade was likewise confined almost exclusively to Saint-Domingue. Before 1775, the French therefore enslaved on average a half to a third of the number of people carried by Britons. After the war, French merchants rushed to meet resurgent colonial demand for enslaved labor by re-entering the trade, a move that was buoyed by a state subsidy. Unlike the sagging British trade, the French boom continued throughout the 1780s; when Clarkson arrived in Bristol in 1787, the French had recently emerged as the largest slave traders in the Atlantic world. Although the French principally achieved their dominance by expanding their trade at their preferred African markets, by 1787 they had begun to elbow their way into West African regions that Britons had previously dominated, such as the Gold Coast and the Bight of Biafra. Seeking profits in the burgeoning French slave trade, numerous British merchants fitted out ships under French colors or relocated to France; others sought revenues abroad by supplying enslaved people to the Spanish colonies.[5]

The double blow of French competition and economic malaise in the British Caribbean drove many Britons out of the slave trade and isolated the business. Merchants had largely abandoned the trade for the duration of the American war; two-thirds of Liverpool's slavers left the business—from a prewar community of 158 traders—and never invested thereafter. The people who returned after

1783 tended to be specialists committed to the trade, rather than general merchants—as Clarkson discovered on his 1787 mission. When he arrived in Bristol, he found a business much reduced from its prewar levels that was largely in the hands of just three men, one of whom was a former slave ship captain. Slave trading had hence become, as one historian writes, "unattractive to all but a small segment of [Bristol's] merchant community" in the 1780s. When Clarkson traveled on to Liverpool, he investigated a much larger business that was equally oligarchic: in 1787, eight firms financed more than half the trade. The two leading firms were headed by former slaving captains who had struck it rich through privateering during the American war; the next-largest firm was controlled by the third generation of a slaving dynasty. Clarkson then headed for Lancaster, where merchants had engaged in the slave trade since the 1740s. He found that although slavers resided in the town, they all "made their outfits at Liverpool, as a more convenient port." Lancaster's slave trade had been all but knocked out by the dislocations of the war. London's slave trade, like Bristol's, was also much reduced: eleven individuals dispatched just eleven ships to Africa in 1787—less than half the number of vessels engaged in the slave trade from that port a century earlier. In London, Bristol, and Liverpool, the number of vessels employed in slaving versus other trades had also shrunk, further marginalizing the traffic; only one in twenty British ships left Liverpool for Africa in 1787, for example, versus one in ten prior to the war. Thus by 1787 Britain's slave trade concentrated in just three ports, within which a handful of specialists outfitted the majority of vessels.[6]

Parliament's inquiries into abolition, which commenced in February 1788, posed a new threat to Britain's languishing slave trade. British slaving merchants were initially startled that Parliament took up abolition, but they remained confident that their business would be quickly exculpated, as it had been when the Quakers petitioned for the ending of the trade in 1783. Instead, a litany of witnesses, many of them found by Clarkson, exposed the traders in men's vicious business methods to public scrutiny, forcing members of Parliament to act. With the clock ticking down on the Parliamentary session and a vote on immediate abolition sure to fail, William Dolben (1727–1814) moved, in May 1788, to regulate the trade by placing a limit on the number of enslaved people that British merchants could embark on their vessels. Despite vociferous opposition by their lobbyists, Britain's slavers were forced to accept regulations that ships could carry five enslaved people for every three tons, to a limit of 201 tons, and one person for every subsequent ton. Fearing that this regulated trade would continue in perpetuity, abolitionists forced a vote on immediate abolition in the 1790 session, but they were defeated, 163 to 88.[7]

The sudden threat of abolition gave Britain's slave trade a short-term boost. Writing from Jamaica in September 1789, John Tailyour informed his Bristol banker: "Proceedings in Parliament relative to the Slave Trade created a general Alarm in this County," the result of which "[has] been to increase the demand for Slaves and the price has consequently risen." Tailyour urged Bristol merchants to fit out ships with the promise that the "great demand" for captive Africans would keep up. He did not exaggerate: the prices of enslaved people increased across the British Caribbean by on average 10 percent between 1788 and 1789—the years when Parliament debated regulating the trade—and a further 10 percent in 1790—when Parliament voted on outright abolition. Britons rushed to get their ships to sea before parliamentary regulations took force on August 1, 1788, driving up the volume of the business; the trade spiked again in 1790, as Britons tried to get ships out before the vote on immediate abolition. This short-term boom only lasted as long as Parliament threatened to abolish the trade, though, especially as the price of sugar remained low. As Tailyour observed in 1790, "Should the British Parliament proceed to take steps which may tend to an Abolition of the Slave Trade, Negroes will be in great demand & sellers may make their own terms." If, however, "the trade is left on the present footing, our demand will not be so great."[8]

The onset of the Haitian Revolution (1791–1804) on Saint-Domingue eliminated French competition and returned British merchants to preeminence in the slave trade. French colonists initially remained confident that the rebellion, which broke out in August 1791, would swiftly be crushed; French slave ships continued to arrive in the colony throughout 1791 and early 1792. Britons were equally sanguine. Writing from Jamaica in November 1791, Tailyour opined that the "favorable accounts" from Saint-Domingue indicated that "matters will soon be quiet again there." In May 1792, though, it became increasingly obvious that the status quo would not be restored, as the rebellion expanded into an island-wide conflict. Saint-Domingue's collapse into civil war blew apart the largest plantation economy in the Americas. Before the revolt, the island had produced 40 percent of the world's sugar, 60 percent of its coffee, and three times as much cotton as the United States. Two years later, these exports had all but disappeared, leaving a gaping hole in world markets that stoked prices for tropical commodities and the people who were forced to produce them; between 1791 and 1799, the prices of sugar and enslaved people rose, in real terms, by 40 percent. France's slave trade simultaneously went into freefall. In 1790, French ships had disembarked forty-five thousand people on Saint-Domingue—more captives than were transported to all the British Americas combined in that year. Five years later, France's slave trade was gone, causing a rapid collapse in the prices of captives in France's favored African markets, particularly on the Loango Coast.[9]

Britons rushed to fill the vacuum. The sudden disappearance of the French from West-Central Africa sparked what one Liverpool merchant called a "race to Angola" among British merchants, who thought slave prices there would be "beyond all comparison lower than at any other part of the Coast." By 1795, embarkations of captives on the Loango Coast by Britons almost exceeded those from the whole of West Africa combined—a remarkable reorientation given that British ships had carried fewer than one in twenty captives from Angola just four years earlier. In the Americas, British captains principally steered their ships for Jamaica, where colonists sought to seize rising produce prices by expanding their plantations and opening mountain coffee estates. Parliament stoked this slaving boom by voting, in April 1792, to abolish the trade within four years. Although the House of Lords would not debate the bill until the 1793 session, the fear of abolition helped to push the trade higher. Writing six months after the abolition bill had been passed, a Liverpool firm exclaimed: "Every thing in the Shape of a Ship that can be come at is fitting out for Africa, and I suppose the money made by the voyage just now concluded exceeds anything ever known." In 1793 alone, British ships disembarked forty-two thousand Africans in the Americas, making Britons once again by far the most numerous slave traders in the Atlantic world.[10]

The outbreak of war with Revolutionary France in February 1793 presented further opportunities. The war initially began poorly; a 1793 credit crisis, the scouring of the African coast by French privateers in 1794, and stalled British military expeditions in the Caribbean had all substantially knocked back Britain's slave trade by 1795. Yet, the war also halted abolition. The House of Commons voted down the gradual abolition bill in February 1793, fearing abolitionism's connection to radical thought, and would not take up the question again until 1799. The war consequently bought Britain's slave traders time, allowing them to expand their business by shipping captives to Surinam, Demerara, Berbice, and Trinidad—all of which had been seized by the Royal Navy in 1796 and 1797. All four colonies were large and fertile, but they were undeveloped compared to the other British Caribbean colonies. The process of converting all four colonies into plantation economies on the Jamaican model began almost immediately after their seizure, opening new markets to British slave traders; Britons forcibly transported 122,000 people to the seized colonies—one in four of the people disembarked by Britons in the Americas in the decade before abolition. The occupations of Martinique, Guadeloupe, and western Saint-Domingue by the British Army provided temporary access to other American slave markets that British merchants also embraced.[11]

British merchants furthered their dominance by exploiting American colonies that also sought to expand plantation agriculture in response to looming abolition and the dislocations of the Haitian Revolution. In 1791, Cuban colonists had begun transforming their island into a "mirror" of prerevolutionary Saint-Domingue by expanding sugar agriculture and opening the island's ports to foreign slave ships. Britons met Cuban demand by shipping almost forty thousand enslaved people to the island between 1793 and 1807. Abolitionist movements in North America and Denmark likewise provided new opportunities in the trade's twilight years. Following Britain's 1792 gradual abolition vote, the Danish Parliament sought to end the slave trade to its Caribbean colonies within a decade. Danish colonists principally turned to Britons to obtain more than twenty thousand Africans before the trade shut down in 1803. The

U.S. Congress looked, in the same period, to close the slave trade to U.S. ports by 1807, when a twenty-year moratorium on abolition lapsed. Planters in the Deep South sought to expand the nascent cotton kingdom by opening American ports to foreign slavers from 1802; the purchase of the Louisiana Territory in the following year further boosted demand for captives. Before 1808, British ships disembarked twenty thousand people in Charleston, most of whom were marched into the cotton fields. Access to these foreign markets further grew the slave trade: between 1793 and 1808, British vessels landed almost one in five Africans at non-British markets.[12]

Parliamentary regulations further enhanced slave traders' ability to supply these various American markets by reducing mortality on the Middle Passage and further driving up slave prices. Slave traders had fulminated against regulations restricting the number of people who could be embarked on ships because, they argued, their vessels could not hold enough people to turn a profit. Ironically, though, regulations ultimately benefited slave traders because they substantially reduced shipboard mortality: death rates halved, from 10 percent to 5 percent of embarked Africans, following Dolben's Act in 1788. British merchants hence delivered more captives alive to the Americas and sold them for prices that were increased by the threat of abolition. Tougher regulations in 1799, which restricted the number of captives on ships according to a vessel's square footage rather than tonnage, further elevated American slave prices and hence potential profits. As one Liverpool merchant wrote shortly after the passage of the new regulations, "Few Ships will answer [under the new regulations], consequently Slaves must sell higher." Outfitters also sought to maximize the number of enslaved people their ships could carry: in the decade after the 1799 regulations came into force, the size of British slave ships increased by a quarter. Abolitionist efforts to improve shipboard conditions for captive Africans therefore inadvertently improved the efficiency of slave traders' businesses.[13]

When abolition finally came in 1807, it thus ended a British slave trade that in the preceding twenty years had been reenergized by the abolitionist movement and the dislocations of the Haitian and French Revolutions. In 1787, Britain had been overshadowed by France and conducted a trade that was largely confined to its stagnant Caribbean colonies. Twenty years later, Britons monopolized almost every African slaving market north of the Congo River—including those previously dominated by the French. In the Americas, British ships disembarked enslaved people in a plethora of markets, the largest of which were colonies Britain seized in the French Revolutionary Wars or foreign colonies open to Britons. Abolition also imposed regulations that finally succeeded in ending the tight packing of people aboard unsanitary slave ships, substantially reducing mortality on the Middle Passage, mitigating the trade's risks, and boosting profits. Britons would have dominated and further expanded this trade long into the nineteenth century had abolition not interceded.

The tectonic changes wrought by abolition and Atlantic revolutions presented unprecedented business opportunities to traders in men, but opportunities offset by considerable risks. African merchants in marginal markets sought to meet the booming demand for enslaved people by expanding the slave trade from their homes—accelerating the trade's geographical expansion in its twilight years. To bypass French competition in West-Central Africa, British merchants began, in the 1780s, to dispatch their vessels to Ambriz and the Congo River—both locations through which caravans of slaves passed on their way to the Loango Coast. Neither location had been a major slaving port before the 1780s, largely because of inaccessibility: Ambriz's rocky shores prevented all but shallow-drafted vessels from anchoring; and the Congo's huge tidal range and treacherous shoals made it difficult for ships to enter and navigate the river. Despite these risks, Britons were attracted to the ports by the lure of low-priced captives. In 1791, for example, people could be purchased in the Congo River for £17–20 per person—compared to £30 at Bonny and the nearby Loango Coast. For African brokers, selling captives to visiting Britons, even at low prices, allowed an entry to the increasingly lucrative slave trade by undercutting their nearby neighbors. Hence both ports emerged as key slaving markets in the twenty years before abolition: sixty-four thousand people would be taken from Ambriz and especially the Congo in that period. In the same era, Porto Novo and Lagos were likewise transformed into major markets, as coastal merchants sought profits from the growing trade in people.[14]

The geographic expansion of the trade in Africa nonetheless failed to satiate American demand for captives, and so brokers in existing markets substantially increased slave prices. In the first half of the eighteenth century, prices had been flat at around £5 per person in Atlantic Africa, indicating that African slave traders were able to satiate demand through the expansion of slaving infrastructure in the interior. In the twenty years prior to the American Revolutionary War, though, slave prices steadily climbed from an average of £6 per person in 1755 to £15 in 1775. Demand for enslaved laborers hence outpaced enslavers' ability to capture people. The pressure placed on African supply networks further increased after 1775 as the export trade increased in volume: between 1775 and 1791, prices per person climbed to £19; by abolition, they had reached £33—a more than fivefold increase across the century. Africans increased slave prices by demanding larger bundles of goods from Europeans; the prices of goods remained largely static, and so inflation did not erode these gains. Africans further increased their earnings by imposing higher port dues and sales taxes on visiting whites. When slave prices were low prior to 1775, these collective fees were small. At Calabar, for example, Britons could purchase people after paying just 819 copper rods in port dues (comey) in 1720. By 1769, though, comey had exploded to 12,500 rods; in 1785, taxes doubled again to 25,000 rods. Gifts (dashes) and taxes on the sales of individual slaves also increased. Unlike with goods used to buy captives, which were mostly passed to slave sellers up-country, coastal brokers retained taxes, boosting their earnings. Imports therefore poured into Africa in immense quantities as Britain's slave trade drew to a close.[15]

The sheer magnitude of this influx of goods is best illustrated by focusing on Bonny—the largest slaving port before abolition. Like merchants elsewhere on the African coast, the Ibani demanded increasingly high prices for captives over the century: from thirteen bars per person in 1700; to thirty-two bars at mid-century; and eighty-five bars by abolition. Accordingly, captives were purchased with sizeable bundles of goods by century's end: in 1759, people had been obtained with just fifteen items; by 1792, people were purchased with as many as seventy-five goods. The Ibani gained further by increasing taxes. In 1759, a British captain paid 1,117 bars' worth of goods in dashes and taxes when he traded at Bonny, in addition to numerous smaller gifts of alcohol, clothing, and firearms to key brokers—fees that amounted to just four bars per person purchased. By 1792, captains gave much more lavish gifts to the king and principal traders and paid fees of forty-five bars per slave, which collectively amounted to seventeen thousand bars. Half a million imports hence flowed annually into Bonny during the twenty years before abolition.[16]

Ibani merchants enriched themselves with these imports. Hugh Crow, a slave ship captain who bought people at Bonny between 1793 and 1807, observed that the "poorer classes" in Bonny lived in mean dwellings and possessed no imports. The "better off"—merchants engaged in the slave trade—lived in "larger, detached, and more numerous" houses "furnished in a superior manner" with "homely articles introduced from Europe." Unlike commoners, who wore a single piece of cloth tied at their waist, slaving merchants wore "shirts and trowsers" and "gold-laced hats," which they had received as gifts from Britons. Ibani traders "secreted" more durable items such as metals under the floorboards of their houses and stored thousands of gunpowder kegs in the thatched eaves, with sometimes disastrous results. The most affluent traders also kept stacks of imported textiles in warehouses "at some distance from the town." Wealth flowing from the slave trade was therefore visible everywhere one looked in Bonny.[17]

In addition to transforming Bonny's society and its built environment, access to imports enabled ambitious Ibani men—many of them formerly enslaved—to open their own trading houses and enter the slave trade. The Ibani, like other African societies, purchased enslaved boys from the interior to employ them within their merchant houses. Apprentices first worked as servants and messengers, allowing them to observe trading transactions and learn English by interacting with white visitors. Boys who showed promise were next charged with superintending the delivery of enslaved people to the ships, where the novice would be paid dashes by captains. Over time, the apprentice could use this accumulating capital to buy small numbers of people at the Aro riverside markets and profitably sell them to ship captains. Once his own business grew sufficiently large, the former apprentice would form his own canoe house under the aegis of his former master. New trading houses were founded throughout the eighteenth century as Bonny's slave trade grew, but they proliferated at century's end as slave prices exploded: King Pepple II (d. 1792), who possessed the largest house at Bonny at mid-century, spawned no fewer than "five major and two minor subordinate houses" before his death in 1792. King Opubo (d. 1830), who succeeded his brother Pepple II to the throne, birthed six satellite canoe houses that formed the backbone of the booming trade in people and—post abolition—the palm oil trade. Increased slave prices driven by abolition and Atlantic revolutions thus accelerated the transformations wrought by the slave trade in African societies and polities.[18]

As with their African counterparts, American slave traders' potential profits soared in the closing years of Britain's slave trade because they earned commissions on the rising value of enslaved people. Before the American Revolutionary War, factors' earnings from the sale of a human cargo ranged between £500 and £1,000, depending on the size of the ship. These sums steadily increased after 1783 as slave prices climbed: by 1792, factors earned a third more from each sale, on average; a decade later their returns had increased by another third. Factors themselves helped to raise slave prices— and hence their own commissions—by pointedly reminding slave buyers that the trade might soon end. Slave buyers responded by rushing to buy people: scramble sales were particularly common in 1789, 1792, 1793, and 1807—all moments when planters feared that Parliament would imminently halt the trade. Factors' gains from selling people quickly and at high prices were offset, however, by the lengthening of credits issued to colonists, which spiked to more than a year, and in some cases three years, between 1784 and 1807. Longer credit increased the already substantial risks of Guinea factoring because economic downturns or wars—frequent occurrences in the Age of Revolutions—might prevent planters from honoring their debts, leaving the factor at risk of default and bankruptcy.[19]

The meteoric rise of Jamaican factor Alexandre Lindo (1742– 1812) illustrates the immense fortunes that Guinea factors could make in the trade's risky, but lucrative, twilight years. Lindo, a Sephardic émigré from France to Jamaica in 1765, entered slave factoring after first working "in Kingston as a retailer, dealing in every sort of commodity that could be bought cheap." Lindo used the capital and contacts he developed through his retail business to sell, between 1782 and 1805, at least forty-two thousand Africans into slavery; he also purchased people at other factors' sales and shipped them off to the Spanish islands. Lindo's intense engagement in the slave trade was enabled by abolition and revolution: in 1792 he part-nered with Richard Lake (1751–1820), a Liverpool merchant who arrived in Kingston with consignments of ships from some of his town's largest slavers. Lindo and Lake joined forces just as Parlia-ment voted to abolish the slave trade and Saint-Domingue collapsed into civil war, boosting Jamaican demand and slave prices—and hence their firm's earnings. Lindo invested his slaving fortune in a portfolio of plantations, town houses, ships, and furniture in Jamaica and London. By 1802, he was so spectacularly wealthy that he lent the French Army £500,000 to finance a near-genocidal attempt to reconquer Saint-Domingue. After the failure of that campaign, the French state refused to honor Lindo's loans, destroying much of his fortune. Even so, Lindo's rise from Kingston retailer to perhaps the largest British American slave trader in history within twenty years demonstrates the opportunities for advancement that were available via the American slave trade before abolition.[20]

The continued expansion of Britain's slave trade—both its vol-ume and its geography—during the Age of Revolutions enabled newcomers such as Lindo to enter the slave trade. In Jamaica, for example, the number of factoring firms increased as the slave trade grew: in 1789, just eleven firms were in operation; by 1793, the peak year of Jamaica's slave trade, twenty-three companies sold people. New firms entered the business by partnering with British merchant houses that were themselves either newcomers or established firms expanding their operations to seize opportunities presented by abo-lition and warfare. Lindo, for example, principally obtained business from Liverpool and London firms that had entered the slave trade after the American Revolutionary War. John Tailyour, who oper-ated alongside Lindo, first began slave trading in 1785 by drawing ships from four houses in London and Bristol—all of them recent entrants to the trade. Tailyour expanded his business in the 1790s by partnering with Liverpool firms that were dispatching extra vessels to access the trade's growing profits. He was able to retire from slave trading in 1795, just thirteen years after he had entered the business, with almost £100,000—a fortune earned through the sale of seventeen thousand people. The opening of new American markets simultaneously presented additional opportunities for merchants to enter Guinea factoring. Shortly after Britain conquered the Dutch Guianas and Trinidad, for example, British merchants sailed into the colonies and established slave factoring firms; twenty firms operated in Demerara alone between 1803 and 1808, all of them staffed by British émigrés.[21]

The road to riches for factors was by no means guaranteed, though, because the same wars, slave rebellions, and economic crises that drove up demand for captive Africans also created uncertainty that could rapidly plunge slave factors into ruin. The Atlantic-wide credit crisis that accompanied the onset of the French Revolutionary Wars in 1793 was particularly disastrous. The largest failures occurred in the militarily vulnerable eastern Caribbean islands, where factors had expanded their businesses prior to 1793 in a bid to access lucrative French markets via the intra-American slave trade. A slave rebellion in Grenada in February 1795 then swept away the island's two largest firms. The eastern Caribbean islands—the backbone of Britain's slave trade prior to 1793—never recovered and became insignificant markets until abolition. An economic downturn at the turn of the nineteenth century likewise affected American slave traders. By 1800, sugar production had increased so rapidly in the British Caribbean that prices plummeted, making it difficult for planters to pay debts incurred for the purchase of people at high prices. Guinea factors' businesses consequently suffered. In 1804, Kingston slave factor David Dick (1769–1833) wrote bitterly that factoring had become much less profitable and that several firms that had "made their fortune[s]" in the early 1790s were now on the verge of failure. One merchant had recently died with a "broke[n] heart," continued Dick, and worth "£50,000 worse than nothing." Another merchant saw his business fall into a "deranged state"; in 1807, Liverpool merchants were still hounding him for the returns he owed from slave sales conducted in 1800. While some, like Tailyour and Lindo, made their fortunes in the high-stakes business of Guinea factoring during the Age of Revolutions, others were ruined.[22]

The potential rewards for British merchants who forcibly trans-ported enslaved people from African merchants to Guinea factors also increased in the Age of Revolutions. Before 1775, an average-size slave ship, which imprisoned three hundred people, cost approx-imately £5,000–£7,000 to outfit. Merchants typically held sixteenth, eighth, or quarter shares in such ships, and so they risked only be-tween £300 and £1,750 on each voyage; smaller ventures absorbed even smaller sums. Profits were correspondingly small. For example, Liverpool merchant William Davenport's returns on investments in 109 slaving voyages ranged from a gain of £1,457 to a loss of £1,039 but averaged a profit of just £130. By thus spreading his investment, Davenport successfully hedged against the trade's risks over a thirty-year career, earning him £34,000 by his death in 1788—one of the largest slaving estates of the era. After the American Revolution-ary War, though, rising slave prices, expanding outfitting expenses, and parliamentary regulations combined to substantially increase the costs of investments: in 1785, the cost of a slave ship carrying three hundred people had risen to approximately £8,000; after 1795, it grew to more than £10,000 and sometimes as high as £24,000. These increasing costs could have been absorbed by bringing in additional partners and hence capital. But moral opprobrium, cou-pled with slaving's notorious risks, dissuaded investors and further concentrated the business in the hands of a small number of houses before abolition. The 1793 credit crisis knocked Bristol out of the trade, leaving London and especially Liverpool merchant houses as-cendant until abolition. Within Liverpool, the number of partners within firms also fell: before the American war, four individuals had invested in each voyage, on average; by the mid-1790s, three indi-viduals held shares; and by the eve of abolition, just two.[23]

The highly capitalized firms who controlled Britain's slave trade in its twilight years stood to make substantial sums through their deadly business. Take, for example, Thomas Leyland (1752–1827), a Liverpool merchant who began slaving in 1783, just as Davenport began to withdraw from the business. Born in a Lancashire village, Leyland apprenticed in Liverpool within the low-risk, low-reward trade to Ireland. In 1776, he won £10,000 in the lottery, a portion of which he sank into one-eighth and one-quarter shares in slave ships as the American Revolutionary War drew to a close. Leyland remained a minor investor in the slave trade throughout the 1780s, as he cautiously awaited the outcome of the abolitionist debates. With slave prices surging as a result of abolition and the Haitian Revolution, Leyland decided to plunge into slaving: between 1789 and 1807, he shipped 21,058 Africans on sixty-five voyages. He held either half, two-thirds, or whole shares in these vessels, and so his investment amounted to approximately £300,000—three times Davenport's outlay over a longer career. Leyland reaped rewards from slaving that far outstripped Davenport's: for fifteen voyages for which accounts survive, his gross profits were £55,657. Even after deducting presumably substantial insurance costs, Leyland must have made far more from those fifteen voyages alone than Davenport earned from 109 ventures; Leyland's earnings from his fifty-seven other ventures likely further boosted his profits. Leyland cannily reinvested his slaving profits in banking, and when he died twenty years after abolition, his estate amounted to £600,000—by far the largest sum left by any British slave-trading merchant over the trade's long history.[24]

The rewards that magnates such as Leyland stood to earn through slaving were offset by increased risks in the era of abolition. No one better epitomizes the rapidity with which the slave trade could make and break British merchants than John Dawson (1738?–1812), the son of a farmer who became the world's largest slave trader on the eve of the French Revolutionary Wars. Dawson left his family farm in rural Cumberland at a young age and by 1768 was helming Liverpool slave ships. During the American Revolutionary War he captained a privateer and captured *Carnatic*, a French East Indiaman valued at £150,000 pounds. Dawson used his share of the booty to establish a merchant house in partnership with his father-in-law, shipbuilder Peter Baker (1731–1796). In 1784, the Spanish Crown granted Baker and Dawson the asiento, and the firm was soon transporting almost three thousand people a year to the Spanish Americas. The loss of the asiento in 1789 did little to slow Dawson's meteoric rise: a year later he further increased his business by directing captives to Alexandre Lindo in Kingston, and his company was capitalized at £157,000. Within three years, though, Dawson's empire lay in ruins as a result of the chaos sparked by the

French Revolutionary Wars. The tightening of transatlantic credit lines after the onset of war caught Dawson out, and within a year he was ordering his captains to seek cash from American slave sales to maintain liquidity. He avoided complete ruin but by 1797 had been forced to abandon slaving and flee to Demerara and Trinidad. He died in 1812, shortly after returning to Liverpool, and left little to his twelve children.[25]

On March 6, 1837, thousands of people lined the streets of Liverpool to pay their final respects to John Bolton (1756–1837), who had died after a long mercantile career. Bolton's hearse passed for two miles through "a continuous stream of human beings" dressed in mourning, before departing the town for the several-day journey north to Storrs Hall, a magnificent country retreat where he had entertained the leading poets, politicians, and aristocrats of the day. Bolton had come far since he first left rural Lancashire as an ambitious teenager in the 1770s. The son of an apothecary, he was apprenticed to a Liverpool West India house after attending a grammar school where he "had not received much education." Aged seventeen, he stepped off one of his employer's ships in Saint Vincent with a sack of potatoes on his back and a cheese under his arm, which he soon sold to turn his first Caribbean profit. Bolton amplified his meager wealth after taking over his deceased employer's merchant office and returned to Liverpool in 1783 with £10,000. Bolton used his West Indian fortune to establish himself as a Liverpool merchant house, and in 1788 he began to take small shares in slave ships. With abolition looming, and Saint-Domingue in flames, Bolton saw an opportunity to increase his wealth: between 1792 and 1807, he outfitted sixty-five vessels—most of them as the sole investor—that took 21,213 people from Africa, especially from Bonny and markets in Angola that had opened with the departure of the French. Bolton sold his victims for high prices in myriad American markets; recently conquered Demerara was particularly key, as he sold almost ten thousand people for cotton—a product that he would trade in Liverpool, helping to steer the town into its second Golden Age in the nineteenth century. By the late 1790s, he was reaping profits of £40,000 a year from his slaving empire, which he ploughed into property, philanthropy, and politics. Like many traders in men before him, Bolton "worked his own way up from poverty to riches" through the enslavement of thousands of Africans.[26]

Bolton died thirty years after abolition and left £180,000 to his wife, by which point the bloody stains on his wealth had been erased. None of his obituaries mentioned the dark source of his family's prosperity; they instead gushed about Bolton's virtue and generosity. The *Gentleman's Magazine* lamented the loss of one of Liverpool's "most honourable merchants and bountiful benefactors" whom "the poor blessed, and whose memory will long be cherished." Another report described Bolton as "universally beloved and respected" for his charity and asked whether Liverpool would ever "see his like again." He was not alone in having his slaving past forgotten. Leyland died ten years before Bolton and was remembered as an "eminent banker, who, from small beginnings, worked his way, by energy, industry, and perseverance, to the possession of immense wealth." That the "energy, industry, and perseverance" of men like Leyland had been directed to slave trading was ignored. Former enslavers instead became "merchants" whose fortunes derived from a vaguely defined world of trade that did not feature enslavement. American factors likewise retired from slaving after abolition without a mark against their names, as they restyled themselves as West Indian merchants who had traded in sugar, coffee, and cotton. The Hibbert family, for example, moved out of the slave trade into the refined world of country living during the nineteenth century; like Bolton, the family furthered its reputation through philanthropy.[27]

The sins of the fathers forgotten, the descendants of slave traders were able to use their inherited wealth to enter polite society. Whereas most British slaving merchants had humble roots, their descendants began life with a leg up on the social ladder. Many moved quickly into manufacturing or mercantile careers, helping to create multigenerational trading dynasties whose foundations in enslavement were buried beneath abolition. The most fortunate attended Oxford or Cambridge before becoming clergymen, army officers, or lawyers; others joined the landed aristocracy, either via their inheritances or through marriage. Bolton's wealth, including Storrs Hall, passed to his nephew, the Reverend Thomas Staniforth (1807–1887)—himself the scion of a Liverpool slaving family—who resided at the estate until his death. As late as 1941, historians still assumed that Storrs, and Bolton, had no connection to the slave trade. The descendants of American factors likewise established mercantile dynasties shorn of their underlying links to slaving. After Alexandre Lindo's death in 1812, his family reinvested what remained of his fortune in enslaved people and then in colonial investments around the Caribbean. By the early twentieth century, the Lindos were once again one of the richest families in the West Indies, with a trading empire that encompassed banana groves, sugar plantations, rum distilleries, and, by the late twentieth century, a major record label that popularized reggae music around the world. The Lindos are principally remembered today as savvy merchants, not slavers.[28]

Many African traders were, like their British and American counterparts, initially able to use their slaving wealth to transition into the post-abolition economy. After a "crisis of adaptation," brokers in the Bight of Biafra struck on palm oil as a lucrative alternative export to selling people. The Ibani and Efik traders were consequently able to further enrich themselves through overseas trade in the early nineteenth century. Other groups fared less well. The Fante were conquered by the Asante empire in 1806 and, a year later, lost the British as partners in the slave trade; Fante merchants would never regain the power that they had commanded before 1807. Some Africans still engaged in the now illegal slave trade, especially in the myriad ports that enterprising British merchants had opened to the slave trade, given that those locations tended to be in creeks and rivers difficult to access and atop cliffs. Many Africans thus fell foul of their erstwhile British partners, who sought to stamp out the slave trade through increasingly aggressive means that included the painting of African merchants who engaged in the slave trade as "uncivilized" people.[29]

Regardless of how the traders in men fared after abolition, their enslaved victims suffered much worse fates. Africans shipped to the British Caribbean continued to toil in bondage until 1838, when they were freed without compensation, while their owners—some of them former slave traders—received reimbursement for the loss of their captive workers; Bolton gained £27,836 after Parliament freed 642 people whom he had enslaved in Saint Vincent and Demerara. After emancipation, former slaves in the British Caribbean tried to scratch new livings as small-holding peasants and wage laborers in colonies still controlled by a small white ruling class. The Africans whom Britons shipped to foreign colonies before the trade shut down suffered in slavery for even longer. Few of the Africans who were marched into the cotton fields of the Deep South would have lived to see emancipation in 1865; none of the people that Britons took to Cuba would see the end of slavery, which did not come until 1886. The stark inequalities between the descendants of enslaved people and their enslavers were taken to be an unfortunate fact for much of the nineteenth and twentieth centuries. The 2020 killing of George Floyd, however, has brought new attention to the injustices that ripple from the history recounted in this book. Two weeks after Floyd's killing, activists in Bristol cast a statue of slaving merchant Edward Colston into the harbor, sparking a raging national debate about Britain's historic connections to the slave trade. Scholars and activists are now unearthing the trade's insidious legacies in financial institutions, manufacturing, insurance, banking, and country houses; Bolton's Storrs Hall has been marked for its association with the trade. While traders in men may have gone to their graves "universally beloved and respected" at the time, their memories are now cursed.[30]

Appendixes

Appendix A. Letters of instruction for British slave ships, 1700–1808

ID in SV	Date	Ship name	British departure	African embarkation	American disembarkation	Source
15124	Aug. 16, 1700	*Blessing*	Liverpool	West-Central Africa	Barbados	Norris Papers, 930 NOR 2/179, LRO
21220	Oct. 22, 1700	*Africa Galley*	London	Bight of Biafra	Virginia	*DIHST*, vol. 4, 72–77
94849	Dec. 18, 1716	*Two Brothers*	Liverpool	Unknown	Antigua	Wadsworth and Mann, *Cotton Trade*, 230
76398	July 15, 1721	*Henry*	London	Gold Coast	Jamaica	Morice Papers, M7/6, Bank of England
76399	Oct. 20, 1722	*Henry*	London	Bight of Benin	N/A: wrecked	Morice Papers, M7/9, Bank of England
76435	Oct. 30, 1722	*Sarah*	London	Gold Coast	N/A: wrecked	Morice Papers, M7/8, Bank of England
76420	May 11, 1724	*Portugal Galley*	London	Bight of Benin	Vera Cruz	Morice Papers, M7/10, Bank of England
16405	Oct. 7, 1725	*Dispatch*	Bristol	Bight of Biafra	Virginia	*The Hobhouse Papers, 1722–1755* (East Ardsley: Micro Methods, 1971)
76559	July 8, 1728	*Judith*	London	Gold Coast	Jamaica	*DIHST*, vol. 2, 366–71
17108	Aug. 13, 1743	*Jason Galley*	Bristol	West-Central Africa	South Carolina	Private Collection; copies at Wilberforce Institute Library, Hull
17170	Mar. 1747	*Bristol Merchant*	Bristol	Bight of Biafra	Jamaica	Morgan, ed., *Bright-Meyler*, 193–96
90178	Apr. 1, 1748	*Chesterfield*	Liverpool	West-Central Africa	Jamaica	Letter and Bill Book 1747–1761, PDAV
90218	June 20, 1748	*St. George*	Liverpool	Bight of Biafra	Jamaica	Letter and Bill Book 1747–1761, PDAV
17296	Jan. 4, 1751	*Molly*	Bristol	Bight of Biafra	Jamaica	Morgan, ed., *Bright-Meyler*, 230–32

90180	May 22, 1751	*Chesterfield*	Liverpool	Bight of Biafra	Barbados	The Earle Collection, D/EARLE/1/1, MMM
17323	Aug. 20, 1752	*Molly*	Bristol	West-Central Africa	Saint Kitts	Accounts of the Molly Snow, SMV/7/2/1/25, Bristol Archives
90478	July 26, 1753	*Charming Nancy*	Liverpool	Senegambia	Barbados	Letter and Bill Book 1747–1761, PDAV
90552	Aug. 20, 1754	*James*	Liverpool	Senegambia	Montserrat	Letter and Bill Book 1747–1761, PDAV
90510	Jan. 24, 1755	*Grampus*	Liverpool	Senegambia	Barbados	Letter and Bill Book 1747–1761, PDAV
90478	Aug. 20, 1755	*Charming Nancy*	Liverpool	Senegambia	Nevis	Letter and Bill Book 1747–1761, PDAV
90641	July 30, 1756	*Charming Nancy*	Liverpool	Senegambia	Tortola	Letter and Bill Book 1747–1761, PDAV
90591	June 8, 1757	*Young Foster*	Liverpool	Windward Coast	Kingston	Liverpool Library
17470	Mar. 5, 1759	*Swift*	Bristol	Bight of Biafra	Antigua	39654(2), Bristol Archives
90858	Feb. 7, 1761	*Tyrrell*	Liverpool	Bight of Biafra	Saint Kitts	Voyages of the Ship "Tyrell," PDAV
90874	Oct. 30, 1761	*Eadith*	Liverpool	Senegambia	Saint Croix	The Eadith Brigt 1760, MMM
90829	Apr. 14, 1762	*Marquis of Grandby*	Liverpool	Bight of Biafra	French Caribbean	Williams, *Liverpool Privateers*, 486–88
91112	Aug. 7, 1764	*Apollo*	Liverpool	Gold Coast	South Carolina	MS11532, Manx National Heritage Library and Archive, Douglas
91000	Apr. 21, 1765	*Cerberus*	Liverpool	Gold Coast	Jamaica	MS11533, Manx National Heritage Library and Archive, Douglas
91081	Sept. 14, 1765	*Henry*	Liverpool	Bight of Biafra	Grenada	Voyages of the Ship "Henry" 1765–1767, PDAV

(continued)

Appendix A. (continued)

ID in SV	Date	Ship name	British departure	African embarkation	American disembarkation	Source
90908	Mar. 6, 1767	*Ranger*	Liverpool	West-Central Africa	Jamaica	Papers relating to the Ship Ranger (1767) 380 TUO/4/2, LRO
91082	July 13, 1767	*Henry*	Liverpool	Bight of Biafra	Grenada	Voyages of the Ship "Henry" 1765–1767, PDAV
91408	Oct. 11, 1767	*King of Prussia*	Liverpool	Bight of Biafra	Grenada	Voyages of the Ship "King of Prussia" 1767–1779, PDAV
91328	July 9, 1768	*Sally*	Liverpool	Windward Coast	Grenada	Papers relating to the Ship Sally (1768) 380 TUO/4/3, LRO
91696	Aug. 3, 1770	*Shark*	Liverpool	Windward Coast	Dominica	Williams, *Liverpool Privateers*, 550
17753	Sept. 1770	*Hector*	Bristol	West-Central Africa	South Carolina	Account Book of slave ship HECTOR (1756) for three voyages, AML/Y/1, NMM
91642	Jan. 19, 1771	*Corsican Hero*	Liverpool	Gold Coast	British Caribbean	Papers relating to the Ships Corsican Hero and Tom (1771), 380 TUO/4/4, LRO
17780	Oct. 30, 1771	*Hector*	Bristol	West-Central Africa	South Carolina	Account Book of slave ship HECTOR (1756) for three voyages, AML/Y/1, NMM
17836	June 26, 1773	*Hector*	Bristol	West-Central Africa	South Carolina	Account Book of slave ship HECTOR (1756) for three voyages, AML/Y/1, NMM

ID	Date	Ship	Port	Region	Destination	Source
92551	Apr. 5, 1774	*Nancy*	Bristol	West–Central Africa	Antigua	Papers relating to Brig Nancy (1774), 380 TUO/4/7, LRO
17846	Oct. 13, 1774	*Africa*	Bristol	Bight of Biafra	Saint Kitts	Accounts of the Snow *Africa*, G2404, Bristol Archives
17886	Aug 1, 1776	*Africa*	Bristol	N/A: wrecked	N/A: wrecked	Accounts of the Snow *Africa*, G2404, Bristol Archives
92728	Sept. 17, 1777	*Swift*	Liverpool	Bight of Biafra	Jamaica	Copy of Letters Commencg Feby 1779, D/DAV/1, MMM
92462	June 1, 1779	*Hawke*	Liverpool	Bight of Biafra	Jamaica	Copy of Letters Commencg Feby 1779, D/DAV/1, MMM
81753	Oct. 25, 1780	*Hawke*	Liverpool	Bight of Biafra	Saint Lucia	Copy of Letters Commencg Feby 1779, D/DAV/1, MMM
80578	July 25, 1782	*Blaydes*	Liverpool	Gold Coast	Jamaica	Papers relating to the Ship Blayds (1782), 380, TUO/4/9, LRO
81731	Sept. 10, 1782	*Harlequin*	Liverpool	Gold Coast	Jamaica	Stanley Dumbell Papers, GB141 MS.10.46, University of Liverpool Library
82415	Jan. 4, 1783	*Madam Pookatta*	Liverpool	West–Central Africa	Tortola	Stanley Dumbell Papers, GB141 MS.10.47, University of Liverpool Library
81344	July 14, 1783	*Experiment*	Liverpool	West–Central Africa	Dominica	Fraser & Ors v Baker & Dawson, E219/380, TNAUK
81906	Dec. 8, 1783	*Ingram*	Liverpool	Bight of Benin	Antigua	Papers relating to the Ship Ingram (1783/4), 380 TUO/4/10, LRO

(continued)

Appendix A. (continued)

ID in SV	Date	Ship name	British departure	African embarkation	American disembarkation	Source
81548	Jan. 24, 1784	*Garland*	London	West-Central Africa	Cuba	Fraser & Ors v Baker & Dawson, E219/380, TNAUK
81818	Mar. 1, 1784	*Hero*	Liverpool	West-Central Africa	Spanish Caribbean	Fraser & Ors v Baker & Dawson, E219/380, TNAUK
83677	Aug. 13, 1784	*Swift*	Liverpool	N/A: wrecked	N/A: wrecked	Fraser & Ors v Baker & Dawson, E219/380, TNAUK
83732	Oct. 19, 1784	*Telemachus*	Liverpool	West-Central Africa	Trinidad	Fraser & Ors v Baker & Dawson, E219/380, TNAUK
82805	Jan. 22, 1785	*Mosley Hill*	Liverpool	Bight of Biafra	Trinidad	Fraser & Ors v Baker & Dawson, E219/380, TNAUK
80797	Feb. 6, 1785	*Champion*	Liverpool	Bight of Biafra	Trinidad	Fraser & Ors v Baker & Dawson, E219/380, TNAUK
81728	Mar. 31, 1786	*Harlequin*	Liverpool	Windward Coast	Antigua	LRB, vol. 1
83562	Oct. 12, 1786	*Sisters*	Liverpool	Bight of Biafra	N/A: wrecked	Fraser & Ors v Baker & Dawson, E219/380, TNAUK
82003	July 2, 1787	*Jenny*	Liverpool	Sierra Leone	Antigua	LRB, vol. 1
82173	June 19, 1788	*Kite*	Liverpool	N/A: abandoned	N/A: abandoned	LRB, vol. 1

81712	June 30, 1789	*Hannah*	Liverpool	Bight of Biafra	Grenada	Thomas Leyland Company account books, 1789–1790, 1792–1793, WCL
80501	Jan. 19, 1790	*Bess*	Liverpool	Senegambia	Dominica	LRB, vol. 2
82004	Nov. 16, 1790	*Jemmy*	Liverpool	Sierra Leone	Jamaica	LRB, vol. 2
80834	June 14, 1791	*Christopher*	Liverpool	West–Central Africa	Dominica	Christopher ship papers, 1791–1792, Duke University Library
81876	Sept. 25, 1791	*Hope*	Lancaster	Bight of Biafra	Jamaica	Accounts and papers concerning the Slave Trade, Lancaster Library, No 2352
82016	Nov. 24, 1792	*Jenny*	Liverpool	West–Central Africa	Jamaica	Thomas Leyland Company account books, 1789–1790, 1792–1793, WCL
81295	Mar. 24, 1794	*Enterprize*	Liverpool	West–Central Africa	Jamaica	Ship Enterprize 3rd Voyage 1794, DX/1732, MMM
83591	June 1795	*Spitfire*	Liverpool	West–Central Africa	Barbados	Stanley Dumbell Papers, GB141 MS.10.49, ULL
81112	Apr 5, 1797	*Earl of Liverpool*	Liverpool	Bight of Biafra	Jamaica	Stanley Dumbell Papers, GB141 MS.10.50, ULL
81113	June 7, 1798	*Earl of Liverpool*	Liverpool	Bight of Biafra	Jamaica	Stanley Dumbell Papers, GB141 MS.10.50, ULL
82379	July 2, 1798	*Lottery*	Liverpool	Bight of Biafra	Jamaica	Thomas Leyland & Co. Account Book of the Ship Lottery (1798–1799), 387 MD 41, LRO
81114	May 31, 1799	*Earl of Liverpool*	Liverpool	West–Central Africa	Jamaica	Stanley Dumbell Papers, GB141 MS.10.50, ULL

(continued)

Appendix A. (continued)

ID in SV	Date	Ship name	British departure	African embarkation	American disembarkation	Source
82382	May 21, 1802	Lottery	Liverpool	Bight of Biafra	Jamaica	Thomas Leyland & Co. Account Book of the Ship Lottery (1802–1811), LRO, 387 MD 42
80455	Mar. 12, 1803	Bedford	London	West-Central Africa	Jamaica	UNKNOWN CAUSE, Thomas Lumley of London, C114/158, TNAUK
81303	July 18, 1803	Enterprize	Liverpool	Bight of Biafra	Jamaica	Thomas Leyland & Co. Account Book of the Ship Enterprize (1803–1804), 387 MD 43, LRO
80456	Aug. 31, 1804	Bedford	London	West-Central Africa	Jamaica	UNKNOWN CAUSE, Thomas Lumley of London, C114/158, TNAUK
81497	Apr. 23, 1805	Fortune	Liverpool	West-Central Africa	Bahamas	Thomas Leyland & Co. Account Book of the Ship Fortune (1805–1807), 387 MD 44, LRO
80457	July 1, 1806	Bedford	London	Gold Coast	Jamaica	UNKNOWN CAUSE, Thomas Lumley of London, C114/158, TNAUK
81305	Sept. 25, 1806	Enterprize	Liverpool	Bight of Biafra	Jamaica	Stanley Dumbell Papers, GB141 MS.10.52, ULL
81512	Dec. 30, 1806	Frederick	London	Bight of Benin	Jamaica	UNKNOWN CAUSE, Thomas Lumley of London, C114/157, TNAUK

Appendix B. Accountbooks recording purchases of enslaved people on the African Coast, 1700–1808

ID in SV	Year/s of voyage	Ship name	British departure	African embarkation	American disembarkation	Source
76398	1721–1722	Henry	London	Gold Coast	Jamaica	Morice Papers, M7/6, Bank of England, London
76399	1722	Henry	London	Whydah, Bight of Benin	Jamaica	Morice Papers, M7/9, Bank of England, London
27329	1722	Sarah	London	Anomabu, Gold Coast	British Caribbean	Morice Papers, M7/9, Bank of England, London
76420	1724–1725	Portugal	London	Bight of Benin	Veracruz	Morice Papers, M7/10, Bank of England, London
77039	1733–1734	Argyle	London	Cabinda, West-Central Africa	Jamaica	HALL V HALLETT (1758), C111/95, TNAUK
17441	1758–1759	Molly	Bristol	Bonny, Bight of Biafra	Virginia	An account book of the slave ship MOLLY at Bonny Island, AML/Y/2, NMM
?	1764–1765	[Africa?]	[Liverpool?]	Benin, Bight of Benin	?	Wilberforce House Museum, Hull
91545	1769–1770	Dobson	Liverpool	Old Calabar, Bight of Biafra	Barbados	Christopher Hassel Papers, Dalemain House, Cumbria
82431	1785–1786	Manlova Grove	Liverpool	Cape Lopez, Mayumba, and Loango, West-Central Africa	Dominica	Add Mss.43841, BL
17996	1787–1789	James	Bristol	Windward Coast	Jamaica	APHLRO, 1790.8

(continued)

Appendix B. (continued)

ID in SV	Year of voyage	Ship name	British departure	African embarkation	American disembarkation	Source
80999	1788–1789	*Diana*	Liverpool	Anomabu and Cape Coast Castle, Gold Coast	Jamaica	*APHLRO*, 1790.8
18124	1791–1792	*Trelawny*	Bristol	Bonny, Bight of Biafra	Jamaica	[Account book of the ship Trelawny], [1791/2], JRP, C107/15, TNAUK
81510	1791–1792	*Francis and Harriot*	London	Anomabu and Cape Coast Castle, Gold Coast	Grenada	"The Journal of an African Slaver, 1789–1792, with an Introductory Note by George A. Plimpton," *Proceedings of the American Antiquarian Society* 39 (1929): 379-465
18146	1792–1793	*Jupiter*	Bristol	Bonny, Bight of Biafra	Jamaica	"Ship Jupiter Old Wages Book," [1793], JRP, C107/59, TNAUK

Appendix C. Logbooks of British slave ships, 1700–1807

ID	Year/s	Ship name	British departure	African embarkation	American disembarkation	Source
9744	1705–1706	*Regard*	London	Gold Coast	Antigua	T70/1218, TNAUK
76720	1730–1731	*Laurence Frigate*	London	West-Central Africa	Montevideo	Log of a voyage of the Lawrance, MssCol 1699, New York Public Library
90350	1750–1751	*Duke of Argyll*	Liverpool	Windward Coast	Antigua	DUKE OF ARGYLE and AFRICAN slave ships. Journal kept by John Newton, LOG/M/46, NMM
90418	1752–1753	*African*	Liverpool	Windward Coast	Saint Kitts	DUKE OF ARGYLE and AFRICAN slave ships. Journal kept by John Newton, LOG/M/46, NMM
90419	1753–1754	*African*	Liverpool	Windward Coast	Saint Kitts	DUKE OF ARGYLE and AFRICAN slave ships. Journal kept by John Newton, LOG/M/46, NMM
17522	1762–1763	*Black Prince*	Bristol	Gold Coast	Antigua	Log & Journal of the Black Prince 1762–1764, 45933/4, Bristol Central Library
90721	1762–1763	*Blakeney*	Liverpool	Windward Coast	Saint Kitts	HCA15/55, TNAUK
17573	1764	*Black Prince*	Bristol	Gold Coast	Antigua	Log & Journal of the Black Prince 1762–1764, 45933/4, Bristol Central Library
91567	1769–1770	*Unity*	Liverpool	Bight of Benin	Jamaica	The Earle Collection, D/EARLE/1/4, MMM
91662	1770–1771	*Glory*	Liverpool	Bight of Benin	Dominica	HCA16/59/18, TNAUK
78123	1773	*Maria*	London	Senegambia	Jamaica	HCA30/714, TNAUK
17889	1776–1777	*Britannia*	Bristol	Bonny	Jamaica	Harlan Crow Library, Dallas, TX
80917	1783–1784	*Compt du Norde*	London	Malembo	South Carolina	Ship's logs of HMS Agamemnon, Count du Nord and Mampookata (vol. 1: 1782–1785), 387 MD 62/1, LRO

(continued)

Appendix C. (continued)

ID	Year/s	Ship name	British departure	African embarkation	American disembarkation	Source
82417	1785–1786	Madam Pookata	Liverpool	Ambriz	Dominica	Ship's logs of HMS Agamemnon, Count du Nord and Mampookata (vol. 1: 1782–1785), 387 MD 62/1, LRO
82418	1786–1787	Madam Pookata	Liverpool	Malembo	Dominica	DX/2277, MMM
82419	1787–1788	Madam Pookata	Liverpool	Malembo	Dominica	DX/2277, MMM
81673	1787–1789	Gregson	Liverpool	Gold Coast	Jamaica	HCA16/81/2087, TNAUK
18040	1789–1790	Crescent	Bristol	Windward Coast	Jamaica	HCA16/83/2218, TNAUK
83272	1789–1790	Ranger	Liverpool	Gold Coast	Jamaica	Log of the Brig Ranger (1789), 387 MD 56, LRO
83600	1793–1794	Spy	London	West-Central Africa	Jamaica	HCA16/88/2765, TNAUK
83502	1793–1794	Sandown	London	Sierra Leone	Jamaica	Log of the slaver-ship SANDOWN . . . , LOG/M/21, NMM
81933	1798–1799	Isabella	London	Gambia	Demerara	HCA16/94, TNAUK
81918	1798–1799	Iris	Liverpool	Bight of Biafra	Jamaica	MS11518/1, MNHLA
81919	1799–1800	Iris	Liverpool	West-Central Africa	Jamaica	MS11518/1, MNHLA
80702	1802	Bruce Grove	London	Gold Coast	Demerara	Wilberforce Institute Library, Hull
18259	1803–1804	Swift	Bristol	Gold Coast	Jamaica	UNKNOWN CAUSE: Account books of the same firm concerning African Trade . . . , C108/214, TNAUK
81194	1805–1806	Eliza	Liverpool	Gold Coast	Demerara	T70/1220, TNAUK
83480	1805–1806	Sally	Liverpool	Windward Coast	Demerara	UNKNOWN CAUSE: Account books of the same firm concerning African Trade . . . , C108/214, TNAUK

Appendix D. Slave sales advertised in newspapers in the Americas, 1700–1808

Colony/ state of publication	Newspaper titles	Place of publication	Year/s	# slave sales advertised
Barbados	Barbados Mercury	Bridgetown	1766, 1770, 1787–1789, 1807	**21**[a]
British Guyana	Essequibo and Demerara Courant	Georgetown	1803–1808	**45**
Grenada	The St. George's Chronicle, and New Grenada Gazette	Saint George	1790–1792	**11**
Antigua	Antigua Gazette	Saint John	1798–1799	**3**
Jamaica	The Royal Gazette	Kingston	1780–1783, 1787, 1791–1799	281
	The Daily Advertizer	Kingston	1789–1790, 1801–1802	45
	The Kingston Mercantile Advertiser	Kingston	1801–1802	17
	Jamaica Mercury and Kingston Weekly Advertizer	Kingston	1779–1780	8
	The Weekly Jamaica Courant	Kingston	1718, 1722, 1753–1754	7
	The Jamaica Gazette	Kingston	1764, 1775	3
	The Kingston Journal	Kingston	1789	1
	The Cornwall Chronicle	Montego Bay	1776–1777, 1781, 1783–1785	57
	The Saint Jago Intelligencer	Spanish Town	1788–1794	3
	The Gazette of Saint Jago de la Vega	Spanish Town	1767–1768	1
	The Savanna-La-Mar Gazette	Savannah-La-Mar	1788	1
				424
Georgia	Georgia Gazette	Savannah	1766–1770, 1774	**10**
South Carolina	The South Carolina Gazette	Charleston	1735, 1749–1774, 1783–1786	215
	Charleston Courier	Charleston	1804–1806	43
				258
Virginia	Virginia Gazette	Williamsburg	1746, 1752, 1766, 1768–1770, 1772	**21**
Maryland	Maryland Gazette	Annapolis	1771	**1**
			Total	794

[a] Numbers in bold are the total number of advertisements for each colony/state.

Appendix E. British American slave sale invoices, 1700–1807

ID in SV	Ship name	African embarkation	American disembarkation	Date sale opened	Length of sale (days)	Captives sold (#)	Captives sold first day (#)	Sickly[a] captives (#)	Died during sale (#)	Source
9729	*Somers*	Gold Coast	Jamaica	Jan. 1700	1	187	Not listed in source (hereafter NL)	42	NL	T70/949, TNAUK, f. 26
9730	*Elkins*	Bight of Benin	Jamaica	Feb. 26, 1700	1	449	449	141	3	Ibid., f. 32
9732	*Fauconberg*	Gold Coast	Antigua	May 20, 1700	29	167	123	9	4	Ibid., ff. 45–46
9732	*Fauconberg*	Gold Coast	Montserrat	May 1700	NL	171	NL	14	4	Ibid., ff. 49–50
9731	*Rainbow*	Unknown	Barbados	Jun. 19, 1700	1	297	297	NL	4	Ibid., f. 40
9733	*Delavall*	Bight of Benin	Nevis	Aug. 15, 1700	30	262	196	NL	23	Ibid., ff. 61–62
9735	*Urban*	Senegambia	Jamaica	Sept. 2, 1700	4	112	26	61	NL	Ibid., f. 64
9736	*Prince of Orange*	Bight of Benin	Barbados	Dec. 17, 1700	11	440	106	217	25	Ibid., ff. 82–83
9737	*Encouragement*	Bight of Benin	Barbados	Dec. 17, 1700	39	378	97	175	3	Ibid., ff. 80–81
9739	*Constantinople*	Bight of Benin	Jamaica	May 12, 1701	2	269	66	93	NL	Ibid., f. 98
9740	*Davers Galley*	Bight of Benin	Newcastle, Nevis	May 30, 1701	119	216	105	9	24	T70/950, TNAUK, ff. 62–64
15034	*Daniel and Hector*	West-Central Africa	Jamaica	July 21, 1701	22	57	9	46	NL	T70/949, TNAUK, f. 107

15035	*Ann and Susanna*	West-Central Africa	Jamaica	Sept. 23, 1701	24	243	4	239	NL	T70/950, TNAUK, f. 3
14992	*Angola*	West-Central Africa	Jamaica	Oct. 1701	NL	199	NL	57	NL	Ibid., f. 7
14993	*Royal Africa*	Bight of Benin	Barbados	Nov. 6, 1701	36	287	60	106	66	Ibid., f. 10
14994	*Larke*	Gold Coast	Barbados	Dec. 23, 1701	84	170	50	58	21	Ibid., f. 34–35
9801	*Evans*	Senegambia	Jamaica	Jan. 13, 1702	25	117	51	43	NL	Ibid., f. 42
14995	*Bridgewater*	Bight of Biafra	Saint John, Antigua	Feb. 2, 1702	26	207	76	25	15	Ibid., ff. 38–40
14997	*Fauconbergh*	Gold Coast	Barbados	Feb. 25, 1702	65	375	54	164	30	Ibid., ff. 50–52
14999	*Gold*	Bight of Benin	Jamaica	June 20, 1702	103	441	21	138	NL	Ibid., ff. 67–68
9727	*William and Jane*	Bight of Benin	Saint John, Antigua	July 25, 1702	17	155	NL	24	NL	Ibid., f. 72
15012	*Royall Africa*	Bight of Benin	Barbados	Nov. 11, 1703	105	436	131	61	7	T70/951, TNAUK, ff. 11–15
20311	*Edward and Francis*	Gold Coast	Barbados	Jan. 25, 1704	23	139	90	22	6	Ibid., ff. 16–17
14984	*Friendship*	Bight of Benin	Nevis	Feb. 3, 1704	22	276	61	4	4	Ibid., ff. 39–40
14986	*Lion and Lamb*	Bight of Benin	Barbados	Apr. 19, 1704	34	371	165	114	7	Ibid., ff. 34–36
14985	*Davers Galley*	Gold Coast	Barbados	May 18, 1704	71	267	152	45	19	Ibid., ff. 32–34
14991	*Mary*	Gold Coast	Nevis	June 13, 1704	95	107	50	35	33	Ibid., f. 64

(continued)

Appendix E. (continued)

ID in SV	Ship name	African embarkation	American disembarkation	Date sale opened	Length of sale (days)	Captives sold (#)	Captives sold first day (#)	Sickly[a] captives (#)	Died during sale (#)	Source
14989	*Fauconbergh*	Bight of Benin	Jamaica	June 23, 1704	32	464	225	67	4	Ibid., ff. 47–49
14934	*Martha*	Bight of Benin	Nevis	June 24, 1704	138	209	28	6	9	Ibid., ff. 41–42
15005	*Postillion*	Senegambia	Virginia	Sept. 1704	NL	69	NL	6	5	T70/952, TNAUK, f. 18
15004	*Whidah*	Bight of Benin	Jamaica	Nov. 7, 1704	59	142	75	1	29	Ibid., f. 13
15007	*Black Eagle*	Bight of Benin	Barbados	Jan. 16, 1705	21	513	281	70	23	Ibid., ff. 30–33
15006	*Lark*	Gold Coast	Barbados	Mar. 27, 1705	21	172	46	13	1	Ibid., ff. 27–28
15010	*Siam*	Bight of Benin	Jamaica	June 13, 1705	18	537	436	17	7	Ibid., ff. 39–40
15011	*Bridgewater*	Gold Coast	Saint John, Antigua	July 17, 1705	50	157	87	29	9	Ibid., f. 52
15009	*Rook*	Gold Coast	Jamaica	July 24, 1705	13	278	48	116	12	Ibid., f. 38
15008	*Saint Lawrence Victorious*	Bight of Benin	Jamaica	July 24, 1705	48	184	48	83	18	Ibid., f. 51
21160	*Davers*	Gold Coast	Montserrat	July 17, 1705	NL	98	NL	9	15	T70/953, TNAUK, ff. 8–9
14938	*Gould Frigate*	Bight of Benin	Jamaica	Nov. 22, 1705	3	385	210	104	16	Ibid., ff. 11–12

15030	*Black Eagle*	Bight of Benin	Barbados	Feb. 20, 1706	31	486	172	96	17	Ibid., ff. 31–37
15002	*Prodigal Son*	Gold Coast	Barbados	Apr. 9, 1706	71	157	11	96	16	Ibid., ff. 39–40
20337	*Content*	Gold Coast	Barbados	Apr. 9, 1706	71	112	47	39	8	Ibid., ff. 41–42
9745	*Union*	Gold Coast	Montserrat	June 1706	NL	281	NL	32	4	T70/954, TNAUK, ff. 13–14
9744	*Regard*	Gold Coast	Saint John, Antigua	Oct. 1706	NL	358	NL	20	NL	Ibid., f. 28
9746	*Bridgewater*	Senegambia	Barbados	Nov. 26, 1706	18	103	4	34	1	Ibid., f. 12
20346	*Royal Consort*	Bight of Benin	Barbados	Jan. 28, 1707	32	441	78	47	1	Ibid., ff. 29–30
9742	*Flying Fame*	Gold Coast	Saint John, Antigua	Aug. 26, 1707	12	114	43	7	0	Ibid., f. 61
20896	*Bridgewater*	Senegambia	Virginia	Aug. 1707	NL	142	NL	19	23	T70/955, TNAUK, f. 69
9757	*Seaford*	Senegambia	Jamaica	Oct. 22, 1707	60	196	48	48	NL	Ibid., ff. 9, 11
9756	*Sherbrow*	Sierra Leone	Barbados	Nov. 20, 1707	56	72	5	24	1	Ibid., f. 15
9755	*Pimdar Galley*	Gold Coast	Jamaica	Jan. 12, 1708	44	280	50	30	NL	Ibid., f. 16
9754	*Elizabeth*	Gold Coast	Jamaica	Jan. 14, 1708	39	232	63	35	NL	Ibid., f. 17
9753	*Amiable*	Senegambia	Saint John, Antigua	Feb. 3, 1708	12	144	16	26	1	Ibid., f. 18
9749	*Katherine*	Bight of Benin	Barbados	Mar. 11, 1708	51	467	157	60	3	Ibid., ff. 44–46

(continued)

Appendix E. (continued)

ID in SV	Ship name	African embarkation	American disembarkation	Date sale opened	Length of sale (days)	Captives sold (#)	Captives sold first day (#)	Sickly[a] captives (#)	Died during sale (#)	Source
9450	Dorothy	Gold Coast	Barbados	Mar. 31, 1708	31	121	32	24	1	Ibid., f. 43
9751	Queen Ann	Gold Coast	Jamaica	Apr. 7, 1708	32	518	69	56	6	Ibid., f. 34
9747	Macklesfield	Bight of Benin	Jamaica	Apr. 30, 1708	44	494	37	130	8	Ibid., f. 33, 48–50
20354	Greyhound	Gold Coast	Barbados	Oct. 8, 1708	14	102	21	56	0	T70/956, TNAUK, f. 11
9767	Flying Fame	Gold Coast	Saint John, Antigua	Oct. 11, 1708	10	110	NL	6	10	Ibid., f. 16
9764	Elizabeth	Gold Coast	Barbados	Nov. 16, 1708	7	254	106	88	12	Ibid., ff. 24–25
9766	Regard	Gold Coast	Saint John, Antigua	Feb. 7, 1709	3	434	189	53	9	Ibid., ff. 20–21
9758 & 9763	Sherbrow & Dolphin	Gold Coast	Barbados	Apr. 21, 1709	21	301	127	111	6	Ibid., ff. 26–27
20918	Amiable	Gold Coast	Saint John, Antigua	Aug. 1709	NL	142	NL	17	NL	Ibid., f. 56
20844	Olive Branch	Gold Coast	Barbados	Dec. 15, 1709	1	159	159	44	NL	Ibid., f. 53
9762	Pindar	Gold Coast	Barbados	May 11, 1710	9	269	170	71	NL	Ibid., ff. 63–64

ID	Ship	Region	Destination	Date						Source
9761 & 9752	*Elizabeth & Dolphin*	Gold Coast	Barbados	Sept. 12, 1710	29	236	101	84	15	Ibid., ff. 78–80
9759	*Camwood Merchant*	Gold Coast	Barbados	Sept. 13, 1711	10	159	57	75	2	Ibid., f. 96
76481	*Royal Africa*	Gold Coast	Barbados	Aug. 16, 1715	10	206	87	102	NL	T70/957, TNAUK, ff. 8–9
9776	*Pindar*	NL	Newcastle, Nevis	June 9, 1716	21	79	41	3	2	Ibid., ff. 11–12
76521	*Sarah Galley*	Gold Coast	Barbados	May 1719	1	232	232	NL	NL	Ibid., f. 45
76525	*Victory*	Gold Coast	Barbados	June 23, 1719	2	156	130	35	2	Ibid., ff. 48–49
76625	*King Solomon*	Gold Coast	Saint Kitts	Mar. 21, 1721	25	285	212	52	NL	Ibid., ff. 61–62
75330	*Dispatch Galley*	Gold Coast	Saint John, Antigua	Aug. 7, 1721	3	104	33	61	NL	Ibid., ff. 78–79
75956	*Otter*	Senegambia	York River, VA	Aug 16, 1721	14	193	42	45	NL	Ibid., ff. 72–73
76460	*Royal Africa Packet*	West-Central Africa	Jamaica	Mar. 13, 1722	46	197	190	2	NL	T70/958, TNAUK, f. 20
75628	*Helden Frigate*	West-Central Africa	Jamaica	Feb. 7, 1723	21	266	137	15	18	Ibid., f. 22
76542	*Diligence*	Gold Coast	Barbados	Mar. 5, 1723	1	182	182	0	1	Ibid., f. 23
75258	*Chandos*	Bight of Benin	Kingston, Jamaica	Mar. 5, 1723	13	433	280	34	NL	Ibid., f. 84

(continued)

Appendix E. (continued)

ID in SV	Ship name	African embarkation	American disembarkation	Date sale opened	Length of sale (days)	Captives sold (#)	Captives sold first day (#)	Sickly[a] captives (#)	Died during sale (#)	Source
76544	*Sherbrow Gally*	West-Central Africa	Jamaica	Mar. 25, 1723	3	269	123	0	NL	Ibid., f. 23
75512	*Francis Galley*	Gold Coast	Jamaica	May 3, 1723	30	279	223	14	8	Ibid., f. 31
9790	*Great Caesar*	Gold Coast	Saint John, Antigua	May 14, 1723	44	138	120	8	4	Ibid., f. 49
76191	*Squirrel*	Bight of Benin	Jamaica	May 30, 1723	19	354	186	27	11	Ibid., f. 50
75181	*Bladen Frigate*	Bight of Benin	Jamaica	June 3, 1723	32	225	140	16	4	Ibid., f. 41
76176	*Sloper*	Gold Coast	Barbados	June 25, 1723	19	195	19	60	8	Ibid., f. 56–57
76546	*Sarah Gally*	Sierra Leone	Barbados	Sept. 26, 1723	14	61	9	41	2	Ibid., f. 69
9784	*Dove*	Senegambia	Jamaica	Nov. 15, 1723	16	113	56	14	5	Ibid., f. 62
76646	*Success*	Bight of Benin	Saint John, Antigua	Apr. 22, 1724	36	42	22	20	2	Ibid., f. 95
75239	*Carleton*	West-Central Africa	Jamaica	June 2, 1724	8	393	273	25	2	Ibid., f. 98

76667	*Shark*	Gold Coast	Montserrat	Nov. 21, 1724	20	46	12	23	NL	T70/959, TNAUK, f. 17
76668	*Sierra Leone*	Sierra Leone	Montserrat	May 4, 1725	1	40	40	3	NL	Ibid., f. 18
76969	*Chandos*	Gold Coast	Jamaica	Aug. 31, 1725	35	458	206	86	7	Ibid., f. 31
76560	*Diligence*	Senegambia	Barbados	May 20, 1729	1	16	16	10	3	T70/960, TNAUK, f. 8
16621	*Freke*	Bight of Biafra	Barbados	Dec. 8, 1730	22	329	122	36	NL	*The Hobhouse Papers, 1722–1755* (East Ardsley: Micro Methods, 1971)
17170	*Bristoll Merchant*	Bight of Biafra	Kingston, Jamaica	Oct. 16, 1747	62	213	1	40	NL	Bright Family Papers, University of Melbourne
90296	*Orrell*	Senegambia	Charleston, SC	Aug. 7, 1751	20	87	NL	37	NL	*DIHST*, vol. 4, 307–9
17296	*Molly*	Bight of Biafra	Savanna-La-Mar, Jamaica	Jan. 2, 1752	24	125	29	21	NL	SMV/7/2/1/25, Bristol Archives
17323	*Molly*	West-Central Africa	Saint Kitts	June 25, 1753	36	193	98	80	NL	Morgan, ed., *Bright-Meyler*, 287–88

(continued)

Appendix E. (continued)

ID in SV	Ship name	African embarkation	American disembarkation	Date sale opened	Length of sale (days)	Captives sold (#)	Captives sold first day (#)	Sickly[a] captives (#)	Died during sale (#)	Source
24025	*Africa*	Gold Coast	Charleston, SC	Aug. 9, 1753	NL	163	NL	28	7	Austin & Laurens Account Book, April 1750–December 1758, Gen. MSS, vol. 184, Beinecke Rare Book and Manuscript Library, Yale University, ff. 12–15 (ALAB)
90298	*Orrell*	Senegambia	Charleston, SC	Sept. 5, 1753	NL	82	NL	13	NL	Ibid., ff. 21–22
90411	*Judith*	Gold Coast	Kingston, Jamaica	Apr. 17, 1754	67	274	2	30	8	CSAB, LRO, ff. 12–13
17339	*Fortune*	Gold Coast	Charleston, SC	July 3, 1754	1	168	168	31	12	ALAB, ff. 54–55
90514	*Orrell*	Senegambia	Charleston, SC	July 31, 1754	NL	164	NL	23	6	Ibid., ff. 56–57
24026	*Africa*	Sierra Leone	Charleston, SC	Sept. 9, 1754	NL	114	NL	26	NL	Ibid., ff. 60–61

90331	*Bulkeley*	Windward Coast	Kingston, Jamaica	Mar. 24, 1755	12	196	65	75	1	CSAB, LRO, f. 41
90140	*Adlington*	NL	Kingston, Jamaica	May 28, 1755	57	146	23	68	2	Ibid., f. 47
17375	*Pearl*	West-Central Africa	Charleston, SC	June 24, 1755	2	243	NL	12	7	ALAB, ff. 91–93
90515	*Orrell*	Senegambia	Charleston, SC	Sept. 5, 1755	2	129	101	27	NL	Ibid., ff. 98–99
90412	*Judith*	Bight of Biafra	Kingston, Jamaica	Sept. 11, 1755	51	192	2	34	3	CSAB, LRO, f. 60
90570	*Swallow*	Windward Coast	Kingston, Jamaica	Oct. 14, 1755	46	101	11	62	NL	Ibid., f. 62
90462	*Swan*	Bight of Biafra	Kingston, Jamaica	Dec. 31, 1755	61	297	17	62	17	Ibid., f. 68
90590	*Young Foster*	Windward Coast	Kingston, Jamaica	Mar. 26, 1756	58	202	12	58	NL	Ibid., f. 70
90597	*Nicholas*	Windward Coast	Kingston, Jamaica	June 14, 1756	118	209	10	44	NL	TNAUK, HCA30/29
36187	*Hare*	Sierra Leone	Charleston, SC	June 29, 1756	15	63	24	19	7	ALAB, ff. 115–16
90315	*Tryton*	Bight of Benin	Kingston, Jamaica	July 8, 1756	72	70	2	36	NL	CSAB, LRO, ff. 12–13
75237	*Carlisle*	Sierra Leone	Charleston, SC	July 8, 1756	36	136	88	18	14	ALAB, ff. 116–18

(*continued*)

Appendix E. (continued)

ID in SV	Ship name	African embarkation	American disembarkation	Date sale opened	Length of sale (days)	Captives sold (#)	Captives sold first day (#)	Sickly[a] captives (#)	Died during sale (#)	Source
24028	Concord	Sierra Leone	Charleston, SC	Aug. 4, 1756	16	46	19	11	3	Ibid., f. 120
77252	Saint Andrew	Senegambia	Charleston, SC	Sept. 1, 1756	50	74	42	13	NL	Ibid., ff. 122–23
24006	Anson	Senegambia	Charleston, SC	Apr. 28, 1757	NL	70	NL	21	NL	Ibid., ff. 133–34
17409	King David	Bight of Biafra	Charleston, SC	Sept. 13, 1757	16	195	83	112	NL	Ibid., ff. 140–42
90591	Young Foster	Windward Coast	Kingston, Jamaica	Jan. 13, 1758	112	268	20	40	NL	CSAB, LRO, ff. 99–100
90542	Chesterfield	Bight of Biafra	Barbados	Feb. 28, 1758	381	381	365	12	NL	The Slave Trade invoice book of the Eadith, Chesterfield and Calveley, 1758–1762, MMM
90466	Rainbow	Bight of Benin	Charleston, SC	May 2, 1758	196	196	NL	24	NL	ALAB, ff. 149–51
17425	Polly	West-Central Africa	Charleston, SC	June 15, 1758	35	364	199	62	NL	Ibid., ff. 156–57

90696	*Polly*	Senegambia	Charleston, SC	July 4, 1758	4	118	74	36	NL	Ibid., ff. 158–59
90964	*Nancy*	Gold Coast	Charleston, SC	Oct. 4, 1758	10	247	114	28	3	Ibid., ff. 166–68
90621	*Phoebe*	Senegambia	Charleston, SC	Oct. 18, 1758	17	140	88	5	NL	Ibid., ff. 168–70
90725	*Molly*	Gold Coast	Charleston, SC	Oct. 18, 1758	23	53	18	7	NL	Ibid., f. 165
90873	*Eadith*	Windward Coast	York River, VA	July 16, 1761	17	149	39	59	NL	The Slave Trade invoice book of the Eadith, Chesterfield and Calveley, 1758–1762, MMM
90858	*Tyrrell*	Bight of Biafra	Saint Kitts	Apr. 1762	NL	277	NL	93	NL	PDAV
90969	*Edgar*	West-Central Africa	Kingston, Jamaica	Feb. 23, 1763	16	378	196	47	NL	CS96/502, National Archives of Scotland
90937	*Plumper*	Windward Coast	Kingston, Jamaica	Aug. 11, 1763	48	257	45	4	3	PDAV
92319	*African*	West-Central Africa	Kingston, Jamaica	Sept. 1764	NL	268	NL	3	NL	*DIHST*, vol. 2, 524–25
91157	*Little Britain*	Bight of Benin	Kingston, Jamaica	July 1765	NL	85	NL	25	3	PDAV
91213	*William*	Senegambia	Charleston, SC	Nov. 5, 1765	23	60	24	14	NL	Ibid.

(continued)

Appendix E. (continued)

ID in SV	Ship name	African embarkation	American disembarkation	Date sale opened	Length of sale (days)	Captives sold (#)	Captives sold first day (#)	Sickly[a] captives (#)	Died during sale (#)	Source
92315	*Sisters*	Bight of Benin	Saint George, Grenada	Mar. 12, 1766	1	209	209	29	NL	Ibid.
91081	*Henry*	Bight of Biafra	Grenada	Dec. 3, 1766	1	115	115	10	NL	Ibid.
91219	*Dalrymple*	Bight of Biafra	Saint John, Antigua	Apr. 25, 1767	5	310	250	50	NL	Ibid.
91408	*King of Prussia*	Bight of Biafra	Saint George, Grenada	Dec. 1768	NL	175	NL	28	28	Ibid.
91427	*Neptune*	Bight of Biafra	Saint George, Grenada	Dec. 13, 1768	15	144	67	73	NL	Ibid.
91215	*William*	Bight of Biafra	Barbados	Jan. 12, 1769	53	121	101	20	6	Ibid.
91428	*Plumper*	Bight of Benin	Kingston, Jamaica	Feb. 9, 1769	99	248	45	59	17	Ibid.
91220	*Dalrymple*	Bight of Biafra	Montego Bay, Jamaica	Mar. 30, 1769	2	220	143	34	NL	Ibid.
91083	*Henry*	Bight of Biafra	Grenada	Dec. 5, 1769	1	103	NL	2	NL	Ibid.
91553	*Fox*	Bight of Biafra	Roseau, Dominica	Dec. 16, 1769	1	177	177	42	NL	Ibid.

91545	*Dobson*	Bight of Biafra	Barbados	Mar. 22, 1770	43	275	110	52	NL	Ibid.
91545	*King of Prussia*	Bight of Biafra	Barbados	May 1, 1770	29	121	50	22	NL	Ibid.
91594	*Andromache*	Bight of Biafra	Dominica	May 25, 1770	1	140	140	14	NL	Ibid.
91573	*Hector*	Bight of Biafra	Dominica	July 6, 1770	1	241	241	35	NL	Ibid.
91585	*William*	Bight of Biafra	Barbados	Sept. 12, 1770	14	103	83	12	NL	Ibid.
91429	*Plumper*	Bight of Benin	Kingston, Jamaica	Oct. 1770	NL	274	NL	141	11	Ibid.
91653	*Swift*	Bight of Biafra	Dominica	Nov. 1, 1770	1	148	148	15	NL	Ibid.
91221	*Dalrymple*	Bight of Biafra	Saint George, Grenada	Dec. 22, 1770	NL	270	NL	23	NL	Ibid.
91621	*Fox*	Bight of Biafra	Saint Kitts	May 3, 1771	1	148	148	62	NL	Ibid.
91643	*True Blue*	Bight of Benin	Kingston, Jamaica	June 1771	NL	204	NL	49	NL	Ibid.
91595	*Andromache*	Bight of Biafra	Dominica	Dec. 23, 1771	1	186	186	26	NL	Ibid.
91668	*Juno*	Sierra Leone	Saint George, Grenada	Jan. 1, 1772	1	226	226	46	NL	Ibid.
91790	*Swift*	Bight of Biafra	Grenada	Feb. 21, 1772	1	192	192	22	NL	Ibid.
91410	*King of Prussia*	Bight of Biafra	Saint Vincent	Mar. 17, 1772	1	200	200	60	NL	Ibid.
91752	*Dalrymple*	Bight of Biafra	Dominica	May 14, 1772	1	198	198	30	NL	Ibid.
91574	*Hector*	Bight of Biafra	Dominica	July 1, 1772	1	204	204	54	NL	PDAV
91723	*Cavendish*	Sierra Leone	Saint Vincent	July 16, 1772	1	287	287	2	NL	C109/401, TNAUK

(continued)

Appendix E. (continued)

ID in SV	Ship name	African embarkation	American disembarkation	Date sale opened	Length of sale (days)	Captives sold (#)	Captives sold first day (#)	Sickly[a] captives (#)	Died during sale (#)	Source
91702	*Lord Cassils*	Bight of Biafra	Dominica	Sept. 1772	NL	130	NL	12	NL	PDAV
91617	*Barbados Packet*	Windward Coast	Zion Hill, Tobago	Oct. 1772	NL	96	NL	26	NL	C109/401, TNAUK
91708	*Meredith*	Sierra Leone	Saint Kitts	Nov. 5, 1772	1	284	284	21	NL	Ibid.
91791	*Swift*	Bight of Biafra	Saint Vincent	Apr. 14, 1773	1	144	144	5	NL	PDAV
91892	*King of Prussia*	Bight of Biafra	Grenada	May 15, 1773	1	224	224	41	NL	Ibid.
91864	*May*	Bight of Biafra	Saint John, Antigua	Sept. 22, 1773	1	100	100	9	NL	Ibid.
91804	*Fox*	Bight of Biafra	Barbados	Oct. 7, 1773	1	153	153	7	NL	Ibid.
91837	*Dreadnought*	Bight of Biafra	Montego Bay, Jamaica	Oct. 1773	NL	170	NL	39	9	Ibid.
91812	*Badger*	Bight of Biafra	Grenada	Nov. 29, 1773	1	186	186	15	NL	Ibid.
91979	*Andromache*	Bight of Biafra	Montego Bay, Jamaica	Feb. 21, 1774	1	186	186	56	NL	Ibid.
91976	*Favourite*	Bight of Biafra	Grenada	Mar. 3, 1774	1	231	231	21	NL	Ibid.
91792	*Swift*	Bight of Biafra	Saint Kitts	May 1774	NL	153	137	16	NL	Ibid.

91893	King of Prussia	Bight of Biafra	Barbados	July 11, 1774	1	224	224	0	NL	Ibid.
92017	King George	Bight of Biafra	Barbados	Nov. 15, 1774	9	81	6	10	NL	Ibid.
91987	Dalrymple	Bight of Biafra	Dominica	Dec. 6, 1774	1	175	175	49	NL	Ibid.
91813	Badger	Bight of Biafra	Barbados	Dec. 7, 1774	9	197	139	37	NL	Ibid.
91977	Favourite	Bight of Biafra	Grenada	Jan. 13, 1775	1	320	320	17	NL	Ibid.
91575	Hector	Bight of Biafra	Saint Kitts	Jan. 13, 1775	12	108	80	28	NL	Ibid.
91865	May	Bight of Biafra	Saint John, Antigua	Feb. 1775	NL	185	NL	38	NL	Ibid.
91838	Dreadnought	Bight of Biafra	Grenada	June 29, 1775	1	186	186	36	NL	Ibid.
92543	Lord Cassils	Bight of Biafra	Roseau, Dominica	July 14, 1775	16	121	86	10	NL	Ibid.
91894	King of Prussia	Bight of Biafra	Roseau, Dominica	Oct. 1775	NL	187	NL	30	NL	Ibid.
91814	Badger	Bight of Biafra	Dominica	Nov. 8, 1775	1	202	202	25	5	Ibid.
91793	Swift	Bight of Biafra	Dominica	Mar. 21, 1776	1	195	195	45	NL	Ibid.
91978	Favourite	Bight of Biafra	Kingston, Jamaica	May 15, 1776	4	178	136	34	NL	Ibid.
91988	Dalrymple	Bight of Biafra	Dominica	May 29, 1776	1	240	240	102	NL	Ibid.
91937	Sam	Bight of Biafra	Barbados	Oct. 1776	NL	208	NL	38	NL	Ibid.

(continued)

Appendix E. (continued)

ID in SV	Ship name	African embarkation	American disembarkation	Date sale opened	Length of sale (days)	Captives sold (#)	Captives sold first day (#)	Sickly[a] captives (#)	Died during sale (#)	Source
91839	*Dreadnought*	Bight of Biafra	Dominica	Nov. 29, 1776	1	130	130	20	NL	Ibid.
91895	*King of Prussia*	Bight of Biafra	Dominica	Jan. 2, 1777	11	242	215	22	NL	Ibid.
91794	*Swift*	Bight of Biafra	Dominica	Apr. 9, 1777	28	186	29	45	NL	Ibid.
91576	*Hector*	Bight of Biafra	Dominica	May 23, 1777	56	216	85	64	4	Ibid.
92536	*Badger*	Bight of Biafra	Dominica	June 10, 1777	38	386	164	84	2	Ibid.
92589	*Dalrymple*	Bight of Biafra	Saint John, Antigua	Jan. 1, 1778	1	234	234	38	NL	Ibid.
92461	*Mars*	Sierra Leone	Old Harbor, Jamaica	Feb. 3, 1780	13	295	169	83	0	Ibid.
81573	*Hawke*	Bight of Biafra	Saint Lucia	July 3, 1781	14	377	179	42	NL	Ibid.
82482	*Mars*	Windward Coast	Saint Kitts	Aug. 14, 1781	2	185	180	5	NL	D/DAV/2, MMM
80458	*Bee*	Sierra Leone	Saint John, Antigua	Dec. 8, 1781	1	60	60	0	NL	PDAV
80251	*Ann*	Windward Coast	Kingston, Jamaica	Dec. 21, 1781	NL	318	NL	57	NL	D/DAV/2, MMM

82324	*Liverpool Hero*	Bight of Biafra	Saint John, Antigua	Mar. 18, 1782	6	418	NL	0	NL	Ibid.
83175	*Preston*	Bight of Biafra	Saint John, Antigua	June 4, 1782	1	205	205	0	NL	PDAV
82415	*Madam Pookata*	West-Central Africa	Tortola	Sept. 1783	NL	208	NL	11	NL	SDP, GB141 MS.10.47, ULL
81731	*Harlequin*	Gold Coast	Kingston, Jamaica	Mar. 17, 1783	1	497	497	4	3	SDP, GB141 MS.10.46, ULL
83266	*Quixote*	Bight of Biafra	Saint Lucia	Oct. 23, 1783	1	381	381	1	NL	PDAV
80253	*Ann*	Bight of Biafra	Tortola	Apr. 1783	NL	442	NL	52	NL	William Davenport & Co. account book relating to ship voyages, 1777–1784, HL
82325	*Liverpool Hero*	Bight of Biafra	Dominica	Feb. 1784	NL	454	NL	65	NL	Ibid.
83176	*Preston*	Bight of Biafra	Saint John, Antigua	Feb. 2, 1784	27	263	29	86	NL	PDAV
17920	*Emilia*	Bight of Biafra	Port Maria, Jamaica	Feb. 5, 1784	17	306	132	131	NL	*HCSP,* vol. 72, 637–40
81311	*Essex*	Windward Coast	Saint Vincent	May 28, 1784	9	280	207	93	11	D/DAV/15, MMM
80587	*Bloom*	Windward Coast	Saint John, Antigua	Aug. 2, 1784	29	307	118	34	NL	Letterbook of Robert Bostock, vol.1, LRO

(*continued*)

Appendix E. (continued)

ID in SV	Ship name	African embarkation	American disembarkation	Date sale opened	Length of sale (days)	Captives sold (#)	Captives sold first day (#)	Sickly[a] captives (#)	Died during sale (#)	Source
80917	Conte du Norde	West-Central Africa	Charleston, SC	Aug. 3, 1784	17	571	189	75	8	E219/377, TNAUK
81606	Golden Age	Bight of Benin	Kingston, Jamaica	Dec. 2, 1784	2	503	245	144	NL	SDP, GB141 MS.10.48, ULL
83267	Quixote	Bight of Biafra	Grenada	Dec. 16, 1784	3	242	119	116	NL	PDAV
81166	Eliza	Sierra Leone	Saint Vincent	Aug. 7, 1787	1	203	203	0	NL	American Papers in the House of Lords Record Office
17981	Active	Gold Coast	Montego Bay, Jamaica	Jan. 7, 1789	39	258	247	28	NL	Ibid.
82420	Madam Pookata	West-Central Africa	Dominica	Jan. 1789	NL	176	NL	22	NL	Ibid.
17983	Alert	Gold Coast	Kingston, Jamaica	Feb. 2, 1789	10	262	205	50	3	Ibid.
17996	James	Windward Coast	Black River, Jamaica	Feb. 4, 1789	4	150	147	14	4	Ibid.
80788	Chambres	Gold Coast	Kingston, Jamaica	Feb. 20, 1789	8	216	175	41	NL	Ibid.
81077	Duke of Buccleugh	Sierra Leone	Grenada	Apr. 1789	NL	351	NL	15	7	Ibid.

80999	*Diana*	Gold Coast	Kingston, Jamaica	July 1789	NL	301	NL	37	3	Ibid.
18276	*Fly*	Sierra Leone	Black River, Jamaica	June 25, 1789	11	45	36	7	0	C107/6, TNAUK
18029	*Ruby*	Sierra Leone	Kingston, Jamaica	Dec. 15, 1789	23	154	70	69	0	C107/13, TNAUK
81713	*Hannah*	Bight of Biafra	Kingston, Jamaica	Jan. 9, 1790	46	294	132	96	6	Thomas Leyland Company account books, 1789–1790, 1792–1793, WCL
18070	*Flora*	Sierra Leone	Montego Bay, Jamaica	Feb. 21, 1791	1	71	71	6	1	C107/5, TNAUK
80834	*Christopher*	West-Central Africa	Dominica	Dec. 1791	NL	270	NL	17	NL	Account books of the *Christopher*, 1791–1792, Duke University Library
18084	*Ruby*	Sierra Leone	Montego Bay, Jamaica	Apr. 11, 1792	1	129	129	46	5	C107/13, TNAUK
18138	*Fame*	Bight of Biafra	Grenada	Sept. 25, 1792	1	126	126	22	7	C107/5, TNAUK
18152	*Mermaid*	Senegambia	Grenada	Nov. 13, 1792	1	128	128	0	0	C107/13, TNAUK
18139	*Fanny*	Sierra Leone	Kingston, Jamaica	Jan. 10, 1793	16	230	104	95	2	C107/59, TNAUK
18129	*African Queen*	Bight of Biafra	Montego Bay, Jamaica	Jan. 18, 1793	4	202	90	70	18	Ibid.

(continued)

Appendix E. (continued)

ID in SV	Ship name	African embarkation	American disembarkation	Date sale opened	Length of sale (days)	Captives sold (#)	Captives sold first day (#)	Sickly[a] captives (#)	Died during sale (#)	Source
18157	Pearl	Bight of Biafra	Barbados	Feb. 5, 1793	24	187	103	82	80	Ibid.
18134	Crescent	Sierra Leone	Old Harbor, Jamaica	Mar. 28, 1793	34	266	228	41	1	Ibid.
18162	Rodney	Bight of Biafra	Kingston, Jamaica	June 3, 1793	33	324	2	143	30	Ibid.
82016	Jenny	West-Central Africa	Kingston, Jamaica	June 4, 1793	55	258	10	128	8	Thomas Leyland Company account books, 1789–1790, 1792–1793, WCL
18169	Swift	Sierra Leone	Barbados	June 19, 1793	2	115	85	14	18	C107/59, TNAUK
18146	Jupiter	Bight of Biafra	Martha Brae, Jamaica	July 3, 1793	1	342	342	100	13	Ibid.
18167	Sarah	Bight of Biafra	Kingston, Jamaica	Sept. 9, 1793	8	127	3	75	10	Ibid.
83815	Tom	Bight of Biafra	Barbados	Jan. 17, 1794	1	39	39	17	1	2352, Lancaster Library
81926	Iris	Bight of Benin	Saint Vincent	Apr. 17, 1794	1	207	207	19	NL	T70/1569, TNAUK
81295	Enterprize	West-Central Africa	Kingston, Jamaica	Dec. 5, 1794	35	356	83	58	4	DX/1732, MMM

ID	Ship	Region	Port of Sale	Date						Source
83591	*Spitfire*	West–Central Africa	Barbados	Jan. 21, 1796	16	418	193	0	NL	SDP, GB141 MS.10.49, ULL
81112	*Earl of Liverpool*	Bight of Biafra	Kingston, Jamaica	Nov. 17, 1797	85	324	62	19	13	SDP, GB141 MS.10.50, ULL
82379	*Lottery*	Bight of Biafra	Kingston, Jamaica	Dec. 13, 1798	3	453	173	84	NL	387 MD 41, LRO
81113	*Earl of Liverpool*	Bight of Biafra	Montego Bay, Jamaica	Dec. 19, 1798	1	344	344	15	NL	SDP, GB141 MS.10.50, ULL
81114	*Earl of Liverpool*	West–Central Africa	Kingston, Jamaica	Feb. 8, 1800	13	279	22	105	NL	SDP, GB141 MS.10.50, ULL
82382	*Lottery*	Bight of Biafra	Montego Bay, Jamaica	Dec. 8, 1802	1	305	305	23	NL	387 MD 42, LRO
81497	*Fortune*	West–Central Africa	Bahamas	Jan. 21, 1806	229	340	10	2	3	387 MD 44, LRO
83199	*Prince of Orange*	West–Central Africa	Trinidad	Dec. 11, 1806	7	142	86	7	NL	E219/340, TNAUK
80457	*Bedford*	Gold Coast	Kingston, Jamaica	May 8, 1807	93	233	7	40	0	C114/158, TNAUK
81305	*Enterprize*	Bight of Biafra	Montego Bay, Jamaica	June 2, 1807	1	231	231	50	NL	387 MD 43, LRO
81512	*Frederick*	Bight of Benin	Kingston, Jamaica	Aug. 6, 1807	91	238	2	31	NL	C114/158, TNAUK

a "Sickly captives" are those who were either denoted as such in the sales invoices (for example, with notations such as "refuse") or sold for two-thirds of the price of a person in the same category of gender and age, or less.

Abbreviations

APHLRO	*American Papers in the House of Lords Record Office, 1621–1917* (Wakefield: Microform, 1983)
BG	Paul Hair, ed., *Barbot on Guinea: The Writings of Jean Barbot on West Africa, 1678–1712*, 2 vols. (London: Hakluyt Society, 1992)
BL	The British Library, London
DAJ	Daybook of Alexander Johnston, 1767–1777, Powel Family Papers Collections, 1582, Historical Society of Pennsylvania
DIHST	Elizabeth Donnan, ed., *Documents Illustrative of the History of the Slave Trade to America*, 4 vols. (Washington, DC: Carnegie Institute, 1930)
HCSP	Sheila Lambert, ed., *House of Commons Sessional Papers of the Eighteenth Century*, 145 vols. (Wilmington: Scholarly Resources, 1975)
JDRH	Nick Hibbert Steele, *The Jamaican Diaries of Robert Hibbert, 1772–1780: Detailing a Family's Involvement in and Defence of the Colonial Slave Trade Based Economy* (Melbourne: Nick Hibbert Steele, 2020)
JRP	Miscellaneous accounts, papers and correspondence of James Roger[s], merchant, of Bristol, C107/1–15, 59, The National Archives, London
LRB	Letterbook, etc., of Robert Bostock, 2 vols., LRO
LRO	Liverpool Record Office, Liverpool
MMM	Merseyside Maritime Museum, Liverpool

MNHLA	Manx National Heritage Library and Archives, Douglas, Isle of Man
NMM	National Maritime Museum, Greenwich
PDAV	Papers of William Davenport. The originals are in Keele University Library, Keele, UK. I consulted them in microfilm: https://microform.digital/boa/collections/12/slave-trading-records-from-william-davenport-co-1745-1797
PHL	Philip M. Hamer, George C. Rogers Jr., David R. Chesnutt, and Maude E. Lyles, eds., *The Papers of Henry Laurens*, 16 vols. (Columbia: University of South Carolina Press, 1968–2003)
PWD	*The Papers of William Davenport and Co., 1745–1797* (Wakefield: Microform, 1998)
SV	*Slave Voyages* (www.slavevoyages.org)
TFP	Tailyour Family Papers, William L. Clements Library, Ann Arbor, MI
TNAUK	The National Archives, Kew, London
ULL	University of Liverpool Library, Liverpool
WCL	William L. Clements Library, University of Michigan, Ann Arbor

Notes

Introduction

1. Justice and Humanity [Thomas Paine], "To Americans," *Postscript to the Pennsylvania Journal and the Weekly Advertiser,* March 8, 1775. Statistics on the slave trade are drawn from *Slave Voyages* (www.slavevoyages.org). Throughout this book "the eighteenth century" is used as a shorthand for the period 1700 to 1808, to encompass the years of the nineteenth century that preceded abolition.

2. For the size of Britain's slave trade pre-1700, see http://www.slavevoyages .org/estimates/Ek7kABFG.

3. Ottobah Cugoano, *Thoughts and Sentiments on the Evil and Wicked Traffic of the Slavery and Commerce of the Human Species, Humbly Submitted to the Inhabitants of Great-Britain* (London: n.p. 1787), 6–12; 5 ("a few"); 7 ("great"); 9 ("a gun," "There"), 10 ("in sight," "base," "succeeding," "thoughts"), 11 ("barbarous," "still," "in similar"), 12 ("delivered").

4. The culmination of the sixty-year effort to quantify the slave trade is *Slave Voyages* and David Eltis and David Richardson, *Atlas of the Transatlantic Slave Trade* (New Haven: Yale University Press, 2010). For "human histories" see Emma Christopher, *Slave Ship Sailors and Their Captive Cargoes, 1730–1807* (Cambridge: Cambridge University Press, 2006); Stephanie E. Smallwood, *Saltwater Slavery: A Middle Passage from Africa to American Diaspora* (Cambridge, MA: Harvard University Press, 2007), 33 ("African"), 153 ("American"); Marcus Rediker, *The Slave Ship: A Human History* (New York: Penguin Books, 2007), 9 ("factory"); Sowande' M. Mustakeem, *Slavery at Sea: Terror, Sex, and Sickness in the Middle Passage* (Urbana: University of Illinois Press, 2016), 6 ("industry").

5. Mustakeem, *Slavery,* 6 ("human"). For the average length of the Middle Passage (sixty-three days), see https://www.slavevoyages.org/voyages/ E6C53cYn.

6. With the exception of Smallwood's volume, which focuses on the late seventeenth century, all of the "human histories" focus principally on the late eighteenth century and then upstream their findings to cover the early and mid-eighteenth century.

7. For the development of plantation slavery on Barbados, see Richard S. Dunn, *Sugar and Slaves: The Rise of the Planter Class in the English West Indies, 1624–1713* (Chapel Hill: University of North Carolina Press, 1972); R. R. Menard, *Sweet Negotiations: Sugar, Slavery, and Plantation Agriculture in Early Barbados* (Charlottesville: University of Virginia Press, 2006); Justin Roberts, *Slavery and the Enlightenment in the British Atlantic, 1750–1807* (Cambridge: Cambridge University Press, 2013); Simon P. Newman, *A New World of Labor: The Development of Plantation Slavery in the British Atlantic* (Philadelphia: University of Pennsylvania Press, 2013); Trevor Burnard, *Planters, Merchants, and Slaves: Plantation Societies in British America, 1650–1820* (Chicago: University of Chicago Press, 2015). For race, see Winthrop D. Jordan, *White over Black: American Attitudes toward the Negro, 1550–1812* (Chapel Hill: University of North Carolina Press, 1968). For gender, see Jennifer L. Morgan, *Laboring Women: Reproduction and Gender in New World Slavery* (Philadelphia: University of Pennsylvania Press, 2004). For North American slavery, see Ira Berlin, "Time, Space, and the Evolution of Afro-American Society on British Mainland North America," *American Historical Review* 85, no. 1 (February 1980): 44–78; Ira Berlin, *Many Thousands Gone: The First Two Centuries of Slavery in North America* (Cambridge, MA, 1998); Ira Berlin, *Generations of Captivity: A History of African-American Slaves* (Cambridge, MA: Harvard University Press, 2004), 21 ("charter"), 51 ("plantation").

8. For differences across place, see Dunn, *Sugar and Slaves*; Philip D. Morgan, *Slave Counterpoint: Black Culture in the Eighteenth-Century Chesapeake and Lowcountry* (Chapel Hill: University of North Carolina Press, 1998); Richard S. Dunn, *A Tale of Two Plantations: Slave Life and Labor in Jamaica and Virginia* (Cambridge, MA: Harvard University Press, 2014); Wendy Warren, *New England Bound: Slavery and Colonization in Early America* (New York: Liveright, 2016).

9. Cugoano, *Thoughts and Sentiments*, 11 ("barbarous").

10. For the regional distribution of national slave trades in Africa before 1808, see http://www.slavevoyages.org/estimates/TGt8ciXG; and for the Americas, see http://www.slavevoyages.org/estimates/auJjT2Ys. The Portuguese embarked almost seven out of ten people in West-Central Africa; most (21 percent) of the remaining people were drawn from the Bight of Benin. The Portuguese presence north of the equator was therefore limited. Ninety-four percent of the captives who survived the Atlantic crossing were landed in Brazil. The non-British and non-Portuguese powers collectively enslaved 2.43 million Africans prior to 1808. Although

colonial American merchants were British subjects before 1775, this book does not include them in its analysis.

11. For works on British slaving merchants, see David Richardson, *The Bristol Slave Traders: A Collective Portrait* (Bristol: Bristol Branch of the Historical Association, 1985); Stephen D. Behrendt, "Markets, Transaction Cycles, and Profits: Merchant Decision Making in the British Slave Trade," *William and Mary Quarterly* 58, no. 1 (January 2001): 171–204; David Pope, "The Wealth and Social Aspirations of Liverpool's Slave Merchants of the Second Half of the Eighteenth Century," in *Liverpool and Transatlantic Slavery*, ed. David Richardson, Anthony Tibbles, and Suzanne Schwarz (Liverpool: Liverpool University Press, 2007), 164–226; Katie McDade, "Liverpool Slave Merchant Entrepreneurial Networks, 1725–1807," *Business History* 53, no. 7 (2011): 1092–1109. For studies of individuals, see David Richardson, "Profits in the Liverpool Slave Trade: The Accounts of William Davenport," in *Liverpool, the African Slave Trade, and Abolition*, ed. Roger Anstey and P. E. H. Hair (Liverpool: Historic Society of Lancashire and Cheshire, 1976), 60–90; David Hancock, *Citizens of the World: London Merchants and the Integration of the British Atlantic Community, 1735–1785* (Cambridge: Cambridge University Press, 1995); Kenneth Morgan, "James Rogers and the Bristol Slave Trade," *Historical Research* 76, no. 192 (2003): 189–216; Peter Earle, *The Earles of Liverpool: A Georgian Merchant Dynasty* (Liverpool: Liverpool University Press, 2015); Matthew David Mitchell, *The Prince of Slavers: Humphry Morice and the Transformation of Britain's Translatlantic Slave Trade, 1698–1732* (London: Palgrave Macmillan, 2020).

12. For a rare study of an individual African merchant, see Stephen D. Behrendt, A. J. H. Latham, and David A. Northrup, *The Diary of Antera Duke: An Eighteenth-Century African Slave Trader* (Oxford: Oxford University Press, 2010). For broader works, see John K. Thornton, *Africa and Africans in the Making of the Atlantic World, 1400–1800*, 2nd edition (Cambridge, MA: Cambridge University Press, 1998); Phyllis Martin, *The External Trade of the Loango Coast, 1576–1870: The Effects of Changing Commercial Relations on the Vili Kingdom of Loango* (Oxford: Oxford University Press, 1972); A. J. H. Latham, *Old Calabar, 1600–1891: The Impact of the International Economy upon a Traditional Society* (Oxford: Oxford University Press, 1973); Alexander X. Byrd, *Captives and Voyagers: Black Migrants across the Eighteenth-Century British Atlantic World* (Baton Rouge: Louisiana State University Press, 2008); Rebecca Shumway, *The Fante and the Transatlantic Slave Trade* (Rochester: University of Rochester Press, 2011); Randy J. Sparks, *Where the Negroes Are Masters* (Cambridge, MA: Harvard University Press, 2014).

13. For studies of Guinea factors, see Kenneth Morgan, ed., *The Bright-Meyler Papers: A Bristol–West India Connection, 1732–1837* (Oxford: Oxford University Press, 2007); David Hancock, "'A World of Business to Do':

William Freeman and the Foundations of England's Commercial Empire, 1645–1707," *William and Mary Quarterly* 57, no. 1 (January 2000): 3–34; Douglas J. Hamilton, *Scotland, the Caribbean and the Atlantic World, 1750–1820* (Manchester: Manchester University Press, 2005), 84–111; Nicholas Radburn, "Guinea Factors, Slave Sales, and the Profits of the Transatlantic Slave Trade in Late Eighteenth-Century Jamaica: The Case of John Tailyour," *WMQ* 72, no. 2 (April 2015): 243–86; Kate Donington, *The Bonds of Family: Slavery, Commerce and Culture in the British Atlantic World* (Manchester: Manchester University Press, 2019).

14. For links between British and African merchants in particular ports, see, for example, David Richardson, *Principles and Agents: The British Slave Trade and Its Abolition* (New Haven: Yale University Press, 2022), 45–66. One nonscholarly work does examine slaving merchants, but it is a survey of the trade and some of its key individual organizers rather than a broad study of slavers across the Atlantic world. See James Pope-Hennessy, *Sins of the Fathers: A Study of the Atlantic Slave Traders, 1441–1807* (New York: Alfred A. Knopf, 1968). For merchants in the U.S. domestic slave trade, see Steven Deyle, *Carry Me Back: The Domestic Slave Trade in American Life* (New York: Oxford University Press, 2005); Edward Baptist, *The Half Has Never Been Told: Slavery and the Making of American Capitalism* (New York: Basic Books, 2014); Calvin Schermerhorn, *The Business of Slavery and the Rise of American Capitalism, 1815–1860* (New Haven: Yale University Press, 2015); Joshua D. Rothman, *The Ledger and the Chain: How Domestic Slave Traders Shaped America* (New York: Basic Books, 2021). For American merchants in the transatlantic slave trade, see Jay Coughtry, *The Notorious Triangle: Rhode Island and the African Slave Trade, 1700–1807* (Philadelphia: Temple University Press, 1981); Leonardo Marques, *The United States and the Transatlantic Slave Trade to the Americas, 1776–1867* (New Haven: Yale University Press, 2016); John Harris, *The Last Slave Ships: New York and the End of the Middle Passage* (New Haven: Yale University Press, 2021).

15. Justice and Humanity [Thomas Paine], "To Americans," *Postscript to the Pennsylvania Journal and the Weekly Advertiser*, March 8, 1775 ("unnatural").

16. Thomas Clarkson, *The History of the Rise, Progress, and Accomplishment of the Abolition of the African Slave-Trade by the British Parliament* (London: R. Taylor, 1808), vol. 1, 25 ("hydra," "many").

17. For works that emphasize the importance of African ethnicity to Atlantic slavery, see Michael Mullin, *Africa in America: Slave Acculturation and Resistance in the American South and the British Caribbean, 1736–1831* (Urbana: University of Illinois Press, 1992); Michael Gomez, *Exchanging Our Country Marks: The Transformation of African Identities in the Colonial and Antebellum South* (Chapel Hill: University of North Carolina Press, 1998); Jose C. Curto and Paul E. Lovejoy, eds., *Enslaving Connections: Changing Cultures of Africa and Brazil during the Era of Slavery* (Amherst: Humanity

Books, 2003); Paul E. Lovejoy and David V. Trotman, eds., *Trans-Atlantic Dimensions of Ethnicity in the African Diaspora* (London: Bloomsbury Academic, 2003); Paul E. Lovejoy, ed., *Identity in the Shadow of Slavery* (New York: Bloomsbury, 2009); Gwendolyn Midlo Hall, *Slavery and African Ethnicities in the Americas: Restoring the Links* (Chapel Hill: University of North Carolina Press, 2009); José C. Curto and Renée Soulodre-LaFrance, *Africa and the Americas: Interconnections during the Slave Trade* (Trenton, NJ: Africa World Press, 2005); Walter Hawthorne, *From Africa to Brazil: Culture, Identity, and an Atlantic Slave Trade, 1600–1830* (New York: Cambridge University Press, 2010).

18. The number of British slaving merchants is based on an analysis of the "vessel owner" field for British flagged vessels in *SV:* https://www.slavevoyages.org/voyages/3Z7KgDpW. For the principal collections of British merchants' papers, see PWD; William Davenport Papers, D/DAV, MMM; JRP. For smaller collections, see *The Humphrey Morice Papers from the Bank of England, London* (Marlborough: Adam Matthews, 2000); *The Hobhouse Letters, 1722–1755: Letters and Other Papers of Isaac Hobhouse & Co., Bristol Merchants* (Wakefield: Microform Academic Publishers, 1971); Tuohy Papers, TUO 4/3, LRO; Thomas Leyland Papers, 387 MD 42, LRO; Letter book, etc. of Robert Bostock, 2 vols., 387 MD 55, Liverpool Record Office; Earle Family Papers, D/EARLE/1/4, LRO; Messrs Thomas Lumley and Co of London (trading with Europe and the West Indies: sugar, rum, cotton, indigo, cloth, and slaves): correspondence and accounts, C114/1–2, 156–58, TNAUK.

19. After its dissolution in 1753, the RAC was succeeded by the Company of Merchants Trading to Africa, a non-monopoly holding company of private slaving merchants that received an annual grant from Parliament to maintain the company's slaving forts. The records for both the RAC and the CMTA are in Company of Royal Adventurers of England Trading with Africa and successors: Records, T70 series, TNAUK.

20. For major collections of Guinea factors' papers, see *PHL*; Austin & Laurens Account Book, April 1750–December 1758, Gen. MSS, vol. 184, Beinecke Rare Book and Manuscript Library, Yale University, New Haven; Morgan, ed., *Bright-Meyler Papers*. For recently discovered papers, see TFP; *JDRH*. For parliamentary testimony, see *HCSP*, vols. 68–73, 82, 99.

21. *SV* grew out of previous efforts to quantify the slave trade, for which see Philip Curtin, *The Atlantic Slave Trade: A Census* (Madison: University of Wisconsin Press, 1969; David Eltis, David Richardson, Stephen Behrendt, and Herbert S. Klein, *The Atlantic Slave Trade: A Database on CD-ROM* (New York: Cambridge University Press, 1999).

22. For works that have used *SV* to detail the volume and direction of the trade, see, for example, David Eltis, "The Volume and Structure of the Transatlantic Slave Trade: A Reassessment," *William and Mary Quarterly* 58, no. 1 (2001): 17–46; David Eltis and David Richardson, eds., *Extending*

the *Frontiers: Essays on the New Transatlantic Slave Trade Database* (New Haven: Yale University Press, 2008); David Eltis and David Richardson, eds., *Routes to Slavery: Direction, Ethnicity and Mortality in the Transatlantic Slave Trade* (London: Routledge, 2013); Alex Borucki, David Eltis, and David Wheat, "Atlantic History and the Slave Trade to Spanish America," *American Historical Review* 120, no. 2 (April 2015): 433–61.

23. Rediker, *The Slave Ship*, 12 ("violence"). For similar critiques, see Paul E. Lovejoy, "Extending the Frontiers of Transatlantic Slavery, Partially," *Journal of Interdisciplinary History* 40, no. 1 (2009): 58–9, 65; Gwendolyn Midlo Hall, "Africa and Africans in the African Diaspora: The Uses of Relational Databases," *American Historical Review* 115, no. 1 (February 1, 2010): 136–50; Paul E. Lovejoy, "The Upper Guinea Coast and the Trans-Atlantic Slave Trade Database," *African Economic History* 38 (2010): 1–27; Toby Green, *The Rise of the Trans-Atlantic Slave Trade in Western Africa, 1300–1589* (Cambridge: Cambridge University Press, 2012), 4–5; Jessica Marie Johnson, "Markup Bodies: Black [Life] Studies and Slavery [Death] Studies at the Digital Crossroads," *Social Text* 36, no. 4 (2018): 57–79. For a study that attempts to meld the quantitative and the qualitative, see Gregory E. O'Malley, *Final Passages: The Intercolonial Slave Trade of British America, 1619–1807* (Chapel Hill: University of North Carolina Press, 2015).

Chapter One. Connecting the Frontiers

1. King Henshaw, Duke Ephraim, and Willy Honesty to [William Davenport?], Old Calabar, June 24, 1780, in *Liverpool General Advertiser*, February 21, 1788, 3. The newspaper reprinted the private 1780 letter, presumably having been given it by the slave trader recipient to combat growing abolitionist sentiment. Robert Norris to Lord Hawkesbury, Liverpool, March 9, 1789, BT6/262, TNAUK. In the year of Norris's letter, Liverpool merchants forcibly embarked 19,952 of the 81,054 captives shipped from Africa (https://www.slavevoyages.org/voyages/XbGUJkue). Liverpool's nearest rival was Nantes, whose traders enslaved 11,615 people (https://www.slavevoyages.org/voyages/oswgn9Sc).

2. For the number of English and African ports before 1700, see https://www.slavevoyages.org/voyages/EG3raRVd. For the number of ports post-1700, see https://www.slavevoyages.org/voyages/plxLkIDj. For the trade from Calabar, Bonny, and Anomabu before 1700, see https://www.slavevoyages.org/voyages/cdzeowRo. For London, Bristol, and Liverpool's dominance of Britain's slave trade, see https://www.slavevoyages.org/voyages/OxYAub2u. For the concentration of the slave trade at large African ports, see Eltis and Richardson, *Atlas*, 90.

3. For the economic forces driving the development of slaving ports, see David Eltis, Paul E. Lovejoy, and David Richardson, "Slave-Trading

Ports: Towards an Atlantic-Wide Perspective, 1676–1832," in *Ports of the Slave Trade (Bights of Benin and Biafra): Papers from a Conference of the Centre of Commonwealth Studies, University of Sterling, June 1998*, ed. Robin Law and Silke Stickrodt (Stirling: Centre of Commonwealth Studies, University of Stirling, 1999), 12–34; Jorge Canizeras-Esguerra, Matt D. Childs, and James Sidbury, eds., *The Black Urban Atlantic in the Age of the Slave Trade* (Philadelphia: University of Pennsylvania Press, 2013); Robin Law, *Ouidah: The Social History of a West African Slaving Port: 1727–1892* (Athens: Ohio University Press, 2004). On credit, see Paul E. Lovejoy and David Richardson, "African Agency and the Liverpool Slave Trade," in *Liverpool and Transatlantic Slavery*, ed. Richardson et al., 43–65. See also, Kenneth Morgan, "Liverpool's Dominance in the British Slave Trade, 1740–1807," in ibid., 14–42.

4. For early European exploration and trade in Africa, see P. E. H. Hair, *Africa Encountered: European Contacts and Evidence, 1450–1700* (Aldershot: Routledge, 1997); Robin Law, "West Africa's Discovery of the Atlantic," *International Journal of African Historical Studies* 44, no. 1 (2011): 1–25; Thornton, *Africa and Africans*, 13–42; Toby Green, *The Rise of the Trans-Atlantic Slave Trade in Western Africa, 1300–1589* (New York: Cambridge University Press, 2012); David Northrup, *Africa's Discovery of Europe*, 3rd edition (Oxford: Oxford University Press, 2014). For the French chartered slaving companies, see Robert Louis Stein, *The French Slave Trade in the Eighteenth Century: An Old Regime Business* (Madison: University of Wisconsin Press, 1979), 3–12. For the Dutch, see Johannes Menne Postma, *The Dutch in the Atlantic Slave Trade: 1600–1815* (Cambridge: Cambridge University Press, 1990), 1–25.

5. For the close connection between the slave trade and the trade in African commodities before 1700, see David Eltis and Lawrence C. Jennings, "Trade between Western Africa and the Atlantic World in the Pre-Colonial Era," *American Historical Review* 93, no. 4 (October 1988): 936–59; Ernst Van Den Boogaart, "The Trade between Western Africa and the Atlantic World, 1600–90: Estimates of Trends in Composition and Value," *Journal of African History* 33, no. 3 (1992): 369–85; David Eltis, "The Relative Importance of Slaves and Commodities in the Atlantic Trade of Seventeenth-Century Africa," *Journal of African History* 35, no. 2 (1994): 237–49. For the RAC's concentration on the "fort" trade in Africa, see also K. G. Davies, *The Royal African Company* (New York: Longmans, Green, 1957), 213–32. For the geography of the pre-1700 slave trade, see *SV*: Estimates, 1501–1699.

6. For the RAC's slave trade, see https://www.slavevoyages.org/voyages/RibGyfaC. For the RAC's myriad economic and political problems, see Davies, *Royal African Company*, 74–96; 122–51; Ann M. Carlos, "Principal-Agent Problems in Early Trading Companies: A Tale of Two Firms," *American Economic Review* 82, no. 2 (May 1992): 140–45; Ann

M. Carlos and Jamie Brown Kruse, "The Decline of the Royal African Company: Fringe Firms and the Role of the Charter," *Economic History Review* 49, no. 2 (May 1996): 291–313; William A. Pettigrew, "Free to Enslave: Politics and the Escalation of Britain's Transatlantic Slave Trade, 1688–1714," *William and Mary Quarterly* 64, no. 1 (January 2007): 3–38; William A. Pettigrew, *Freedom's Debt: The Royal African Company and the Politics of the Atlantic Slave Trade, 1672–1752* (Chapel Hill: University of North Carolina Press, 2013).

7. For the regional configuration of Britain's pre-1750 slave trade, see https://www.slavevoyages.org/voyages/24iKo5QL. For Bristol, see Kenneth Morgan, *Bristol and the Atlantic Trade in the Eighteenth Century* (Cambridge: Cambridge University Press, 1993), 128–51; David Richardson, *Bristol, Africa and the Eighteenth-Century Slave Trade to America*, 4 vols. (Bristol: Bristol Record Society's Publications, 1986–1996); Madge Dresser, *Slavery Obscured: The Social History of the Slave Trade in an English Provincial Port* (London: Bloomsbury, 2016), 7–52; Richardson, *Bristol Slave Traders*; David Richardson, "Slavery and Bristol's 'Golden Age,'" *Slavery and Abolition* 26, no. 1 (April 2005): 35–54. For London, see James A. Rawley, "The Port of London and the Eighteenth Century Slave Trade: Historians, Sources, and a Reappraisal," *African Economic History* 9 (1980): 85–100. For Whitehaven, see David Richardson and M. M. Schofield, "Whitehaven and the Eighteenth-Century British Slave Trade," *Transactions of the Cumberland and Westmoreland Antiquarian and Archaeological Society* XCII (1992): 183–204. For Lancaster, see Melinda Elder, *The Slave Trade and the Economic Development of 18th Century Lancaster* (Halifax: Ryburn, 1992). For other outports, see M. M. Schofield, "The Slave Trade from Lancashire and Cheshire Ports Outside Liverpool, c. 1750–c. 1790," *Transactions of the Historic Society of Lancashire and Cheshire* 126 (1976): 30–73; Nigel Tattersfield, *The Forgotten Trade: Including the Log of the "Daniel and Henry" of 1700 and Accounts of the Slave Trade from the Minor Ports of England, 1698–1725* (London: Jonathan Cape, 1991).

8. For London's population, see Jan de Vries, *European Urbanization, 1500–1800* (London: Routledge, 2006), 195. For Liverpool and the northwest, see Kenneth Morgan, "Liverpool's Dominance in the British Slave Trade, 1740–1807," in *Liverpool and Transatlantic Slavery*, ed. Richardson et al., 17; Jon Stobart, *The First Industrial Region: North West England, c. 1700–60* (Manchester: Manchester University Press, 2004), 34–37. For Bristol, see David Harris Sacks, *The Widening Gate: Bristol and the Atlantic Economy, 1450–1700* (Berkeley: University of California Press, 1991). Colonial American merchants in at least twenty ports, especially in New England, likewise embraced the slave trade after the RAC's collapse. See Coughtry, *Notorious Triangle*, 5–21; Sparks, *Where the Negroes*, 163–185.

9. Alfred Wadsworth and Julia de Lacy Mann, *The Cotton Trade and Industrial Lancashire, 1600–1780* (Manchester: Manchester University Press,

1931), 311 ("not so much"). For the growth of England's population, see De Vries, *European Urbanization*, 36. For Liverpool, see Diana E. Ascott, Fiona Lewis, and Michael Power, *Liverpool 1660–1750: People, Prosperity and Power* (Liverpool: Liverpool University Press, 2006), 37. For Bristol, see W. E. Minchinton, "Bristol: Metropolis of the West in the Eighteenth Century: The Alexander Prize Essay," *Transactions of the Royal Historical Society* 4 (1954): 69–89; Henry Rees, "The Growth of Bristol," *Economic Geography* 21, no. 4 (October 1945): 269–75.

10. For tobacco imports, see *Historical Statistics of the United States Colonial Times to 1957* (Washington, DC: Bureau of the Census, 1961), 765–67. For sugar, see Richard B. Sheridan, *Sugar and Slavery: An Economic History of the British West Indies, 1623–1775*, reprint edition (Kingston: Canoe Press, 2000), 22. For the growth of Atlantic port cities, see De Vries, *European Urbanization*, 141.

11. For the London merchant societies' grip on European trade during the seventeenth century, see Robert Brenner, *Merchants and Revolution: Commercial Change, Political Conflict, and London's Overseas Traders, 1550–1653* (Princeton: Princeton University Press, 1993), 3–50; 113–195 ("new men"). Sacks, *The Widening Gate*, 251–77; 267 ("the chance"). For Bristol's merchant society, see also E. M. Carus-Wilson, "The Merchant Adventurers of Bristol in the Fifteenth Century," *Transactions of the Royal Historical Society* 11 (1928): 61–82. Writing of London, Nuala Zahedieh describes the "plantation trades" attracting "crowds of investors" in London because they were "largely open, and unregulated" (*The Capital and the Colonies: London and the Atlantic Economy, 1660–1700* [Cambridge: Cambridge University Press, 2012], 57, 63).

12. For Liverpool merchants' strategies, see Paul G. E. Clemens, "The Rise of Liverpool, 1665–1750," *Economic History Review* 29, no. 2 (May 1976): 211–25. For London sugar imports, see Zahedieh, *Capital and the Colonies*, 200. For Bristol sugar imports, see Morgan, *Bristol and the Atlantic Trade*, 169–75. For Bristol's trade, see also W. E. Minchinton, "The Trade of Bristol in the Eighteenth Century," *Bristol Record Society Publications* 20 (1957); Kenneth Morgan, "Shipping Patterns and the Atlantic Trade of Bristol, 1749–1770," *William and Mary Quarterly* 46 (1989): 506–38; Kenneth Morgan, "Bristol and the Atlantic Trade in the Eighteenth Century," *English Historical Review* 107, no. 424 (July 1992): 626–50; Kenneth Morgan, "Bristol West India Merchants in the Eighteenth Century," *Transactions of the Royal Historical Society* 3 (1993): 185–208; Evan T. Jones, "Illicit Business: Accounting for Smuggling in Mid-Sixteenth-Century Bristol," *Economic History Review* 54, no. 1 (February 2001): 17–38.

13. Thomas Hodgson to Richard Miles, Liverpool, February 18, 1783, T70/1549/2, TNAUK ("Golden Voyages"). Testimony of John Newton, May 12, 1790, in *HCSP*, vol. 73, 146 ("lottery"). For the slave trade's risks, see Sheryllynne Haggerty, "Risk and Risk Management in the Liverpool

Slave Trade," *Business History* 51, no. 6 (November 2009): 817–34. For the profitability of the transatlantic slave trade, see David Richardson, "Profits in the Liverpool Slave Trade: The Accounts of William Davenport, 1757–1784," in *Liverpool, the African Slave Trade, and Abolition*, ed. Roger Anstey and P. E. H. Hair (Liverpool: Historic Society of Lancashire and Cheshire, 1976), 60–90; J. E. Inikori, "Market Structure and the Profits of the British African Trade in the Late Eighteenth Century," *Journal of Economic History* 41, no. 4 (December 1981): 745–76.

14. Elder, *Slave Trade*, 205 ("marginal"). Data on the Bristol slave traders are drawn from an analysis of the city's apprenticeship records (*Transcripts and Indexes of the Bristol Apprenticeship Books*, 2 vols. [Bristol: Bristol and Avon Family History Society, 2012–2019]), and burgesses records (*Index to the Bristol Burgess Books, Volumes 1 to 21, 1557–1995* [Bristol: Bristol and Avon Family History Society, 2005]). These records detail the fathers' occupations for 248 of the 568 Bristol slave traders recorded in *SV*: https://www.slavevoyages.org/voyages/ZSDalfiH. Of those 248, fifty-seven were the sons of merchants and forty-four sons of gentlemen or "esquire." The remainder were sons of tradesmen engaged in a variety of professions, including anchorsmiths; apothecaries; bakers; blacksmiths; clerks; coopers; maltsters; market gardeners; soap makers; and tobacconists.

15. For the Earle family, see Earle, *The Earles of Liverpool*; T. Algernon Earle, "Earle of Allerton Tower," in *Transactions of the Historic Society of Lancashire and Cheshire*, 42 (1890): 15–76; Alexandra Robinson, "'Citizens of the World': The Earle Family's Leghorn and Venetian Business, 1751–1808," in *Slavery Hinterland: Transatlantic Slavery and Continental Europe, 1680–1850*, ed. Felix Brahm and Eve Rosenhaft (Woodbridge: Boydell Press, 2016), 45–64; Brian W. Refford, "The Bonds of Trade: Liverpool Slave Traders, 1695–1775," unpublished Ph.D. dissertation, Lehigh University, 2005, 86–106. For Clayton, see "CLAYTON, William (aft. 1650–1715), of Fulwood, nr. Preston and Water Street, Liverpool, Lancs.," in *The History of Parliament: The House of Commons, 1690–1715*, ed. Eveline Cruickshanks, Stuart Handley, and David W. Hayton (Cambridge: Cambridge University Press, 2002).

16. Pettigrew, *Freedom's Debt*, 25, 45 ("powerful"), 59 ("emerged"). For Colston, see Kenneth Morgan, "Edward Colston and Bristol," *Bristol Branch of the Historical Association Local History Pamphlets* 96 (Bristol: Bristol Branch of the Historical Association, 1999). For the origins of London merchants, see Zahedieh, *Capital and the Colonies*, 63–64. For Morice, see "MORICE, Humphry (c. 1671–1731) of The Grove, Chiswick, Mdx., and Mincing Lane, London," in *The History of Parliament: The House of Commons, 1690–1715*, ed. Cruickshanks, Handley, and Hayton; James A. Rawley, *London, Metropolis of the Slave Trade* (Columbia: University of Missouri Press, 2003), 40–56; James A. Rawley, "Morice, Humphry (bap. 1679, d. 1731)," *Oxford Dictionary of National Biography* (Oxford: Oxford

University Press, 2004); Mitchell, *Prince of Slavers*, 103–143. John Atkins, *A Voyage to Guinea, Brasil and the West Indies; in His Majesty's Ships, the Swallow and Weymouth* . . . , 2nd edition (London: Ward and Chandler, 1737), 159 ("greatest"). Morice died in disgrace after it was discovered that he had embezzled £29,000 from the Bank of England. Richard Harris, Robert Heysham, and Abraham Houlditch—the three other leading London slavers—mirrored Morice's elite background and connections to the colonial trades.

17. For voyage patterns in the early eighteenth century, see, for example, the logbook of the *Regard*, November 20, 1705–July 13, 1706 (1705/6), and the account books of the ships *Henry* (1721–1722; 1722–1723), *Sarah* (1722–1723), and *Portugal* (1724) within Morice's papers (M7/6–10, Bank of England, London). For citations to logbooks, see my Appendix C. See also the cargo books of the RAC's voyages, which include numerous vessels that ran along the coast to get a complete human cargo at Benin (T70/910–923, TNAUK). In 1675, six hundred people could be purchased at Ardra with a cargo costing £1,787 ("Invoice of Goods Laden on board the St George . . . ," T70/910, TNAUK). In 1700, by contrast, 221 people were exchanged at Whydah for a cargo costing £2,140 ("Invoice of Sundry Goods Laden on board ye Larke Frigatt . . . ," T70/919, TNAUK). In the same year, a person could be purchased at Calabar for just under £5 ("Invoice of Sundry Goods Laden on board ye Bridgewater Frigatt . . . ," ibid). For the high prices of captives on the Gold Coast and in the Bight of Benin, and the low prices of people elsewhere in Africa, see "Copy of Petitions Presented by the Royal African Company of England From November the 20th 1707 To May the 5th 1712," T70/175, TNAUK. Currencies are sterling unless stated otherwise.

18. For the purchase of captives at Whydah, see Thomas Phillips, *A Journal of a Voyage Made in the Hannibal of London, Ann. 1693, 1694* . . . (London: Walthoe, 1732), 214–30. For fraught relations on the Windward Coast, see *BG*, vol. 1, 239–302; Atkins, *Voyage*, 58–59, 167. Fewer than five thousand people are recorded as embarked at Sierra Leone and the Windward Coast before 1700 (https://www.slavevoyages.org/voyages/DiR2JgqJ). This number understates the numbers of captives carried from the two regions because vessels often embarked people there before completing the loading of their cargoes farther down the coast. Nonetheless, both regions were minor and dangerous markets compared to busier locations to the east.

19. For the cargoes used to buy people at Calabar, see, for example, "Invoice of Sundry Goods Laden on board ye Bridgewater Frigatt . . . ," May 10, 1701, T70/919, TNAUK. For cargoes at Whydah, see "Invoice of Sundry Goods Laden on Board ye Gold Frigatt . . . ," June 24, 1701, T70/919, TNAUK. For the manning of slave ships from the outports' hinterlands, see Stephen D. Behrendt, "Human Capital in the British Slave Trade," in

Liverpool and Transatlantic Slavery, ed. Richardson et al., 75–82. For the importance of Bristol's metal industry to the town's slave trade, see Richardson, "Slavery and Bristol's 'Golden Age,'" 43–44.

20. Instructions for the *Blessing*, 1700. For the citation to these instructions, see my Appendix A. Just six English ships are known to have traded on the Loango coast in the five years before 1700. See https://www.slavevoyages .org/voyages/yUH6rkos/. The *Two Brothers* orders are quoted in Wadsworth and Mann, *Cotton Trade*, 230 ("try all," "be so"). The latitude that outport traders gave to their captains in selecting a trading region in Africa likely explains why there are so few African trading locations listed for the vessels of non-London slave ships in the *SV* (see https://www .slavevoyages.org/voyages/95WbYzHO).

21. For the opening of new African markets by Liverpool merchants, see Morgan, "Liverpool's Dominance," in *Liverpool and Transatlantic Slavery*, ed. Richardson et al., 26–27. For the Gambia, see Elder, *The Slave Trade*, 55–57. For Liverpool's expansion of the trade in Upper Guinea, see Kenneth Morgan, "Liverpool Ascendant: British Merchants and the Slave Trade on the Upper Guinea Coast, 1701–1808," in *Slavery, Abolition and the Transition to Colonisation in Sierra Leone*, ed. Paul Lovejoy and Suzanne Schwarz (Trenton, NJ: Africa World Press, 2015), 29–50. For the Isles de Los, see Bruce J. Mouser, "Iles de Los as Bulking Center in the Slave Trade, 1750–1800," *Revue française d'histoire d'outre-mer* 83, no. 313 (1996): 77–91. For Bance Island, see Hancock, *Citizens of the World*, 172–220. For new markets in the Bight of Benin, see Silke Strickrodt, *Afro-European Trade in the Atlantic World: The Western Slave Coast, c. 1550–c. 1885* (Woodbridge: Boydell and Brewer, 2015).

22. For Davenport and Cameroon, see Nicholas Radburn, "William Davenport, the Slave Trade, and Merchant Enterprise in Eighteenth-Century Liverpool," unpublished M.A. thesis, Victoria University of Wellington, 2009. *Racoon* was captured by the French, but its captain returned to Liverpool and, presumably, gave Davenport intelligence on Cameroon. The reference to secrecy is to a 1767 voyage that Davenport cofinanced to explore the markets of Cape Lopez, the Nazareth River, and Gabon, which were near Cameroon. See Thomas Staniforth & Co. to Captain Samuel Richardson, Liverpool, October 11, 1767, in Trading Accounts of the King of Prussia 1767–1779, PWD ("so unknown"). These ventures must have been failures—likely because of the hostility of the resident Africans; Davenport and his partners did not outfit further vessels to those ports.

23. For Davenport's Cameroon voyages, see https://www.slavevoyages.org/ voyages/NM5douMd. Davenport's Cameroon ships carried off much larger numbers of males (averaging 74 percent of the human cargo, versus 60 percent at Calabar) and acquired enslaved people at lower prices than at other, more competitive markets. For Davenport's profits from

his Cameroon investments, see Richardson, "Profits"; Radburn, "William Davenport," 88.

24. Atkins, *Voyage*, 158 ("rejected"), 159 ("the Windward"). For regional West African consumer demand, see David Richardson, "West African Consumption Patterns and Their Influence on the Eighteenth-Century English Slave Trade," in *The Uncommon Market: Essays in the Economic History of the Atlantic Slave Trade*, ed. Henry A. Gemery and Jan S. Hogendorn (New York: Academic Press, 1979), 303–30; Stanley B. Alpern, "What Africans Got for Their Slaves: A Master List of European Trade Goods," *History in Africa* 22 (1995): 5–43. For Davenport's supply chain to different African ports, see Radburn, "William Davenport," 42–71.

25. For the importance of credit in acquiring Guinea cargoes, see B. L. Anderson, "The Lancashire Bill System and Its Liverpool Practitioners: The Case of a Slave Merchant," in *Trade and Transport: Essays in Economic History in Honour of T. S. Willan*, ed. W. H. Chaloner and B. M. Ratcliffe (Manchester: Manchester University Press, 1977), 59–97; Inikori, "Market Structure," 756–58. For interconnections between outport merchants, see Refford, "The Bonds of Trade"; Richardson, *Bristol Slave Traders*.

26. For the growth of powder and gun exports to Africa from Britain, see Joseph E. Inikori, "The Imports of Firearms into West Africa, 1750–1807: A Quantitative Analysis," *Journal of African History* 18, no. 3 (1977): 339–68. The link between the gunpowder industry and the slave trade are detailed in the records of five power mills that were established to supply the trade at Woolley (Somerset Heritage Centre, Taunton, DD/SH/27); Thelwall (Derbyshire Record Office, D157/MT); Haverthwaite (Lancashire Archives, DDLO); Sedgwick (Kendal Archive Centre, WD/W); and Littleton (*The Diary of William Dyer: Bristol in 1762*, ed. Jonathan Barry [Bristol: Bristol Record Society, 2012]). For the shift of gun making to Birmingham, see Priya Satia, *Empire of Guns: The Violent Making of the Industrial Revolution* (Palo Alto: Stanford University Press, 2019).

27. For dock development, see Richard Brooke, *Liverpool as It Was during the Last Quarter of the Eighteenth Century, 1775 to 1800* (Liverpool: J. Mawdsley and Son, 1853), 97; Francis Edwin Hyde, *Liverpool and the Mersey: An Economic History of a Port, 1700–1970* (Newton Abbot: David and Charles, 1971), 14; Kenneth Morgan, "Building British Atlantic Port Cities: Bristol and Liverpool in the Eighteenth Century," in *Building the British Atlantic World: Spaces, Places, and Material Culture, 1600–1850*, ed. Daniel Maudlin and Bernard L. Herman (Chapel Hill: University of North Carolina Press, 2016), 212–28. New stone quays were also constructed at Lancaster and Whitehaven in the mid-eighteenth century, facilitating both ports' entry into the slave trade.

28. For "wealth in people," see Jane I. Guyer, "Wealth in People and Self-Realization in Equatorial Africa," *Man* 28, no. 2 (June 1993): 243–65; Thornton, *Africa and Africans*, 74–90.

29. John Ogilby, *Africa: Being an Accurate Description of . . . the Land of Negroes, . . . Collected and Translated from Most Authentick Authors . . . by John Ogilby* (London: Tho. Johnson, 1670), 423 ("chiefest"). For Fante origins, see Shumway, *Fante*, 25–52; John Kofi Fynn, "The Political System of the Fante of Ghana during the Pre-Colonial Period," *Universitas* 9 (1987): 108–20; Rebecca Shumway, "The Fante Shrine of Nananom Mpow and the Atlantic Slave Trade in Southern Ghana," *International Journal of African Historical Studies* 44, no. 1 (2011): 27–44; Robin Law, "The Government of Fante in the Seventeenth Century," *Journal of African History* 54, no. 1 (March 2013): 31–51. For polities on the coast, see Thornton, *Africa and Africans*, xi.

30. Quoted in Shumway, *Fante*, 25 ("complete"). Ray A. Kea, *Settlements, Trade, and Polities in the Seventeenth-Century Gold Coast* (Baltimore: Johns Hopkins University Press, 1982), 27 ("gunpowder"). For the introduction of firearms to the Gold Coast, see Ray A. Kea, "Firearms and Warfare on the Gold and Slave Coasts from the Sixteenth to the Nineteenth Centuries," *Journal of African History* 12, no. 2 (1971): 185–213. For warfare on the Gold Coast, see Ogilby, *Africa*, 462; *BG*, vol. 1, 607–8; John K. Thornton, *Warfare in Atlantic Africa, 1500–1800* (London: Routledge, 1999), 55–74. For the importation of enslaved people into the Gold Coast, see Walter Rodney, "Gold and Slaves on the Gold Coast," *Transactions of the Historical Society of Ghana* 10 (1969): 13–28.

31. For Asante's rise, see John Kofi Fynn, *Asante and Its Neighbours, 1700–1807* (London: Longman, 1971), 27–56; Kwame Yeboa Daaku, *Trade and Politics on the Gold Coast, 1600–1720: A Study of the African Reaction to European Trade* (Oxford: Clarendon Press, 1970), 66–72. For Akwamu, see Ivor Wilks, "The Rise of the Akwamu Empire, 1650–1710," *Transactions of the Historical Society of Ghana* 3, no. 2 (1957): 25–62. For Asante's conquests, see John Kofi Fynn, "The Structure of Greater Ashanti: Another View," *Transactions of the Historical Society of Ghana* 15, no. 1 (June 1974): 1–22; Ivor Wilks, *Asante in the Nineteenth Century: The Structure and Evolution of a Political Order* (Cambridge: Cambridge University Press, 1975), 67–71; Benedict G. Der, *The Slave Trade in Northern Ghana* (Accra: Woeli, 1998), 8–15; Kwame Osei Kwarteng, "The Asante Conquest of Ahafo in the 18th Century: A Historical Legacy," *Transactions of the Historical Society of Ghana* 6 (2002): 59–66; Sparks, *Where the Negroes*, 124–26. For slave-raiding wars between the peoples of the Gold Coast, see the testimony of enslaved people from the region within Christian Georg Andreas Oldendorp, *C. G. A. Oldendorp's History of the Mission of the Evangelical Brethren on the Caribbean Islands of St. Thomas, St. Croix, and St. John*, ed. and trans. Johann Jakob Bossard, Arnold R. Highfield, and Vladimir Barac (Ann Arbor, MI: Karoma, 1987), 163–65.

32. *BG*, vol. 2, 416 ("heavily"). Willem Bosman, *A New and Accurate Description of the Coast of Guinea: Divided into the Gold, the Slave, and the Ivory Coasts*

(London: James Knapton, 1705), 56 ("circumjacent"). For the Fante's military campaigns in the early eighteenth century, see James Sanders, "The Expansion of the Fante and the Emergence of Asante in the Eighteenth Century," *Journal of African History* 20, no. 3 (1979): 349–64, 356–57 ("exclusive"); Daaku, *Trade and Politics*, 166–170; Shumway, *Fante*, 94–101.

33. For the Great Roads, see Wilks, *Asante*, 1–42; Akosua Adoma Perbi, *A History of Indigenous Slavery in Ghana: From the 15th to the 19th Century* (Accra: Sub-Saharan, 2004), 37–41; Sparks, *Where the Negroes*, 130–33. Enslaved people were sold in slave markets along the Great Roads and in and around Kumasi, only some of whom were subsequently marched to the sea. Asante slaveholders purchased captives to work at a wide variety of tasks, but especially agriculture; gold mining; domestic service; and military service. For domestic slavery, see Ivor Wilks, *Forests of Gold: Essays on the Akan and the Kingdom of Asante* (Athens: Ohio University Press, 1995), 77; T. C. McCaskie, *State and Society in Pre-Colonial Asante* (Cambridge: Cambridge University Press, 2003), 88–101.

34. For Anomabu, see Sparks, *Where the Negroes*, 7–34; Trevor R. Getz, "Mechanisms of Slave Acquisition and Exchange in Late Eighteenth Century Anomabu: Reconsidering a Cross-Section of the Atlantic Slave Trade," *African Economic History* 31 (2003): 77–79; Shumway, *Fante*, 71–86; Daaku, *Trade and Politics*, 17–18; Randy J. Sparks, "Gold Coast Merchant Families, Pawning, and the Eighteenth-Century British Slave Trade," *William and Mary Quarterly* 70, no. 2 (April 2013): 332.

35. For pawnship, see Sparks, *Where the Negroes*, 28; Sparks, "Gold Coast Merchant Families," 320–32; Paul E. Lovejoy and David Richardson, "The Business of Slaving: Pawnship in Western Africa, c. 1600–1810," *Journal of African History* 42, no. 1 (January 2001): 67–89. For African children in Liverpool, see John Matthews, James Penny and Robert Norris to John Tarleton, Liverpool, April 16, 1788, BT 6/7, TNAUK ("about fifty"). For Brew and his descendants, see M. A. Priestley, "Richard Brew: An Eighteenth-Century Trader at Anomabu," *Transactions of the Historical Society of Ghana* 4, no. 1 (1959): 29–46; M. A. Priestley, *West African Trade and Coast Society: A Family Study* (Oxford: Oxford University Press, 1969).

36. For Anomabu as a key grain market, see Randy J. Sparks, "The Peopling of an African Slave Port: Annamaboe and the Atlantic World," *Almanack* 27 (2020): 1–39, 6 ("principal granary"). For slave ship provisioning, see Alexander Dalrymple-Smith and Ewout Frankema, "Slave Ship Provisioning in the Long 18th Century: A Boost to West African Commercial Agriculture?" *European Review of Economic History* 21, no. 2 (2017): 185–235. The seasonality of the Gold Coast slave trade is based on an analysis of the slave purchases of British fort officer Richard Miles at Tantumquerry, Anamabo, and Cape Coast Castle, which are recorded in Slave Barters by R. Miles at Tantumquerry, Accra and Annamaboe, 1772–1776, T70/1264, TNAUK; Slave barters by R. Miles at Annamaboe . . . ,

1776–1777, T70/1265, TNAUK; R. Miles: Tantumquerry; rough day book, 1771–1772, T70/1488, TNAUK. Miles's transactions have been cross-referenced with rainfall levels from Wilks, *Forests of Gold*, 57.

37. For ships completing their purchases at Anomabu, see Atkins, *Voyage*, 169. Logbook of the *Black Prince*, October 18, 1762–February 28, 1763. For ships principally embarking captives at Anomabu, see also the logbook of the *Gregson*, January 1–November 18, 1788. For London's focus on Cape Coast Castle, see https://www.slavevoyages.org/voyages/zMoqvjUo. For the outport's focus on Anomabu, see https://www.slavevoyages.org/voyages/jQAYOmzD. For London merchants' continued concentration on the "fort trade," see Behrendt, "Human Capital," 82–84.

38. For the origins of the captives taken from Biafra in the early seventeenth century, see Alonso de Sandoval, *Treatise on Slavery: Selections from De Instauranda Aethiopum Salute*, trans. Nicole von Germeten (Indianapolis: Hackett, 2008), 47; Ogilby, *Africa*, 483; A. J. H. Latham, *Old Calabar, 1600–1891: The Impact of the International Economy upon a Traditional Society* (Oxford: Oxford University Press, 1973), 9. For the volume of the Bight of Biafra slave trade, see *SV*: Estimates Section, Embarkation Region: Bight of Biafra, 1618–1808.

39. *BG*, vol. 2, 672 ("thrown," "malignity"), 700 ("pray," "alive," "lost"). "A Journall of my Intended Voyage for ye Gold Coast . . . Ship James," June 15, 1676, T70/1211, TNAUK ("Bite slaves"). For the decline in the Dutch trade to Biafra, see https://www.slavevoyages.org/voyages/gykL91Nd; for the London trade, see https://www.slavevoyages.org/voyages/GWUDwyHh. For captives carried from the Gold Coast and Biafra, see http://www.slavevoyages.org/estimates/JDGC3AiF.

40. Oldendorp, *History of the Mission*, 210 ("contentious"). For the Aro and their slave trade, see David Northrup, *Trade without Rulers: Pre-Colonial Economic Development in South-Eastern Nigeria* (Oxford: Clarendon Press, 1978), 34–36, 114–45; Kenneth Onwuka Dike and Felicia Ifeoma Ekejiuba, *The Aro of South-Eastern Nigeria, 1650–1980: A Study of Socio-Economic Formation and Transformation in Nigeria* (Ibadan: University Press, 1990); G. Ugo Nwokeji, *The Slave Trade and Culture in the Bight of Biafra: An African Society in the Atlantic World* (Cambridge: Cambridge University Press, 2010), 22–81.

41. *BG*, vol. 2, 691 ("above," "up"), 693 ("fetch"), map 53 ("Hackbous Country"). For the Aro slave-trading network, see Dike and Ekejiuba, *Aro*, 94–123; Northrup, *Trade*, 85–113; Ukwu I. Ukwu, "The Development of Trade and Marketing in Iboland," *Journal of Historical Society in Nigeria* 3, no. 4 (June 1967): 647–62; David Northrup, "The Growth of Trade among the Igbo before 1800," *Journal of African History* 13, no. 2 (1972): 217–36; Paul E. Lovejoy and David Richardson, "'This Horrid Hole': Royal Authority, Commerce and Credit at Bonny, 1690–1840," *Journal of*

African History 45, no. 3 (January 2004): 380–82. *SV*: Estimates Section, Embarkation Region: Bight of Biafra, 1700–1808.

42. For Europeans trading at multiple ports in the western Bight, see *BG*, vol. 2, 673–91, 690 ("to and fro," "circumjacent"); "A Journall of a voyage att New Callabarr in the shipp the Arthur . . . ," February 12, 1678, T70/1213, TNAUK; Instructions for the *Africa*, 1699; *Dispatch*, 1725. For the dispersed nature of the early Old Calabar slave trade, see Behrendt et al., *Diary of Antera Duke*, 52–53. For the Rio Rel Rey and Santo Domingo trades, see Ogilby, *Africa*, 482–83.

43. *BG*, vol. 2, 677 ("drove"). For the early history of the Efik, see A. K. Hart, *Report of the Enquiry into the Dispute over the Obongship of Calabar* (Enugu: Government Printer, 1964); Ene Antigha Eyo, "Efik Origins, Migrations and Settlements," unpublished Ph.D. thesis, University of Nigeria, Nsukka, 1977; Behrendt et al., *Diary of Antera Duke*, 14–21.

44. Logbook of the *Vine*, November 10–17, 1681, HCA30/661, TNAUK. For the blocking of the Akpa, see Dike and Ekejiuba, *Aro*, 102–3, 39 ("shut off"). For Efik dominance of the trade from c. 1720 onward, see Behrendt et al., *Diary of Antera Duke*, 53–54; Latham, *Old Calabar*, 49–51.

45. For the *King Amboe*, see https://www.slavevoyages.org/voyages/2yjOfjoX. For Ambo's death, see "Extract of a Letter from on Board the Ship Castle of Bristol, Captain Montgomery, dated at Old Malabar [Calabar], March 10, 1729," *London Journal*, August 16, 1729. For personal networks between Britons and the Efik, see Behrendt et al., *Diary of Antera Duke*, 68–78; Radburn, "William Davenport," 49–63; Paul E. Lovejoy and David Richardson, "Letters of the Old Calabar Slave Trade, 1760–1789," in *Genius in Bondage: Literature of the Early Black Atlantic*, ed. Vincent Carretta and Phillip Gould (Lexington: University Press of Kentucky, 2001), 89–115.

46. Liverpool captain Ambrose Lace noted, in a recently discovered document, that the Efik were "all one Town" when he visited in 1748. See "Account of what happen'd at Callabar, between the Old & New Town in 1767 or 1768," KCM 99/67/5, Slavery Manuscript Collection, File 5, Killie Campbell Africana Library, University of KwaZulu-Natal, Durban, South Africa ("being Stopt"). For maps showing only Creek Town, see, for example, "A Chart of ye Coast of Biafra . . . ," in Jer. Seller and Cha. Price, *The Fifth Part of the English Pilot Describing . . . Africa* (London: J. Matthews, 1701). For the seizure of the cannon, see Captain James Berry to [Ambrose Lace?], Old Calabar, April 3, 1763, in Gomer Williams, *History of the Liverpool Privateers and Letters of Marque with an Account of the Liverpool Slave Trade* (Liverpool: Edward Howell, 1897), 533–34. For the massacre of 1767, see Behrendt et al., *Diary of Antera Duke*, 22–24, 40–41; Randy J. Sparks, *The Two Princes of Calabar: An Eighteenth-Century Atlantic Odyssey* (Cambridge, MA: Harvard University Press, 2009), 10–32; Latham, *Old Calabar*, 49–51.

47. For Dutch voyages to the Rio Real, see Ogilby, *Africa*, 482 ("pretty," "Great," "the chiefest"). For English visitors in the late seventeenth century, see *BG*, vol. 2, 691 ("g[o]t," "two," "eight"). Instructions for the *Africa Galley*, 1700 ("The people"). Bonny did have one geographic advantage: the river before the town was much deeper than at New Calabar, and so larger ships could anchor there. For Bonny, see Byrd, *Captives and Voyagers*, 17–31.

48. For kingship at Bonny and the sequence of monarchs, see Ebiegberi J. Alagoa and Adadonye Fombo, *A Chronicle of Grand Bonny* (Ibadan: Ibadan University Press, 1972), 3–16, 7 ("supreme"); G. I. Jones, *The Trading States of the Oil Rivers: A Study of Political Development in Eastern Nigeria* (Oxford: Oxford University Press, 1963), 26. Precisely dating the reigns of the Bonny monarchs is difficult because they are principally remembered in oral history. For the centrality of kingship to Bonny's slave trade, see Lovejoy and Richardson, "'This Horrid Hole,'" 363–92. For the Ibani's religious beliefs, see Dike and Ekejiuba, *Aro*, 146. For *Ekpe*, see Behrendt et al., *Diary of Antera Duke*, 27–36.

49. For Bonny's conquests, see Alagoa and Fombo, *Grand Bonny*, 3–16, 10 ("great"). For villagers fleeing the rivers, see E. J. Alagoa, "The Slave Trade in Niger Delta Oral Tradition and History," in *Africans in Bondage: Studies in Slavery and the Slave Trade*, ed. Paul E. Lovejoy (Madison: University of Wisconsin Press, 1986), 130–31. James Barbot Sr. met King Halliday in 1699, and so the Andoni War occurred after that date, perhaps during the War of the Spanish Succession (1701–1714) or the War of the Austrian Succession (1739–1748). For political organization at Andoni and New Calabar, see Silas Eneyo, *The Andoni Monarchy: An Introduction to the History of the Kingship Institution of the Andoni People* (Port Harcourt: Riverside, 1991); Robin Horton, "From Fishing Village to City-State: A Social History of New Calabar," in *Man in Africa*, ed. Mary Douglas and Phyllis M. Kaberry (London: Routledge, 1969), 37–58.

50. Chinua Achebe, *Things Fall Apart* (New York: Anchor Books, 1959), 19 ("king," "a man's," "women's"). Of the captives departing Biafran ports between 1601 and 1864, 41.5 percent were females, versus 33.9 percent on the Gold Coast. See Nwokeji, *Slave Trade*, 151. For seasonality in the Biafran slave trade, see Stephen D. Behrendt, "Ecology, Seasonality, and the Transatlantic Slave Trade," in *Soundings in Atlantic History: Latent Structures and Intellectual Currents, 1500–1830*, ed. Barnard Bailyn (Cambridge, MA: Harvard University Press, 2009), 60–68.

51. For the purchase of slaves according to the fairs' schedule, see John Adams, *Sketches Taken During Ten Voyages to Africa Between the Years 1786 and 1800 . . .* (Liverpool, 1822), 38 ("wholesale"); Testimony of James Fraser in *HCSP*, vol. 71, 17–20; Testimony of Alexander Falconbridge in *HCSP*, vol. 72, 587. Captains learned to time their purchases according to the rhythm of the fairs at Bonny. See, for example, Captain John Elworthy

to Baker & Dawson, Bonny, January 1, 1787, E/112/1529/191, TNAUK; Captain William Woodville Jr. to James Rogers, Bonny, April 23, 1791, JRP, C107/13, TNAUK. Letters from ship captains trading at Old Calabar in the same period do not mention the fairs as a source of slaves. For Calabar's commercial hinterland, see Behrendt et al., *Diary of Antera Duke*, 104–19, 102 ("vast"); Latham, *Old Calabar*, 28–29.

52. Venture Smith, *A Narrative of the Life and Adventures of Venture, A Native of Africa: But resident above sixty years in the United States of America* (New London: C. Holt, 1798), 5–13, 9 ("laid," "speedily," "violent"), 13 ("taken"). Olaudah Equiano, *The Interesting Narrative of the Life of Olaudah Equiano or Gustavus Vassa, The African. Written by Himself*, 3rd edition (London, 1790), 1–46, 33 ("bathing," "small"). I have followed Paul Lovejoy in locating Equiano's birthplace in Africa. See Paul E. Lovejoy, "Olaudah Equiano or Gustavus Vassa—What's in a Name?" *Atlantic Studies* 9, no. 2 (June 2012): 165–84. Vincent Carretta has raised important questions about the origins of Equiano, who, he suggests, may have been born in South Carolina. If correct, Equiano's work likely combines the oral histories of Igbo people enslaved in Carolina. See Vincent Carretta, *Equiano, the African: Biography of a Self-Made Man*, reprint edition (New York: Penguin Books, 2007); Vincent Carretta, "Olaudah Equiano or Gustavus Vassa? New Light on an Eighteenth-century Question of Identity," *Slavery and Abolition* 20, no. 3 (December 1999), 96–105.

Chapter Two. Cross-Cultural Trade and the Sale of Enslaved People in Atlantic Africa

1. Captain W[illia]m Read, Old Calabar, to Royal African Company, April 15, 1702, T70/175, TNAUK. Read was not exaggerating about his long stay: it took him a year to reach the Americas from the time he left London. See https://www.slavevoyages.org/voyages/zKGmUumR.

2. Instructions for the *Enterprize*, 1794 ("long stay"); *Madam Pookata*, 1783 ("ruin"); *Hector*, 1771 ("Dispatch is"). William Snelgrave, *A New Account of Some Parts of Guinea, and the Slave-Trade . . .* (London: James, John, and Paul Knapton, 1734), 173 ("either," "kill[ing]," "a great"). Grandy King George to Ambrose Lace, Old Calabar, January 13, 1773, in Williams, *Liverpool Privateers*, 545 ("No"). Captain Phillips wrote that drawn-out purchases in Africa meant that "those you have on board are dying while you are buying others ashore." See Phillips, *A Journal*, 227.

3. For credit, see Lovejoy and Richardson, "'This Horrid Hole.'" For the indiscriminate purchase of enslaved people in Africa, see, for example, Smallwood, *Saltwater Slavery*, 33–64; Audra A. Diptee, *From Africa to Jamaica: The Making of an Atlantic Slave Society, 1775–1807* (Gainesville: University of Florida Press, 2010), 50–72; Sparks, *Where the Negroes*, 139–61. Byrd, *Captives and Voyagers*, 27–31, Rediker, *The Slave Ship*, 108–19.

For an analysis that instead emphasizes the selectiveness of British slave traders in Africa, see Mustakeem, *Slavery at Sea*, chapter 2. For African agency in the slave trade, see Thornton, *Africa and Africans*, 43–71. For works that argue for the importance of the African slave trade in shaping who entered the Atlantic slave trade, see, for example, G. Ugo Nwokeji, "African Conceptions of Gender and the Slave Traffic," *William and Mary Quarterly* 58, no. 1 (2001): 47–68; Jennifer L. Morgan, *Laboring Women: Reproduction and Gender in New World Slavery* (Philadelphia: University of Pennsylvania Press, 2004), 50–68; David Eltis and Stanley L. Engerman, "Was the Slave Trade Dominated by Men?" *Journal of Interdisciplinary History* 23, no. 2 (1992): 237–57; David Eltis and Stanley L. Engerman, "Fluctuations in Sex and Age Ratios in the Transatlantic Slave Trade, 1663–1864," *Economic History Review* 46, no. 2 (1993): 308–23; Paul E. Lovejoy and David Richardson, "Competing Markets for Male and Female Slaves: Prices in the Interior of West Africa, 1780–1850," *International Journal of African Historical Studies* 28, no. 2 (1995): 261–93. For children, see Audra A. Diptee, "African Children in the British Slave Trade during the Late Eighteenth Century," *Slavery and Abolition* 27, no. 2 (August 2006): 183–96. For the pricing of enslaved people, see Daina Raimey Berry, *The Price for Their Pound of Flesh: The Value of the Enslaved, from Womb to Grave, in the Building of a Nation* (New York: Beacon Press, 2017); Caitlin Rosenthal, *Accounting for Slavery: Masters and Management* (Cambridge, MA: Harvard University Press, 2018), 121–56.

4. Alexander Falconbridge, *An Account of the Slave Trade on the Coast of Africa* . . . (London: J. Phillips, 1788), 13 ("of all"). Auguste Chambon, *Traité général du commerce de l'Amérique* . . . , vol. 2 (Amsterdam: Marc-Michel Rey, 1783), 399 ("old people"). Adams, *Sketches*, 9–10 ("meagre"). Testimony of Richard Miles in *HCSP*, vol. 69, 41 ("Sores"). Testimony of Robert Heatley in ibid., 30 ("very"). Quoted in Byrd, *Captives and Voyagers*, 24 ("bad"). For mortality on the march to the coast, see Joseph C. Miller, *Way of Death: Merchant Capitalism and the Angolan Slave Trade, 1730–1830* (Charlottesville: University of Virginia Press, 1988), 379–87.

5. Smallwood, *Saltwater Slavery*, 51 ("equally"). Instructions for the *James*, 1754 ("Slaves"); *Saint George*, 1749 ("suitable"); *Molly*, 1761 ("Prime"); *Dispatch*, 1725 ("none"); *Experiment*, 1783 ("well"); *Africa Galley*, 1700 ("Thirty").

6. Instructions for the *Dispatch*, 1725 ("most"); *Marquis of Grandy*, 1762 ("stand"). For "stand the purchase," see Instructions for the *Enterprize*, 1806. Pieter Gallandat, *Necessary Instructions for the Slave Traders*, trans. Lieneke Timpers (Middelburg, Netherlands: Pieter Gillissen, 1769), ("young").

7. Gallandat, *Necessary Instructions* ("at first," "blemishes," "attention"). Paul Erdmann Isert, *Letters on West Africa and the Slave Trade: Paul Erdmann Isert's Journey to Guinea and the Caribbean Islands in Columbia (1788)* (Ac-

cra: Sub-Saharan, 2007), 115 ("if they"). For white men's fascination with African women's breasts, see Jennifer L. Morgan, "'Some Could Suckle over Their Shoulder': Male Travelers, Female Bodies, and the Gendering of Racial Ideology, 1500–1770," *William and Mary Quarterly* 54, no. 1 (January 1997): 167–92. Slave traders sometimes subdivided captives into "men-boys" and "women-girls": that is, teenage boys and girls.

8. Gallandat, *Necessary Instructions* ("carefully," "no wounds," "fevers"). Ludewig Ferdinand Romer, *A Reliable Account of the Coast of Guinea (1760)*, trans. and ed. Selena Axelrod Winsnes (New York: Diasporic Africa Press, 2013), 226 ("four hours"). For inspections, see also Phillips, *A Journal*, 218; Bosman, *A New and Accurate Description*, 364.

9. Equiano, *Interesting Narrative*, 46 ("handled"). Gallandat, *Necessary Instructions* ("severe," "killed"). Atkins, *Voyage* 179 ("Beasts"). Testimony of Anders Sparman in *HCSP*, vol. 69, 25 ("trembled"). Johannes Rask, *Two Views from Christiansborg Castle, Volume 1: A Brief and Truthful Description of a Journey to and from Guinea*, trans. Selena Axelrod Winsnes (Accra: Sub-Saharan, 2009), 189 ("cut off"). Louis de Grandpre, *Voyage à la côte occidentale d'Afrique, fait dans les années 1786 et 1787*, vol. 2 (Paris, 1801), 56 ("often"); my translation. H. C. Monrad, *Two Views from Christianborg Castle, Volume 2: A Description of the Guinea Coast and Its Inhabitants* (Accra: Sub-Saharan, 2009), 223 ("crying"). Awnsham Churchill, *A Collection of Voyages and Travels . . .* (London: John Walthoe, 1732), vol. 5, 507 ("the king," "for decency").

10. Testimony of John Newton in *HCSP*, vol. 69, 60 ("all"). Testimony of Robert Heatley in ibid. ("never"). Testimony of John Matthews, Archibald Dalzell and Robert Norris in ibid. ("generally"). Romer, *Reliable Account*, 181 ("when").

11. Instructions for the *Molly*, 1751 ("imposed"). Testimony of John Barnes in *HCSP*, vol. 69, 22 ("the lowest," "seldom"). Logbook of the *Duke of Argyll*, January 13 ("positive") and March 22 ("small"), 1751. Testimony of John Anderson in *HCSP*, vol. 69, 45 ("as few"). Newton later stated that children "from 8 to 16 years [old]" composed "about a fourth" of his prisoners on his numerous voyages. Newton must have rejected captives below the age of eight. See Testimony of John Newton in *HCSP*, vol. 73, 143. For four feet as the minimum height of slaves, see, for example, Testimony of James Arnold in ibid., 50; "Slaves Purchased & c & c & c on Board of the Ship Tom, George Maxwell master, in the River Congo," *APHLRO*, 1794; Instructions for the *Young Foster*, 1757; *Mosley Hill*, 1785; *Abram*, 1785. For Miles's transactions, see R. Miles: Tantumquerry; rough day book, T70/1488, TNAUK; Slave Barters by R. Miles at Tantumquerry, Accra and Annamaboe, 1772–1776, T70/1264, TNAUK; Slave barters by R. Miles at Annamaboe . . . , 1776–1777, T70/1265, TNAUK. Miles likely acquired comparatively few children because he was in the business of selling captives at high prices to slave ships that neared their departure

from the coast. The lowest heights of the children were 3′ 2″ (*Duke of Buccleugh*), 3′ 9″ (*Eliza*), and 3′ 11″ (*Tom*). See "A Report of the Commissioners Appointed to Enquire into Losses Which May Have Been Sustained by Owners of Ships or Vessels Engaged in the African Trade . . . ," in *American Papers in the House of Lords Record Office* (Wakefield: Microform, 1983), 1788.2 (*Eliza*), 1790.8 (*Duke of Buccleugh*), 1794.12 (*Tom*). On the *Daniel*, there were six boys and nine girls under 4′, out of 126 people. See Henry Laroche to James Rogers, Grenada, October 1, 1791, JRP, C107/12.

12. Monrad, *Description*, 222 ("small," "could"). John Riland, *Memoirs of a West-India Planter* (London: Hamilton, Adams, 1827), 52 ("reduced," "afford[ed]," "fed"). Romer, *Reliable Account*, 182 ("takes"). Antoine Edme Pruneau de Pommegorge, *Description of La Négritie* (Amsterdam: Maradan, 1789), 209 ("at the"), 209–10 ("endless"). Testimony of James Towne in *HCSP*, vol. 82, 22 ("It is"). Towne added that the infants of two women on the ships he served on both died. The mothers "grieved after them" and then died themselves shortly thereafter. John Newton, *Thoughts Upon the African Slave Trade* (London, 1788), 18 ("threw," "disturbed"). Captains also rejected sickly, elderly, and adolescent captives to maximize space. For example, a Liverpool merchant advised his captain that "bad [captives] count the same as good ones and fetch nothing at market." See Robert Bostock to Captain James Fryer, Liverpool, November 19, 1788, Letter book, etc. of Robert Bostock, vol. 1, 387 MD 55, Liverpool Record Office. For accounts detailing women with infants, see logbook of the *Madam Pookata*, November 23, 1786, and September 9, 1787; and the slave purchasing records for the *Ned*, 1789; *Duke of Buccleugh*, 1789; *Africa*, 1792; and *Fly*, 1792, in *APHLRO*.

13. Testimony of James Arnold in *HCSP*, vol. 69, 55 ("plagued"). Testimony of John Ashley Hall in *HCSP*, vol. 72, 515 ("always"). Captain Arthur Bold to Richard Miles, Cape Coast Road, [1773?], T70/1533, TNAUK ("very good"). Ashley Hall added that he saw only one instance of a child accompanying their parent in his lengthy time in the trade when he saw "a woman" sold "with a child, about six weeks old, sucking at the breast."

14. Testimony of James Arnold in *HCSP*, vol. 69, 54 ("with"; "in great"; "in the"). Romer, *Reliable Account*, 182 ("from the"). Romer wrote that he had personally seen "discarded children" on the Gold Coast "left, lying like a kitten, until, at night, a wolf may have dragged them off." The Danish fort officers took abandoned children and gave them to the "female company slaves" to raise them. "None," Romer concluded, had "reached adulthood." For captains rejecting children, see also David Mill to Richard Miles, [Cape Coast Castle], April 20, 1774, T70/1532, TNAUK; Richard Miles to Captain Edward Williams, Cape Coast Castle, November 13, 1774, T70/1479/5, TNAUK; Captain Joseph Fayrer to John Bartlett, Anamabo Road, February 18, 1775, T70/1479/5, TNAUK.

15. Instructions for the *Corsican Hero*, 1742 ("sell"). For orders not to purchase elderly people, see also Instructions for the *Henry*, 1767; *Sisters*, 1786; and *Jemmy*, 1787. Bosman, *New and Accurate*, 364 ("above," "grey"). Logbook of the *Duke of Argyll*, November 3 ("long breasted"), 13 ("old"), 1750. Captain Clement Noble to Samuel Gwyther, Anamabo, September 21, 1775, T70/1533, TNAUK ("old, dropsical"). Testimony of Henry Ellison in *HCSP*, vol. 73, 362 ("too old"). Testimony of John Ashley Hall in *HCSP*, vol. 69, 50 ("seldom").

16. Captain Thomas Goodwin to Richard Miles, Anamabo, February 18, 1773, T70/1533, TNAUK ("prime"). Captain Thomas Blundell to Richard Miles, Anamabo, December 19, 1776, T70/1533, TNAUK ("a Benin").

17. Falconbridge, *Account*, 17 ("defects," "If"). Phillips, *A Journal*, 218 ("greatest"). Captain Peter Lawson to Thomas Miles, undated, [1776?], T70/1533, TNAUK ("ill"). Testimony of William James in *HCSP*, vol. 69, 49 ("No sickly"). Testimony of [James Towne] in Thomas Clarkson, *The Substance of the Evidence of Sundry Persons on the Slave-Trade . . .* (London: James Phillips, 1789), 74 ("All").

18. Testimony of John Fountain in *HCSP*, vol. 68, 200 ("even," "purchase"). Captain Richard Rogers to James Rogers, Old Calabar, March 26, 1788, JRP, C107/12 ("6 & 7"). Captain James Paisley to Richard Miles, Anamabo Road, October 5, 1779, T70/1538, TNAUK ("only"). Testimony of James Arnold in *HCSP*, vol. 69, 50 ("full as"). Testimony of James Fraser in *HCSP*, vol. 71, 43 ("twice"). Falconbridge, *Account*, 22. Richard Miles's correspondence with captains is scattered through T70/1479, T70/1483, T70/1531–4, T70/1538, T70/1549, TNAUK. For Newton's voyages, see logbook of the *Duke of Argyll*, 1750–1751, and *African*, 1752–1753; 1753–1754.

19. Philip D. Curtin, *Economic Change in Precolonial Africa: Senegambia in the Era of the Slave Trade* (Madison: University of Wisconsin Press, 1975), 175 ("young"), 237 ("systematic"), 239 ("comparative"). Miller, *Way of Death*, 67 ("standard"). Quoted in G. I. Jones, "Native and Trade Currencies in Southern Nigeria during the Eighteenth and Nineteenth Centuries," *Africa* 28, no. 1 (January 1958): 43 ("slaves," "copper"), 47 ("A slave"). For African conceptions of value and exchange, see also Jane I. Guyer, *Marginal Gains: Monetary Transactions in Atlantic Africa* (Chicago: University of Chicago Press, 2004).

20. For inflation, see Jones, "Native and Trade," 50–51; Jan Hogendorn and Marion Johnson, *The Shell Money of the Slave Trade* (Cambridge: Cambridge University Press, 1986), 109–13; Toby Green, *A Fistful of Shells: West Africa from the Rise of the Slave Trade to the Age of Revolutions* (London: Penguin, 2019), 167–68.

21. For the development of assortment and African trade currencies, see Jones, "Native and Trade"; Marion Johnson, "The Ounce in Eighteenth-

Century West African Trade," *Journal of African History* 7, no. 2 (1966): 197–214; Karl Polanyi, "Sortings and 'Ounce Trade' in the West African Slave Trade," *Journal of African History* 5, no. 3 (November 1964): 381–93. For the changing compositions of trading cargoes, see the outward invoices for RAC ships in T70/910–919, TNAUK.

22. George Metcalf, "Gold, Assortments and the Trade Ounce: Fante Merchants and the Problem of Supply and Demand in the 1770s," *Journal of African History* 28, no. 1 (1987): 29. Stacey Sommerdyk, "Trade and the Merchant Community of the Loango Coast in the Eighteenth Century," unpublished Ph.D. thesis, University of Hull, 2012, 160. Forty-eight Ibani merchants sold enslaved people to the captain of the *Molly* in 1759. See African account book of the *Molly*, 1759. For citations to these accounts, see my Appendix B.

23. Prices of goods at Bonny have been ascertained by examining the extant account books and invoices of voyages to the port over the eighteenth century: *Africa Galley*, 1700 (*DIHST*, vol. 2, 77–79); *Bristol Merchant*, 1747 (Bright Family papers, University of Melbourne Library); *Swift*, 1759 (39654(2), Bristol Archives); *Molly*, 1759 (AML/Y/2, NMM); *Trelawny*, 1792 (C107/15, TNAUK); *Jupiter*, 1793 (C107/59, TNAUK); *Earl of Liverpool*, 1797, 1798 (GB141 MS.10.50, ULL). For prices in Miles's barters, see Metcalf, "Gold, Assortments," 35–41. For the static prices of goods, see also Martin, *External Trade*, 109–10; Polanyi, "Sortings," 381–93; Johnson, "Ounce," 203.

24. Grandpre, *Voyage*, vol. 2, 60 ("between," "if the," my translation). William Richardson and Edmund Spencer Eardley Childers, *A Mariner of England; an Account of the Career of William Richardson from Cabin Boy in the Merchant Service to Warrant Officer in the Royal Navy (1780 to 1819) as Told by Himself*, ed. Colonel Spencer Childers (London, 1908), 52 ("bite," "strike"). For "shops" aboard the ship, see "Mr Parfitts Information respecting Trade between Sierra Leone & Cape Lopez, including the Islands St Thomas &c," Add.Mss.12131, BL. For screws on guns, see Chambon, *Traité général*, vol. 2, 383; Governor Meyer to the Directors of the West India and Guinea Company, Christianborg, February 1, 1704, in Ole Justesen, ed., *Danish Sources for the History of Ghana, 1657–1754*, trans. James Manley (Copenhagen: Royal Danish Academy of Sciences and Letters, 2005), vol. 1, 177.

25. *BG*, vol. 2, 687 ("because," "until"), 688 ("king"). Testimony of James Fraser in *HCSP*, vol. 71, 20 ("br[oke]"). When the *Molly* arrived at Bonny on February 1, 1759, the king sold the captain a man for twenty-two bars as the first transaction. The captains of the *Guerrier*, *Trelawny*, and *Jupiter*, which traded at Bonny in 1790, 1791, and 1793, respectively, also bought an adult male slave from the king as their first transaction; the *Jupiter* and *Guerrier*'s commanders both wrote in their ledgers that this occurred

when they "broke trade." See my Appendix B for citations of account books recording the acquisitions of enslaved people in Africa.

26. Churchill, *A Collection*, vol. 5, 504 ("no," "privately"). Grandpre, *Voyage*, vol. 2, 44 ("price"). Metcalf, "Gold, Assortments," 37 ("trade," "price"). Phillips, *A Journal*, 217 ("attended," "samples," "agreement"), 218 ("the bell"). Romer, *Reliable Account*, 225 ("at which").

27. *BG*, vol. 2, 689. African account book of the *Molly*, 1759. Isert, *Letters*, 115. According to Isert, Danish officers priced enslaved men taller than 4′ 4″ at 160 thalers and enslaved women taller than 4′ at 128 thalers, when he visited the Gold Coast in 1784. Danes reduced the price offered for children by eight thalers per inch below those heights. The account book of one British ship trading in Sierra Leone in 1787 shows that at least one captain did use such a system, as the price he paid for enslaved children was directly proportional to their height and the price of prime adults. See *HCSP*, vol. 68, 55.

28. Testimony of John Fountain in *HCSP*, vol. 68, 195 ("defects," "The," "objectionable," "would"). For price deductions, see also Monrad, *Description*, 220; Isert, *Letters*, 115; Romer, *Reliable Account*, 226; Grandpre, *Voyage*, vol. 2, 44–45. Only at the infamously pestilential port of Old Calabar did captains purchase enslaved people at heavy discounts: the account book of the *Dobson* shows the captain purchasing enslaved adults at prices that were sometimes 50 percent lower than for other captives, likely because the people arriving from the interior were so sickly that he took enslaved people who would be rejected at other ports; African account book of the *Dobson*, 1769–70.

29. Nathaniel Cutting Journal and Letterbooks, 1786–98, January 7, 1790, Massachusetts Historical Society. Gray was conducting the barter on behalf of another trader named "Mr Benin." Cutting observed: "The Current price of each article of Merchandize, rated in Barr, is well known to all who trade at this mart, either Black or White." The "quality of the merch[an]d[i]ze" was also "generally known." Isert, *Letters*, 115 ("pick[ing] and choos[ing]"). John Fountain told Parliament that he had been "two hours, frequently, in the purchase of one slave." See Testimony of John Fountain in *HCSP*, vol. 68, 165. For similar descriptions of the barter methods in Africa, see Joseph Corry, *Observations Upon the Windward Coast of Africa . . .* (London: G. and W. Nicol, 1807), 58; Grandpre, *Voyage*, vol. 2, 58–59; "Mr Parfitts Information respecting Trade between Sierra Leone & Cape Lopez, including the Islands St Thomas &c," Add. Mss.12131, BL.

30. Isert, *Letters*, 112 ("young"), 115 ("without").

31. Isert, *Letters*, 114 ("must," "or the"). Francis Moore, *Travels into the Inland Parts of Africa . . .*, 2nd edition (London: D. Henry and R. Cave, 1738), 32 ("Heads"). For *grandes* and *petites merchandises*, see Martin, *External*

Trade, 107–8; Captain Thomas Phillips, who traded at Whydah in the late seventeenth century, likewise understood the distinction between the two types of goods. He wrote, "Near half the cargo value must be cowries or booges, and brass basons, to set off the other goods that we buy cheaper, as coral, rangoes, iron & c., else they [the Africans] will not take them." See Phillips, *A Journal*, 227. For "commanding articles," see Instructions for the *Blaydes*, 1782, and *Hope*, 1791.

32. Instructions for the *Africa Galley*, 1700 ("no certainty," "those"). Smith, *A Narrative*, 13 ("four"). For the much larger bundles of goods paid for enslaved adults versus children, see, for example, R. Miles: Tantumquerry; rough day book, T70/1488, TNAUK.

33. William Earle to Kenyon & Southwark, Liverpool, April 22, 1761, Letter-book of William Earle, 1760–1761, MMM ("it is not"). For merchant decision making in selecting African slaving ports, see Behrendt, "Markets, Transaction Cycles, and Profits," 188–91.

34. Chambon, *Traité général*, vol. 2, 400 ("key," "regulated," "in greater"). Instructions for the *Earl of Liverpool*, 1797 ("propose," "shew"); *Blaydes*, 80578, 1782 ("part"). The *Blaydes* traded at Whydah, but, as the owners of the vessel pointed out, the captain was to follow the instructions "at whatever place you slave off at." For orders to offer low prices upon arrival, see also Instructions for the *Tyrrel*, 1761 (Old Calabar); *Apollo*, 1764 (Sierra Leone); and *Nancy*, 1774 (Loango Coast).

35. Captain Peter Potter to William Davenport & Co., June 23, 1775, D/DAV/7, MMM ("oaths," "very"); Captain Peter Potter to William Davenport & Co., November 22, 1776, D/DAV/10, MMM ("a whole"). *BG*, vol. 2, 687 ("also objected"). On the Loango Coast, the mafouk could stop the trade of captains who refused to pay his prices by "blocking all the brokers" from trading with that captain on pain of a steep fine. See François Vanstabel to Bonaventure Tresca, Malembo, December 24, 1783, Musée des beaux-arts de Dunkerque.

36. Instructions for the *Africa*, 1774 ("Signs"); *Hector*, 1771 ("half"); *Bristol Merchant*, 1747 ("keep"). African account book of the *Molly*, 1759. In 1757 the captain of the *Carter* wrote that he had arrived at Bonny two months earlier and found another ship anchored there, which was "half slaved, and then paying 50 Barrs" for adult male slaves. The *Carter*'s captain had "only yet purchased 15 slaves at 30 and 35 Barrs" but "propose[d] giving more" once another ship had left the river. There was thus a two-thirds increase in slave prices over the period of the purchase. See Captain John Baillie to Foster Cunliffe & Sons, Bonny, January 31, 1757, in Williams, *Liverpool Privateers*, 481. Thomas Phillips writes, "[A captain must be] cautious in making his report to the king [of Whydah] at first, of what sorts and quantities of goods he has. And be sure to say his cargo consists mostly in iron, coral, rangoes, chints, &c."—the lowest-priced goods— "so that he may dispose of those goods as soon as he can, and at last his

cowries and brass will bring him slaves as fast as he can buy them." See Phillips, *A Journal*, 227.

37. Testimony of James Fraser in *HCSP*, vol. 71, 20 ("The ships"). Captain Charles Gwynn to Richard Prankard & Co., Malembo, December 15, 1754, Gloucester Record Office, P74/MI ("turn"). Captain Henry Madden to Ambrose Lace, Old Calabar, November 23, 1768, Private Collection. For the staggering of prices in Benin, see Testimony of [James Morley] in Clarkson, *Substance*, 74. On the Gold Coast, prices increased at the conclusion of a ship's time on the coast because captains purchased large groups of captives from white traders, who typically sold enslaved people at a premium. See, for example, Atkins, *Voyage*, 169. A captain labeled those who tried to vault the queue "burners" (*brûleurs*) because they consumed their cargoes too quickly. See François Vanstabel to Bonaventure Tresca, Malembo, February 6, 1784, Musée des beaux-arts de Dunkerque.

38. Captain William Woodville to James Rogers, Bonny, April 23, 1791, JRP, C107/13 ("pay"). Testimony of Alexander Falconbridge in *HCSP*, vol. 72, 587 ("been"). Testimony of Anon. in Clarkson, *Substance*, 64 ("regular"). The number of captives brought back from the fairs varied, depending on the number of slave ships anchored in the river, which increased over the century. See https://www.slavevoyages.org/voyages/a76uKfJo. William James, who sailed to Bonny as a surgeon in the 1760s, said that the fleets going up to the fairs consisted of "twenty or thirty canoes," each of which returned with "twenty or thirty slaves." That is, between four hundred and nine hundred captives. See Testimony of William James in *HCSP*, vol. 69, 48 ("oiled"). Falconbridge, who traded at Bonny in the early 1780s also as a surgeon, wrote that the traders purchased "from twelve to fifteen hundred" slaves "at one fair." See Falconbridge, *Account*, 12 ("opulence," "forty"). John Adams, who visited the port in the 1790s as a captain, said that the "Bonny people" returned with "1500 or 2000 slaves" (Adams, *Sketches*, 39).

39. Adams wrote that the slaves were "sold to Europeans the evening after their arrival" (Adams, *Sketches*, 39). A captain who bought people told his employers that he found slaves "very scarse" soon after his arrival at Bonny because several vessels that had recently departed had "ended" their purchase at "40 or 50 bars," and had bought most of the captives coming from the fairs (Captain Joseph Pitman to John Strattens, Bonny, December 9, 1738, P74 MI, Gloucester Record Office). African account books of the *Molly*, 1758–1759; and *Trelawny*, 1791–1792. The commander of the *Jupiter* purchased eighty-six "boys" and "girls" near the end of his purchase, but at the same price as adults, implying that they were teenagers who met the height requirement of adults. See African account book of the *Jupiter*, 1792–1793. A Liverpool captain wrote in his memoirs that "ten or twelve" vessels had "priority" over him "in receiving their Cargoes," and so he went hunting because he had so much time on his hands while the

other captains were purchasing captives. See Hugh Crow, *Memoirs of the Late Captain Hugh Crow of Liverpool* . . . (Liverpool: G. and J. Robinson, 1830), 142.

40. Testimony of Alexander Falconbridge in *HCSP*, vol. 69, 48 ("cruelly"). Testimony of James Fraser in *HCSP*, vol. 71, 19 ("youngest," "kept," "sent," "old," "goods"). Testimony of [James Morley] in Clarkson, *Substance*, 73 ("refused," "sent," "who"). Falconbridge said that the traders at New Calabar "dropped their canoes under the stern" of slave ships and "instantly beheaded [un-sold captives], in sight of the captain" (Falconbridge, *Account*, 18). Enslaved people themselves feared that they would be executed by their owners if they were rejected. See James Albert Ukawsaw Gronniosaw, *A Narrative of the Most Remarkable Particulars in the Life of James Albert Ukawsaw Gronniosaw* . . . (Kidderminster: W. Gye, 1772), 9.

41. Simon J. Hogerzeil and David Richardson, "Slave Purchasing Strategies and Shipboard Mortality: Day-to-Day Evidence from the Dutch African Trade, 1751–1797," *Journal of Economic History* 67, vol. 1 (March 2007), 160–90, 184 ("bias"). Grandpre, *Voyage*, vol. 2, 47 ("the rejects"). François Vanstabel to Bonaventure Tresca, Malembo, December 14, 1783, Musée des beaux-arts de Dunkerque.

42. Testimony of [James Morley] in Clarkson, *Substance*, 73 ("from experience"). Testimony of John Anderson in *Report of the Lords* [. . .] ([London?], 1789), 45 ("rejected"). David Mill to Richard Miles, Cape Coast Castle, May 25, 1775, T70/1533, TNAUK ("rejected"). Thomas Westgate to Richard Brew, Winnebah, [March 1774?], T70/1536, TNAUK ("very," "long," "objected," "approved"). Captain Archibald Robe to Richard Miles, November 28, 1776, T70/1534, TNAUK ("ye refusal"). Richard Brew to [Richard Miles?], Anamabo, February 22, 1776, T70/1534, TNAUK ("very").

43. Thomas Westgate to Richard Brew, Winnebah, July 10, 1774, T70/1536, TNAUK (all quotes). The woman would have also encountered whites in Lagoe itself, as several traders were resident in the town. See Richard Miles to David Mill, Tantumquerry, August 11, 1773, T70/1479/6, TNAUK. For enslaved people becoming "raving mad" on their arrival at the ships, especially women, see Falconbridge, *Account*, 32. For the rejection of insane people, see, for example, Captain Arthur Bold to Richard Miles, [February 1773?], Cape Coast Road, T70/1533, TNAUK.

44. Testimony of John Newton in *HCSP*, vol. 73, 144 ("separated," "as sheep"). Gronniosaw, *A Narrative*, 7 ("without").

Chapter Three. Merchants and the Creation of the Floating Dungeon

1. Instructions for the *Africa Galley*, 1700 (all quotes). "Accompts submitted by the Plaintiff in the Court of Chancery suit Capt. James Westmore, commander, v. Thomas Starke, owner of the slaver 'Affrican Galley' con-

cerning expenses incurred by Westmore on a voyage from London to Virginia via St Thomas' Island, Gulf of Guinea, and back, 20 Apr. 1701–4 Dec. 1702," Add. Ms. 45123, BL.

2. For the concept of the "floating dungeon," see James Field Stanfield, *The Guinea Voyage: A Poem in Three Books* (London: James Phillips, 1789), 26; Rediker, *The Slave Ship*, 132–56, 9 ("war machine"). For resistance, see David Richardson, "Shipboard Revolts, African Authority, and the Atlantic Slave Trade," *William and Mary Quarterly* 58, no. 1 (January 2001): 69–92; Stephen D. Behrendt, David Eltis, and David Richardson, "The Costs of Coercion: African Agency in the Pre-Modern Atlantic World," *Economic History Review* 54, no. 3 (August 2001): 454–76; Eric Robert Taylor, *If We Must Die: Shipboard Insurrections in the Era of the Atlantic Slave Trade* (Baton Rouge: University of Louisiana Press, 2006). For mortality on the Middle Passage, see Charles Garland and Herbert S. Klein, "The Allotment of Space for Slaves aboard Eighteenth-Century British Slave Ships," *William and Mary Quarterly* 42, no. 2 (April 1985), 238–48; Herbert S. Klein, *The Atlantic Slave Trade* (New York: Cambridge University Press, 1999), 130–60; Robin Haines, John McDonald, and Ralph Shlomowitz, "Mortality and Voyage Length in the Middle Passage Revisited," *Explorations in Economic History* 38, no. 4 (October 2001): 503–33; Herbert S. Klein et al., "Transoceanic Mortality: The Slave Trade in Comparative Perspective," *William and Mary Quarterly* 58, no. 1 (January 2001): 93–118; Sowande' Mustakeem, "'I Never Have [*sic*] Such a Sickly Ship Before': Diet, Disease, and Mortality in 18th-Century Atlantic Slaving Voyages," *Journal of African American History* 93, no. 4 (Fall 2008): 474–96; Nicolas J. Duquette, "Revealing the Relationship between Ship Crowding and Slave Mortality," *Journal of Economic History* 74, no. 2 (June 2014): 535–52. For the impacts of the Middle Passage on mental health, see Smallwood, *Saltwater Slavery*, 122–52.

3. Anon., "The Slave Trade from West Africa to the Cape Verde Islands in the Sixteenth Century," in *The Portuguese in West Africa, 1415–1670*, ed. and trans. Malyn Newitt (Cambridge: Cambridge University Press, 2012), 154 ("the men," "naked"), 155 ("not do"). Francesco Carletti, "The Slave Trade in the Cape Verde Islands, 1594," in ibid., 158 ("below," "lodged"). Information on pre-1600 slaving voyages is patchy: "Very little evidence exists for conditions on board slave ships in the early seventeenth century," write Linda A. Newson and Susie Minchin, *From Capture to Sale: The Portuguese Slave Trade to Spanish South America in the Early Seventeenth Century* (Leiden: Brill, 2007), 101–35.

4. De Sandoval, *Treatise*, 56 ("shackled"), 57 ("closed," "Even," "looking"). A missionary who sailed on a Portuguese slave ship in 1666 observed that the men were in the hold "fastened to another with stakes, for fear they should rise and kill the whites," whereas the women were "between the decks" and in the crew cabins. See "A Curious and Exact Account

of a Voyage to Congo, in the Years 1666, and 1667," in *A Collection of Voyages and Travels* . . . , vol. 1 (London: Awnsham and John Churchill, 1704), 637. For recorded insurrections, see https://www.slavevoyages.org/voyages/r2mzHH8F. For mortality on pre-1700 Portuguese voyages, see https://www.slavevoyages.org/voyages/xCdfUpMo. For the poor health of captives who survived the Middle Passage, see Newson and Minchin, *From Capture to Sale*, 121–35. In the eighteenth-century Portuguese trade, crewmen continued to keep enslaved men between decks and women in the cabins. They seldom—if ever—washed the ship and did not allow enslaved people above deck to wash, for fear that they would "hurl themselves into the sea." See Miller, *Way of Death*, 412.

5. The Guinea Company to Bartholomew Haward, London, December 9, 1651, in *DIHST*, vol. 1, 130 ("veary"). *BG*, vol. 2, 774 ("placed"). [Thomas Tryon], *Friendly advice to the gentlemen-planters of the East and West Indies* . . . (London: Andrew Sowle, 1684), 83 ("suffocated"). *BG*, vol. 2, 781 ("great"), 553 ("long," "two"). The English likely copied Portuguese methods that they witnessed on captured slaving vessels. Englishmen also employed Portuguese sailors to serve on their vessels and, no doubt, advise them how to control the captives. See, for example, *DIHST*, vol. 1, 11. For shackles and handcuffs on early English ships, see also "Ship Friezland Book, 1674," T70/1210, TNAUK. For the "mustering" of captives above deck, see, for example, logbook of the *Arthur*, March 28, 1678, T70/1213, TNAUK; "An Account of the several Mustering of the Negroes on board of the Shipe Hannah Capt Charles Danbers Commander," 1689, T70/1217, TNAUK. For the first mention of the "boys' room," see logbook of the *Duke of Argyll*, December 20, 1750. For mortality on English ships pre-1700, see https://www.slavevoyages.org/voyages/fSx1rr2b.

6. *BG*, vol. 2, 553 ("save," "render"), 780 ("a handful"), 781 ("large," "proper," "a full"). For the purported benefits of beans, see also Phillips, *A Journal*, 229. For provisions brought from Europe, see also the RAC's outward invoices in T70/910–935, TNAUK. For knowledge transfer from the Dutch trade, see Thornton, *Africa and Africans*, 156. The Portuguese made several modifications to their own shipping methods in the eighteenth century. Although men slaves were still locked below, their captors provided them with more food and water than in previous eras. When combined with a shortening in voyage lengths (from an average of seventy-four days pre-1700 to fifty-one days post-1700), these changes reduced mortality rates on Portuguese-flagged voyages, circa 1700 to 1808, to an average of 9 percent of embarked captives. See Milller, *Way of Death*, 379–442; https://www.slavevoyages.org/voyages/BKKBgJJw.

7. *BG*, vol. 2, 775 ("a mess," "as they"), 779 ("thrice"), 780 ("twice," "by turns"). For "dancing," see ibid., 780. Phillips, *A Journal*, 229; Churchill, *A Collection*, vol. 5, 513.

8. *BG*, vol. 2, 775 ("liberty," "deprive," "as many"). Phillips, *A Journal*, 229 ("always," "yaun"). For an identical regime, see "Voyage to Guinea," [c. 1714], Add.Mss.39946, BL. For the importance of advances in firearm technology for shaping shipboard regimes in the slave trade, see Stephanie E. Smallwood, "African Guardians, European Slave Ships, and the Changing Dynamics of Power in the Early Modern Atlantic," *William and Mary Quarterly* 64, no. 4 (October 2007): 701–3.

9. Phillips, *A Journal*, 229 ("surprised"). Churchill, *A Collection*, vol. 5, 513 ("about," "severely"). *BG*, vol. 2, 775 ("chopping," "terrify"), 780 ("not hear"). "Voyage to Guinea," [c. 1714], Add.Mss.39946, BL ("cut"). Bosman, *New and Accurate*, 365–66. For terror as a deliberate strategy to quell resistance, see also Snelgrave, *New Account*, 182–85.

10. *BG*, vol. 2, 780 ("We"), 782 ("Some," "hinders"). Phillips, *A Journal*, 229 ("the time," "aptest"). Crewmen constructed toilet blocks on the side of the vessel that captives were permitted to visit in small groups of four at a time during the night. See ibid. and Snelgrave, *New Account*, 169. Barbot understood the link between voyage length, mortality, and venture profits well. See *BG*, vol. 2, 782.

11. Instructions for the *Judith*, 1728 ("quarters," "Great," "Enemies," "may"). John Smith, *The sea-mans grammar and dictionary explaining all the difficult terms in navigation: and the practical navigator and gunner: in two parts . . .* (London: Randal Taylor, 1691), 11 ("to clear"). Wood was shipped out from England on slave ships to construct the "platforms" and "bulkheads"; see John Perry to The Com[issioner]s for Transports, [London?], October 18, 1711, T70/175, TNAUK.

12. William Falconer, *An universal dictionary of the marine . . .* , New Edition (London: T. Cadell, 1769), "Barricade" ("a strong," "intercept"). For the "baracado" as a device to "keepe off small shott," see Henry Teonge, *The Diary of Henry Teonge, Chaplain on Board His Majesty's Ships Assistance, Bristol, and Royal Oak, Anno 1675 to 1679* (London: C. Knight, 1825), 260. For the small number of crew before the barricado, see Henry Smeathman (ed. Deidre Coleman), "Oeconomy of a Slave Ship," in *Slavery and the Cultures of Abolition: Essays Marking the Bicentennial of the British Abolition Act of 1807*, ed. Brycchan Carey and Peter J. Kitson (Rochester: D. S. Brewer, 2007), 141–42. The captain seldom passed beyond the barricado because the men slaves "always aim[ed] at the chief Person in the Ship." See Snelgrave, *New Account*, 190.

13. Isert, *Letters*, 235 ("cannot"). For "deck chains," see also Smeathman (ed. Coleman), "Oeconomy of a Slave Ship," 142; Richardson and Childers, *Mariner of England*, 50. For quarter netting, see Falconer, *An universal dictionary*, "quarter-netting"; William Hutchinson, *A treatise on practical seamanship; with hints and remarks relating thereto* (Liverpool: Cowburne, 1777), 168–69. The first mention of netting employed on slave ships is in Instructions for the *Dispatch*, 1725.

14. Samuel Robinson, *A Sailor Boy's Experience aboard a Slave Ship* (Broughton Gifford: Cromwell Press, 1996), 55 ("the poor"). Behrendt, Eltis, and Richardson, "The Costs of Coercion," 463 ("Successful"). Snelgrave, *New Account*, 190 ("occasioned"). On the Rhode Island ship *Thames* off the Gold Coast in 1776, about one hundred male slaves on the main deck tried "to get down the Barricado, or over it for upwards of 40 minutes" but "could not effect it." See *DIHST*, vol. 3, 323. For the factors that limited the chances of success in revolts, see Taylor, *If We Must Die*, 67–84. Although insurrections were almost always thwarted, resistance nonetheless had an important effect on the overall contours of the slave trade: because merchants spent large sums on precautions to prevent resistance, they invested less in the trade. As a result, as many as a million people were saved from enslavement. See Richardson, "Shipboard Revolts," 74–75.

15. This account is drawn largely from Smeathman (ed. Coleman), "Oeconomy of a Slave Ship." It is corroborated by slave ship logbooks, the testimony of numerous witnesses in *HCSP*, and Clarkson, *Substance of the Evidence*. The time of day that the slaves were brought up varied between seven and ten in the morning. See, for example, logbook of the *Glory*, July 16–August 11, 1771.

16. *BG*, vol. 2, 778 ("strong"). Instructions for the *Africa Galley*, 1700 ("as much"); "Accompts submitted by the Plaintiff in the Court of Chancery suit Capt. James Westmore, commander, v. Thomas Starke, owner of the slaver 'Affrican Galley' . . ." Add. Ms. 45123, BL ("Bulkhead"). Royal African Company to Captain Andrew Seale, London, August 3, 1704, T70/63, TNAUK ("divert"). Captain William Snelgrave to John Magnus, [Whydah?], [1723?], Morice Papers, Bank of England, London ("barricado"). Atkins, *Voyage*, 173 ("Rule[s]"). Testimony of Robert Norris in *HCSP*, vol. 68, 4 ("usual Manner"). A 1702 dictionary described a "Barricado" as a "kind of warlike defence, made of barrels fill'd with Earth & c" and made no mention of its use aboard ships, confirming that it was a later invention. See John Kersey, *A new English dictionary* . . . (London: P. Scolar, 1702), 20. For surviving logbooks, see my Appendix C.

17. For mortality circa 1650–1699, see https://www.slavevoyages.org/voyages/nAo4UDmo. For mortality circa 1700–1788, see https://www.slavevoyages.org/voyages/BVsVkqQr. Parliamentary regulations came into force after 1788, which further altered shipboard regimes, and so I have excluded the years 1789–1808 from this analysis.

18. T[homas] Aubrey, *The Sea-Surgeon, or the Guinea Man's Vade Mecum* . . . (London: John Clarke, 1729), 102 ("Nature"), 105 ("raw"), 106 ("Relicks"), 117 ("evil"). *BG*, vol. 2, 779 ("bad"). For ship surgeons' medical ideas, see also Richard B. Sheridan, "The Guinea Surgeon on the Middle Passage: The Provision of Medical Services in the British Slave Trade," *International Journal of African Historical Studies* 14, no. 4 (1981): 601–25; Kenneth F. Kiple, *The Caribbean Slave: A Biological History* (Cambridge:

Cambridge University Press, 1984), 57–75; Mustakeem, "'I Never Have Such a Sickly Ship Before,'" 474–96. Medical knowledge in the slave trade still remained limited after abolition. See Manuel Barcia Paz, *The Yellow Demon of Fever: Fighting Disease in the Nineteenth-Century Transatlantic Slave Trade* (New Haven: Yale University Press, 2020).

19. For mortality rates by African region, see https://www.slavevoyages.org/voyages/E6C53cYn.

20. Phillips, *A Journal*, 230 ("great"), 237 ("To"); Aubrey, *The Sea-Surgeon*, 132 ("what a"). Innovation to shipboard management is striking by its absence in the voluminous papers of slave-trading merchants after 1720.

21. Anon., "The Slave Trade from West Africa to the Cape Verde Islands in the Sixteenth Century," in *Portuguese in West Africa*, ed. and trans. Newitt, 158 ("pressed"). "A Curious and Exact Account," in *Collection of Voyages and Travels . . .*, vol. 1, 637 ("pressed together"). *BG*, vol. 2, 778 ("as close"), 779 ("so crouded"). Newton, *Thoughts*, 33 ("With").

22. The slave ships have been isolated in the registers, which are at the MMM (C/EX/L/4), and then cross-referenced with *Slave Voyages*. Of the 762 slave ships in the database, just 179 undertook their first slaving voyage within two years of their construction—an indication that they had been built for the slave trade. Another third were between three and ten years old, and the final third were more than ten years old; forty-one vessels had been at sea for more than twenty years before being used in the trade. Only a third (208) of the ships were built in Liverpool; 36 percent (222) had been constructed in either a British town besides Liverpool or a British colony; and the remainder (178, or 29 percent) came from America, France, Spain, or the Netherlands, mostly as prizes taken in the American and French Revolutionary Wars. When Bristol merchant James Rogers wanted a ship for the Windward Coast trade in 1789, his captain advised him that he would have to obtain a "small vessel" and should avoid those that were "too large." See Captain William Roper to James Rogers, Liverpool, June 22, 1789, JRP, C107/5. For the addition of the quarterdeck during the voyage, see logbook of the *Madam Pookata*, May 18, 1785.

23. George Pinckard, *Notes on the West Indies . . .* (London: Longman, Hurst, Rees, and Orme, 1806), vol. 1, 237 ("stand"). For differing statures and ages of enslaved people embarked at African markets, see James Jones to Lord Hawkesbury, Bristol, July 26, 1788, Add. Mss. 38416, BL.

24. Testimony of James Jones in *HCSP*, vol. 68, 43 ("a great," "small"). For platforms in the early Portuguese trade, see de Sandoval, *Treatise*, 56. For platforms in the early French and English trade, see *BG*, vol. 2, 778. "Dimensions Of The Following Ships in the Port of Liverpool, employed in the African Slave Trade," 1788, BT6/7, TNAUK. According to Robert Norris, "small Vessels" and "long low Vessels" did not have platforms. See *HCSP*, vol. 68, 9. Shipbuilders could change the height of the space between decks on new ships "to the convenience of the purchasers," and

so merchants must have deliberately built their vessels with low space between decks. See Captain William Roper to James Rogers, Liverpool, June 22, 1789, C107/5, TNAUK.

25. Testimony of James Jones in *HCSP*, vol. 68, 43–44 ("general"), 45 ("judge of"), 46 ("Four," "how"). For the Liverpool slave traders, see Testimony of James Penny in ibid., 39; Testimony of John Matthews in ibid., 41.

26. For the production of the *Brooks* diagram, see Clarkson, *History*, vol. 2, 113 ("how many"), 114 ("without"). For the *Brooks*, see Marcus Wood, "Imaging the Unspeakable and Speaking the Unimaginable: The 'Description' of the Slave Ship *Brookes* and the Visual Interpretation of the Middle Passage," *Lumen* 26 (1997): 211–45; Rediker, *The Slave Ship*, 308–42.

27. Nicholas Radburn and David Eltis, "Visualizing the Middle Passage: The *Brooks* and the Reality of Ship Crowding in the Transatlantic Slave Trade," *Journal of Interdisciplinary History* 49, no. 4 (Spring 2019): 541–49.

28. The deck area for the slaves aboard the *Marie-Séraphique* was calculated by taking the horizontal area of her rooms (1,637 feet square) and adjusting for the platforms in the women's room, which measured twenty-three feet by six feet on either side of the room. The platforms in the women's room increased the deck area by 276 feet square, bringing the total area to 1,913 square feet.

29. Newton, *Thoughts*, 33 ("close"). Testimony of [James Towne] in Clarkson, *Substance*, 52 ("lie exceedingly"). Testimony of [James Morley] in Clarkson, *Substance*, 75 ("stowed," "12"). Testimony of George Millar in *HCSP*, vol. 73, 388 ("there"). Testimony of William James in *HCSP*, vol. 69, 137 ("stowing," "adjusting"). Testimony of James Morley in *HCSP*, vol. 73, 157 ("as close"). Testimony of Thomas Trotter in ibid., 84 ("spoonways," "Those").

30. James Irving to Mary Irving, Tobago, December 2, 1786, in Suzanne Schwarz, *Slave Captain: The Career of James Irving in the Liverpool Slave Trade* (Liverpool: Liverpool University Press, 2008), 87 ("almost"). For water barrels occupying space on deck, see also Testimony of John Knox in *HCSP*, vol. 68, 90. For livestock on slave ships, see, for example, logbook of the *Maria*, August 6, 1773. Captain Phillips purchased a "young tiger" at Cape Coast that he kept in a "wooden cage upon the quarter-deck," which mauled an enslaved woman's leg. See Phillips, *A Journal*, 230–31. Crewmen stored provisions in the tops to further maximize space. On the *Spy*, a bunch of plantains that had been lodged in the sails came loose, fell, and "shaterd one slaves arm all to pieces" and wounded two others. See logbook of the *Spy*, March 27, 1794.

31. Testimony of John Knox in *HCSP*, vol. 68, 88 ("at a"). Testimony of [Alexander Falconbridge?] in Clarkson, *Substance*, 131 ("no interval," "shrieks"). Falconbridge, *Account*, 33 ("even"). John & Thomas Hodgson to Richard Miles, Liverpool, October 14, 1783, T70/1549/1, TNAUK ("yet").

32. Testimony of George Millar in *HCSP*, vol. 73, 388.

33. Logbook of the *Duke of Argyll*, October 8, 1750 ("marked off," "began"), December 7, 1750 ("swivel"). For the construction of the gratings, see logbook of the *Unity*, September 28, 1769. Once the slaves had been sold, the carpenter "sheathed" the gratings, presumably to prevent water washing below on the return voyage to Europe. See logbook of the *Black Prince*, May 25, 1763. Constructing the barricado was a drawn-out task: on one ship, the barricado was still "half built" two weeks after construction had begun (logbook of the *Gregson*, December 24, 1787).

34. William Butterworth, *Three Years Adventures of a Minor, in England, Africa, the West Indies, South-Carolina and Georgia* (Leeds: Thomas Inchbold, 1851), 39 ("cleaning"). Richardson and Childers, *Mariner of England*, 62 ("a number"). Smeathman (ed. Coleman), "Oeconomy of a Slave Ship," 143 ("pounding"). Logbook of the *Duke of Argyll*, December 18, 1750 ("with chains"). For captives sleeping in half-finished rooms, see logbook of the *Spy*, February 8–March 14, 1794. On the *Mermaid*, the men slaves "rose" on the carpenter and seized his hammer as he worked on a "Stanchion to Prevent the Slaves from Breaking the Main Gratings." A crewman subsequently guarded the carpenter in his work "with a Loaded Pistol in his Hands." See "Statement from Captain Edward Taylor," August 1793, C107/13, TNAUK.

35. Henry Smeathman to Mr. Drury, Sierra Leone, July 10, 1773, MS D.26, no. 2, University Library, Uppsala University ("eating," "ten"). Testimony of Thomas Trotter in *HCSP*, vol. 73, 89 ("look"). Trotter added that visiting African traders were not permitted to "go forward after our barricado was put up." See ibid., 90. Testimony of James Towne in *HCSP*, vol. 82, 22 ("look"). For the distribution of beads and dice, see, for example, Testimony of James Penny in *HCSP*, vol. 69, 117. On one ship, the crew threw broken ship biscuits from the top of the barricado to the enslaved children to entertain them. See Smeathman (ed. Coleman), "Oeconomy of a Slave Ship," 144.

36. Captain William Thoburn to Richard Miles, [Cape Coast Castle?], October 22, 1776, T70/1534, TNAUK ("shove in"). James Field Stanfield, *Observations on a Guinea Voyage, In a Series of Letters Addressed to the Rev. Thomas Clarkson* (London: James Phillips, 1788), 32 ("boat-load," "packed"). The measurements of the *Golden Age* are in "Dimensions Of The Following Ships in the Part of Liverpool, employed in the African Slave Trade," 1788, BT6/7, TNAUK. By cross-referencing the measurements with the slave purchases for the same vessel recorded in *APHLRO*, 1794, I have calculated the amount of space per person throughout the purchasing period on the African coast. The same collections detail the dimensions and loading of the Liverpool ship *Jane*, which sailed to Bonny in the same year, detailing the same pattern as the *Golden Age*.

37. Logbook of the *Ranger*, July 7, 1790. Testimony of Robert Norris in *HCSP*, vol. 68, 16 ("full-grown," "moved," "Space," "sufficient," "down").

Riland, *Memoirs*, 56 ("little"). Archibald John Monteith, "Archibald John Monteith: Native Helper and Assistant in the Jamaica Mission at New Carmel," *Callaloo* 13, no. 1 (Winter 1990): 114 ("heartrending").

38. Testimony of Robert Norris in *HCSP*, vol. 68, 17 ("a double"). Testimony of Henry Ellison in *HCSP*, vol. 73, 366 ("30," "messed"). Captain James Charles to Richard Miles, Cape Coast Castle, November 4, 1783, T70/1549/1, TNAUK ("filling," "well," "like"). Captain William Thoburn, who traded on the Gold Coast in the same period as Charles, likewise told Miles that he only had "Room for small slaves" aboard his ship as it neared departure from the coast. See Captain William Thoburn to Richard Miles, Cape Coast Castle, August 2, 1783, T70/1549/1, TNAUK).

39. Smeathman (ed. Coleman), "Oeconomy of a Slave Ship," 145. Falconbridge, *Account*, 30 ("permitted," "allowed"). Logbook of the *Charlotte*, February 15, 1806.

40. Logbook of the *Bruce Grove*, July 20 ("wringing") and July 21 ("fresh"), 1802. Robinson, *Sailor Boy's Experience*, 93 ("nothing"). For the removal of restraints at sea, see Phillips, *A Journal*, 229. For shackling throughout the voyage, see Newton, *Thoughts*, 14–15. For the unshackling of supposedly "peaceable" nations and the chaining of "vicious" people at sea, see, for example, James Fraser in *HCSP*, vol. 71, 26, 34. Captives taken from ports in Upper Guinea were most apt to rebel, a fact that was well understood by the captain, who typically kept male captives from that region chained throughout the voyage. See Richardson, "Shipboard Revolts," 76–77.

41. Logbook of the *Isabella*, August 15 ("all bad"), 16 ("eat nothing"), 18 ("eat," "washed"), 1798. Falconbridge, *Account*, 26 ("ease"), 32 ("resembled"). For the lax cleaning regime, see, for example, logbook of the *Britannia*, November 11, 1776–January 1, 1777. For "flux," and the increased likelihood of its spread on crowded vessels, see Richard H. Steckel and Richard A. Jensen, "New Evidence on the Cause of Slave and Crew Mortality in the Atlantic Slave Trade," *Journal of Economic History* 46, no. 1 (March 1986): 66–68.

42. Falconbridge, *Account*, 35 ("flesh," "shoulder"). Darold D. Wax, "A Philadelphia Surgeon on a Slaving Voyage to Africa, 1749–1751," *Pennsylvania Magazine of History and Biography* 92, no. 4 (October 1968): 484 ("so cramped"). Riland, *Memoirs*, 57 ("fully"). Testimony of James Arnold in *HCSP*, vol. 69, 126 ("driven," "only"). Thomas Trotter, *Observations on the Scurvy . . .* , 2nd edition (London: T. Longman, 1792), 53 ("custom"). For measles, see Testimony of James Penny in *HCSP*, vol. 68, 37. For smallpox, see logbook of the *Gregson*, December 1–15, 1788; Phillips, *A Journal*, 237. For yaws, see Aubrey, *The Sea-Surgeon*, 110–26. On the Danish slaver *Christianbourg* the captives could "exercise" above deck only "every second day" because their "number [was] so great." See Isert, *Letters*, 235.

43. Testimony of [James Towne] in Clarkson, *Substance*, 52 ("bathed"). Testimony of Anon. in Clarkson, *Substance*, 64 ("water"). Robinson, *Sailor Boy's Experience*, 54 ("hot iron"). Logbook of the *African*, May 14 ("very sharp,"

"upon") and 17, 1753 ("keep ye"); *Isabella*, August 30, 1798 ("always"); *Black Prince*, March 1–May 7, 1763. Newton, *Thoughts*, 34 ("The heat"). Riland, *Memoirs*, 51 ("extremely").

44. Testimony of Thomas Trotter in *HCSP*, vol. 73, 84 ("heave," "we are," "to the," "in a"). Testimony of James Morley in ibid., 158 ("up on," "take"). Silas Told, *An Account of the Life, and Dealings of God with Silas Told . . .* (London: W. Cowdroy June, 1805), 25 ("universal," "ailed," "wild," "devil"). Mass panic, and wild attacks on neighbors to escape, is a common reaction when people are trapped in dark crowded spaces with diminishing air. See Albert D. Biderman, Margot Louria, and Joan Bacchus, *Historical Incidents of Overcrowding* (Washington, DC: Bureau of Social Science Research, 1963), 17–24. These captives on the *Royal George* were likely afflicted by carbon dioxide poisoning, which causes panic, convulsions, and, in the most extreme cases, death.

45. For dehydration on the Middle Passage, see Kenneth F. Kiple and Brian T. Higgins, "Mortality Caused by Dehydration during the Middle Passage," *Social Science History* 13, no. 4 (1989), 421–37.

46. Aubrey, *The Sea-Surgeon*, 124 ("mere"). Medical Log of a slaver the Lord Stanley by Christopher Bowes, 1792, Royal College of Surgeons of England Library. Logbook of the *Eliza*, July 19–September 19, 1805; *Swift*, September 14–November 3, 1803.

47. Testimony of James Ramsay in *HCSP*, vol. 69, 142 ("a Fifth," "refuse"). For mortality, see https://www.slavevoyages.org/voyages/XAsglvoB (1676–1699); https://www.slavevoyages.org/voyages/mMVCZgEM (1700–1788); https://www.slavevoyages.org/voyages/OG95NtaS (1789–1808). Haines and Shlomowitz claim that the decline in mortality rates post-1789 was driven by slave ship surgeons' improved medical knowledge. The abruptness of the drop in mortality rates after the passage of Dolben's Act, however, indicates that parliamentary regulation did indeed have an important impact on the trade. See Robin Haines and Ralph Shlomowitz, "Explaining the Mortality Decline in the Eighteenth-Century British Slave Trade," *Economic History Review*, 53, no. 2 (May 2000): 262–83. The proportion of sickly captives across time was: 1700–1725, 21 percent; 1726–1750, 15 percent; 1751–1775, 18 percent; 1776–1800, 18 percent; 1801–1808, 12 percent.

48. For the differing conditions of enslaved people arriving in the Americas, see Testimony of James Ramsay in *HCSP*, vol. 69, 141–42.

49. Testimony of [James Bowen?] in Clarkson, *Substance*, 45 ("in healthy," "unhealthy"). Testimony of James Ramsay in *HCSP*, vol. 69, 142 ("Proportion").

50. Butterworth, *Three Years Adventures*, 102–32, 103 ("fierce"), 117 ("resented"), 120 ("simultaneous"), 122 ("flogged," "without," "a strong"), 127 ("raged"), 129 ("evinced"). For the *Hudibras*'s voyages, see https://www.slavevoyages.org/voyages/QlLlCmp8.

51. Ninety percent of the 10,229 British slaving voyages sailing circa 1700–1808 disembarked their captives in the Americas. See https://www .slavevoyages.org/voyages/Pt3qNpTE.

Chapter Four. Guinea Factors and the Forced Migrations of Enslaved People within the Americas

1. Butterworth, *Three Years Adventures*, 130 ("glutted").
2. For the intra-American slave trade, see Gregory E. O'Malley, *Final Passages: The Intercolonial Slave Trade of British America, 1619–1807* (Chapel Hill: University of North Carolina Press, 2015); Gregory E. O'Malley, "Beyond the Middle Passage: Slave Migration from the Caribbean to North America, 1619–1807," *William and Mary Quarterly* 66, no. 1 (2009): 125–72; Alex Borucki, David Eltis, and David Wheat, "Atlantic History and the Slave Trade to Spanish America," *American Historical Review* 120, no. 2 (April 2015): 433–61; Intra-American Slave Trade-Database (https://slavevoyages.org/american/database).
3. For the early history of Barbados, see Sheridan, *Sugar and Slavery*, 84–116; Dunn, *Sugar and Slaves*, 46–116. For the Leewards, see Dunn, *Sugar and Slaves*, 117–48; Sheridan, *Sugar and Slavery*, 148–83; Natalie A. Zacek, *Settler Society in the English Leeward Islands, 1670–1776* (New York: Cambridge University Press, 2010). Although the Leewards were an archipelago, merchants often considered them to be a "single freight zone" because of their proximity. See Ian K. Steele, *The English Atlantic, 1675–1740: An Exploration of Communication and Community* (Oxford: Oxford University Press, 1986), 29. For Jamaica, see Dunn, *Sugar and Slaves*, 149–87; Sheridan, *Sugar and Slavery*, 208–33; Nuala Zahedieh, "Trade, Plunder, and Economic Development in Early English Jamaica, 1655–89," *Economic History Review* 39, no. 2 (May 1996): 205–22. For landings of Africans in the English Americas pre-1700, see http://www.slavevoyages .org/estimates/cwzauJLJ.
4. For colonial North American slavery, see Allan Kulikoff, *Tobacco and Slaves: The Development of Southern Cultures in the Chesapeake, 1680–1800* (Chapel Hill: University of North Carolina Press, 1986); Peter H. Wood, *Black Majority: Negroes in Colonial South Carolina from 1670 through the Stono Rebellion* (New York: W. W. Norton, 1996); Lorena S. Walsh, *Motives of Honor, Pleasure, and Profit: Plantation Management in the Colonial Chesapeake, 1607–1763* (Chapel Hill: University of North Carolina Press, 2012); Warren, *New England Bound*. For slave landings in English North America, see http://www.slavevoyages.org/estimates/JSexwtoF.
5. For Jamaican ports, see https://www.slavevoyages.org/voyages/bSVAhMjn. For Charleston as a slave market, see Daniel C. Littlefield, "Charleston and Internal Slave Redistribution," *South Carolina Historical Magazine* 87, no. 2 (April 1986): 93–105; Gregory E. O'Malley, "Slavery's Converging

Ground: Charleston's Slave Trade as the Black Heart of the Lowcountry," *William and Mary Quarterly* 74, no. 2 (2017): 271–302. For Georgia's slave trade, see Paul M. Pressly, *On the Rim of the Caribbean: Colonial Georgia and the British Atlantic World* (Athens: University of Georgia Press, 2013). During the Seven Years' War, British merchants shipped thirty thousand enslaved people to Martinique and Guadeloupe before the islands were returned to France in 1763. British ships likewise brought six thousand captives to Cuba after the capture of Havana in 1762. See https://www .slavevoyages.org/voyages/YJ6vi7Ix.

6. For the shifting contours of slave landings in the British Americas during the eighteenth century, see https://www.slavevoyages.org/voyages/ E6C53cYn. For duties placed on slave imports by North American legislatures, see, for example, *DIHST*, vol. 4, 14–15, 23–29 (Maryland); 102–17, 120–56 (Virginia); 281–90 (South Carolina).

7. A. P. Thornton, "The Organization of the Slave Trade in the English West Indies, 1660–1685," *William and Mary Quarterly* 12, no. 3 (July 1955): 408 ("sought-after"). For the RAC's factors, see Davies, *Royal African Company*, 291–343; David Galenson, *Traders, Planters and Slaves: Market Behavior in Early English America* (Cambridge: Cambridge University Press, 1986); Trevor Burnard, "Who Bought Slaves in Early America? Purchasers of Slaves from the Royal African Company in Jamaica, 1674–1708," *Slavery and Abolition* 17, no. 2 (August 1996): 205–28; Hancock, "'A World of Business to Do,'" 8–15. For factors' correspondence with London, see "Letters Received. From Africa and the West Indies," T70/1, TNAUK; "Letters Received. Abstracts for the Committee Of Correspondence. From Africa and the Indies," T70/10–12, TNAUK.

8. For the importance of American debt for the RAC's collapse, see Davies, *Royal African Company*, 57–63, 316–25; Galenson, *Traders, Planters*, 150–51.

9. Quoted in Morgan, ed., *Bright-Meyler*, 121 ("Loss"). For factors' remittances from slave sales, see Jacob M. Price, "Credit in the Slave Trade and Plantation Economies," in *Slavery and the Rise of the Atlantic System*, ed. Barbara L. Solow (New York: Cambridge University Press, 1991), 293–340; Kenneth Morgan, "Remittance Procedures in the Eighteenth-Century British Slave Trade," *Business History Review* 79, no. 4 (Winter 2005): 715–49; Robin Pearson and David Richardson, "Social Capital, Institutional Innovation and Atlantic Trade before 1800," *Business History* 50, no. 6 (November 2008): 765–80; Nicholas Radburn, "Keeping 'the Wheel in Motion': Trans-Atlantic Credit Terms, Slave Prices, and the Geography of Slavery in the British Americas, 1755–1807," *Journal of Economic History* 75, no. 3 (September 2015): 660–89.

10. Smith & Baillies to Henry Bright, St. Kitts, June 21, 1763, in Morgan, ed., *Bright-Meyler*, 373 ("not inconsiderable," "at least"); see n. 454 for the breakdown of profits. Richard Meyler II to Jeremiah Meyler, Bristol,

April 28, 1761, in ibid., 365 ("the only"). There are no records that comprehensively detail the identity of Guinea factors trading across the British Americas. Rather, there are colony specific snapshots in various official and unofficial records. I have cross-referenced these sources with *SV* to ascertain the identities of factors for the 2,396 voyages. For the small amounts of capital needed to finance slave sales when credit transactions were timed correctly, see, for example, Levinius Clarkson to William Neale, Charleston, December 5, 1772, in *DIHST*, vol. 4, 452.

11. I have identified factors by cross-referencing the sources in my Appendixes D and E with voyages in *SV*. For factors' origins, see Hamilton, *Scotland, the Caribbean*, 84–111; S. D. Smith, *Slavery, Family, and Gentry Capitalism in the British Atlantic: The World of the Lascelles, 1648–1834* (Cambridge: Cambridge University Press, 2006), 195–207; Morgan, ed., *Bright-Meyler*, 20–47; Radburn, "Case of John Tailyour," 247–53.

12. For South Carolina factors, see Record of the Public Treasurers of South Carolina, 1725–76, no. M/3, South Carolina Department of Archives and History, Columbia. For Jamaica, see "A List of Ships and Vessels arrived in Jamaica from the Coast of Guinea between 22d September 1752 and 22d December 1753," CO 142/16, TNAUK; for Barbados, see "An Account of what number of New Negroes are imported into [Barbados]," CO 28/30, TNAUK. For Grenada, see "List of Slaves sold in Grenada since its restoration to the English in 1784," CO 101/28/47, TNAUK.

13. John Tailyour to William Miles Jr., Kingston, November 22, 1789, Letterbook 1788–89, TFP ("Every"). Taylor, Ballantine & Fairlie to John Tailyour, Kingston, January 13, 1793, Box 6, TFP ("country interest"). For the difficulties of obtaining consignments of ships, see Levinius Clarkson to David Van Horne, Charleston, February 23, 1773, in *DIHST*, vol. 4, 456 ("the preference"). The value of ships has been calculated by multiplying the average cash price of enslaved people by the average number of people disembarked, both of which are detailed in *SV*. Using that metric, the average values were: 1700–1725, £4,800; 1726–1750, £5,688; 1751–1775, £8,208; 1776–1800, £14,858; 1801–1808, £19,530. See https://www.slavevoyages.org/voyages/dhT7tGm9. For links between British firms and factoring houses, see Radburn, "Case of John Tailyour," 257. For Hibbert, see Donington, *Bonds*, 50–77.

14. For the Rainfords, see Sheryllynne Haggerty and John Haggerty, "Visual Analytics of an Eighteenth-Century Business Network," *Enterprise and Society* 11, no. 1 (March 2010): 1–25, 6 ("over"), 11 ("sub-nets"); Sheryllynne Haggerty, *"Merely for Money"? Business Culture in the British Atlantic, 1750–1815* (Liverpool: Liverpool University Press, 2012), 181–88. Jonathan Blundell Junior to Rainford, Blundell & Rainford, Liverpool, June 4, 1787, Papers of Chaffers, 920 CHA/1, LRO ("young").

15. John Tailyour to Camden, Calvert & King, Kingston, May 16, 1790, Letterbook 1790–91, TFP ("respectable"). John Tailyour to William Miles, Kingston, May 16, 1790, ibid. ("folly"). For credit terms, see Rad-

burn, "Keeping 'the Wheel.'" Record of the Public Treasurers of South Carolina, 1725–76, no. M/3, South Carolina Department of Archives and History, Columbia; "An Account of what number of New Negroes are imported into [Barbados]," CO 28/30, TNAUK; "List of Slaves sold in Grenada since its restoration to the English in 1784," CO 101/28/47, TNAUK. Factors who took ships from other firms faced ire, including challenges to a duel. See *JDRH*, November 14–24, 1775.

16. David Hancock, *Oceans of Wine: Madeira and the Emergence of American Trade and Taste* (New Haven: Yale University Press, 2009), xvii ("further"). For merchants expanding and integrating the British Empire through their profit-motivated decisions, see also Hancock, *Citizens of the World.*

17. [Edgar Corrie] to Lord Hawkesbury, [London?], August 31, 1788, Liverpool Papers, BL, MS.38416 ("four," "will," "the remittance," "involves"). For the risks enumerated by Corrie, see Sheryllynne Haggerty, "Risk and Risk Management in the Liverpool Slave Trade," *Business History* 51, no. 6 (November 2009): 817–34; Radburn, "Keeping 'the Wheel,'" 660–86.

18. "Account book for a slaving voyage of the Jason gally and later household accounts for the Becher family, 1743–1818," Bristol Archives, 45167/1.

19. For the importance of winds and currents in the navigation of British slave ships, see Behrendt, "Ecology, Seasonality," 46–53.

20. Instructions for the *Lottery*, 1802 ("the want"). Munro, McFarlane & Co. to James Rogers, Grenada, June 14, 1792, C107/10, JRP ("Barbados," Capt[ain]s"). For factors lodging intelligence in the eastern Caribbean, see, for example, Henry Laurens to Captain William Jenkinson, Charleston, August 13, 1755, in *PHL*, vol. 1, 315–16. For islands as entrepôts in the reexport slave trade, see O'Malley, *Final Passages,* 328–31.

21. For the concept of "limits" and credit lengths at different American markets, see Radburn, "Keeping 'the Wheel,'" 663–68.

22. [Edgar Corrie] to Lord Hawkesbury, [London?], August 31, 1788, Liverpool Papers, BL, MS.38416 ("ultimate"). Lytcott & Maxwell to James Rogers, Barbados, March 3, 1789, C107/9, JRP ("without"). Instructions for the *Charming Nancy*, 1753 ("at a"). For the *Bedford*, see Thomas Lumley & Co. to Captain William Beamish Lane, London, March 12, 1803, C114/156, TNAUK. For the difficulty of sailing from west to east in the Caribbean, see Steele, *English Atlantic*, 32; The Memorial of the Merchants in Liverpool, Traders to Africa . . . , [1776?], BT6/2, TNAUK. For the low North American demand for slaves in winter, see Edmund Jennings to the Board of Trade, Virginia, January 11, 1710, in *DIHST*, vol. 4, 90–91. On some ships, clothing for the captives was stored in the hold specifically for the voyage north. See, for example, The Royal African Company: Minutes of Committee, July 16, 1722, in ibid., 269.

23. Baillies & Hamilton to William Davenport & Co., St. Vincents, November 17, 1784, D/DAV/13, MMM ("some," "lengthening"). Instructions for the *Sally*, 1768 ("be healthy"). Robert Bostock to Captain James Fryer,

Liverpool, December 16, 1790, Letter book, etc. of Robert Bostock, vol. 2, 387 MD 55, Liverpool Record Office ("sickly," "make," "for fear"). For orders to sell sickly people in eastern markets, see also Instructions for the *James*, 1754; *Swift*, 1759.

24. Logbook of the *African*, June 3, 1753 ("drop," "Jamaica"). Richard Meyler II to Tilghman & Ringold, Bristol, October 6, 1753, in Morgan, ed., *Bright-Meyler*, 288 ("buried"), 289 ("sett"). William Barton to James Rogers, Barbados, March 6, 1793, C107/59, JRP ("very," "buryed," "proceeded"). Munro, McFarlane & Co. to James Rogers, Grenada, September 4, 1792, C107/5, JRP ("cruelty"). Henry Laurens to Captain Valentine Powell, Charleston, November 9, 1756, in *PHL*, vol. 2, 348 ("should," "do"). For the laws, see "Act for Establishing Quarantine, 1744," in *DIHST*, vol. 4, 299–300 (South Carolina); "Repeal of the Act Excluding Negroes, 1750," in ibid., 610–11 (Georgia). Captains also stopped their ships if large numbers of crewmen had died on the Middle Passage. See, for example, Munro, McFarlane & Co. to James Rogers, Grenada, November 18, 1792, C107/13, JRP.

25. Logbook of the *African*, June 3, 1753 ("worn," "orders," "intelligence," "as good"). For captains forcing unhealthy slaves on additional voyages, see also Captain John Kennedy to James Rogers, Barbados, March 11, 1793, C107/59, TNAUK; Captain James Cream Hunt to James Rogers, Barbados, May 11, 1793, C107/59, TNAUK. For the 1772 crisis and its effects on the geography of the slave trade, see Radburn, "Keeping 'the Wheel,'" 673–75.

26. Radburn, "Keeping 'the Wheel,'" 675–80. For similar shifts in Britain's slave trade circa 1792–1796 and circa 1799–1801, see ibid., 680–84.

27. Instructions for the *Hector*, 1771 ("refreshments"). Butterworth, *Three Years*, 129 ("oranges"). Trotter, *Observations on the Scurvy*, 69 ("must"). For purchases of provisions in the eastern Caribbean, see, for example, "Ship *Hannah*'s Disbursements in Barbados," "Ship *Hannah*'s disbursements in Dominica," in Thomas Leyland Company account books, 1980. M-1933, William L. Clements Library, University of Michigan, Ann Arbor.

28. Logbook of the *Spy*, May 3 ("survey[ed]," "save"), May 15 ("boiling," "the water"), May 16 ("induced"), and June 4, 1794, HCA16/88, TNAUK. For provisions almost running out before reaching an American port, see Captain John Kennedy to James Rogers, St. Vincents, November 7, 1788, C107/2, TNAUK. For ships putting in at ports because they were low on water, see, for example, Captain William Blake to James Rogers, Barbados, August 16, 1793, C107/59, JRP; "News Items Relating to the Slave Trade, 1759," in *DIHST*, vol. 4, 374.

29. Testimony of William James in *HCSP*, vol. 69, 137 ("in great," "walk"). For the difficulty of navigating to Barbados, see Steele, *English Atlantic*, 24–25. For slave ships overshooting islands, see, for example, Captain John Goodrich to James Rogers, Martha Brae, June 15, 1793, C107/59, JRP.

For captains bypassing islands in wartime, see, for example, Instructions for the *Swift*, 1759; *Earl of Liverpool*, 1797. For the *Zong*, see James Walvin, *The Zong: A Massacre, the Law and the End of Slavery* (New Haven: Yale University Press, 2011), 76–101. For the throwing of people overboard, see "News Items Relating to the Slave Trade, 1759," in *DIHST*, vol. 4, 373; Carl B. Wadstrom, *An Essay on Colonization, particularly applied to the Western coast of Africa . . . in Two Parts* (London: Darton and Harvey, 1794), 29–30.

30. Butterworth, *Three Years*, 124–25 ("very"), 125 ("procured"), 128 ("eagerly"), 128–29 ("they saw"), 129 ("lost"). For an experience identical to that of the *Hudibras*'s captives, see Equiano, *Interesting Narrative*, 54–55. Although most vessels anchored for only a few hours, others remained in port for several days for repairs or to await a convoy to the other islands. For longer stays, see, for example, logbook of the *Sandown*, April 28–May 3, 1794. For enslaved people's fears of being cannibalized, see Smallwood, *Saltwater Slavery*, 122–52. For slaves mustering on deck in American ports, see also Journal of Jonathan Troup, May 11, 1789, University of Aberdeen Special Collections, GB 231 MS 207; J. B. Moreton, *West India Customs and Manners . . .* (London, 1793), 145.

31. Logbook of the *Britannia*, January 3 ("came") and 4 ("Oyld," "many," "Came"), 1777. Captain Edward Holden to Isaac Hobhouse, York River, May 26, 1723, in *DIHST*, vol. 4, 100 ("25"). For factors viewing slaves before the ship departed for another market, see also Samuel & James King Wents to William Davenport & Co., Barbados, October 30, 1775, D/DAV/7, MMM; Lycott & Maxwell to James Rogers, Barbados, March 3, 1789, C107/9, JRP. For the sale of sickly slaves in the eastern Caribbean, see also Richardson, *Bristol, Africa*, vol. 1, 62, 101–2, 105–6, 108–12, 118–20, 124, 132, 138, 140, 143, 152, 161, 171.

32. Logbook of the *African*, June 3, 1753 ("so long"). Butterworth, *Three Years*, 130 ("out," "like"). Henry Laurens to John Knight, Charleston, December 31, 1756, in *PHL*, vol. 2, 389 ("grow," "turn[ed]"). For enslaved people's desire to reach land, see also logbook of the *Eliza*, September 13, 1805; Sir James Wright to Lord Dartmouth, Savannah, September 16, 1775, in *DIHST*, vol. 4, 629. For ships touching at islands on either side of the Atlantic, see logbook of the *Britannia*, November 13, 1776–January 15, 1777.

33. Butterworth, *Three Years*, 132 ("fertile," "engaged"). For ships running along Jamaica's coasts, see logbook of the *Gregson*, January 20, 1789. For ships running up the rivers in the Chesapeake region, see Captain Edward Holden to Isaac Hobhouse, York River, May 26, 1723, in *DIHST*, vol. 4, 100; Phillip Lee to Governor Samuel Ogle, North Patowmeck, June 27, 1741, in ibid., 28; "New Items Relating to the Slave Trade, 1766," in ibid., 46.

34. I have determined the lengths of fifty-one voyages by cross-referencing logbooks and shipping records with *SV*. I have also analyzed voyage

lengths of ships departing from British Caribbean colonies for other markets in *The Intra-American Slave Trade* database in *SV.* For the voyage from the Leewards to Jamaica, see logbook of the *Maria*, September 9–16, 1773. For the diagonal route to Jamaica from Barbados, see logbook of the *Swift*, October 24–November 4, 1803. For the voyage from the Caribbean to Virginia, see Captain Edward Holden to Isaac Hobhouse, York River, May 26, 1723, in *DIHST*, vol. 4, 100. For voyage lengths within the Caribbean, see also Steele, *English Atlantic*, 29–32.

35.   Samuel Richards to James Rogers, Barbados, March 11, 1791, C107/10, JRP ("in great"); Captain Samuel Stribling to James Rogers, Barbados, March 12, 1791, C107/12, JRP ("in a"). Crow, *Memoirs*, 153 ("daily"), 157 ("toilsome," "r[a]n"). Captain John Kennedy to James Rogers, Montego Bay, March 13, 1791, C107/14, JRP ("the worst"). "Joseph Banfield memoirs, not before 1796," mssHM 57345, Huntington Library, San Marino ("Suffocated"). For poor weather within the Caribbean, see also Captain William Woodville Jr. to James Rogers, Grenada, August 10, 1791, C107/13, JRP.

36.   Henry Laurens to Robert & John Thompson, Charleston, July 24, 1756, in *PHL*, vol. 2, 269 ("buffeted," "five weeks"). Henry Laurens to Walter Caddell, Charleston, August 15, 1755, in *PHL*, vol. 1, 318 ("destroy'd"). For vessels driven away from Carolina by winds, see also "Negroes Imported into South Carolina, 1760," in *DIHST*, vol. 4, 376, n. 4. For the *Britannia*, see "Negroes Imported Into South Carolina, 1765," in ibid., 413, n. 27. For the *Republican*, see "News Items Relating to Slave Trade, 1804," *DIHST*, vol. 4, 509, n. 3. The closing of North American ports by legislatures also turned slave ships away—killing captives who were forced to undertake extra voyages against the winds. See, for example, "News Item Relating to Slave Trade, 1775," in *DIHST*, vol. 4, 470; Testimony of James Fraser in *HCSP*, vol. 73, 33; Sir James Wright to Lord Dartmouth, Savannah, October 14, 1775, in *DIHST*, vol. 4, 629; *JDRH*, September 28, 1775.

37.   Logbook of the *Eliza*, September 18 ("took," "little") to September 20, 1805. *Jamaica Courant*, Kingston, September 12, 1722 ("most of"). Testimony of James Fraser in *HCSP*, vol. 71, 38 ("scarcity"). The *Racehorse* likewise struck land off North Carolina after spending "three weeks" trying to find her way out of "thick foggy weather." The captives were eventually rowed to Charleston and sold. See "Negroes Imported into South Carolina, 1760," in *DIHST*, vol. 4, 376, n. 5. For similar cases, see "Negroes Imported into South Carolina, 1806," in *DIHST*, vol. 4, 514, n. 13; Henry Laurens to Richard Oswald, Charleston, February 4, 1771, in *DIHST*, vol. 4, 439. For Africans sold from wrecked ships, see also *JDRH*, June 24, 1774; June 13, 1776. In 1778, 234 captives from the *Mermaid* were killed when shipwrecked on Jamaica's coast. The six survivors were sold in Kingston. See *JDRH*, July 15–16, 1778.

38. Crow, *Memoirs*, 71 ("wounded"). Williams, *Liverpool Privateers*, 472 ("one man"). For the large numbers of privateers lurking off the British islands, see Steele, *English Atlantic*, 36–37; Williams, *Liverpool Privateers*, 196, 200–201, 245, 488. For slave ships fending off privateers, see ibid., 207, 286, 294, 484, 491. When the *Mary* engaged what the captain thought to be a French privateer, a cannon blasted into the men's room and "wounded a great number of blacks, five of whom soon after died." The "enemy" vessel transpired to be a British man-of-war. See Williams, *Liverpool Privateers*, 110. For enslaved people wounded in action, see ibid., 491 (*Hector*, three captives killed), 563 (*Jane*, one enslaved boy killed); "Negroes Imported Into South Carolina, 1805," in *DIHST*, vol. 4, 509 (*Margaret*, eighteen slaves wounded); logbook of the *Swift*, 18259, October 18, 1803 (one man killed).

39. Logbook of the *Spy*, May 13, 1794 ("a number"). Captain Clement Noble to [Thomas Rumbold?], Montego Bay, April 26, 1777, in Williams, *Liverpool Privateers*, 561 ("fight," "fight," "killed," "fought"). Captain William Stevenson to [Joseph Caton?], Old Harbour, April 28, 1781, in ibid., 565 ("very well," "shot," "hurt"). In 1757, the captain of the *Knight* also armed "several of his negroes," who fought "gallantly with small arms" alongside the crew against a French privateer that later sank. See Williams, *Liverpool Privateers*, 484.

40. Crow, *Memoirs*, 102 ("selected," "and in"), 103 ("a pair," "dram," "were very"). William Beamish Lane to Thomas Lumley & Co, Bedford, on her passage to Demerara, November 13, 1803, C114/158, TNAUK ("harassed," "chose," "knocked," "three"). For preferential treatment shown to enslaved men who worked with the crew, see also Smallwood, "African Guardians."

41. "Extract of a Letter from Messrs. Ashburner, Hinde & Co dated Grenada 17th March 1777 to Messrs. Tarleton & Backhouse of Liverpool," SP78/32, TNAUK ("carried"). "Account of Piracies on the Virginia Coast, 1724," in *DIHST*, vol. 4, 119 ("38"). [Merchant of St. Vincent] to [Merchant of Liverpool], St. Vincent, May 5, 1777, in Williams, *Liverpool Privateers*, 201 ("cheaper").

42. Snelgrave, *New Account*, 190 ("attempted"). "Letter on Board the *Prince of Orange*," in *DIHST*, vol. 2, 460 ("resolv'd," "the Injury"), 461 ("proceeding"). "Memoirs of Joseph Senhouse: 1776–1779," March 23, 1778, Senhouse Papers, Cumbria County Council Archives, f.155 ("whole," "made," "through"). Taylor, *If We Must Die*, 181–210. Seven of the twelve revolts ended with the captives gaining control of the vessel, but in six of those seven the ship was retaken. The fate of the seventh vessel—a ship that was taken by the slaves in the Caribbean in 1772—is unknown, but Taylor assumes the captives managed to escape ashore. Crewmen were also prone to mutiny in American waters. See, for example, Captain Henry Laroche

to James Rogers, Grenada, October 1, 1791, C107/12, TNAUK. For the unshackling of captives once in the Americas, see Trotter, *Observations on the Scurvy*, 69; Newton, *Thoughts*, 36. Some captains kept African men, especially those from the Gambia River, in shackles until their final sale. See, for example, logbook of the *Maria*, September 18–22, 1773.

43. Butterworth, *Three Years*, 132 ("the land"), 133 ("a number," "for the," "ready"). Richardson, *Mariner of England*, 64 ("were glad," "they gave," "plunge"). Newton, *Thoughts*, 36 ("transient"). For Africans imprisoned in American ports being "very noisy & troublesome," see *JDRH*, February 6, 1780.

44. Newton, *Thoughts*, 36 ("short-lived").

Chapter Five. Many Middle Passages

1. Rough Diary of Sir William Fitzherbert (1st Baronet) Visiting Barbados, December 27, 1770, Fitzherbert Family Papers, Derbyshire Record Office, Matlock ("The," "was," "all," "miserable," "all"). John Gabriel Stedman, *Narrative of a Five Years' Expedition, against the Revolted Negroes of Surinam . . .* (London: J. Johnson, 1806), vol. 1, 209 ("behold," "They were," "a resurrection"), 210 ("worr[ied]"). For visitors to the Americas describing slave ships in harbors, see also Hans Sloane, *A Voyage to the Islands Madera, Barbados, Nieves, S. Christophers and Jamaica . . .* (London, 1707), vol. 1, lxxiii; Jonathan Troup: Journal, 5 December 1788–c. April 1790, May 11, 1788, University of Aberdeen Library, GB 231 MS 2070; Pinckard, *Notes on the West Indies*, vol. 1, 238.

2. Stedman, *Narrative*, vol. 1, 209 ("men," "risen"). For American sales, see Kenneth Morgan, "Slave Sales in Colonial Charleston," *English Historical Review* 113, no. 453 (September 1998), 905–27; Trevor Burnard and Kenneth Morgan, "The Dynamics of the Slave Market and Slave Purchasing Patterns in Jamaica, 1655–1788," *William and Mary Quarterly* 58, no. 1 (January 2001), 205–28; Galenson, *Traders, Planters*, 53–85; Rediker, *The Slave Ship*, 152–54; Sean Kelley, "Scrambling for Slaves: Captive Sales in Colonial South Carolina," *Slavery and Abolition* 34, no. 1 (January 2013), 1–21. For works that appreciate the importance of enslaved people's diversity within American sales, see Smallwood, *Saltwater Slavery*, 153–81; Diptee, *From Africa to Jamaica*, 25–49; Mustakeem, *Slavery at Sea*, chap. 5.

3. Emma Hart, *Trading Spaces: The Colonial Marketplace and the Foundations of American Capitalism* (Chicago: Chicago University Press, 2019), 13–68, 24 ("rich," "act[ing]"). Jamaica's Assembly passed a law in 1789 that mandated that slave sales could no longer take place aboard ships, and that factors should strive to keep families together. The second part of the act was quietly shelved soon thereafter because, factors argued, it was inoperable. No similar law was enforced elsewhere in the Americas. See *The New Act*

of Assembly of the Island of Jamaica . . . Commonly Called the New Consolidated Act . . . (London: B. White and Son, 1789), 16.

4. Quoted in Dunn, *Sugar and Slaves*, 57 ("over," "very"). Abbot Emerson Smith, *Colonists in Bondage: White Servitude and Convict Labor in America* (Chapel Hill: University of North Carolina Press, 1947), 19 ("displayed"). Marcelus Rivers and Oxenbridge Foyle, *England's Slavery, or Barbados Merchandize . . .* (London, 1659), 5 ("according").

5. The Company of Royal Adventurers to Francis Lord Willoughby, London, January 10, 1662, in *DIHST*, vol. 1, 156–57. See also The Guinea Company to Francis Soane, London, December 9, 1651, in ibid., 132–33.

6. For the RAC's sales methods, see Galenson, *Traders, Planters*, 71–92, 62 ("accommodate," "roughly"), 87 ("2.5"). Edwyn Stede & Stephen Gascoigne to RAC, Barbados, March 15, 1684, T70/16, TNAUK ("croud"). For the social structure of Barbados, see Dunn, *Sugar and Slaves*, 84–116. The RAC's directors did not ordinarily mandate how their factors organized sales, and so it was left to American agents to devise their methods; the RAC's directors reminded one factor, "Our business is to sell our Negroes by such Methods as may be most to our Advantage." RAC to Stede, Harding & Prideaux, Barbados, December 29, 1692, T70/57, TNAUK.

7. For colonists trying to drive down the prices of lots of slaves, see Hender Molesworth and Charles Penhallow to RAC, Barbados, September 11, 1683, T70/16, TNAUK. For the intermixing of healthy and unhealthy captives within the RAC's lots, see John Heyler to William Heyler, Port Royal, Sept 22, 1686, DD/WHh 1089/3, Somerset Heritage Centre. For the *William*, see T70/936, TNAUK. For the *Henry and William*, see T70/938, TNAUK. For Jamaica's comparatively flatter social structure, see Trevor Burnard, "'A Pack of Knaves': The Royal African Company, the Development of the Jamaican Plantation Economy and the Benefits of Monopoly, 1672–1708," *Journal of Colonialism and Colonial History* 21, no. 2 (Summer 2020).

8. RAC Directors to Edwin Stede, Benjamin Shutt and William Harding, London, November 11, 1690 ("Inch," "publish," "all"), T70/57, TNAUK; RAC Directors to Walter Ruding & Samuel Barnard, London, August 4, 1691 ("openly"). For the ending of the experiment, see RAC Directors to William Beeston & Samuel Barnard, London, Oct 13, 1692.

9. Sale invoice of the *African*, 1694. For citations of sale invoices, see my Appendix E. The number of large slave buyers in Jamaica increased rapidly during the 1680s and 1690s as wealth became consolidated on the island: "In the 1670s, the top decile of purchasers bought on average seven slaves at each purchase. By the 1680s the comparable number had risen to 18 and after 1690 large purchasers typically bought their slaves in very large lots of 28 slaves each purchase." See Burnard, "Who Bought Slaves." For the "lotting" of enslaved people in Virginia, see, for example, Colonel William Byrd to Perry and Lane, Virginia, September 10, 1686,

in *DIHST*, vol. 1, 61–62. For buyers selecting captives themselves in Virginia, see Sale invoice of the *Postillion*, 1704.

10. Oldendorp, *History of the Mission*, 219 ("strong," "sick"). Dieudonné Rinchon, *Pierre Ignace-Lievin Van Alstein Captain Négrier, Gand 1733–Nantes 1793* (Dakar: Ifan Press, 1964), 193 ("age"), 194 ("tail"), 313–14. For sales methods in the British colonies, see Testimony of John Knox in *HCSP*, vol. 68, 104; Testimony of William James in *HCSP*, vol. 69, 138; Testimony of John Castles in *HCSP*, vol. 71, 218; Testimony of Alexander Falconbridge in *HCSP*, vol. 72, 596; Testimony of Thomas Trotter in *HCSP*, vol. 73, 87; Testimony of Clement Noble in ibid., 118–19; Testimony of James Morley in ibid., 159; Testimony of Thomas Clappeson in *HCSP*, vol. 82, 212; Testimony of William Fitzmaurice in ibid., 233.

11. Logbook of the *Madam Pookata*, March 7 ("French"), 1787. Instructions for the *Ranger*, 1767 ("friend"). John Tailyour to James Jones, Kingston, May 30, 1788, Letterbook 1788–89, TFP ("country"). On the *Madam Pookata*'s subsequent voyage to Dominica, 188 of the 192 Africans were sold to a merchant from Saint Kitts within a week of arrival. See logbook of the *Madam Pookata*, February 13–17, 1788. The figures for the number of private sales overstates their frequency because the sale invoices for the second half of the eighteenth century are disproportionately drawn from the papers of William Davenport, who principally shipped captives to the eastern Caribbean islands. If factors elected not to sell a human cargo, the captain offered the prisoners to another factoring house in the town or upped anchor and headed for another port. See, for example, *JDRH*, July 28, 1773; August 9, 1773; May 11–12, 1774; May 24, 1774. For merchants purchasing large numbers of captives from ships soon after their arrival, see also ibid., December 7–8, 1773; December 30, 1773; July 25, 1775; December 5–6, 1775; February 17, 1776; August 27, 1776.

12. John Tailyour to Simon Taylor, Kingston, January 24, 1789, Taylor and Vanneck-Arcedeckne Papers, Plantation Life in the Caribbean (PLC) Series: Pt. 1, Jamaica, c. 1765–1848, London, XIV/38 ("every"). John Perry to James Rogers, Montego Bay, January 21, 1793, C107/13, JRP ("a long," "dying," "a good"). The opening day has been determined by cross-referencing advertisements and invoices for slave sales in my Appendixes D and E with *Slave Voyages*. Sales opened on Monday 207 times; Tuesday 246; Wednesday 258; Thursday 200; Friday 129; Saturday 34. In South Carolina, Wednesday was a particularly common opening day, presumably to allow ample time for people to come in from the distant countryside after the Sabbath. In Jamaica, by contrast, Monday was the most common day, perhaps to provide as many days as possible for the sale to run before it temporarily closed on Sunday.

13. *Royal Gazette*, Kingston, September 28, 1782 ("had the"); *Royal Gazette*, Kingston, June 1, 1793 ("were all"); *South Carolina Gazette*, Charleston, March 23, 1769 ("after"). For the *Margaret*, see the *Weekly Jamaica*

Courant, Kingston, February 11, 1718. For different images of Africans in advertisements, see, for example, the *Royal Gazette*, Kingston, April 26, 1783 (captives standing); *Royal Gazette*, Kingston, December 29, 1780 (wielding hoes); *South Carolina Gazette*, Charleston, June 6, 1771 (carrying bows); *South Carolina Gazette*, Charleston, May 30, 1785 (smoking); *South Carolina Gazette*, Charleston, April 4, 1771 (with children); *South Carolina Gazette*, Charleston, May 31, 1771 (carrying children). For the clustering of advertisements, see the *South Carolina Gazette*, Charleston, April 13, 1769.

14. *South Carolina Gazette*, Charleston, June 20, 1754 ("all in"). Henry Laurens to Henry Weare & Co., Charleston, July 2, 1755, August 30, 1755, in *PHL*, vol. 1, 281 ("scabby"), 327 ("the most"). Henry Laurens to Law, Satterthwaite, & Jones, Charleston, December 14, 1755, in *PHL*, vol. 2, 38 ("very low"). *South Carolina Gazette*, Charleston, December 25, 1755 ("in good"). *Royal Gazette*, Kingston, May 25, 1793 ("healthy"). Grove, Harris & Papps to James Rogers, Kingston, July 14, 1793, C107/59, JRP ("Meagre").

15. For South Carolina colonists' preferences for captives from Upper Guinea and dislike for people from the Bight of Biafra, see Henry Laurens to Smith and Clifton, Charleston, July 17, 1755, in *PHL*, vol. 1, 295; Henry Laurens to Jonathan Blundell & Co., Charleston, May 16, 1756, *PHL*, vol. 2, 182; Henry Laurens to Richard Oswald, Charleston, May 17, 1756, in ibid., 186. For planter preferences in the Low Country and their importance for shaping the slave trade, see also Daniel C. Littlefield, *Rice and Slaves: Ethnicity and the Slave Trade in Colonial South Carolina* (Baton Rouge: Louisiana State University Press, 1981); Wood, *Black Majority*. Judith Ann Carney, *Black Rice: The African Origins of Rice Cultivation in the Americas* (Cambridge, MA: Harvard University Press, 2009). For Jamaican planters' preferences for captives from the Gold Coast and Biafra, see John Tailyour to John and Alexander Anderson, Kingston, July 12, 1784, Letterbook 1781–85, TFP. For Jamaican planters' dislike for "Windward Coast" slaves, see Simon Taylor to John Tailyour, Kingston, July 12, 1793, Box 7, TFP, WCL.

16. Sale invoices of the *True Blue*, 1771 ("several"); *Crescent*, 1793 ("past[ed] up"); *Orrel*, 1753 ("disper[sed]"); *Iris*, 1794 ("intimate"). John Tailyour to Simon Taylor, Kingston, January 24, 1789, Simon Taylor Papers, Senate House Library, University of London, ICS 120, 14/A/42 ("the cargo," "hop[ed]," "if not"). Richardson and Childers, *Mariner*, 64 ("with"). For criers, see Phillip Waldeck, *Eighteenth-Century America: A Hessian Report on the People, the Land, the War, as Noted in the Diary of Chaplain Philipp Waldeck (1776–1780)*, trans. Bruce E. Burgoyne (Bowie: Heritage, 2008), 104–5. For walking slaves on shore before their sale, see also logbook of the *Maria*, September 24, 29, 1773; *Bruce Grove*, September 5, 8, 1802. For factors "writ[ing] letters to Planters," see *JDRH*, June 8, 1774.

17. Henry Laurens to Gidney Clarke, Charleston, January 31, 1756, in *PHL*, vol. 2, 84 ("success"). Henry Laurens to Law, Satterthwaite, & Jones, Charleston, January 12, 1756, in ibid., 65 ("draws," "remote"). Henry Laurens to Henry Weare & Co., Charleston, August 30, 1755, in *PHL*, vol. 1, 327 ("70"). "Memoirs of Joseph Senhouse: 1776–1779," vol. 2, August 15, 1776, Senhouse Papers, Cumbria County Council Archives, 30 ("exorable") 31 ("full," "led," "deep," "up"). Diary of Nathaniel Phillips, 1781, in *Jamaican Material in the Slebech Papers, British Records Relating to America in Microform (BRRAM)* (Wakefield: Microform, 2004), 9411.

18. Equiano, *Interesting Narrative*, 54 ("Many"), 54–55 ("put us"), 55 ("pointed," "we should," "some," "were not," "every," "filled"). For bringing Africans aboard to calm the new arrivals, see also Testimony of George Baillie in *HCSP*, vol. 71, 189. Unlike captives brought to the Caribbean, enslaved people entering Charleston were forced to spend ten days ashore in quarantine prior to their sale on Sullivan's Island, a sand bar at the entrance to the harbor. For conditions on the island, see Pelatiah Webster and Thomas Perrin Harrison, *Journal of a Voyage to Charlestown in So. Carolina by Pelatiah Webster in 1765* (Charleston, 1898). For factors hiring enslaved linguists ("Negro speakers"), see *JDRH*, July 18, 1772.

19. Logbook of the *Maria*, September 18, 1773 ("Nockt"). Sale invoice of the *Freke*, 1730 ("clouts"); *William*, 1770 ("pluck"). Captain William Jenkins to James Rogers, Grenada, September 4, 1792, C107/5, JRP ("I am"). Logbook of the *Gregson*, January 21–29, 1789. While the captives ate offal on the ships, captains enjoyed lavish meals ashore with factors. See, for example, *JDRH*, March 24, 1772; December 14, 1773; January 1, 1774.

20. Moreton, *West India Customs and Manners*, 145 ("hurt[ing]," "the dead," "concealed"). Robinson, *Experience*, 105 ("floating"). "News Items Relating to the Slave Trade, 1807," in *DIHST*, vol. 4, 526–27. For deaths after arrival but before sale, see Herbert S. Klein, Stanley L. Engerman, Robin Haines, and Ralph Shlomowitz, "Transoceanic Mortality: The Slave Trade in Comparative Perspective," *William and Mary Quarterly*, 58, no. 1 (January 2001): Table II; Appendix E. For the 1785 Jamaica health crisis, see Marcus Rediker, "History from below the Water Line: Sharks and the Atlantic Slave Trade," *Atlantic Studies* 5, no. 2 (August 2008): 292.

21. Testimony of Thomas Clappeson in *HCSP*, vol. 82, 212 ("butcher's"). [Dr. Collins], *Practical Rules for the Management and Medical Treatment of Negro Slaves in the Sugar Colonies. By A Professional Planter* (London: J. Barfield, 1803), 45 ("Guinea-yards"); Falconbridge, *Account*, 34 ("thrown"). For captives escaping from anchored ships, see the *Daily Advertiser*, Kingston, February 11, 1790; *Charleston Courier*, December 28, 1807, 270. Africans from the *Squirrel* were sold at a "Yard" in Bridgetown, Barbados, that was "opposite the Dwelling-House" of the factor. See *Barbados Mercury*, Bridgetown, February 1, 1766. For locations of sales, see sale invoice of the *King of Prussia*, 1772 (tavern); *South Carolina Gazette*, Charleston,

June 9, 1739 (house); *Essequibo and Demerara Courant*, Georgetown, November 19, 1803 (plantation); *Barbados Mercury*, Bridgetown, April 18, 1807 (sail loft). For sales "upon the Wharf," see *JDRH*, February 4, 1780.

22. John Tailyour to John & Alexander Anderson, Kingston, June 8, 1785, Letterbook 1781–1785, TFP ("fixed," "goodness"). Henry Laurens to Captain Samuel Linnecar, Charleston, May 8, 1756, in *PHL*, vol. 2, 178 ("wholly"). Testimony of George Baillie in *HCSP*, vol. 73, 182 ("ranged"). For the pricing of enslaved Africans, see also Kelley, "Scrambling," 7–9. In shipboard sales, the captives remained divided by sex. "The men are on the main deck," a Liverpool captain told Parliament, "and the women all on the quarter deck." See Testimony of Clement Noble in *HCSP*, vol. 73, 118.

23. Testimony of [James Bowen?] in Clarkson, *Substance*, 46 ("laughed," "unusual," "it was"). *Two Reports (one presented the 16th of October, the other on the 12th of November, 1788) from the Committee of the Honourable House of Assembly of Jamaica* . . . (London: B. White, 1789), 30 ("astringent," "blacking"). Diary of Thomas Thistlewood, March 17, 1761, Beinecke Rare Book and Manuscript Library, Yale University, New Haven, OBB MSS 176 ("They"). Richardson and Childers, *Mariner*, 65 ("the purchasers"). For "darkening" the ship, see logbook of the *Britannia*, January 27, 1777. The practice of shaving and glossing slaves originated with the RAC's sales. See Invoice Books: Homewards, T70/936, TNAUK, f.161; "James: journal of intended voyage," May 24, 1675, T70/1211, TNAUK.

24. Allan, White & Co. to James Rogers, January 27, 1793, C107/6, TNAUK ("diseased," "not," "mere"). For selling of sickly people ashore before the sale opening, see Falconbridge, *Account*, 33. For unhealthy people not "appear[ing] in the yard," see also Henry Laurens to Richard Oswald, Charleston, July 10, 1756, in *PHL*, vol. 2, 246.

25. Logbook of the *Glory*, August 22, 1771 ("great"). Diary of Thomas Thistlewood, July 15, 1776, Beinecke Rare Book and Manuscript Library, Yale University, New Haven, OBB MSS 176 ("200"). Pinckard, *Notes on the West Indies*, vol. 2, 326 ("quite," "arrayed," "a day," "period"). Sale invoice of the *Dreadnought*, 1775 ("fife"). The same invoice included "Ham Turkey Punch & c" for the buyers and rent of "a house to sell the slaves." For the "crowd" of buyers at slave sales, see also *JDRH*, April 2, 1772.

26. Henry Laurens to John Knight, Charleston, July 12, 1756, in *PHL*, vol. 2, 250 ("tollerable," "but," "with," "we"). Henry Laurens to Wells, Wharton, & Doran, Charleston, August 12, 1755, in *PHL*, vol. 1, 314 ("choose," "make"). Diary of Thomas Thistlewood, August 12, 1776, Beinecke Rare Book and Manuscript Library, Yale University, New Haven, OBB MSS 176 ("abate," "about," "others"). For the "stated price" of slaves at sales, see William Dickson, *Letters on Slavery* (London: J. Phillips, 1789), 111. For factors' "power to choose purchasers" when demand was high, see John Tailyour to William Miles, February 17, 1788, Letterbook 1788–89,

TFP. Factors often did not note the names of cash buyers in their sale invoices, indicating that their identity was irrelevant. Colonists unknown to factors who wanted to purchase on credit could have their reputations vouched for by others. See, for example, *JDRH*, June 21–22, 1774. The Jamaican pound was worth 1.4 pounds sterling across the eighteenth century.

27. Dickson, *Letters*, 110 ("The sale"). Advertisements seldom noted the opening time of sales, and so they must have been well known to the buyers. Of the forty-four adverts that did mention the starting time, they were: "early in the forenoon" (one sale); 9 A.M. (four sales); 10 A.M. (twenty-four); 11 A.M. (fourteen); midday (one). Just eight advertisements noted the closing time of the sale, all at 2 P.M. These sales were all held in early nineteenth-century Charleston, though, so it is difficult to determine the closing times of sales elsewhere in the British Americas. There was apparently a lull in the sale while factors and buyers lunched. See *JDRH*, August 8, 1775; August 29, 1776.

28. Testimony of James Ramsay in *HCSP*, vol. 69, 141 ("healthy," "certain"). Malcolm Laing to William Phillip Perrin, Blue Mountain, November 27, 1771, Fitzherbert Family Papers, Derbyshire Record Office, Matlock, 16730 ("mere," "housed," "not," "young," "Meagre"). Henry Laurens to Samuel & William Vernon, Charleston, August 10, 1756, in *PHL*, vol. 2, 277 ("Wrong"). Henry Laurens to Law, Satterthwaite, & Jones, Charleston, January 12, 1756, in *PHL*, vol. 2, 65 ("Whilst"). John Tailyour to William Miles, Kingston, February 17, 1788, Letterbook 1788–89, TFP ("No"). John Tailyour to James Jones, May 30, 1788, Letterbook 1788–89, TFP ("Planters"). For planters' preference for teenagers and young adults, see Diary of Thomas Thistlewood, March 17, 1761, Beinecke Rare Book and Manuscript Library, Yale University, New Haven, OBB MSS 176. Factors sometimes allowed favored colonists a "private choice" of the captives before the sale opened. See, *JDRH*, January 3, 1774; Radburn, "Case of John Tailyour," 271.

29. Simon Taylor to Chaloner Arcedeckne, Kingston, November 11, 1765, in Betty Wood, ed., "The Letters of Simon Taylor of Jamaica to Chaloner Arcedekne, 1765–1775," in *Travel, Trade and Power in the Atlantic, 1765–1884*, Camden Miscellany XXXV, Camden 5th Series, ed. Betty Wood and Martin Lynee (Cambridge: Cambridge University Press, 2002), 28 ("fine," "ch[o]se"). Falconbridge, *Account*, 34 ("encircl[e]"). Richardson and Childers, *Mariner of England*, 65 ("tallies"). Testimony of George Baillie in *HCSP*, vol. 73, 182 ("pick[ing]," "hurried"); Testimony of Alexander Falconbridge in *HCSP*, vol. 72, 596 ("cr[ied]"). John Tailyour to James Jones, May 31, 1789, Letterbook 1788–89, Letterbook 1788–89, TFP ("purchasers," "Had"). For enslaved assistants at sales, see Diary of Thomas Thistlewood, April 29, 1765, Beinecke Rare Book and Manuscript Library, Yale University, New Haven, OBB MSS 176.

30. For the *Marie-Séraphique*, see Bertrand Guillet, *La marie-séraphique navire négrier* (Nantes: Éditions MeMo, 2010); Nicholas Radburn and David Eltis, "Visualizing the Middle Passage: The *Brooks* and the Reality of Ship Crowding in the Transatlantic Slave Trade," *Journal of Interdisciplinary History* 49, no. 4 (Spring 2019): 533–65.

31. "Observations made by the Reverand Mr Ramsay of Teston on the condition in which African slaves are imported into the W Indies," James Ramsay Papers, Bodleian Library, University of Oxford, MSS.Brit.Emp.S.2 ("second"). Diary of Thomas Thistlewood, August 12, 1776, Beinecke Rare Book and Manuscript Library, Yale University, New Haven, OBB MSS 176 ("girl"). Thomas Rose to John Foster Barham, St. Elizabeths, March 20, 1785, Clarendon Papers, Bodleian Library, University of Oxford, MS Clar.Dep.c357 ("Carpenter," "three"). Henry Laurens to Robert & John Thompson & Co., Charleston, April 20, 1757, in *PHL*, vol. 2, 524 ("very Mauger," "application"). For "second day slaves," see also Testimony of John Knox in *HCSP*, vol. 68, 104.

32. "Observations made by the Reverend Mr Ramsay of Teston on the condition in which African slaves are imported into the W Indies," James Ramsay Papers, Bodleian Library, University of Oxford, MSS.Brit.Emp.S.2 ("diseased," "fallen"). Henry Laurens to Richard Oswald & Co., Charleston, July 19, 1756, in *PHL*, vol. 2, 266 ("Carr[ied]"). Testimony of Hercules Ross in *HCSP*, vol. 73, 261 ("had," "landed," "in the"). Testimony of Drewery Ottley in *HCSP*, vol. 82, 184 ("made a"). For captives perishing during or immediately after an auction, see James Baillie Jr. & Co. to James Rogers, Grenada, October 31, 1781, C107/8, JRP.

33. François Vanstabel to Bonaventure Tresca, Malembo, January 20, 1784, Musée des beaux-arts de Dunkerque ("new arrivals"). For the *Comte du Norde*, see "Baillie & anr v Hartley: exhibits re SS Comte du Nord and slave trade: schedule, correspondence (Penny and Barber, Ball, Jennings & Co. to Hartley), accounts," E219/377, TNAUK; "Captured ship: L'Oiseau, master M. le Chevalier de Tarade. Nationality: French ship of war," HCA32/416/5, TNAUK. For Barber, see Elder, *Slave Trade*, 148–50. For "great Opposition from the French Ships" that Penny faced, see Testimony of James Penny, *HCSP*, vol. 68, 37. James Penny to Miles Barber, Malembo, May 22, 1784, E219/377, TNAUK.

34. Miles Barber to James Penny, London, March 11, 1784 ("truly great"). Captain James Penny to Miles Barber, Saint Christophers, July 1, 1784, E219/377, TNAUK ("six & seven"). James Penny to Miles Barber, Charleston, July 24, 1784, E219/377, TNAUK ("dreadful"). For the mortality suffered by the *Comte du Norde*'s captives, see logbook of the *Comte du Norde*, May 30–July 1, 1784; Testimony of James Penny in *HCSP*, vol. 68, 37. For Ball, Jennings & Co., see Miles Barber to James Penny, London, March 11, 1784, E219/377, TNAUK. Ball and Jennings had been engaged in the slave trade in the Caribbean before moving to

Charleston. Being "entire strangers" in South Carolina Ball & Jennings partnered with Smith, Dessausure & Darrell in Charleston, "an old established house" that had "never been in the Guinea Line" before. See James Penny to Miles Barber, July 24, 1784, E219/377, TNAUK.

35. Sale invoice of the *Comte du Norde*, 1784.

36. The identities of Charleston slave buyers have been ascertained by cross-referencing the *Comte du Norde*'s sale invoice with James W. Hagy, *People and Professions of Charleston, South Carolina, 1782–1802* (Baltimore: Genealogical, 1999). Planter purchasers have been identified by cross-referencing with genealogical databases, such as *Ancestry* and *Familysearch*. For Woodruff, see Karen H. Hebling, "Joseph Woodruff," *Savannah Biographies*, vol. 104 (1987). The sixty-one Africans from the slave ship *Hare* were likewise scattered over a long distance by numerous buyers after their sale in Charleston in 1755. See Sean M. Kelley, *The Voyage of the Slave Ship Hare: A Journey into Captivity from Sierra Leone to South Carolina* (Chapel Hill: University of North Carolina Press, 2016), 135–44.

37. For the scramble, see, for example, Kelley, "Scrambling"; Rediker, *The Slave Ship*, 152–53; Byrd, *Captives and Voyagers*, 59–61. One former ship officer who was in the trade on seven voyages circa 1758–1775 observed that he was "never in any ship" where the Africans were sold by a scramble. See Testimony of [James Morley?] in Clarkson, *Substance*, 77.

38. Thomas Hibbert Jr. to Nathaniel Phillips, Kingston, August 20, 1772, in *Slebech Papers*, BRRAM, 9212. Thomas Barritt to Nathaniel Phillips, Pleasant Hill, May 10, 1790, in ibid., 8356 ("pick'd up"). *Royal Gazette*, Kingston, January 12, 1793 ("in the"). Thomas Samson to Henry Goulburn, August 1, 1805, in "Papers Relating to the Jamaican Estates of the Goulburn Family of Betchworth House," BRRAM, 304J/1/12/10(a) ("course"). For the Bahamas sale, see Sale invoice of the *Fortune*, 1806.

39. Henry Laurens to Peter Furnell, Charleston, June 12, 1755, in *PHL*, vol. 1, 262 ("glorious"). Henry Laurens to Devonshire, Reeve, & Lloyd, Charleston, June 24, 1755, in ibid., 268 ("ran off"). For the number of buyers at the *Pearl* sale, see Henry Laurens to Robert & John Thompson & Co, Charleston, July 5, 1755, in ibid., 289. Sale invoice of the *Pearl*, 1755 ("sick & refuse"); *Adlington*, 1755.

40. For the "glutted" Jamaica market, see Jeremiah Meyler to Henry Bright, Savannah-la-Mar, March 9, 1751, in Morgan. ed., *Bright-Meyler*, 236; Henry Bright to Richard Meyler II, Kingston, July 25, 1749, in ibid., 217. For the ending of the asiento, see ibid., 226, n. 182. For the number of captives exported from Jamaica, see O'Malley, *Final Passages*, 361–64. For sugar prices, see Sheridan, *Sugar and Slavery*, 497. For the collapse of the reexport slave trade from Jamaica, see https://www.slavevoyages.org/voyages/2ri1EKkm.

41. Quoted in Morgan, *Slave Counterpoint*, 159 ("an excellent"). In 1750, the Charleston price of best-copper indigo was 2.74 shillings per pound, and 63,100 lbs. were exported. In 1755, the price was 4.33 shillings per pound, and exports were 303,500 lbs. See R. C. Nash, "South Carolina Indigo, European Textiles, and the British Atlantic Economy in the Eighteenth Century," *Economic History Review* 63, no. 2 (2010): 371. For rice prices, see R. C. Nash, "South Carolina and the Atlantic Economy in the Late Seventeenth and Eighteenth Centuries," *Economic History Review* 45, no. 4 (November 1992): 680. For the *Pearl*, see Henry Laurens to Devonshire, Reeve, & Lloyd, Charleston, June 24, 1755, in *PHL*, vol. 1, 268; Henry Laurens to John Knight, Charleston, June 26, 1755, in ibid., 270; Henry Laurens to Robert & John Thompson & Co., Charleston, July 5, 1755, in ibid., 289. For the *Prince George*, see Henry Laurens to Thomas Easton & Co., Charleston, July 31, 1755, in ibid., 306–7.

42. Henry Laurens to John Holden, Charleston, June 19, 1755, in *PHL*, vol. 2, 227–28 ("the demand"). Henry Laurens to Richard Oswald & Co., Charleston, July 10, 1756, in ibid., 245 ("entirely"). Henry Laurens to Robert & John Thompson & Co., Charleston, July 24, 1756, in ibid., 269 ("the planters").

43. Dickson, *Letters*, 110 ("crowd"), 110–11 ("rush[ed]"), 111 ("instantly," "f[e]ll," "embrac[ed]"). Falconbridge, *Account*, 34 ("climb[ing]), 35 ("shriek[ed]"). Testimony of Clement Noble in *HCSP*, vol. 73, 119 ("a general"). Henry Laurens to Corsley Rogers & Son, Charleston, August 1, 1755, in *PHL*, vol. 1, 308 ("pulling," "good"). For the duel, see the *Cornwall Chronicle*, Montego Bay, November 20, 1784.

44. Diary of Thomas Thistlewood, August 12, 1776, Beinecke Rare Book and Manuscript Library, Yale University, New Haven, OBB MSS 176 ("long"). Henry Laurens to Richard Oswald & Co., Charleston, August 14, 1756, in *PHL*, vol. 2, 283 ("full"). For the *Venus*, see Jamaica accts forward, 1757, Samuel and William Vernon, 1756–1799, 1756–1799, Slavery Collection, 1709–1899, NYHS, Series 1, Sub-Series 2, Box 2, Folder 15 ("Negro guide"). For sales opening and factors "Sell[ing] very few" captives, see also *JDRH*, June 17, 1773; November 15, 1773.

45. For the movement of Africans beyond the ships, see Nicholas Radburn, "'[M]anaged at First as if They Were Beasts': The Seasoning of Enslaved Africans in Eighteenth-Century Jamaica," *Journal of Global Slavery* 6 (2021): 15–18. Africans were usually guided to the plantations by enslaved people rather than the white buyer. See, for example, *JDRH*, July 19–20, 1774.

46. Testimony of Hercules Ross in *HCSP*, vol. 82, 257 ("speculated"). Falconbridge, *Account*, 35 ("examin[ed]," "stand," "When"). Diary of Thomas Thistlewood, October 2, 1771, Beinecke Rare Book and Manuscript Library, Yale University, New Haven, OBB MSS 176 ("The Rem[ain]d[e]r,"

"little," "a poor"). Sale invoice of the *Ruby*, 1789. Refuse slaves were often rowed ashore at the conclusion of a shipboard sale and sold from the factor's "store." See, for example, *JDRH*, December 20, 1773. For factors inviting merchants to purchase captives in bulk at the end of sales, see *JDRH*, January 11, 1775; November 1, 1775; November 11, 1775; December 16, 1775. For buyers examining "refuse slaves" and deciding not to purchase them, see also *JDRH*, February 26, 1775.

47. Testimony of Baker Davison in *HCSP*, vol. 82, 184 ("make"). Testimony of James Morley in *HCSP*, vol. 73, 160 ("poorer," "contrary," "more," "the beech," "in a"). Sale invoice of the *Alert*, 1789.

48. John Tailyour to James Jones, May 30, 1788, Letterbook 1788–89, Tailyour Family Papers ("fatten[ed]"). Louis Nelson, *Architecture and Empire in Jamaica* (New Haven: Yale University Press, 2016), 32 ("slave," "barrel," "single," "illuminated"). *JDRH*, June 21 ("refuse," "Mrs"), October 9, 1774. Hibbert went to inspect "sick slaves" on a ship a day after a drunken night of champagne consumption. See *JDRH*, May 12–13, 1775. For Hibbert's purchases of refuse slaves, see also ibid., November 11, 1776; December 22, 1778. For buyers visiting Hibbert's pen to "choose Negroes," see ibid., December 22, 1774; January 13, 1775. For recuperating Africans working at Hibbert's pen, see ibid., October 19, 1775. John Cunningham to James Rogers, Montego Bay, February 4, 1793, C107/59, JRP ("sick"). John Perry to James Rogers, Montego Bay, March 10, 1759, C107/59, TNAUK ("boast"). For the imprisonment of more than a hundred Africans, see the *Royal Gazette*, Kingston, December 1, 1791. For the four men's elopement, see the *Royal Gazette*, Kingston, March 3, 1790.

49. John Tailyour to James Jones, May 30, 1788, Letterbook 1788–89, Tailyour Family Papers ("retail"). Hercules Ross likewise stated that speculators bought refuse slaves "either for the purpose of carrying them to the country, and retailing them, or for being shipped off the island to foreign parts." See Testimony of Hercules Ross in *HCSP*, vol. 82, 257. For captives imported and reexported, see *Journals of the Assembly of Jamaica* (Kingston: Alexander Aikman, 1810), vol. 10, 367–72. Jamaican merchants likewise reexported large numbers of captive Africans after the American Revolutionary War, when demand for slaves in Cuba and Saint-Domingue was high, while domestic demand was flat. See https://www.slavevoyages.org/voyages/8FdZlBRZ.

50. For the experiences of captives at sea in the intra-American slave trade, see O'Malley, *Final Passages*, 48–60. Foreign buyers either worked through British factors or attended slave sales themselves. On December 16, 1773, for example, several "Spaniards" made a "proposal" to purchase 164 people from two slave ships consigned to the Hibberts, the largest factoring firm in Kingston, Jamaica. The next day the Spanish merchants, accompanied by Robert Hibbert, visited both vessels and "ch[o]se out of both"

the Africans, who were bought with bullion. See *JDRH*, December 16–17, 1773. See also ibid., March 18, 1774.

51. Falconbridge, *Account*, 35 ("unable"). For advertisements by slave retailers, see, for example, the *Royal Gazette*, Kingston, December 7, 1782 (Kingston); July 3, 1790 (Spanish Town); December 10, 1790 (Montego Bay); March 17, 1792 (Saint Ann's); November 2, 1792 ("25"), October 9, 1793 (Clarendon). For the *Thomas*'s sale, see the *Royal Gazette*, October 20, 1792; Taylor, Ballantine & Fairlie to John Tailyour, Kingston, October 22, 1792, TFP. Jones also purchased twenty-six captives from the *Diana* in 1789, and forty people from the *Rodney* in 1795; both vessels landed their captives at Kingston. See Sale invoice of the *Diana*, 1789; *Royal Gazette*, Kingston, June 13, 1795. For Jones's other sales, see the *Royal Gazette*, March 17, 1792; June 13, 1795.

52. DAJ, July 9, 1770 ("about"), August 31, 1770 ("a man"), June 1771. For the slave-purchasing strategies of middling whites in Jamaica, see Nicholas Radburn and Justin Roberts, "Gold versus Life: Jobbing Gangs and British Caribbean Slavery," *William and Mary Quarterly* 76, no. 2 (2019): 223–56. For Johnston, see Alan Karras, "The World of Alexander Johnston: The Creolization of Ambition, 1762–1787," *Historical Journal* 30, no. 1 (March 1987), 53–76.

53. For the purchase of the Africans from the ship, see DAJ, December 1, 1769. For Betty's purchase and sale, see ibid., November 23, 1767, March 8, 1768. For Romeo's purchase and sale, see ibid., January 1, 1770, October 2, 1770.

54. DAJ, January 1, 1771 ("a dropsy"). DAJ, June 1771 ("inexperienced"). For deaths, see DAJ, September 4 (Sally), 26 (Little Polly; two women bought from Lousada). Johnston paid £117 in Jamaican currency to Draper & Holden for the three Africans, or £39 per person (DAJ, July 9, 1770), and £52 for Junius (DAJ, August 31, 1770). By contrast, 230 healthy enslaved people sold at Kingston for £48 each in September 1764 (Sale invoice of the *African*, 1764).

55. Johnston bought four women for £65 in Jamaican currency per person on November 3, 1775 (DAJ); twelve women from the *Jane* for £63 per person (DAJ, November 23, 1775); twelve women and eight teenage girls for £58 per person (DAJ, March 21, July 3, 1776); thirteen men, two teenage boys, and one woman from the *Gregson*, paying £58 for the men and £56 for the boys and the woman (DAJ, October 17, 1776); he bought the man and three girls he called "refuse" also from the *Gregson* on the same day. He later acquired another twelve women and eight teenage girls and paid £60 for the women and £55 for the girls (DAJ, September 16, 1777). For the deaths of the four "refuse" slaves and the one man (whom Johnston had renamed Lucius), see DAJ, December 3, 1776.

56. James Ramsay, *Objections to the abolition of the slave trade, with Answers . . .*, 2nd edition (London: J. Phillips, 1788), 71 ("not more"). Testimony of

James Ramsay in *HCSP,* vol. 69, 42 ("almost"). For large numbers of "refuse" slaves perishing shortly after their sale from ships, see also *JDRH,* January 26, 1774; Sale invoice of the *King David,* 1757; James Baillie Jr. & Co. to James Rogers, Grenada, October 31, 1791, C107/8, TNAUK. For mortality rates during "seasoning," J. R. Ward, *British West Indian Slavery, 1750–1834: The Process of Amelioration* (Oxford: Clarendon Press, 1988), 127; Michael Craton, "Jamaican Slave Mortality: Fresh Light from Worthy Park, Longville and the Tharp Estates," *Journal of Caribbean History* 3 (1971), 26; Morgan, *Slave Counterpoint,* 444; Klein, *Atlantic Slave Trade,* 172–73; Radburn, "'[Managed] at First,'" 27–28. For mortality before and during sales, see my Appendix E; *Two Reports,* 25. For deaths on the Middle Passage, which are estimated at 430,956 on British ships circa 1700–1808, see http://www.slavevoyages.org/estimates/lbRGNBQ8.

57. *Daily Advertiser,* Kingston, June 26, 1790 ("paraded," "a sort," "very," "chintz," "two," "dan[ced]," "signs," "ea[se]"). John Tailyour to John and Alexander Anderson, Kingston, June 27 ("foreigners," "wish"), July 19, 1790 ("a considerable," "at vendue"), Letterbook 1790–91, TFP.

Epilogue

1. Henry Laurens to Ross & Mill, Charleston, September 1768, in *PHL,* vol. 6, 311 ("the wheel").
2. *The Works of The Rev. John Newton* . . . (Edinburgh: Peter Brown and Thomas Nelson, 1830), 4 ("genteel"). For abolitionism, see Adam Hochschild, *Bury the Chains: The British Struggle to Abolish Slavery* (London: Pan, 2007); Christopher Leslie Brown, *Moral Capital: Foundations of British Abolitionism* (Chapel Hill: University of North Carolina Press, 2006); Seymour Drescher, *Abolition: A History of Slavery and Antislavery* (Cambridge: Cambridge University Press, 2009); Manisha Sinha, *The Slave's Cause: A History of Abolition* (New Haven: Yale University Press, 2017). The last British slave ship to reach the Americas before abolition was the *Royal Edward,* which disembarked 316 people in Surinam in October 1808. See https://www.slavevoyages.org/voyages/Ah9cF00s. For compensation of slave owners, see *Legacies of British Slave Ownership* (https://www.ucl.ac .uk/lbs/); Catherine Hall et al., *Legacies of British Slave-Ownership: Colonial Slavery and the Formation of Victorian Britain* (Cambridge: Cambridge University Press, 2014).
3. For "decline," see Eric Williams, *Capitalism and Slavery* (Chapel Hill: University of North Carolina Press, 1944), 108–208; Selwyn H. H. Carrington, *The British West Indies during the American Revolution* (Leiden: Brill, 1988); David Beck Ryden, *West Indian Slavery and British Abolition, 1783–1807* (Cambridge: Cambridge University Press, 2009). For "econocide," see Seymour Drescher, *Econocide: British Slavery in the Era of Abolition* (Pittsburgh: University of Pittsburgh Press, 1977); David Eltis, *Economic*

Growth and the Ending of the Transatlantic Slavery Trade (New York: Oxford University Press, 1987); James Walvin, "Why Did the British Abolish the Slave Trade? *Econocide* Revisited," *Slavery and Abolition* 32, no. 4 (2011): 583–88.

4. Clarkson, *History*, vol. 1, 293 ("melancholy," "Trembling," "arduous," "subvert," persecution"), 294 ("even"). See also "Diary of travels in the West Country and Wales," 25 June 1787–25 July 1787, Saint John's College Special Collections, Cambridge, Clarkson/Folder 1–5/Doc 1. For the slave trade's collapse in the American Revolutionary War, see Radburn, "Keeping 'the Wheel,'" 660–89. For the huge profits earned in the war's aftermath, see Inikori, "Market Structure," 745–76. For profits in the British Caribbean, see Ward, *British West Indian Slavery*, 48. Britain's slave trade was partially kept afloat in the 1780s by the intra-American trade, through which 29,459 of the 117,561 Africans (one in four people) arriving in the British Caribbean were reshipped between 1784 and 1787. See https://www.slavevoyages.org/voyages/5OvSlhgD. For the volume of Britain's slave trade circa 1775–1789, see http://www.slavevoyages.org/estimates/c8AZ4bsu.

5. For British competition in Africa, see Robert Louis Stein, *The French Slave Trade in the Eighteenth Century: An Old Regime Business* (Madison: University of Wisconsin Press, 1979); "Mémoire du commerce du Calbar," 1762, C736, Chambre du commerce de Nantes, Archives départmentales Loire-Atlantique. For Britons working for the French and Spanish, see "Ships fitted out, in the following Ports for the Coast of Africa, supposed to be for Account of Spanish & French Subjects from the 1st of January 1787 to the 1st of May 1788," Liverpool Papers, MS.38416, BL, ff.89–90. For the British and French trades' volumes circa 1775–1791, see http://www.slavevoyages.org/estimates/gQtTRMOO.

6. Richardson, *Bristol, Africa*, vol. 1, xxxvi ("unattractive"). Clarkson, *History*, vol. 1, 370–414, 410 ("made"). Bristol's slave trade had by 1787 dropped by approximately a third versus its prewar level. See https://www.slavevoyages.org/voyages/A5hnWXrM. Of the twenty Bristol voyages in 1787, five were financed by James Jones, five by James Rogers, and three by James McTaggart, who had helmed ships between 1756 and 1766. Four individuals organized the remaining seven voyages. For the collapse of Lancaster's slave trade, which ended in 1793, see Elder, *Slave Trade*; https://www.slavevoyages.org/voyages/ZlUp7XXE. For the proportion of slaving vessels leaving Liverpool, see Holt & Gregson Papers, vol. 10, LRO, 942 HOL 10, f.363. For London's slave trade in 1787, see https://www.slavevoyages.org/voyages/XrsBMlJ9. For market structure in Liverpool, see James Wallace, *A General and Descriptive History of the Ancient and Present state, of the Town of Liverpool . . .* (Liverpool: R. Phillips, 1795), 244.

7. For the Parliamentary debates over abolition through 1790, see Clarkson, *History*, vol. 1, 469–572; vol. 2, 1–345. For the inquiries into the trade,

including debates over Dolben's Act, see *HCSP*, vols. 67–73, 82, 99. For Dolben's Act, see 28 Geo. III, c.54.

8. John Tailyour to William Miles Jr., Kingston, September 15, 1789, Letterbook 1788–89, TFP ("proceedings"). John Tailyour to William Miles, Kingston, January 24, 1790, Letterbook 1788–89, TFP ("Should," "the trade"). For the threat of abolition increasing slave prices, see also Robert Bostock to Captain James Fryer, Liverpool, May 17, 1789, Letter book, etc. of Robert Bostock, vol. 2, 387 MD 55, Liverpool Record Office. The intra-American slave trade slumped as British colonists sought to buy captives before abolition: in 1788 and 1789, just one in eight Africans were reexported from the British Caribbean, versus one in four circa 1784–1787. For sugar and slave prices, see David Eltis, Frank D. Lewis, and David Richardson, "Slave Prices, the African Slave Trade, and Productivity in the Caribbean, 1674–1807," *Economic History Review* 58, no. 4 (2005): 679; https://www.slavevoyages.org/voyages/PVFaY5de.

9. John Tailyour to Simon Taylor, Kingston, November 29, 1791, Taylor and Vanneck-Arcedeckne Papers, PLC, Reel 15 ("favourable"). For arrivals of slave ships in Saint-Domingue during the rebellion, see, for example, Nathaniel Cutting Journal and Letterbooks, 1786–98, January 1, January 19, 1792, Massachusetts Historical Society, Boston. For slave and sugar prices, see Eltis, Lewis, and Richardson, "Slave Prices," 679. For the collapse of the French Atlantic system, see Alan Forrest, *The Death of the French Atlantic: Trade, War, and Slavery in the Age of Revolutions* (Oxford: Oxford University Press, 2020). For rising slave and commodity prices because of the "devestations in the French Islands," see also Tarleton & Rigg to John Tailyour, Liverpool, February 17, 1794, Box 6, TFP.

10. Edgar Corrie to John Tailyour, Liverpool, January 6, 1794, Box 2, TFP ("race"). Clayton Tarleton to Thomas Tarleton, Liverpool, September 24, 1792, 920 TAR 1, LRO ("Every"). For Jamaica's "coffee boom," see B. W. Higman, "Jamaican Coffee Plantations, 1780–1860: A Cartographic Analysis," *Caribbean Geography* 2, no. 2 (October 1986): 73–91. For the spur given to slave prices by the April 1792 abolition vote, see, for example, Robert Bostock to Captain Thomas Flint, Liverpool, May 3, 1792, Letter book, etc. of Robert Bostock, vol. 2, 387 MD 55, Liverpool Record Office. For the geography of Britain's slave trade in Africa circa 1791–1807, see http://www.slavevoyages.org/estimates/wq21XvJH.

11. For the impact of the French Revolutionary Wars on Britain's slave trade circa 1793–95, see Radburn, "Keeping 'the Wheel.'" Slaving merchants hoped that Britain's 1793 invasion of Saint-Domingue would enable them to seize control of the island along with its immense slave trade. See Edgar Corrie to John Tailyour, Liverpool, January 30, 1794, Box 2, TFP. The much smaller islands of Martinique and Guadeloupe proved much more lucrative markets for Britain's slavers, who shipped approximately

thirty thousand Africans to the two islands between 1793 and 1808. For the transformation of the Guianas into plantation colonies, see Randy M. Browne, *Surviving Slavery in the British Caribbean* (Philadelphia: University of Pennsylvania Press, 2017). For shipments of captives to the Guianas and Trinidad, see http://www.slavevoyages.org/estimates/pvIgbKni. For military action in the Caribbean during the French Revolutionary Wars, see Michael Duffy, *Soldiers, Sugar and Seapower: The British Expeditions to the West Indies and the War against Revolutionary France* (New York: Clarendon Press, 1987).

12. For Cuba's transformation, see Ada Ferrer, *Freedom's Mirror: Cuba and Haiti in the Age of Revolution* (Cambridge: Cambridge University Press, 2014). For the U.S. slave trade before abolition, see James A. McMillan, *Final Victims: Foreign Slave Trade to North America, 1783–1810* (Columbia: University of South Carolina Press, 2004). For demand for Africans from cotton planters, see the numerous letters from the Charleston slave factoring firm Tunno and Price to London merchants Thomas Lumley circa 1805–1806, in C114/1, TNAUK. For the Danish trade, see Erik Gobel, *The Danish Slave Trade and Its Abolition* (Leiden: Brill, 2016). For the growth of Britain's slave trade to foreign markets, see http://www.slavevoyages.org/estimates/xtNNcXCS. Cognizant of the importance of foreign markets to British slave traders, abolitionists passed the Foreign Slave Trade Abolition Bill in 1806, which barred Britons from carrying Africans to foreign territories.

13. Ralph Fisher to Captain Thomas Taylor, Liverpool, August 8, 1799, Letterbook of Ralph Fisher, 1798–1803, Cumbria Archive Centre, Kendal ("few"). For the 1799 act, see 39 Geo III, c.80. For tonnages and mortality rates, see https://www.slavevoyages.org/voyages/SMiZ7U8a.

14. For the growth of the British slave trade at Ambriz and the Congo River, see James Penny to Robert Norris, Liverpool, June 25, 1791, BT6/8, TNAUK. For the cost of buying captives at the Congo River, see, for example, the account books of the *Christopher*, 1791–92, Duke University Library; *Jenny*, 1792–93, William L. Clements Library, University of Michigan, Ann Arbor; and *Enterprize*, 1794–95, MMM. Porto Novo's growth was concentrated in the period 1785 to 1791, when exports of enslaved people rose from near zero to three thousand people a year, on average. Lagos emerged as a key slaving port in the five years preceding abolition. See Kristen Mann, *Slavery and the Birth of an African City, Lagos, 1760–1900* (Bloomington: Indiana University Press, 2007). For the numbers of captives taken from these ports, see https://www.slavevoyages.org/voyages/P3VFRGlJ.

15. For rising slave prices in Africa, see David Richardson, "Prices of Slaves in West and West-Central Africa: Toward an Annual Series, 1698–1807," *Bulletin of Economic Research* 43, no. 1 (January 1991): 21–56. For

the increase in comey at Calabar, see Behrendt et al., *Diary of Antera Duke*, 67.

16. For prices of enslaved people at Bonny, see *BG*, vol. 2, 687 (1700); African account book of the *Molly*, 1759; *Jupiter*, 1793; Accountbook of the *Earl of Liverpool*, 1797–1800, Stanley Dumbell Papers, GB141 MS.10.50, ULL; Crow, *Memoirs*, 202. The African account book of the Bristol ship *Trelawny* 1791/2 itemizes the 17,888 goods that were exchanged for 334 enslaved people at Bonny in 1792. Each person was hence bought with approximately fifty-four items, most of which were individual goods, such as a gun, a piece of cloth, or a barrel of gunpowder, but also groups of items considered a single object in trade, such as a dozen knives or a bunch of beads. Multiplying this figure by the 6,722 people purchased at Bonny per year circa 1789–1808 gives the number of annual imports used to purchase people: 362,998. The addition of taxes and fees brings total annual imports to approximately half a million. For the numbers of captives taken from Bonny, see https://www.slavevoyages.org/voyages/hyH2okVm. For the increasing sizes of the bundles used to buy people over the eighteenth century, see Richardson, "Prices of Slaves," 40–41.

17. Crow, *Memoirs*, 196 ("poorer," "better," "homely"), 217 ("larger," "shirts," "gold-laced"), 251 ("secreted," "at some"). For gifts of ostentatious clothing to Ibani brokers, see Richardson and Childers, *Mariner*, 48–49.

18. Sylvanus John Sodienye Cookey, *King Jaja of the Niger Delta: His Life and Times, 1821–1891*, 2nd edition (New York: Nok, 1974), 22 ("become"), 31 ("five"). For canoe houses, see Kenneth Onwuka Dike, *Trade and Politics in the Niger Delta, 1830–1885* (London: Oxford at The Clarendon Press, 1966), 34–37; Jones, *Trading States*, 51–57. For lineage at Bonny, see Alagoa and Fombo, *Grand Bonny*, 6–16. The retention of captives to work in canoe houses likely explains why so few boys were carried from Bonny versus other African slaving ports. See Radburn, "Long Middle Passage," 61–62.

19. Earnings from sales have been calculated from the invoices listed in Appendix E. For shifting credits issued for slave sales, see Radburn, "Keeping 'the Wheel.'" For interest as a share of factors' earnings, see Radburn, "Case of John Tailyour," 280. For factors deliberately pushing demand, see, for example, Thomas Lumley to John Hinde & Co, London, February 7, 1807, Letterbook 1806–1812, C114/1, TNAUK.

20. For Lindo, see Jackie Ranston, *The Lindo Legacy* (London: Toucan Books, 2000), 14–20. For Lake's consignments of "5 to 6,000 [slaves] annually" from Liverpool merchants, see Taylor, Ballantine & Fairlie to John Tailyour, Kingston, December 10, 1792, Box 6, TFP. For Lindo's purchases of people from ships, see, for example, Sales invoice for the *Golden Age*, 1784. For Lindo's extensive offices and wharf in Kingston, see "Plan and Elevations of the House, Stores, and Wharf Belonging to Alexander Lindo Esquire Situate in Princess Street in the City of Kingston in the Island of Jamaica. 1805." MPH1/152, TNAUK.

21. For the numbers of firms in Jamaica and Tailyour's business and profits, see Radburn, "Case of John Tailyour." The number of factoring firms in Demerara is drawn from the *Essequebo en Demerarische Courant*, Georgetown, 1793–1808. Lindo had particularly strong ties to Anthony Calvert of London and John Dawson of Liverpool, both of whom had substantially expanded their slaving businesses after the American Revolutionary War.

22. David Dick to John Tailyour, Kingston, August 29, 1804, Box 2, TFP ("made"). George & Robert Todd to Captain Thomas Brassey, Liverpool, December 3, 1807, DX/1908/6, MMM ("deranged"). For Guinea factors' substantial losses, see also David Dick to John Tailyour, Kingston, February 14, 1802, and November 18, 1803, Box 2, TFP. For the 1793 credit crisis, see Francis E. Hyde, Bradbury Parkinson, and Sheila Mariner, "The Port of Liverpool and the Crisis of 1793," *Economica* 18, no. 72 (November 1951): 363–78. For the impacts of the crisis on the slave trade, see Radburn, "Keeping 'the Wheel,'" 680–83. For the overproduction of sugar, see Ryden, *West Indian Slavery*, 216–53. For the collapse of the slave trade to the eastern Caribbean islands (Trinidad excepted) after 1795, see http://www.slavevoyages.org/estimates/VOcbM27d.

23. For Davenport's investments, see Radburn, "William Davenport," 119–22; Richardson, "Profits." For outfitting costs circa 1770–1808, see Inikori, "Market Structure," 773. Data on the numbers of investors is drawn from the ownership records for Liverpool ships in *SV*. The trade likewise became concentrated in the hands of smaller partnerships in Bristol before that town's trade collapsed. See Richardson, *Bristol, Africa*, xx; Morgan, "James Rogers."

24. For Leyland, see David Richardson, "Leyland, Thomas (1752?–1827)," *Oxford Dictionary of National Biography* (Oxford: Oxford University Press, 2004); John Hughes, *Liverpool banks [and] bankers, 1760–1837, a history of the circumstances which gave rise to the industry, and of the men who founded and developed it* (Liverpool: Henry Young and Sons, 1906), 169–82. For Leyland awaiting the outcome of the abolitionist debates, see Thomas Leyland to Samuel Galton & Son, Liverpool, December 30, 1787, Letter Book of Thomas Leyland (May 1786–Sept 1788), 387 MD 59, LRO. For Leyland's wealth, see Pope, "Wealth," 208–15. For Leyland's investments, see https://www.slavevoyages.org/voyages/C16a3ZpI. For Leyland's profits, see Inikori, "Market Structure," 773; and the account books for the *Harlequin*, 1783; *Madam Pookata*, 1783; *Hannah*, 1790; *Christopher*, 1791; *Jenny*, 1793; *Enterprize*, 1794, 1804, 1807; *Spitfire*, 1796; *Earl of Liverpool*, 1797, 1798, 1800; *Lottery*, 1798, 1802; and *Fortune*, 1806, all of which are cited in my Appendix E.

25. For Dawson's origins, see Jeremiah Finch Smith, *The Admission Register of the Manchester School . . . from A.D. 1776 to A.D. 1807* (Manchester: Chetham

Society, 1878), vol. 2, 211. For the *Mentor's* capture, see Sales of the Ship *Carnatic's* Cargo, Prize to the Ship *Mentor*, C114/36, TNAUK; Williams, *Liverpool Privateers*, 239–40. The firm Baker and Dawson also fitted out the privateers *Telemachus* and *Ulysses*, which captured the Spanish frigate *Soledad*, reputed to be worth one million pounds sterling. See David Starkey, *British Privateering Enterprise in the Eighteenth Century* (Liverpool: Liverpool University Press, 1990), 233. For Dawson's investment in the slave trade, see *HCSP*, vol. 71, 500. For Dawson in Trinidad, see Pierre F. McCallum, *Travels in Trinidad . . .* (Liverpool: W. Jones, 1805), 237–46. For Dawson's wealth at his death, see PROB 11/1539/297, TNAUK. For Dawson, see also James Rawley and Stephen D. Behrendt, *The Transatlantic Slave Trade: A History* (Lincoln: 2005), 186–87. Dawson's contemporary William Boats (1716–1794) initially followed a similar career trajectory: from humble beginnings he elevated himself into one of Liverpool's largest slaving merchants, via captaining slave ships and then outfitting privateers. Unlike Dawson, though, Boats died with substantial wealth from his slaving career, which he bequeathed to his son and two daughters. See Williams, *Liverpool Privateers*, 484–85.

26. *Westmoreland Gazette*, Kendal, March 11, 1837 ("continuous"); James Aspinall, *Liverpool a few years since: By an Old Stager* (Liverpool: Adam Holden, 1885), 33 ("worked"), 34 ("had not"). For Bolton, see George Baillie, *Interesting letters addressed to John Bolton Esq. of Liverpool, merchant, and Colonel of a regiment of volunteers* (London: J. Gold, 1809); Godfrey W. Mathews, "John Bolton, a Liverpool Merchant, 1756–1837," *Transactions of the Historic Society of Lancashire and Cheshire*, vol. 93 (1941); David Pope, "Bolton, John (1756–1837)," *Oxford Dictionary of National Biography* (Oxford: Oxford University Press, 2016). For Bolton's dealing in cotton, see Alexey Krichtal, "Liverpool and the Raw Cotton Trade: A Study of the Port and Its Merchant Community, 1770–1815," unpublished M.A. thesis, Victoria University of Wellington, 2013, 35, 45.

27. *Gentleman's Magazine*, vol. 161 (April 1837), 431 ("most," "the poor"). *Westmoreland Gazette*, Kendal, March 11, 1837 ("universally," "see"). Aspinall, *Liverpool*, 37 ("eminent"). Leyland's engagement in the slave trade is likewise downplayed in Hughes, *Liverpool banks [and] bankers*, 172. For the Hibberts' post-slaving careers, see Donington, *The Bonds of Family*, 282–92.

28. For slave traders' descendants, see Pope, "Wealth," 177; Earle, *Earles of Liverpool*, 239–62. For the Staniforths, see Jane Longmore, "Portrait of a Slave-Trading Family: The Staniforths of Liverpool," in *Britain's History and Memory of Transatlantic Slavery: Local Nuances of a "National Sin,"* ed. Katie Donington, Ryan Hanley, and Jessica Moody (Liverpool: Liverpool University Press, 2016), 60–82. For the Lindo family, see Ranston, *Lindo Legacy*. For recent reportage that overlooks the Lindo family's connec-

tions to Atlantic slavery, see, for example, Ian Thomson, "Blanche Blackwell [nee Lindo] Obituary," *Guardian*, London, August 29, 2017.

29. For the transition to the palm oil trade in Biafra, see Jones, *Trading States*. For British attempts to stamp out the slave trade at Bonny, see Dike, *Trade and Politics*, 81–96. For the conquest of Fante, see Shumway, *Fante*, 11, 22; William St. Clair, *The Door of No Return: The History of Cape Coast Castle and the Atlantic Slave Trade* (New York: BlueBridge, 2007), 192–99.

30. *Westmoreland Gazette*, Kendal, March 11, 1837 ("universally"). For Bolton's compensation claim, see Mathews, "John Bolton" (https://www .ucl.ac.uk/lbs/person/view/7760/). Slave traders now have the dubious distinction of being categorized, alongside pirates, torturers, and mosquitoes, as "enemies of all mankind" (*hostis humani generis*).

Index

Abolition Act of 1807, 18, 197, 204, 211–15

abolition/abolitionists: as a boost to the slave trade, 200–213; campaign in parliament, 197, 201–3; fates of enslaved people after, 215–16; fates of slaving merchants after, 214–15; fixation of campaign on Middle Passage, 5, 146; increase in costs of slave trading prior to, 135; investigation into the slave trade by, 198–99; size of Britain's slave trade before, 2, 25; production of *Brooks* diagram by, 109–11; publicization of scramble sales by, 182; regulation of slave trade following campaign, 106, 204–5

Accra, 43, 44

Adams, John, 281n38–39

Africa (ship), 63, 81, 91, 103

African (ship), 121, 164

African Queen, 166, 189

African slave sales, 59–90; captives sold at the Aro fairs, 48–49, 54–55, 272n51, 281n38; enslaved woman and child sold on the Gold Coast, 88–89; in the Asante empire, 43; increasing earnings from as abolition neared, 204–8; increasing prices

paid for people over time, 82–85, 280n36, 281n37; inspection of captives at, 64–66; of Broteer Furro and Olaudah Equiano, 57; order in which people purchased at, 85–88, 281n39; pricing of people and goods at, 71–82, 279n27, 279n29, 280n31; rejection of captives by ship captains at, 66–71, 276n12, 276n14; selectiveness of European buyers at, 62–64, 279n28; separation of families at, 68–69, 276n13; similarity of to American slave sales, 172; unsold captives beaten and killed, 86, 282n40

African slave traders, 40–58, 198–99, 205–8, 215, 289n35; conquest of competitors by, 43, 50–53, 55, 272n49; construction of infrastructure by, 43–44, 49; demand of for imports, 37–39; disgust of at inspections of captives, 66; divergent paths of post-abolition, 215; early interactions of with Europeans, 22–24; friction with visiting whites, 34–35, 59–60, 266n22, 280n35; gains of, 40, 54, 206–7; haggling by with whites, 76–78, 83–84, 279n29, 280–81n36; inspection of imported

barricado (*continued*)
    construction of, 115, 289n33; de-
    velopment of, 99–103, 286n16; en-
    slaved people divided by, 116, 177
beads, 38, 73, 75, 80, 83, 116, 316n16
beans, 46, 56, 95, 145
Becher, Michael, 139
Bedford (ship), 141, 153
Bende, 49, 54
Benguela, 23
Benin, 69, 72, 117
Berbice River, 151, 203
Bernal, Abraham, 189
Betty, 191–93
Bight of Benin: as a key market for
    French slavers, 199; as a key market
    for Portuguese slavers, 256n10;
    construction of slaving forts at, 23;
    cost of a human cargo at, 265n17;
    crowding of slaves aboard at, 116–
    17; expansion of slave trade within,
    36; height of slaves purchased at,
    108; impacts of slaves-for-cowries
    trade at, 72–74; murder of an en-
    slaved man at, 69; numbers of cap-
    tives carried from by Britons, 21;
    preference for among Europeans,
    47; preference for captives from, 48;
    rising prices of slaves at, 33. *See also*
    Ardra, Benin, Lagos, Porto Novo,
    and Whydah
Bight of Biafra, 47–56; deadliness of
    climate at, 47–48; early slave trade
    at, 72–73; expansion of French
    slave trade at, 199; export of low-
    priced guns to, 39; geography of,
    47; growth of palm oil trade at,
    215; higher proportions of enslaved
    women carried from, 108, 272n50;
    high mortality rates of captives
    taken from, 105; kidnapping of
    Olaudah Equiano within, 57; low
    prices of enslaved people at, 33;
    numbers of captives carried from

by Britons, 21; planter opinions on
people carried from, 168; smallness
of seventeenth-century slave trade
at, 24; trade currencies at, 74. *See
also* Andoni (place); Aro; Bonny;
Cameroon River; New Calabar;
Old Calabar
bills of exchange, 132–33, 138, 162
Bimbia Island, 68
Birmingham, 39
Bissau, 23
Black Prince (ship), 46, 121
Blaydes (ship), 83, 280n34
Blessing (ship), 36
Blundell, Bryan, 136
Blundell, Jonathan Sr., 136
Blundell, Jonathan Jr., 136
Blundell family, 136
Boats, William, 30, 136, 318n25
Boats family, 30, 136
Bolton, John, 213–16
Bonny, 53–56, 85–86, 206–8; as one
of several key slaving ports in the
Rio Real, 50; breaking trade at, 76,
278n25; children working aboard
slave ships at, 115; crowding of
captives aboard slave ships at, 114;
depth of river at, 272n47; difficulty in dating ruling monarchs at,
272n48; high prices of people at,
205; increasing prices paid for captives over time at, 84; John Bolton's
trade for people at, 213; *Kitty's
Amelia's* deadly voyage from, 149–
50; negotiations over slave prices
at, 83; numbers of captives brought
to in Ibani canoe fleets, 281n38;
numbers of captives carried from by
Britons, 21; prices of children at, 81,
281n39; prices of men and women
at, 77, 281n39; purchase of captives
at by James Fraser, 71; retention of
enslaved boys at, 316n18; shipping
of Olaudah Equiano from, 57; static

to from Jamaica, 190, 310n49; slave sales on, 165, 177–78; *Zong* assumed to be off, 146. *See also* Haitian Revolution
Saint George's Bay (Grenada), 154
Saint Helena (South Carolina), 181
Saint Kitts: arrival of *Comte du Norde* at, 180; as a node in the re-export slave trade, 140, 302n11; James Ramsay on slave sales at, 124, 193; landing of Africans on, 142–43; lodging of letters from British slaving merchants on, 138; mass suicide attempt of Africans aboard *Prince of Orange* at, 154; profits of factoring firms on, 133; settlement of, 129
Saint Lucia, 144, 153
Saint Thomas, 190
Saint Vincent, 142, 148–49, 152–53, 213, 215
Sally, 191, 193
Sanders, James, 43
Sandoval, Alonso de, 93–94
Santo Domingo River, 50
São Jorge da Mina, 23, 41, 43
São Tome, 148
Savannah, 130, 181
Savanna-la-Mar, 175, 185
Scotland, 191
Scottish slave traders, 36, 134, 191
scramble sale, 159, 182–84, 195, 208, 308n37
Senegal River, 23
Senegambia, 21, 23, 65, 72, 108
Senhouse, Joseph, 169
Sephardic slave traders, 187, 191, 208
Seven Years' War, 131, 184, 293n5
Sierra Leone, 21, 23, 36, 33–36, 115–16, 168, 265n18, 279n27
slave sales advertisements, 167–69, 180
slave ship captains: arming slaves to fight off attackers at sea, 151–53, 299n38, 299n39; as a focus of

"human histories," 9; attempt of to keep shipmates together at American sales, 173; crowding enslaved people on ships, 113–19; dining with Guinea factors ashore, 304n19; emulating the practices of other captains, 94–96; heading largest British slaving firms before abolition, 200, 212–13, 318n25; held to ransom at Old Calabar, 51; ignorance of slave mortality, 105–6; importance of for bonds to African merchants, 51–53, 207; inspecting enslaved people in Africa, 64–66; instructed to seek out African markets, 36–77, 266n20, 266n22; instructions issued to on purchasing people, 62–64, 280n34; killed by enslaved people, 101; licking enslaved males' faces, 64–65; marching captives to American slave markets, 185; murdering captives, 98, 145–46; navigating ships to American markets, 127, 138–50, 202, 296n24, 296n25, 302n11; negotiating with merchants in Africa, 76–78, 280n31, 280n35, 280n36; purchasing a tiger in Africa, 288n30; purchasing enslaved people in Africa, 78–87, 116, 179–80, 272–73n51, 273n2, 276n12, 278n25, 279n27, 279n28, 281n37, 281n39; purchasing foodstuffs from African brokers, 45–46; recruited from slaving ports' hinterlands, 35; rejecting enslaved people in Africa, 66–71; releasing captives from shackles, 154, 170; selling sickly captives in the eastern Caribbean, 147; sexual assault of enslaved women by, 118; steps taken by to prevent revolts, 96–101, 114–15, 125, 285n12, 290n40, 300n42; violence of toward coastal Africans, 59